Dog Owner's Home Veterinary Handbook

A healthy puppy is a happy puppy with a happy owner. This is Kate Giffin and her three-month-old Great Pyrenees.

Dog Owner's Home Veterinary Handbook

Revised and Expanded

DELBERT G. CARLSON, D.V.M.

AND

JAMES M. GIFFIN, M.D.

PRENTICE HALL

Library of Congress Cataloging-in-Publication Data

Carlson, Delbert G.
    Dog owner's hom veterinary handbook / Delbert G. Carlson
and James M. Giffin.
        p.   cm.
    Includes index.
    ISBN 0-13-085632-0 (ppc)   ISBN 0-87605-537-4 (c)
    1. Dogs—Diseases—Hnadbooks, manuals, etc. I. Giffin, James M.
II. Title.
SF991.C25   1992
636.7'089—dc20   91-43575
                                                           CIP

Printed in the United States of America

10 9 8 7 6 5 4 3

ISBN 0-13-085632-0 (ppc)

PRENTICE HALL
Paramus, NJ 07652

On the World Wide Web at http://www.phdirect.com

*Dedicated
with love
to our families*

The Authors

DELBERT G. CARLSON, D.V.M.

Dr. Del Carlson, a practicing veterinarian with long-standing experience in the medical and surgical care of dogs, makes his home in Springfield, Missouri. He received his medical degree from the University of Minnesota Veterinary School in 1954 and interned at the Rawley Memorial Hospital in Springfield, Massachusetts.

Dr. Delbert G. Carlson

Dr. James M. Giffin

He and Mrs. Carlson have found the time to raise and show horses through-out the Midwest, breed Afghan Hounds and Borzois and put five children through college. He is an avid fly fisherman.

Dr. Carlson is a member of the Missouri Veterinary Medical Association and a past president of the Greene County Humane Society. He is the coauthor of the *Cat Owner's Home Veterinary Handbook* (Howell Book House).

JAMES M. GIFFIN, M.D.

Dr. Jim Giffin is the coauthor of the award-winning book *The Complete Great Pyrenees*, as well as coauthor of the *Cat Owner's Home Veterinary Handbook* and the *Horse Owner's Veterinary Handbook* (Howell Book House). He has been active in breeding and showing dogs, and has served on the board of directors of the Great Pyrenees Club of America, Inc.

Dr. Giffin received his medical degree from Yale University School of Medicine and completed his surgical residency at Barnes Hospital in St. Louis. He served as chief of surgery at the 45th Surgical Hospital in Vietnam, and was activated from the Armed Forces Reserve to serve in Operation Desert Storm.

Dr. Giffin enjoys outdoor sports, including skiing, fishing and hiking with the dogs.

Finding it quick in
DOG OWNER'S HOME
VETERINARY HANDBOOK:

A special INDEX OF SIGNS AND SYMPTOMS is on the inside front cover page for fast referral. Consult this if your dog exhibits unexplained behavior. It will help you locate the problem.

The detailed CONTENTS outlines the organs and the systems that are the usual sites of disease. If you can locate the problem anatomically, consult it first.

The GENERAL INDEX begins on page 413 and gives you a comprehensive guide to the book's medical information. Where a page number is in boldface, it indicates a more detailed coverage of the subject.

CROSS-REFERENCES note pertinent supplementary information. Where the reference is in large and small caps (SKIN), it identifies a chapter title; in italics, it identifies a subdivision of a chapter.

Contents

Introduction

IF MY DOG were able to sit down at my computer, I believe she would type something like the following:

> "TO WHOM IT CONCERNS:
> IT HAS COME TO MY ATTENTION
> THAT YOU HAVE WHOLE-HEARTEDLY
> AND WITH FIRM INTENT TAKEN MY HEART.
> IF YOU DO NOT CEASE AND DESIST AT ONCE,
> YOU SHOULD BE PREPARED TO ACCEPT
> EVERLASTING DEVOTION."

Veterinary medicine has progressed so rapidly that much of what was new in the 1980s is now on the verge of obsolescence. For this reason the time has come to revise, expand and update the *Dog Owner's Home Veterinary Handbook* to insure that you, our readers, have the latest and best information to care for your dog: as much as your dog cares for you.

Modern technology has brought new methods to the practicing veterinarian—making diagnosis more specific and treatment more accurate. We have attempted to show how these advances will impact veterinary medicine in the 1990s and beyond.

In this edition you will find that we have incorporated newer and safer medications, including those used for vaccinating, deworming and treating insect parasites, heartworms and infectious diseases.

More space has been devoted to the epidemiology of infectious diseases, their modes of transmission and how you can protect yourself as well as your pet.

A number of new diseases have been recognized—Lyme disease is an example. We now know more about autoimmune skin diseases, central nervous system diseases, inherited and congenital defects and disorders of the digestive tract. The text has been expanded accordingly.

Over the years we have received your questions. We have learned what you want to know and what was not covered in sufficient detail, and we have used this important information to anticipate your needs.

The *Dog Owner's Home Veterinary Handbook* was the first in a series that now includes the *Cat Owner's Home Veterinary Handbook* and the *Horse Owner's Veterinary Handbook* (all from Howell Book House). The experience gained in keeping abreast of veterinary progress has helped us greatly in planning and executing this revision.

In writing this book, we have attempted to describe the signs and symptoms that will help you arrive at a preliminary diagnosis—so you can weigh the severity of the problem. Some health problems are not potentially serious and can be treated at home. Others are not. Knowing when to call your veterinarian is of great importance. Delays can be costly.

At the same time we have sought to provide guidance for the acute or emergency situations that common sense dictates you should handle on your own. Life-saving procedures such as artificial respiration, heart massage, the treatment of bloat, management of obstetrical emergencies, poisonings, seizures, heat stroke and the like are illustrated and explained in a step-by-step fashion.

A veterinary handbook is not intended to be a substitute for professional care. Book advice can never be as helpful or as safe as medical assistance. No text can replace the interview and physical examination, during which the veterinarian elicits the sort of information that leads to a speedy and accurate diagnosis. But the knowledge provided in this book will enable you to work in better understanding and with more effective cooperation with your veterinarian. You'll be more alert to the symptoms of disease and be better able to describe them.

In this book you will find the basics of health care and disease prevention for the young and the old. A well-cared-for dog suffers fewer illnesses and infirmities in the aging process.

Chapters on Sex and Reproduction, Pregnancy and Whelping, Pediatrics and Geriatrics provide comprehensive coverage on matters of importance to all dog breeders.

The combined efforts of many people make this book possible.

Dr. James Clawson, Krist Carlson and Jim Giffin contributed many fine photographs to the first edition of this book. Liisa Carlson, now in veterinary practice with her father, consulted with us on this revision and brought to us the perspective of the newly graduated veterinarian.

Rose Floyd, Sydney Giffin Wiley and Karen Wyatt created the many fine drawings. Diane Saia was a great help to us in the preparation of the manuscript. We would like to express our appreciation to Bristol-Myers Squibb and the editors of American Veterinary Publications and Canine Medicine for giving us permission to use pictures from their publications.

Recognition would not be complete without mentioning the many researchers, clinicians and educators whose works have served as a source for our information. Among them are *Current Veterinary Therapy X* (edited by Robert W. Kirk, D.V.M.); *Small Animal Dermatology* (George W. Muller, D.V.M., and Robert W. Kirk, D.V.M.); *Canine Ophthalmology* (William G. Magrane, D.V.M.); *Veterinary Internal Medicine*, Third Edition (Stephen J. Ettinger, D.V.M.) and the numerous contributors to *The Veterinary Clinics of North America* (W. B. Saunders Company).

To Howell Book House and Sean Frawley, who gave us the opportunity to produce this work, and to Marcy Zingler, who did such a splendid job of editing, we are indeed grateful.

—DELBERT G. CARLSON
—JAMES M. GIFFIN

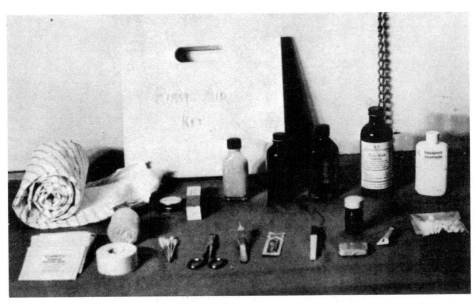

Home Emergency and Medical Kit

1. Container
2. Cotton role
3. Gauze pad (3″ × 3″)
4. Gauze roll (3″)
5. 1″ roll adhesive
6. Q-tips
7. Tweezers
8. Scalpel, scissors
9. Thermometer
10. Hydrogen peroxide (3%)
11. Pepto-Bismol
12. Furacin ointment
13. Panolog ear drops
14. Charcoal suspension
15. Kaopectate
16. Milk of Magnesia
17. Dramamine
18. Aspirin
19. Gastric tube

1

Emergencies

ACUTE PAINFUL ABDOMEN
(may include Bloat)

THE ACUTE abdomen is an emergency that may lead to the death of the individual unless treatment is started as soon as possible.

This condition is characterized by the *sudden onset* of abdominal pain along with vomiting, retching, extreme restlessness and inability to find a comfortable position, whining and crying, grunting and labored breathing. The abdomen is extremely painful when pressed on. A characteristic position sometimes seen is one in which the dog's chest rests against the floor with the rump in the air (prayer position). As the condition advances, the dog's pulse becomes weak and thready, the mucus membranes pale and the dog goes into shock.

One of the following may be the cause:

Bloat
Torsion of the stomach and intestines
Urinary stones
Trauma to the abdomen with internal injury
Rupture of the bladder
Poisoning
Rupture of the pregnant uterus
Peritonitis
Acute pancreatitis
Intestinal obstruction

Veterinarians will tell you that a dog with **Bloat** or any other form of acute abdomen is critically ill and should have **immediate veterinary attention**.

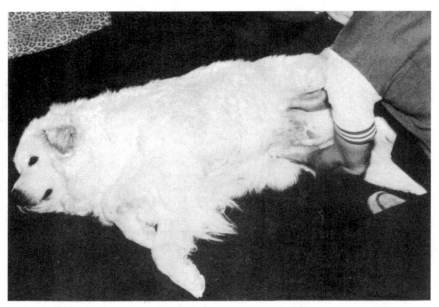

Feeling for a painful abdomen. An *acute* abdomen is tender and feels rigid.

ARTIFICIAL RESPIRATION AND HEART MASSAGE

Artificial respiration is an emergency procedure used to assist breathing in an unconscious dog. Heart massage is used when no heartbeat can be heard or felt. When combined with artificial respiration, it is called *cardiopulmonary resuscitation*. As cessation of breathing is soon followed by heart stoppage, and vice versa, cardiopulmonary resuscitation frequently is required to sustain life.

Heart massage by itself provides for both movement of air and pumping of blood. For best results, combine heart massage with forced mouth-to-nose breathing. This requires two people, one to administer heart massage and one to give mouth-to-nose breathing.

The following emergencies may require artificial respiration and/or heart massage:

Shock	Head Injury
Poisoning	Electric Shock
Prolonged Seizure	Obstructed Airways (Choking)
Coma	Sudden Death

In artificial respiration, two methods are used. The *chest compression* technique consists of applying force to the chest wall, which pushes air out and allows the elastic recoil of the chest to draw air back in. It is the easiest to perform.

Mouth-to-nose forced respiration is used when the compression technique is ineffective, or when the chest is punctured (pneumothorax).

2

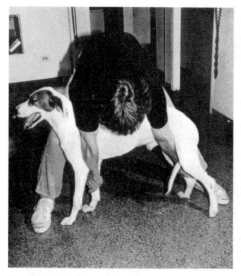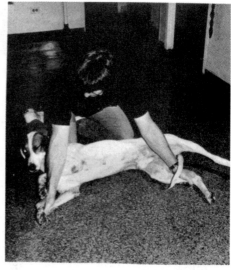

How to lay the dog on its side.

Artificial Respiration

Steps in Chest Compression:

1. Feel for pulse or heartbeat.
2. Open mouth and clear away secretions. Check for a foreign body. If found, remove if possible. If impossible to reach, execute the Heimlich maneuver (see RESPIRATORY SYSTEM: *Laryngeal Blockage*).

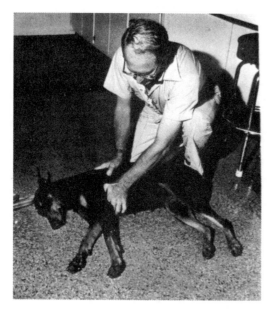

The chest *compression* technique for giving artificial respiration.

3. Lay the dog on a flat surface with the *right* side down.
4. Place both hands on the chest and press down sharply. Release quickly. If properly performed, you should be able to hear air moving in and out. If you can't, proceed with mouth-to-nose resuscitation.
5. Continue until the dog breathes on its own, or as long as the heart beats.

Steps in Mouth-to-Nose Resuscitation:

1. Perform steps 1 and 2 in *Chest Compression*.
2. Pull the tongue forward and close the mouth. Seal the lips with your hand.
3. Place your mouth over the dog's nose and blow in steadily for three seconds. The chest will expand. Release to let the air come back out.
4. Continue until the dog breathes on its own, or as long as the heart beats.

Heart Massage

Steps in Small Dogs and Puppies:

1. Perform steps 1 and 2 in *Chest Compression*.
2. Lay the dog on its side. Place your thumb on one side of the sternum and your fingers on the other, just behind the elbows.
3. Compress the chest firmly six times. Wait five seconds to let the chest expand; then repeat.
4. Continue until the heart beats on its own, or until no heartbeat is felt for five minutes.

Heart Massage: Note the placement of the hands behind the elbow and over the heart. Heart massage alone provides for movement of air as well as pumping of blood.   (*J. Clawson*)

Steps in Larger Dogs:

1. Repeat steps 1 and 2 in *Chest Compression*.
2. Lay the dog on a flat surface with the *right* side down.
3. Place the heel of your hand on the rib cage just behind the elbow (over the heart).
4. Compress the chest firmly six times. Wait five seconds to let the chest expand; then repeat.
5. Continue until the heart beats on its own, or until no heartbeat is felt for five minutes.

BURNS

Burns are caused by heat, chemicals, electric shocks and radiation. Sunburn is an example of radiation burn. It occurs on the nose of dogs with insufficient pigment (see NOSE: *Collie Nose*), and on the skin of white-coated dogs who are clipped close in summer.

Skin damage depends upon the length and intensity of exposure. With a superficial burn, you will see redness in the skin, sometimes blisters and perhaps slight swelling. The burn will be tender. With deep burns, the skin will appear white, the hair will come out easily when pulled and pain will be severe. If more than 15 percent of the body surface is involved in a deep burn, the outlook is poor. In such cases fluid seeps from the damaged area. This can lead to shock.

Treatment: For small burns, apply cold water soaks or ice packs for 20 minutes to relieve pain. Clip away hair and wash gently with a surgical soap. Blot dry. Apply a topical antibiotic ointment (Furacin, Neosporin). Neosporin can be purchased over the counter without a prescription. Protect the area from rubbing by applying a loose-fitting gauze dressing.

Treat chemical burns by flushing them with copious amounts of water. Acid on the skin is neutralized by rinsing with baking soda (four tablespoons to a pint of water). Alkali is neutralized by rinsing with a weak vinegar solution (two tablespoons to a pint of water). Blot dry and apply antibiotic ointment. Bandage loosely.

COLD EXPOSURE

Hypothermia (Abnormal Low Temperature)

Prolonged exposure to cold results in a drop in body temperature. It is most likely to occur when a dog is wet. It is seen most often in Toy breeds and those with short hair. Hypothermia also occurs in shock, after a long anesthetic and in newborn pups. Prolonged chilling burns up the available energy and predisposes the body to low blood sugar.

The signs of hypothermia are violent shivering followed by listlessness and apathy, a rectal temperature below 97 degrees F (which is diagnostic) and, finally, collapse and coma.

Treatment: Wrap your dog in a blanket or coat and carry it into the house. If your dog is wet (having fallen into ice water), give the animal a warm bath. Rub vigorously with towels to dry the skin.

Warm chilled dogs by applying warm water packs to the axilla (armpit), chest and abdomen. The temperature of the packs should be about that of a baby bottle (warm to the wrist: 105–108 degrees F). Continue to change the packs until the rectal temperature reaches 100 degrees F. Warming with a hair dryer or air comb works well. As sensation returns it can be painful, and the dog may attempt to bite at the skin.

As the dog begins to move about, give some honey or glucose (four tablespoons of sugar added to a pint of water).

How to warm a chilled puppy is discussed in PEDIATRICS: *Warming a Chilled Puppy*.

Frostbite

Frostbite affects the toes, ears and scrotum. The skin at first is pale white. With the return of circulation, it becomes red and swollen and may begin to peel. Eventually it looks much like a burn, with a line of demarcation between the live and dead tissue. Dead skin separates in one to three weeks.

Treatment: Warm frostbitten parts with warm water soaks for fifteen to twenty minutes as described above, but don't rub too vigorously. Prevent infection by applying an antibiotic ointment. Cover with a bandage as described in *Bandaging* at the end of this chapter. As sensation returns it can be painful. Prevent the dog from biting at the skin and causing injury.

DEHYDRATION

Dehydration is excess loss of body fluids. Usually it involves loss of both water and electrolytes, which are minerals such as sodium, chloride and potassium. During illness, dehydration may be caused by an inadequate fluid intake. Fever increases the loss of water. This becomes significant if the dog does not drink enough to offset it. Other common causes of dehydration are prolonged vomiting and diarrhea.

One sign of dehydration is loss of skin elasticity. When the skin along the back is picked up into a fold, it should spring back into place. In dehydration, the skin stays up in a ridge. Another sign is dryness of the mouth. Late signs are sunken eyes and circulatory collapse.

Treatment: If your dog is noticeably dehydrated, you should seek veterinary attention. Treatment is directed at replacing fluids and preventing further losses.

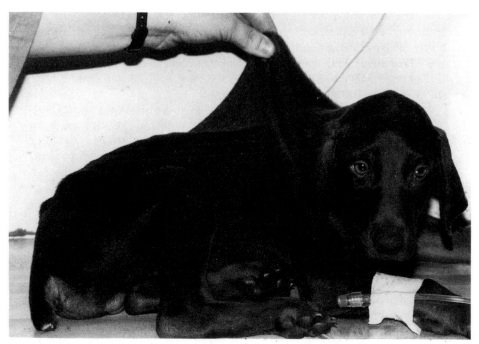

Loss of skin elasticity in severe dehydration. Note intravenous fluids, which are of extreme importance.

In mild cases without vomiting, fluids can be given by mouth. If the dog won't drink, you can give an electrolyte solution into the cheek pouch by bottle or medicine syringe (see APPENDIX). Balanced electrolyte solutions for treating dehydration in children are available at drug stores. Ringer's lactate, mixed half and half with 5% dextrose in water, and a solution called Pedialyte are suitable for dogs. They are given at the rate of two to four cc per pound body weight per hour depending upon the severity of the dehydration (or as directed by your veterinarian).

The treatment of dehydration in infant puppies is discussed in PEDIATRICS: *Common Feeding Problems*.

DROWNING AND SUFFOCATION

Conditions that prevent oxygen from getting into the lungs and blood cause *asphyxiation*. They are carbon monoxide poisoning, inhalation of toxic fumes (smoke, gasoline, propane, refrigerants, solvents), drowning and smothering (which can happen when a dog is left too long in an airtight space). Other causes are foreign bodies in the airways and injuries to the chest that interfere with breathing.

The symptoms of lack of oxygen are straining to breathe, gasping for breath (often with the head extended), extreme anxiety and weakness progressing to loss of consciousness as the dog begins to succumb. The pupils begin to dilate. The tongue and mucus membranes turn blue, which is a reflection of insufficient oxygen in the blood. One exception to the blue color is carbon monoxide poisoning, in which the membranes are a bright red.

Treatment: The most important consideration is to provide your dog with fresh air to breathe. (Better yet, give oxygen if available.) If respirations are shallow or absent, begin immediately by giving mouth-to-nose respiration.

If there is an open wound in the chest, which you can diagnose if you hear air sucking in and out as the dog breathes, seal off the chest by pinching the skin together over the wound.

When the situation is one of drowning, turn the dog upside down, suspended by the legs, and let the water run out of the dog's windpipe. Then position the dog with the head lower than the chest (on a slope, or with a roll beneath the chest) and begin artificial respiration. Mouth-to-nose forced respiration may be required. With heart stoppage, heart massage should be attempted. Continue efforts to resuscitate until the dog breathes naturally or until no heartbeat is felt for five minutes. (See *Artificial Respiration and Heart Massage* in this chapter.)

Once the immediate crisis is over, veterinary aid should be sought. Pneumonia from inhalation is a frequent complication.

ELECTRIC SHOCKS AND BURNS

Electric shocks occur in puppies that chew on electric cords. Occasionally a dog comes into contact with a downed wire or is struck by lightning. Burns of the mouth from electric cords are discussed in the chapter ORAL CAVITY. Dogs that receive an electric shock may be burned. They may show signs of circulatory collapse and difficulty breathing. Electric current damages the capillaries of the lungs and leads to the accumulation of fluid in the air sacs (pulmonary edema).

Treatment: If your dog is unconscious and not breathing, administer artificial respiration. Pulmonary edema must be treated by a veterinarian.

HANDLING AND RESTRAINT OF AN INJURED DOG

Any dog in pain, or severely injured, cannot be held responsible for its actions. No matter how docile a dog may be, you should recognize that under certain circumstances your dog may turn and bite. This is an understandable reflex. You should take proper precautions so as not to be injured.

Apprehension is another cause of panic and aggressive behavior. If you plan to give an injection, or must do something that is apt to cause your dog pain, approach it with quiet confidence and a minimum of fanfare. Dogs are quick to sense anxiety in their owners.

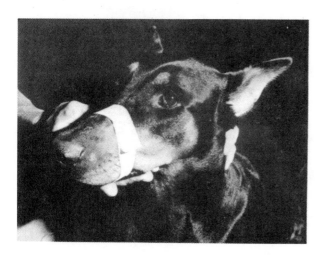

A strip of adhesive tape makes a good temporary muzzle.

(J. Clawson)

Take precautions *before* doing anything that might excite or hurt your dog. Properly restrained, a dog usually will settle down and accept the treatment. A good assistant is a real asset.

There are several good ways to restrain a dog. They are illustrated in the photographs. An emergency muzzle can be made from tape, a necktie, silk stocking, piece of linen or anything suitable at hand. A good muzzle can be made by looping a leash around the jaws and fastening the end to a doorknob as shown in the illustration. Pillows and blankets around the neck are good for short procedures such as giving a shot, but an assistant is required to hold them in place.

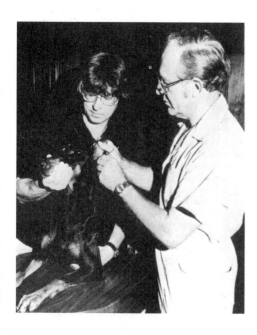

How to restrain your dog for medical care.

(J. Clawson)

9

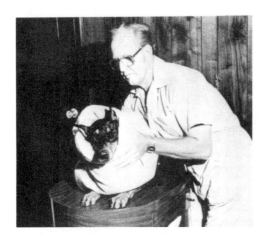

Pillows around the neck are good for short procedures such as giving a shot.

(J. Clawson)

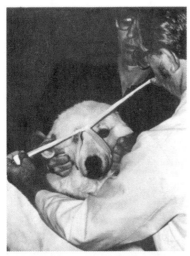

A piece of linen can be used in an emergency. It should be tied behind the head to keep the dog from pawing it off.

(J. Clawson)

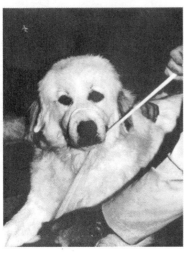

Lifting a small dog that must be restrained.

HEAT STROKE

Heat stroke is an emergency that requires immediate recognition and prompt treatment. Dogs do not tolerate high temperatures as well as humans. They depend upon rapid breathing to exchange warm air for cool air. Accordingly, when air temperature is close to body temperature, cooling by rapid breathing is not an efficient process. Dogs with airway disease also have difficulty with excess heat.

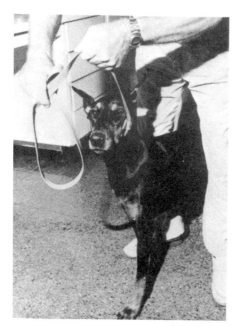

The leash muzzle is useful when you don't have an assistant. Tie the end to a door knob.

(J. Clawson)

11

Common situations that predispose to overheating or heat stroke in dogs are:

1. Being left in a car in hot weather.
2. Being confined on concrete runs; chained without shade in hot weather.
3. Being of a short-nosed breed, especially a Bulldog or Pug.
4. Being muzzled while put under a dryer (this can happen in a grooming parlor).
5. Suffering from airway disease or any condition that impairs breathing.

Heat stroke begins with rapid, frantic, noisy breathing. The tongue and mucus membranes are bright red, the saliva is thick and tenacious and the dog frequently vomits. Its rectal temperature is high, sometimes over 106 degrees F. The cause of the problem usually is evident by the typical appearance of the dog; it can be confirmed by taking its temperature.

If the condition is allowed to go unchecked, the dog becomes unsteady and staggers, has diarrhea that often is bloody and becomes progressively weaker. Coma and death ensue.

Treatment: Emergency measures must begin at once. Mild cases respond to moving the dog to a cooler surrounding, such as an air-conditioned building or car. If the dog's temperature is over 104 degrees F, or if unsteady on its feet, the dog should be cooled by immersion in a tub of cold water. If this is impossible, hose your dog down with a garden hose. For a temperature over 106 degrees F, or if the dog is near collapse, give a cold water enema. A more rapid temperature drop is imperative. Cool to a rectal temperature of 103 degrees F.

Heat stroke can be associated with swelling of the throat. This aggravates the problem. A cortisone injection by your veterinarian may be required to treat this.

Prevention:

1. Do not expose dogs with airway disease or impaired breathing to prolonged heat.
2. Restrict exercise during the heat of the day in summer.
3. Breed dogs in air-conditioned quarters.
4. Crate a dog only in an open wire cage.
5. Provide shade and cool water to dogs living in outdoor runs.

INSECT STINGS

The stings of bees, wasps, yellow jackets and ants all cause painful swelling at the site of the sting. If stung many times, an animal could go into shock as a result of absorbing toxins. Rarely, hypersensitivity reactions develop in dogs that have been stung before (see SKIN: *Allergies*).

The stings of black widow and Missouri brown spiders, and tarantulas, also are toxic to animals. The signs are sharp pain at the sting site. Later the dog can develop chills, fever, labored breathing. Shock can occur.

The stings of centipedes and scorpions cause local reaction and at times a severe illness. The bites heal slowly.

The bite of a female wood tick rarely can cause a paralysis (see NERVOUS SYSTEM: *Tick Paralysis*). Other common insect parasites are discussed in the SKIN chapter.

Treatment of Insect Bites:

1. Identify the insect.
2. Remove a stinger when accessible with tweezers. (Only bees leave their stingers behind.)
3. Make a paste of baking soda and apply it directly to the sting.
4. Ice packs relieve swelling and pain.
5. Calamine lotion relieves itching.

If there are signs of an acute hypersensitivity or toxic reaction, take your dog to the veterinarian.

POISONING

A poison is any substance harmful to the body. Animal baits are palatable poisons that encourage ingestion. This makes them an obvious choice for intentional poisoning.

Dogs are curious by nature and have a tendency to hunt small game, or explore out-of-the-way places such as wood piles, weed thickets and storage ports. This puts them into contact with insects, dead animals and toxic plants. It also means that in many cases of suspected poisoning the actual agent will be unknown. The great variety of potentially poisonous plants and shrubs makes identification difficult or impossible—unless the owner has direct knowledge that the dog has eaten a certain plant or product. Most cases suspected of being malicious poisoning actually are not.

In some types of vegetation, only certain parts of the plant are toxic. In others, all parts are poisonous. Ingestion causes a wide range of symptoms. They include mouth irritation, drooling, vomiting, diarrhea, hallucination, seizures, coma and death. Other plant substances cause skin rash. Some toxic plants have specific pharmacological actions that are used in medicines.

The following tables of toxic plants, shrubs and trees are included for reference.

Poisonous Houseplants

Toxic Houseplants:

A. That give rash after contact with the skin or mouth:

Chrysanthemum	Poinsettia
Creeping fig	Pot mum > might produce dermatitis
Weeping fig	Spider mum > " " "

B. That are irritating to mucus membranes (toxic oxalates); the mouth especially gets swollen; painful tongue; sore lips:

Arrowhead vine	Majesty
Boston ivy	Neththytis ivy
Collodium	Pathos
Drunk cane	Red princess
Emerald duke	Saddle leaf (philodendrum)
Heart leaf (philodendrum)	Split leaf (philodendrum)
Marble queen	

C. That may contain a wide variety of poisons. Most cause vomiting, abdominal pain, cramps. Some cause tremors, heart and respiratory and/or kidney problems, which are difficult for owners to interpret:

Amaryllis	Elephant ears	Pot mum
Asparagus fern	Glocal ivy	Ripple ivy
Azalea	Heart ivy	Spider mum
Bird of paradise	Ivy	Sprangeri fern
Creeping Charlie	Jerusalem cherry	Umbrella plant
Crown of thorns	Needlepoint ivy	

Outdoor Plants with Toxic Effects

A. *Outdoor plants* that produce vomiting and diarrhea in some cases:

Delphinium	Poke weed	Indian tobacco
Daffodil	Bittersweet	Wisteria
Castor bean	woody	Soapberry
Indian turnip	Ground cherry	
Skunk cabbage	Foxglove	
	Larkspur	

B. *Trees and shrubs* that are poisonous and may produce vomiting, abdominal pain and in some cases diarrhea:

Horse chestnut	Western yew	Apricot,
Buckeye	English holly	almond
Rain tree	Privet	Peach, cherry
Monkey pod	Mock orange	Wild cherry
American yew	Bird of paradise	Japanese plum
English yew	Black locust	Balsam pear

C. *Outdoor plants* with varied toxic effect:

Rhubarb	Buttercup	Moonseed
Spinach	Nightshade	Mayapple
Sunburned	Poison hemlock	Dutchman's
potatoes	Jimsonweed	breeches

Tomato vine	Pigweed	Mescal bean
Locoweed	Water hemlock	Angel's
Lupine	Mushrooms	trumpet
Dologeton		Jasmine
		Matrimony
		vine

D. *Hallucinogens:*

| Marijuana | Nutmeg | Peyote |
| Morning glory | Periwinkle | Locoweed |

E. *Outdoor plants* that produce convulsions:

| Chinaberry | Moonweed | Water |
| Coriaria | Nux vomica | hemlock |

If you think that your dog may have been poisoned, the first thing to do is try to identify the poison. Most products containing chemicals are labeled for identification. Read the label. If this does not give you a clue to its possible toxicity, call the Poison Control Center.

Poison Control Centers are located throughout the United States and Canada. All available information on the toxic ingredients in thousands of medicines, insecticides, pesticides and other registered commercial products has been placed confidentially in the centers by the government in these Poison Control Centers. It is estimated that 1,500 new items are added each month. The local Poison Control Center's telephone number is listed in the front of most telephone directories. Alternately, you can call the emergency room of your local hospital and ask them to request the information that you require.

The first step in treatment is to eliminate the poison from your dog's stomach by making it vomit. The second step is to delay absorption of the poison from the dog's intestinal tract by coating it with a substance that binds it. This is followed by a laxative to speed elimination.

Note: Do not induce vomiting or give charcoal by mouth if your dog is severely depressed, comatose, unable to swallow or experiencing seizures. Before proceeding, consult *Vomiting, How to Induce* in this chapter.

How to Delay or Prevent Absorption

1. Mix activated charcoal (one tablet to 10 cc water). Give one teaspoonful per two pounds body weight and follow with a pint of water. Depending upon the dog's condition, this may need to be given by stomach tube. Veterinary assistance usually is required.
2. Thirty minutes later, give sodium sulphate (Glauber's salt), one teaspoonful per ten pounds body weight, or Milk of Magnesia, one teaspoonful per five pounds body weight.

Note: If these agents are not available, coat the bowel with milk, egg whites or vegetable oil and give a warm water enema.

If your dog has a poisonous substance on the skin or coat, wash it well with soap and water or give a complete bath in *lukewarm* (not cold) water, as described in the SKIN chapter. Even if the substance is not irritating to the skin, it should be removed. Otherwise, the dog may lick it off and swallow it. Soak gasoline and oil stains with mineral or vegetable oil. Work in well. Then wash with a mild detergent, such as Ivory soap.

When signs of nervous system involvement begin to show, the dog is in deep trouble. At this point, your main objective is to *get your dog to a veterinarian as quickly as possible*. Try to bring with you a sample of vomitus, or better yet the poison in its original container. If the dog is convulsing, unconscious or not breathing, see *Shock* and *Artificial Respiration*. (Also see NERVOUS SYSTEM: *Fits*).

The poisons discussed below are included because they are among the most frequently seen by veterinarians.

Strychnine

Strychnine is used as a rat, mouse and mole poison. It is available commercially as coated pellets dyed purple, red or green. Signs of poisoning are so typical that the diagnosis can be made almost at once. Onset is sudden (less than two hours). The first signs are agitation, excitability and apprehension. They are followed rather quickly by intensely painful tetanic seizures that last about sixty seconds, during which the dog throws the head back, can't breathe and turns blue. The slightest stimulation, such as tapping the dog or clapping the hands, starts a seizure. This characteristic response is used to make the diagnosis. Other signs associated with nervous system involvement are tremors, champing, drooling, uncoordinated muscle spasms, collapse and paddling of the legs.

Seizures caused by strychnine and other central nervous system toxins sometimes are misdiagnosed as epilepsy. This would be a mistake as immediate veterinary attention is necessary. Epileptic seizures are self-limited; the signs usually appear in a certain order, and each attack is the same. They are over before the dog can get to a veterinarian. Usually they are not considered emergencies (see NERVOUS SYSTEM: *Epilepsy*).

Treatment: With signs of central nervous involvement, don't take time to induce vomiting. It is important to avoid loud noises or unnecessary handling that trigger a seizure. Cover your dog with a coat or blanket and drive to the nearest veterinary clinic.

If your dog is showing signs of poisoning, is alert and able to swallow and hasn't vomited, induce vomiting as discussed above.

Sodium Fluroacetate (1080)

This chemical, used as a rat poison, is mixed with cereal, bran and other rat feeds. It is so potent that cats and dogs can be poisoned just by eating the dead rodent. The onset is sudden and begins with vomiting followed by excitation, straining to urinate or defecate, an aimless staggering gait, atypical fits or true convulsions and then collapse. Seizures are *not* triggered by external stimuli as are those of strychnine poisoning.

Treatment: Immediately after the dog ingests the poison, induce vomiting. Care and handling is the same as for strychnine.

Arsenic

Arsenic is combined with metaldehyde in slug and snail baits, and may appear in ant poisons, weed killers and insecticides. Arsenic is also a common impurity found in many chemicals. Death can occur quickly before there is time to observe the symptoms. In more protracted cases the signs are thirst, drooling, vomiting, staggering, intense abdominal pain, cramps, diarrhea, paralysis and death. The breath of the dog will have a strong smell of garlic.

Treatment: Induce vomiting. A specific antidote is available but requires professional use.

Metaldehyde

This poison (often combined with arsenic) is used commonly in rat, snail and slug baits. The signs of toxicity are excitation, drooling and slobbering, uncoordinated gait, muscle tremors and weakness that leads to inability to stand in a few hours. The tremors are not triggered by external stimuli.

Treatment: Immediately after the dog ingests the poison, induce vomiting. The care and handling are the same as for strychnine.

Lead

Lead is found in insecticides and is a base for many paints used commercially. Intoxication occurs primarily in puppies and young dogs that chew on substances coated with a lead paint. Other sources of lead are linoleum, batteries, plumbing materials, putty, lead foil, solder, golf balls and some roofing materials. Lead poisoning can occur in older dogs after ingestion of insecticides containing lead. A chronic form does occur.

Acute poisoning begins with abdominal colic and vomiting. A variety of central nervous system signs are possible. They include fits, uncoordinated gait, excitation, continuous barking, attacks of hysteria, weakness, stupor and blindness. Chewing and champing fits might be mistaken for the encephalitis of distemper, especially in young dogs.

Treatment: When ingestion is recent, induce vomiting. Otherwise, coat the bowel as described above. Specific antidotes are available through your veterinarian.

Phosphorus

This chemical is present in rat and roach poisons, fireworks, matches and match boxes. A poisoned dog's breath may have a garlic odor. The first signs of intoxication are vomiting and diarrhea. They may be followed by a free interval, then by recurrent vomiting, cramps, pain in the abdomen, convulsions and coma. There is no specific antidote. Treat as you would for strychnine.

Zinc Phosphide

This substance also is found in rat poisons. Intoxication causes central nervous system depression, labored breathing, vomiting (often of blood), weakness, convulsions and death. There is no specific antidote. Treat as you would for strychnine.

Warfarin (Decon, Pindone)

Warfarin is incorporated into grain feeds for use as a rat and mouse poison. It causes death by interfering with the blood clotting mechanism. This leads to spontaneous bleeding. There are no observable signs of warfarin poisoning until the dog begins to pass blood in the stool or urine, bleeds from the nose or develops hemorrhages beneath the gums and skin. The dog may be found dead with no apparent cause. A single dose of warfarin is not as serious as repeated doses.

Treatment: Induce vomiting. Vitamin K (for clotting) is a specific antidote. It is given intramuscularly (or in cases where there are no symptoms it can be given by mouth as a preventative).

Antifreeze (Ethylene Glycol)

Poisoning with antifreeze is not uncommon because ethylene glycol has a sweet taste that appeals to dogs and cats. In dogs, a toxic dose is one half teaspoonful per pound body weight. Signs of toxicity, which appear suddenly, are vomiting, uncoordinated gait (seems ''drunk''), weakness, mental depression, coma and death in twelve to thirty-six hours. Convulsions are unusual. Dogs that recover from the acute phase may have damage to the kidneys and go on to kidney failure.

Treatment: Induce vomiting. Coat the bowel to prevent further absorption. Intensive care in an animal hospital may prevent kidney complications.

Organophosphates and Carbamates

These substances are used on dogs to kill fleas and other parasites. The common ones are dichlorvos, ectoral and sevin, but there are others. They also are used in garden sprays and in some dewormers. Improper application of insecticides to the dog can lead to absorption of a toxic dose through the skin. These drugs effect the nervous system primarily. For more information, see SKIN: *Insecticides.*

Treatment: For topical insecticides, bathe your dog immediately using warm soapy water to remove residual compounds from the coat. Call your veterinarian.

Chlorinated Hydrocarbons

These compounds, like the organophosphates, are incorporated into some insecticide preparations for use on the dog. The common products in veterinary use are chlordane, toxaphene, lindane and methoxychlor. The treatment is the same as for organophosphates.

Corrosives (Acid and Alkali)

Corrosives and caustics are found in household cleaners, drain decloggers and commercial solvents. They cause burns of the mouth, esophagus and stomach. Severe cases are associated with acute perforation, or late stricture, of the esophagus and stomach.

Treatment: If acid is ingested, rinse out your dog's mouth. Give an antacid (Milk of Magnesia or Pepto-Bismol) at the rate of one to two teaspoons per five pounds body weight. If an alkali, use vinegar or lemon juice. Vinegar is mixed one part to four parts of water. The amount to give is judged by the size of the dog. Do not induce vomiting; this could result in rupture of the stomach or burns of the esophagus.

Petroleum Products (Gasoline, Kerosene, Turpentine)

These volatile liquids can cause pneumonia if aspirated or inhaled. The signs of toxicity are vomiting, difficulty of breathing, tremors, convulsions and coma. Death is by respiratory failure.

Treatment: Do not induce vomiting. Administer an ounce or two of mineral oil, olive oil or vegetable oil by mouth; then follow it in thirty minutes with Glauber's salt. Be prepared to administer artificial respiration.

Garbage Poisoning (Food Poisoning)

Food poisoning is common, as dogs are notorious scavengers and come into contact with carrion, decomposing foods, animal manure and other noxious substances (some of which are listed in DIGESTIVE SYSTEM: *Common Causes of Diarrhea*). Signs of poisoning begin with vomiting and pain in the abdomen; they are followed in severe cases by diarrhea (often bloody) in two to six hours. If the problem is complicated by bacterial infection, shock may develop. Mild cases recover in a day or two.

Treatment: Induce vomiting. Afterward, coat the intestines to delay or prevent absorption. The condition may require antibiotics. (See also NERVOUS SYSTEM: *Botulism.*)

Chocolate Poisoning

All dogs like chocolate, but chocolate can be dangerous. Chocolate contains a caffeinelike alkaloid called theobromine. While not toxic to people in the amounts present in commercial foods, theobromine in these amounts can be quite harmful to the dog.

Signs of chocolate toxicity occur within hours after the dog ingests the chocolate. They include vomiting, diarrhea, increased heart rate, rapid breathing, muscle tremors, seizures and coma.

A small dog weighing five to ten pounds can die after eating four to sixteen ounces of milk chocolate; a medium-sized dog weighing twenty to forty pounds can die after eating sixteen to thirty-two ounces; a larger dog after eating about two pounds. Individual variations do occur. Unsweetened chocolate (used for baking) contains higher concentrations of theobromine and is therefore more toxic. A large dog can die after eating just four ounces.

Treatment: If you know your dog has eaten chocolate, induce vomiting (see *Vomiting, How to Induce*). If two or more hours have passed, administer activated charcoal to prevent the toxin from becoming absorbed.

Don't feed your dog chocolates. To prevent accidental ingestion, keep chocolate candy in the refrigerator.

Toad Poisoning

Since all toads have a bad taste, dogs who mouth them slobber, spit and drool. In southern states a tropical toad (*Bufo marinus*) secretes a potent toxin that appears to affect the heart and circulation of dogs, bringing on death in as short a time as fifteen minutes. There are twelve species of *Bufo* toads worldwide.

Symptoms in dogs depend upon the toxicity of the toad and the amount of poison absorbed. Signs vary from merely slobbering to convulsions and death.

Treatment: Flush your dog's mouth out with a garden hose and attempt to induce vomiting. Be prepared to administer artificial respiration.

People Medicines

Veterinarians frequently are called because a dog has swallowed pills intended for the owner, or has eaten too many dog pills. (Some dog pills are flavored to encourage dogs to eat them.) Drugs most often involved are antihistamines, sleeping pills, diet pills, heart preparations and vitamins.

Treatment: Induce vomiting and coat the bowel as described (p. 15) to prevent further absorption. Discuss possible side effects of the drug with your veterinarian.

SNAKE BITES

If your dog is bitten by a snake, there may be no cause for concern, as the majority of snakes are nonpoisonous. The bites of harmless snakes show teeth marks in the shape of a horseshoe, but there are no fang marks.

In the United States, there are four poisonous varieties: Cottonmouth moccasins, rattlesnakes, copperheads and coral snakes. The diagnosis of poisonous snake bite is made by the appearance of the bite, by the behavior of the animal and by identification of the species of snake. (Kill it first, if possible.)

Pit Vipers (Rattlesnakes/Moccasins/Copperheads)

Identify these species by their large arrow-shaped heads, pits below and between the eyes, elliptical pupils, rough scales and the presence of fangs in the upper jaws.

The bite: There are two puncture wounds in the skin (fang marks). Signs of local reaction appear *quickly* and include swelling, excruciating pain, redness and hemorrhages in the skin.

Behavior of the animal: Signs and symptoms depend on the size and species of the snake, location of the bite and amount of toxin absorbed into the system. The first signs are extreme restlessness, panting, drooling and weakness. They are followed by diarrhea, collapse, sometimes seizures, shock and, in severe cases, death.

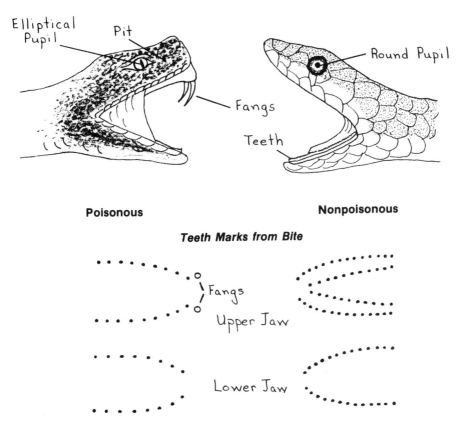

Except for the coral snake, all poisonous species in North America are pit vipers. Note the elliptical pupil, pit below the eye, large fangs and characteristic bite.   *(Rose Floyd)*

Coral Snake

Identify this snake by its rather small size, small head with black nose and vivid colored bands of red, yellow, white and black—the red and yellow bands always next to each other. Fangs are present in the upper jaw.

The bite: There is less severe local reaction but the pain is excruciating. Look for the fang marks.

Behavior of the animal: Coral snake venom primarily is neurotoxic. Signs include vomiting, diarrhea, urinary incontinence, paralysis, convulsions and coma.

Treatment of All Bites:

First identify the snake and look at the bite. If it appears your dog has been bitten by a poisonous snake, proceed as follows:

1. Restrain the dog. Snake bites are extremely painful.
2. Apply a flat tourniquet above the bite. It should not be as tight as an arterial tourniquet (see *Wounds*) but should be tight enough to keep venous blood from returning to the heart.
3. Using a knife or razor blade, make parallel cuts one-quarter inch deep through the fang marks. On a leg, make them up and down. Blood should ooze from the wound. If not, loosen the tourniquet.
4. Apply mouth suction unless you have a cut or open sore in your mouth. Spit out the blood. If poison is swallowed, the stomach will inactivate it. Continue for thirty minutes.
5. Loosen the tourniquet for thirty seconds every half hour.
6. *Keep the dog quiet.* Excitement, exercise and struggling increase the rate of absorption. Carry your dog to the veterinarian.

Specific antivenoms are available through veterinarians. Snake bites become infected. Antibiotics and dressings are indicated.

SHOCK

Shock is lack of adequate blood flow to meet the body's needs. Adequate blood flow requires effective heart pumping, open intact vessels and sufficient blood volume to maintain flow and pressure. Any condition adversely affecting the heart, vessels or blood volume can induce shock.

At first the body attempts to compensate for the inadequate circulation by speeding up the heart, constricting the skin vessels and maintaining fluid in the circulation by reducing output of urine. This becomes increasingly difficult to do when the vital organs aren't getting enough oxygen to carry on these activities. After a time, shock becomes self-perpetuating. Prolonged shock causes death.

Common causes of shock are dehydration (prolonged vomiting and diar-

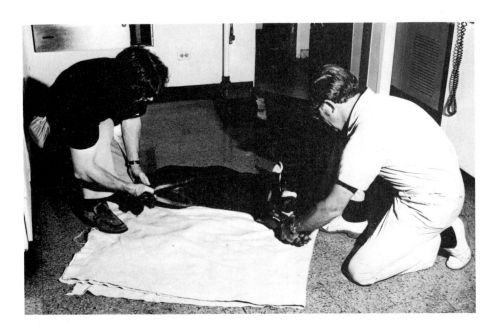

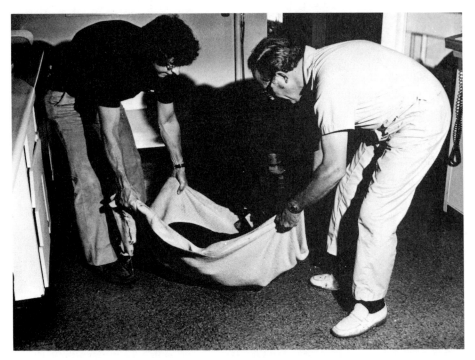

Transporting a dog in shock. Muzzle only when absolutely necessary.   (J. Clawson)

rhea), heat stroke, severe infections, poisoning and hemorrhage. *Being hit by a car is the most common cause of traumatic shock in the dog.*

The signs of shock, which are caused by the effects of poor circulation and the adjustments made to compensate for this, are a drop in body temperature; shivering; listlessness and mental depression; weakness; cold feet and legs; pale skin and mucus membranes; a weak faint pulse.

Treatment: First evaluate the signs present. Is the dog breathing? Is there a heartbeat? What are the extent of the injuries? Is the dog in shock? If so, proceed as follows:

1. If not breathing, proceed with artificial respiration.
2. If no heartbeat or pulse, administer heart massage.
3. If unconscious, check to be sure the airway is open; clear secretions from the mouth with your fingers; pull out the tongue to keep the airway clear of secretions. Keep the dog's head lower than the body.
4. Control bleeding (as described under *Wounds* section that follows).
5. To prevent further aggravation of shock:
   a. Calm your dog and speak soothingly.
   b. Let the dog assume the most comfortable position, and adopt the one with the least pain. Don't force your dog to lie down—it may make breathing more difficult.
   c. When possible, splint or support broken bones before moving the dog (see MUSCULOSKELETAL SYSTEM).
   d. Cover your dog with a coat or blanket. Do not wrap tightly.
   e. Transport large dogs on a flat surface or in a hammock stretcher. Carry small dogs with injured parts protected.
   f. Muzzle only when absolutely necessary. It may impair breathing.

VOMITING, HOW TO INDUCE

Do Not *Induce Vomiting If Your Dog:*

1. Swallows an acid, alkali, solvent or heavy-duty cleaner;
2. Is severely depressed or comatose;
3. Swallows a petroleum product;
4. Swallows tranquilizers (which prevent vomiting);
5. Swallows sharp objects (which could lodge in the esophagus or perforate the stomach);
6. Or if more than two hours have passed since the poison was swallowed.

Induce Vomiting By Giving:

1. Syrup of ipecac (one teaspoonful per ten pounds body weight);
2. Hydrogen peroxide 3% (one to three teaspoonfuls every ten minutes; repeat three times);
3. One half to one teaspoonful of salt, placed at the back of the tongue.

WOUNDS

In the care of wounds, the two most important objectives are first to stop the bleeding, and then to prevent infection. Since wounds are painful to the dog, be prepared to restrain or muzzle before you treat the wound.

Control of Bleeding

Bleeding may be *arterial* (the spurting of bright red blood), or *venous* (oozing of dark red blood), or sometimes both. Do not wipe a wound that has stopped bleeding. This will dislodge the clot. Don't pour hydrogen peroxide on a fresh wound. Bleeding then will be difficult to control.

The two methods used to control bleeding are the pressure dressing and the tourniquet:

The Pressure Dressing: Take several pieces of clean or sterile gauze, place them over the wound and bandage snugly. Watch for swelling of the limb below the pressure pack. This indicates impaired circulation. The bandage must be loosened or removed.

An alternate method to control bleeding is to apply pressure over the artery in the groin or axilla. (See CIRCULATORY SYSTEM: *Pulse*). Often this will control bleeding long enough to permit an assistant to apply a pressure dressing.

If material is not available for bandaging, place a pad on the wound and press it firmly. Hold in place until help arrives.

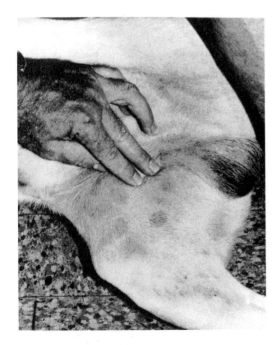

Apply pressure over the artery in the groin to control arterial bleeding in the leg. *(J. Clawson)*

25

The Tourniquet: A tourniquet may be needed to control a spurting artery. It can be applied to the tail or leg above the wound (between the wound and the heart). Take a piece of cloth or gauze roll and loop it around the limb. Then tighten it by hand, or with a stick inserted beneath the loop and twisted around until bleeding is controlled. If you see the end of the artery, you might attempt to pick it up with tweezers and tie it off with a piece of cotton thread. When possible, this should be left to a trained practitioner.

A tourniquet should be loosened every thirty minutes for two to three minutes to let blood flow into the limb.

Treating the Wound

All wounds are contaminated with dirt and bacteria. Proper care and handling will prevent some infections. Before handling a wound, make sure your hands and instruments are clean. Starting at the edges of a fresh wound, clip the hair back to enlarge the area. Cleanse the edges of the wound with a damp gauze or pad. Irrigate the wound with clean tap water. Apply antibiotic ointment. Bandage as described below.

Older wounds with a covering of pus and scab are cleansed with 3% hydrogen peroxide solution or a surgical soap. Blot dry. Apply antibiotic ointment and bandage as described below.

Dressings over infected wounds should be changed frequently to aid in the drainage of pus, and to allow you to apply fresh ointment.

Fresh lacerations over one-half inch long should be sutured to prevent infection, minimize scarring and speed healing. Wounds over twelve hours old are quite likely to be infected. Suturing is questionable.

Bites are heavily contaminated wounds. Often they are puncture wounds. They are quite likely to get infected. *They should not be sutured.* Antibiotics are indicated.

With all animal bites, the possibility of rabies should be kept in mind (see INFECTIOUS DISEASES: *Rabies*).

Bandaging

The equipment you will need is listed in the *Home Emergency and Medical Kit*, in the photo at the beginning of this chapter.

Foot and Leg Bandages. To bandage the foot, place several sterile gauze pads over the wound. Insert cotton balls between the toes and hold in place with adhesive tape looped around the bottom of the foot and back across the top until the foot is snugly wrapped.

For leg wounds, begin by wrapping the foot as described. Then cover the wound with several sterile gauze pads and hold in place with strips of adhesive tape. Wrap the tape around the leg but don't overlap it so that the tape sticks to the hair. This keeps the dressing from sliding up and down, as often happens

26

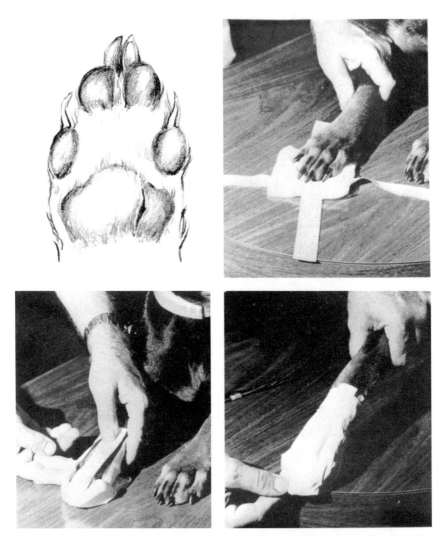

A method of applying a foot bandage for a lacerated pad. Tape loosely to allow good circulation. *(J. Clawson)*

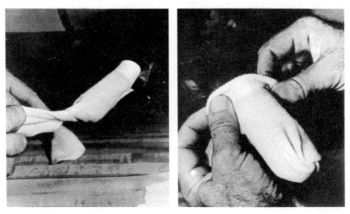

A sock slipped over a gauze square is a good bandage for ease of dressing change. *(J. Clawson)*

when a roll gauze bandage is used. Flex the knee and foot several times to be sure the bandage is not too tight and there is good circulation and movement at the joints.

When a dressing is to be left in place for some time, check on it every few hours to be sure the foot is not swelling. If there is any question about the sensation or circulation to the foot, loosen the dressing.

Many-Tailed Bandage. This bandage is used to protect the skin of the neck or abdomen from scratching and biting and to hold dressings in place. It is made by taking a rectangular piece of linen and cutting the sides to make tails. Tie the tails together over the back to hold it in place.

A many-tailed bandage may be used to keep puppies from nursing infected breasts.

Eye Bandage. At times your veterinarian may prescribe an eye bandage in the treatment of an eye ailment. Place a sterile gauze square over the affected eye and hold it in place by taping around the head with one inch adhesive. Be careful not to get the tape too tight. Apply the dressing so that the ears are free.

You may be required to change the dressing from time to time to apply medication to the eye.

The ear bandage is discussed in the chapter EARS.

Elizabethan Collar. An Elizabethan Collar, named for the high neck ruff popular in the reign of Queen Elizabeth, is a useful device to keep a dog from scratching at the ears and biting at a wound or skin problem. They are recommended for certain disorders discussed in the SKIN chapter. They can be purchased from some veterinarians or pet stores, or can be made from plastic and cardboard. Plastic flowerpots, wastebaskets and buckets work well.

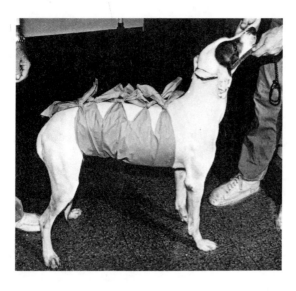

Many-tailed bandage.
(J. Clawson)

Eye bandage, properly applied. *(J. Clawson)*

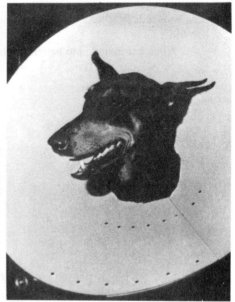
Elizabethan collar. *(J. Clawson)*

The size of the collar is tailored to the dog. Cut just enough out of the bottom to let the dog's head slip through, then fasten the device to a leather collar by strings passed through holes punched in the sides of the plastic. The neck of the collar should be short enough to let the dog eat and drink. Most dogs adjust to them quite well after a few minutes. Others won't eat or drink with the collar in place. In that case, temporarily remove the collar.

Typical appearance of a puppy suffering from intestinal parasites.

2

Worms—Intestinal Parasites

MOST OWNERS believe that if parasites are found in the stool, then the dog is suffering from a disease state.

This is not necessarily the case. Most dogs are infested at one time or another with intestinal parasites. Some are born with them and others acquire them later in life. When they recover, they develop a certain amount of immunity. This helps to keep the worms in check.

One should distinguish a disease state from the mere presence of a parasite. For example, demodectic mange mites live on the skin, and in most dogs they produce no disease and require no treatment. The same may be true of intestinal parasites.

If worms are causing disease, there should be some change in the appearance of the stool. In turn, this is reflected by a decline in the general health of the dog. You should note decreased appetite, loss of weight, upset stomach, anemia, mucus and/or blood in the feces.

Dogs are capable of developing a resistance to certain worms—those having a larvae phase that migrates in their tissues (roundworms, hookworms and threadworms). The effect is on the maturation cycle. The larvae remain dormant as cysts in the tissues instead of becoming adults in the intestine. Whipworms and tapeworms have no migratory stage and thus cause little buildup of immunity.

Resistance to roundworms appears age-related. Experimentally, it is difficult to induce a heavy infestation (over ten worms in the gut) in dogs over six months of age.

Immunosuppressive drugs such as cortisone have been shown to activate large numbers of hookworm larvae lying dormant in the dog's tissue. Stressful events such as trauma, surgery, severe disease and emotional upsets (i.e., shipping a puppy) also can activate dormant larvae. This leads to the appearance of parasites in the stool.

During pregnancy, roundworm larvae are activated and migrate to the unborn puppies. Accordingly, a heavy parasite problem may appear in a litter even when the mother was effectively dewormed. This can happen because none of the deworming agents are effective against larvae encysted in the tissue.

DEWORMING PUPPIES AND ADULT DOGS

Most **puppies** are infested with roundworms. Other worms may be present, too. It is advisable to have your veterinarian check your puppy's stool before treating for roundworms. Otherwise, other worms may go undetected.

Deworming Agents

Drug	Type of Worm Involved				Comments
	Hook	Round	Whip	Tape	
CANOPAR (*Thenium Closylate*)	****	----	----	----	Do not use in a nursing bitch. Use one size of pill only. May induce vomiting.
DNP (*Disophenol*)	****	----	----	----	Use with caution in anemic dogs or those with respiratory problems. Do not overdose.
DRONCIT (*Praziquantel*)	----	----	----	****	Available as pill or injection.
NEMEX (*Pyrantel Pamoate*)	****	****	----	----	Can be given to nursing puppies. Available as liquid or tablets.
PANACUR (*Bunamide*)	****	****	****	**	Granular formulation. No contraindications.
PIPERAZINE	----	***	----	----	Do not overdose.
SCOLABAN (*Bunamidine*)	----	----	----	****	Occasional sudden death in large dogs. Do not use with Styquin or in dogs with heart condition, severe debilitation, impaired liver function. Do not crush tablets before administering.

STYRID CARICIDE (*Diethylcarbamizine and Strylpyridium*)	*	*	–––	–––	Do not use if dog has heartworms.
TASK (*Dichlorvos*)	****	****	–––	–––	Do not use if dog has heartworms. Do not use concurrently with insecticides. Injectable form is good for whips.
TELMINTIC (*Mebendazole*)	****	****	****	*	Wide margin of safety. Give to the dog for 3 to 5 days.
THIABENDAZOLE (*Mintezol*)	–––	–––	–––	–––	Vomiting sometimes occurs. Can be used in threadworm treatment.
VERCOM PASTE (*Febantel and Praziquantel*)	****	****	****	****	Administer to adults by mouth or in food without regard to feeding schedule. Administer to puppies less than 6 months of age only by mouth on a full stomach.
IVERMECTIN	****	****	–––	–––	Not approved for dogs as a dewormer, only for heartworm prevention. May cause seizures in Collies and Collie mixes.
FILARBITS PLUS (*Oxibendazole and Diethylcarbamizine*)	**	**	**	–––	Used primarily in heartworm prevention, but is contraindicated if microfilariae are present in blood. Can be used in puppies 8 weeks or older as daily tablet.
INTERCEPTOR (*Milbemycin Oxime*)	**	–––	–––	–––	One tablet a month prevents heartworms and controls hookworms. Can be used in puppies 8 weeks and older. Wide margin of safety. Does not cause problem in Collies.

**** Excellent *** Good ** Fair * Poor ––– No effect

Worm infestations are particularly harmful in puppies subjected to over-feeding, chilling, close confinement and a sudden change in diet. Stressful conditions such as these should be corrected before administering a deworming agent.

Puppies should be dewormed at two to three weeks of age and again at five to six weeks. If eggs or worms are still found in the stool, subsequent courses should be given.

There are a number of dewormers on the market. No one preparation is advisable for all occasions. If you decide to use one of these preparations, be sure it is safe and effective; follow the recommendations supplied by the manufacturer.

Many veterinarians recommend that **adult** dogs be dewormed only when there are specific signs of an infestation. A stool examination is the most effective way of making an exact diagnosis and choosing the best agent.

Most dogs carry *roundworms* as encysted larvae, but intestinal infestation by the adult worm in the healthy dog is a rare occurrence. *Hookworms* are likely to be a problem during periods of stress. Routine deworming may catch an intestinal phase but is not effective against encysted larvae. When *whipworms* are present, usually several courses of treatment are required to eliminate the infestation. *Tapeworms* are common in the dog. The worm segments are easy to detect in the stool. Fortunately, they cause very little difficulty. *Threadworms* are not common. Very few agents are effective against this parasite.

Many kennel owners believe that their dogs are kept in better condition if they deworm them once or twice a year. In such cases, Panacur is a good choice. It has a wide spectrum of activity and no known contraindications.

Problems may be caused by overworming with harsh preparations. They are stressful to the dog, irritate the intestines and actually may lower resistance to worms.

Consult the accompanying table to learn about some of the currently recommended deworming agents. Certain dewormers should not be given to dogs with coexistent illnesses, such as heartworms. Others can react adversely with drugs your dog has taken recently. It is not safe to use certain drugs on breeding animals or those who are pregnant. It is best to check with your veterinarian before using one of those preparations.

Before breeding a **brood bitch**, have her stool checked. If parasites are found, she should receive a thorough deworming. This will not protect puppies from all worm infestation; however, it will help to put her in the best condition for a healthy pregnancy.

How to Control Worms

The life cycles of most canine worms are such that the possibility of reinfestation is great. To keep worms under control, you must destroy eggs or larvae *before* they infest the dog. This means good sanitation and maintaining clean, dry quarters for your dog.

Dogs should not be kenneled on dirt runs. A watertight surface, such as cement, is the easiest to keep clean. Hose it down daily and allow it to dry thoroughly. Disinfect with boiling water and Lysol. Gravel is a good substitute. Usually it provides good drainage and it is easy to remove stools from gravel.

Gravel can be disinfected with lime or salt. Lime is an alkaline corrosive and should not be consumed. Pens should be hosed down after using lime. Remove stools from the pens daily.

Lawns should be cut short and watered only when necessary. Stools in the yard should be removed at least once a week.

Fleas, lice, mice and other rodents are intermediate hosts for the tapeworm. It is necessary to get rid of these pests in order to control their disease (see SKIN: *Premises Control*).

Dogs should not be allowed to roam and hunt. They could catch and devour raw meat, ingest carrion or parts of dead animals. Be sure to cook thoroughly all fresh meat before feeding it to your dog (*see Tapeworms*).

Kennels that have continuous problems with worms often have other problems, too. They include skin, bowel and respiratory difficulties. Steps should be taken to improve the management of the kennel, especially sanitation measures.

Heartworm preparations, given to prevent dirofilaria immitis, also are partially effective against roundworms (Caricide), and round and hookworms (Styrid-Caricide). These agents are given daily in low dosages. The effect lasts only as long as you give the medication. Used in this manner, they serve mainly to *prevent* infection.

DISEASES CAUSED BY WORMS

Roundworms (*Ascarids*)

Adult roundworms, which live in the intestine, are one to seven inches long. A female may lay 200,000 eggs in a day. These eggs are protected by a hard shell. They are extremely hardy and can live for months or years in the soil.

Dogs acquire the disease through contact with soil containing the eggs. Eggs, entering via the oral route, hatch in the intestine. Larvae are carried to the lungs by the bloodstream. Here, they become mobile, crawl up the windpipe and are swallowed (this may cause bouts of coughing and gagging). They return to the intestine and develop into adults. This sequence occurs mainly in the young puppy.

In the older dog, only a few larvae return to the intestine. The others encyst in tissue and remain dormant. During the late stages of pregnancy, these dormant larvae are released, reenter the circulation and are carried to the unborn puppies. Circulating larvae also get to puppies via the breast milk.

Deworming the dam before or during pregnancy does not prevent roundworm infestation of unborn puppies; medications do not work on encysted larvae. Accordingly, many puppies are born with roundworms.

Roundworms do not cause much difficulty in adult dogs. A severe infestation in puppies, however, can lead to death. Puppies with a heavy roundworm infestation have a potbellied appearance and a dull coat. The usual signs are vomiting (sometimes of worms), diarrhea, loss of weight and failure to thrive. Worms may be passed in the stool. Typically, they look like white earthworms or strands of spaghetti that are alive and moving.

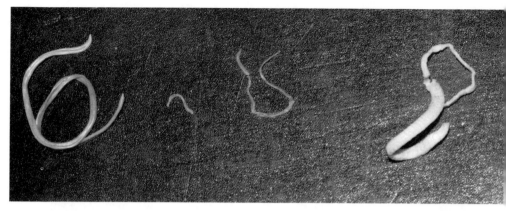

| ROUNDWORM | HOOKWORM | WHIPWORM | TAPEWORM |

Common adult canine worms, showing relative size and appearance of adult worms and eggs. (Roundworm eggs: two species).

Roundworms can cause a disease in humans called *visceral larva migrans*. A few cases are reported each year, usually from areas with a mild climate. There is often a history of dirt-eating (of soil contaminated by the eggs). Children are most likely to be affected. Because man is not the normal host, the immature worms do not become adults. Instead, they migrate into tissues and wander aimlessly, causing fever, anemia, liver enlargement, pneumonia and other ill effects. Usually, the disease runs its course in about a year. It is prevented most effectively by controlling infestation in the dog through periodic deworming and good sanitation (see SKIN: *Premises Control*).

Treatment: Nemex (pyrantel pamoate) is one of the safest dewormers for roundworms and hookworms and can be given to nursing puppies. This makes it the agent of choice for these youngsters. Puppies should be dewormed by three weeks of age to prevent contamination of their quarters by roundworm eggs. A second course should be given two to three weeks later to kill any adult worms that were in the larvae stage at the first deworming.

Pyrantel pamoate dewormers can be obtained from your veterinarian. You do not have to fast your dog before using this agent. Be sure to follow the directions of the manufacturer in regard to dosage.

Dichlorvos (Task) is effective against roundworms, hookworms and whipworms. It is somewhat harsher than other preparations. Note that there are better and safer dewormers on the market than Task. It is no longer recommended as a first-line choice. It should not be given to heartworm-positive dogs. Dogs that have been treated with insecticides, and those wearing a flea collar, should not be treated within a week. Use only under veterinary guidance.

Panacur and Telmintic (mebendazole) are effective against roundworms, hookworms and some tapeworms and whipworms. Vercom paste also is effective against roundworms, hookworms, tapeworms and whipworms. All three dewormers have the disadvantage that they must be given for three to five consecutive days. They should be used under veterinary guidance.

Caricide and Styrid-Caricide given in low doses to prevent heartworms also keep roundworms under control. It is advisable to treat first with a more effective agent and then to maintain a wormfree state with these products. Styrid-Caricide also helps control hookworms.

Hookworms (*Ancylostoma*)

Hookworms are small thin worms about one-fourth to one-half inch long. They fasten to the wall of the small intestine and draw blood from the host.

The dog acquires the disease through contact with larvae in contaminated soil or feces. The immature worms migrate to the intestine where they become adults. In about two weeks, the dog begins to pass eggs in the feces.

Unborn puppies can acquire hookworms while still in the uterus, but this is uncommon (1 to 2 percent). The majority of infections are acquired through ingestion of the dam's milk during the first three weeks of life. These puppies can sicken and die rapidly.

The typical signs of *acute* hookworm infestation are anemia and diarrhea. Stools characteristically are bloody, wine-dark or tarry-black. Usually this condition affects puppies at two to eight weeks of age. Occasionally it is seen in older dogs.

Chronic hookworm infection usually is not a problem in the adult dog. When it occurs, the signs are diarrhea, anemia, weight loss and progressive weakness. The diagnosis is made by finding the eggs in the feces.

Many puppies and adults that recover from the disease become carriers via cysts in the tissue. During periods of stress or some other illness, a new outbreak can occur as the larvae are released.

A disease in humans called *cutaneous larvae migrans* (creeping eruption) is caused by the hookworm (*A. brasiliense*). Larvae present in soil penetrate the skin. It causes lumps, streaks beneath the skin and itching. The condition is self-limited.

Treatment: A number of agents, as shown in the accompanying table, are effective against hookworms. Nemex, Panacur, Task (dichlorvos), Vercom Paste and Telmintic are effective against other worms as well (see *Roundworms*). Disophenol (DNP) is a hookworm preparation that must be given by subcutaneous injection. Consult your veterinarian before using any of these agents.

Puppies with acute signs and symptoms require intensive veterinary management.

Tapeworms (*Cestodes*)

These worms also live in the small intestine. The scolex (head) of the parasite fastens itself to the wall of the gut by hooks and suckers. The body is composed of segments containing the egg packets. Tapeworms vary in length from less than an inch to several feet. To cure tapeworm infection, the scolex must be killed and purged.

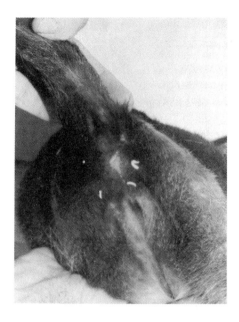
Tapeworm segments.

The body segments containing the eggs are passed in the feces. Fresh moist segments are capable of moving. They are about a quarter of an inch long. Sometimes you will see them adhering to the fur about your dog's anus or in the stool. When dry, they resemble kernels of rice.

Dogs can acquire several different kinds of tapeworm. One is due to eating uncooked meat or discarded animal parts. Another is acquired by eating raw fresh fish. Commonly, the disease is transmitted by the flea. The dog must bite or swallow the flea that harbors the immature tapeworms in its intestine. Fleas acquire the parasite by eating tapeworm eggs.

Apart from a change in the texture and condition of the coat, the common tapeworm rarely causes significant ill effects. Severe infestations can cause mild diarrhea, loss of appetite or reduction in weight. Unless there is a heavy infection, probably you will not notice tapeworm segments in the feces.

Children can acquire a tapeworm if they accidentally swallow an infective flea.

A more serious disease in humans is caused by the tapeworm *Echinococcus granulosus*. This disease is found in cattle, sheep, deer, elk, pigs, horses and other domestic livestock. The dog acquires the infection by eating uncooked meat or the carcass of an animal infected with *Echinococcus granulosus* larvae. Man acquires the disease directly by contact with eggs present in the feces of the dog.

The eggs do not produce worms in humans, as man is not a natural host. Instead, they produce large cysts in the liver, lungs and brain. These cysts are called *hydatids*. A serious or even fatal illness can result.

Prevention: The common dog tapeworm can be prevented by controlling fleas and other insects (see SKIN: *Premises Control*).

Echinococcus granulosus is found in the southern, western and southwestern United States, in areas where sheep and cattle are common. A number of cases are reported each year. Dogs should not be permitted to have access to dead animals or offal. Do not give your dog uncooked meat or raw game to eat.

If you live in a rural area where *Echinococcus granulosus* could be a problem, ask your veterinarian to check your dog's stools for tapeworms twice a year. This species of tapeworm can be identified only after the head has been recovered by effective deworming. Accordingly, dogs infected with a tapeworm of unknown type must be handled with extreme caution to avoid fecal contamination of the hands and food, until a definite diagnosis is forthcoming.

Treatment: Droncit (praziquantel) is effective against all the common dog tapeworms. Other suitable remedies are Scolaban (bunamidine) and Vercom Paste. Use under veterinary guidance.

Whipworms (*Trichuris vulpis*)

The adult whipworm is two to three inches long. It is threadlike for the most part but is thicker at one end. This gives it the appearance of a whip.

The adult lives in the first part of the large intestine (cecum). It fastens itself to the wall of the gut. The female lays fewer eggs than most worms. Infestations are frequently light. Therefore, it is sometimes difficult to detect the presence of whipworms, even after several stool examinations.

Heavy infestations do occur in dogs where the soil is badly contaminated with eggs. These dogs lose weight, appear unthrifty and frequently have diarrhea. Periodic stool checks are advisable in such areas to identify the presence of these worms.

Treatment: A number of preparations are effective against whipworms. They include Panacur (bunamide), Telmintic (mebendazole) and Vercom Paste (febantel and praziquantel). Repeated stool checks are required to assure success, as false negatives are common. Usually several courses of treatment over a prolonged period (three months) are required to eliminate the infestation.

Threadworms (*Strongyloides stercoralis*)

Threadworms are small round worms that live in the intestine and are able to infect both man and dogs. Eggs and/or larvae are passed in the feces. The life cycle of the threadworm is complex. The disease may be acquired by ingestion of the larvae or direct penetration of the skin by larvae present in contaminated soil.

Puppies with threadworms may suffer from profuse watery diarrhea and signs of lung infection. The disease might be mistaken for distemper.

The hazard to human health is variable. There are several geographically separate strains that vary in their ability to infect man. Humans living in tropical climates are affected most commonly. Only a few cases are reported in temperate zones.

Treatment: At present, the deworming agent of choice is Thiabendazole (mintezol). It must be given once a day for five days, and repeated monthly as required. Several negative stool examinations should be obtained before concluding that your dog is free of threadworms.

Uncommon Worm Parasites

Pinworms are a common cause of concern to families having pets and children. However, dogs and cats do not present a source of human pinworm infection as they do not acquire or spread this disease.

Trichinosis is a disease acquired through ingestion of uncooked pork containing the encysted larvae of *Trichina spiralis*. In humans only a few cases are reported each year. The incidence is probably somewhat higher in dogs. Prevent trichinosis by keeping your dog from roaming, especially if you live in the country. Cook all fresh meat—both your own and your dog's.

Flukes are flatworms ranging in size from a few millimeters up to an inch or two in length.

Lung flukes cause a disease in dogs living around the Great Lakes, the Midwest and the southern United States. They are acquired by eating aquatic snails and crayfish. Cysts develop in the lungs. The signs are those of a chronic cough. Rarely a cyst ruptures and causes a collapsed lung.

Intestinal flukes are found in the Pacific Northwest. They are acquired by eating raw fish. The problem is complicated by a rickettsia in the fluke that produces the disease *Canine Salmon Poisoning* (see Infectious Diseases).

Flukes are difficult to treat. Some of the newer dewormers show promise. Prevent infection by cooking fish and restricting hunting.

Lungworms are slender hairlike parasites under an inch in length. Infection is spread from dog to dog through the ingestion of eggs in the sputum or feces.

Capillaria aerophilia resides in the nasal cavity and upper air passages. Most infections are asymptomatic. There may be a chronic cough.

Filaroides osleri is a tracheal/bronchial infection that tends to be a kennel-related problem, especially in Greyhounds. Signs are those of a mild chronic illness with a persistent cough; occasionally there is loss of weight or exercise intolerance. Bronchoscopy discloses small nodules in the wall of the trachea. Larvae may be seen peeking out of these growths.

Treatment of lungworms with various deworming agents is possible, but reactions do occur and treatment is sometimes prolonged.

3

Infectious Diseases

INFECTIOUS DISEASES are caused by bacteria, viruses, protozoa, fungi and rickettsia that invade the body of a susceptible host and cause an illness.

Infectious diseases are often transmitted from one animal to another by contact with infected urine, feces and other bodily secretions or by inhalation of germ-laden droplets in the air. A few are transmitted via the genital tract when dogs mate. Others are acquired by contact with spores in the soil that get into the body through a break in the skin.

Bacteria are single-celled germs, while the virus, the tiniest germ known and even more basic than a cell, is simply a package of molecules. Although germs exist virtually everywhere, only a few cause infection. Fewer still are contagious, i.e., capable of being transmitted from one animal to another. Many infectious agents are able to survive for long periods outside of the host animal. This information is especially useful in controlling the spread of infectious diseases.

ANTIBODIES AND IMMUNITY

An animal that is *immune* to a specific germ has chemical substances in the system called antibodies, which attack and destroy that germ before it can cause an illness.

Natural immunity exists that is species-related. A dog does not catch a disease that is specific for a horse, and vice versa. Some infectious diseases are not specific. They are capable of causing illness in several species of animals.

If susceptible and exposed to an infectious disease, an animal will become

41

ill and begin to make antibodies against that particular germ. When the dog recovers, these antibodies afford protection against reinfection. They continue to do so for a variable length of time. The dog then has acquired *active immunity*.

Active immunity can be induced artificially by vaccination. Through vaccination the animal is exposed to heat-killed germs, live or attenuated germs rendered incapable of disease, or toxins and germ products. They stimulate the production of antibodies that are specific for the vaccine.

Since active immunity tends to wane with the passage of time, booster shots should be given at regular intervals to maintain a high level of antibody in the system.

Antibodies are produced by the *reticuloendothelial system*. It is made up of white blood cells, lymph nodes and special cells in the bone marrow, spleen, liver and lungs. The special cells act along with antibodies and other substances in the blood to attack and destroy germs.

Antibodies are highly specific. They destroy only the type of germ that stimulated their production. Some drugs depress or prevent antibody production. They are called *immunosuppressive drugs*. Cortisone is such a drug.

Run-down, malnourished, debilitated dogs may not be capable of responding to a challenge by developing antibodies or building immunity to germs. Such dogs can be vaccinated but should be revaccinated when in a better state of health. Puppies under three weeks of age may not be able to develop antibodies because of physical immaturity or passive immunity.

There is another type of immunity called *passive immunity*. It is acquired from one animal to another. A classic example is the immunity puppies acquire from the colostrum, or first milk, of the dam. Puppies are best able to absorb these special proteins through their intestines during the first twenty-four to thirty-six hours after birth. The length of protection is dependent upon the antibody level in the blood of the dam when the pups were born. Dams vaccinated within a few months have the highest levels. The maximum length of protection is sixteen weeks. If the dam was never vaccinated against a disease, her pups would receive no protection against it.

Passive antibodies can "tie-up" vaccines given to stimulate active immunity, rendering them ineffective. This is one reason why vaccinations do not always "take" in very young puppies.

VACCINATIONS

There are two types of vaccines. The first is a *modified live virus* preparation. The attenuated live virus particles must reproduce to a certain extent to stimulate an adequate immune response. The second is an *inactivated* or *killed virus* vaccine. Repeated administration is necessary to maintain an adequate level of antibody. In general, modified live vaccines are more effective and produce longer-lasting protection.

While vaccines are highly effective in preventing certain infectious diseases in dogs, failures do occur. They can be due to improper handling and storage, incorrect administration or the inability of the dog to respond. Trying to stretch out the vaccine by dividing one ampule between two dogs is another reason for failure to take.

The nutritional state of the dog is also an important consideration. Malnourished dogs can be vaccinated but should be revaccinated when in better condition. A concurrent illness depresses the immune response, as does the administration of an immunosuppressive drug such as cortisone. If a dog is already exposed to an illness, vaccinating will not alter the course of the disease.

Because each pup or adult is an individual case and proper handling and administration of the vaccine is so important, vaccination should be given only by those familiar with the techniques. When you go to your veterinarian for a booster shot, your dog will get a physical checkup. The veterinarian may detect some important change that you have overlooked.

Young puppies are highly susceptible to certain infectious diseases and should be vaccinated against them as soon as they are old enough to build an immunity. These diseases are distemper, infectious hepatitis, parvovirus, leptospirosis, parainfluenza and coronavirus. Rabies is another problem that continues to be a serious threat to the dog.

To be effective, vaccinations must be kept current (see the *Vaccination Schedule*).

Distemper Vaccine

The first distemper shot should be given shortly after weaning and before a puppy is placed in a new home and is exposed to other dogs. Many veterinarians recommend that six-week-old puppies be vaccinated with the combination canine distemper–measles–parainfluenza vaccine and first-dose parvo vaccine. A high percent of puppies do not get a satisfactory response from a distemper shot because of circulating maternal antibodies that neutralize the distemper virus in the vaccine. The measles virus, which is quite similar to the distemper virus, is not so affected. It is able to stimulate antibodies that protect against distemper, but it does not cause any disease in dogs as it does in humans.

This combination vaccine has been found to build temporary immunity in most young puppies. The distemper-measles vaccine should not be used more than once. Instead, follow it with the DHLPP + Corona vaccination. Booster shots are required.

Infectious Hepatitis Vaccine

The infectious hepatitis vaccine contains one of the canine adenovirus preparations (CAV-I or CAV-2). Either vaccine protects against hepatitis and the adenovirus implicated in the kennel cough complex.

Vaccines containing CAV-1 cause clouding of the clear window of the eye (see EYES: *Blue Eye*). This problem appears one to two weeks after vaccination. For this reason *most* vaccines employed today contain only CAV-2. Vaccines are incorporated into the DHLPP vaccines. Booster shots are required.

Leptospirosis Bacterin

Leptospira bacterin protects against two bacteria that cause leptospirosis. The first shot should be given at three to four months of age. Leptospira vaccine is incorporated into the DHLPP vaccine. Booster shots are required.

In areas where the disease is prevalent, vaccinations at eight and ten weeks of age are indicated. A booster vaccination is advisable every six months.

Parvovirus Vaccine

Virulent parvovirus can infect puppies one to four weeks before we can actively immunize them with many of our current vaccines. Generally, modified live virus vaccines provide greater immunity than killed vaccines. It is difficult to tell at what age a puppy loses its mother's immunity. In high risk situations, vaccinate every two weeks beginning at six weeks of age. Continue until the puppy is sixteen weeks old. Parvovirus vaccine is incorporated in the DHLPP shot. Annual boosters are required.

Coronavirus Vaccine

Coronavirus vaccine is available only in a killed form. It is recommended for puppies twelve weeks of age or older but can be given as early as six weeks. If given at six weeks, puppies should be revaccinated every two weeks until they reach twelve weeks of age. In either case, the pup should be vaccinated again at sixteen weeks. An annual booster is required.

Rabies Vaccine

There are two general types of rabies vaccines. One is a modified live virus preparation and the other is an inactivated virus. *It is important to read and follow the manufacturer's recommendations carefully with respect to frequency of dosage and route of administration.* Be sure that the product is made specifically for dogs.

The first injection should be given at three to four months of age, with booster shots every one to three years, depending upon the vaccine used and local and state ordinances.

Canine Parainfluenza Vaccine (CPI)—Kennel Cough

The parainfluenza is one of the germs implicated in the kennel cough complex. CPI vaccine will protect against this virus, while hepatitis vaccine will protect against two adenoviruses.

Bordetella bronchiseptica vaccine (bacterin) is of aid in the control of the kennel cough complex. Show dogs and dogs living in kennels may benefit from this additional protection. Discuss this with your veterinarian. For more information, see *Bordetella Bronchiseptica*.

Vaccination Schedule

This suggested vaccination schedule should provide adequate protection at minimum cost. It should be modified under the following circumstances:

Vaccination Schedule

Age of Dog	Vaccine Recommended
At 6 to 8 weeks	Canine distemper–measles–parainfluenza (CPI) Parvovirus
At 8 to 12 weeks	DHLPP (distemper, hepatitis [CAV-2], leptospirosis, parainfluenza, parvovirus) Corona* Rabies (at 12 weeks)
At 16 weeks	DHLPP +/− Corona*
At 12 months	Rabies
Annual Booster	DHLPP +/− Corona* Rabies (1 or 3 years, depending on manufacturer's recommendations).

*Corona vaccination is optional. Give first shot at 12 weeks of age.

1. If the puppies receive no colostrum, special immunization procedures will be required (see PEDIATRICS).
2. Females should be given a DHLPP booster shot *before* being bred.
3. Do not vaccinate a pregnant female until you have discussed it with your veterinarian.
4. Some strains of rabies vaccine require booster shots at one year intervals, others at three years. Follow the recommendations of the manufacturer of the vaccine or those of your veterinarian.
5. Parainfluenza and leptospirosis vaccinations are indicated *more frequently* in endemic areas.

CANINE BACTERIAL DISEASES

Brucellosis

This disease is caused by a bacteria called *Brucella canis*. It is an important cause of reproductive failure in dogs. It is the leading cause of late abortions (forty-five to fifty-five days gestation). It may be at fault when a bitch delivers stillborn puppies, or puppies that sicken and die shortly after birth. It can produce sterility in a dog and bitch without causing obvious signs of disease.

Dogs with active infection may show enlargement of the lymph nodes in the groin or beneath the jaw. Fever is absent. Joints may become swollen and painful. The testicles of the male may swell up, then go on to atrophy as the sperm-producing cells are destroyed. In others the disease goes unsuspected until there is evidence of reproductive failure. These animals are able to transmit the infection. In the male, bacteria may be found in the prostate gland and testicle (epididymis); in the female, in the uterus and vagina.

The bacteria is present in vaginal discharges, the products of abortion, blood, mother's milk and the semen of the male. The most common mode of transmission is by contact with infected vaginal discharges. In a kennel it can spread rapidly from dog to dog in this manner. Venereal transmission is important in that males can harbor the bacteria for months or years.

A brucellosis test is available through your veterinarian. It should be done on all dogs before mating. False positives indicate the need for more detailed laboratory tests.

Treatment: At present there is no effective vaccine or treatment for the prevention and cure of brucellosis in dogs. Long-term treatment with antibiotics may be undertaken but relapse is likely to occur when the drugs are stopped. Pet dogs should be castrated or spayed to keep them from transmitting the disease.

To control the spread of brucellosis in a kennel, all animals must be tested and those infected removed from the premises. Follow-up tests must be run every three months to identify new cases.

Leptospirosis

Canine leptospirosis is a disease caused by a bacteria called a *spirochete*. There are two common species that infect the dog. Leptospira also infect cattle, sheep, wild animals, rats and man. The disease is spread in the urine of an infected animal. Rats appear to be one of the main reservoirs of the infection.

Spirochetes enter a dog's system through a break in the skin or via the alimentary route when the dog drinks water or eats food contaminated by infected urine. Most cases are mild or subclinical.

Signs of illness appear within five to fifteen days. Fever is present in the early stage of the disease. It is accompanied by listlessness, loss of appetite and mental depression.

Leptospirosis affects many systems but primarily the kidneys. Symptoms include a "hunched-up" gait because of pain in the kidney area, the formation of ulcers on the mucus membranes of the mouth and tongue, the appearance of a thick brown coating on the tongue, bleeding from the mouth or the passage of bloody stools and severe thirst with increased urination.

The whites of the eyes may turn yellow. This indicates liver involvement.

Persistent vomiting and diarrhea are common. Dogs have difficulty eating and swallowing because of sores in the mouth.

Treatment: A presumptive diagnosis can be made on the basis of the dog's clinical signs and physical findings. This can be confirmed by finding spirochetes in its urine or blood and by blood tests.

Severely ill dogs should be hospitalized for public health reasons and to provide more intensive care. Antibiotic combinations are effective. Supportive measures include control of vomiting and diarrhea, replacement of fluids and maintenance of nutrition.

Some dogs develop chronic progressive kidney failure. They become "carriers" and shed bacteria in their urine for up to a year.

Leptospira cause a disease in humans called *Weil's disease*. Precautions should be taken when handling sick dogs or cleaning up their quarters to avoid contact with infected secretions.

It is advisable to vaccinate dogs in areas where leptospirosis is a problem (see *Vaccinations*).

Tetanus (Lockjaw)

This disease can affect almost all animals including man. It is not contagious. It is caused by a bacteria called *Clostridium tetani*. Dogs possess some natural resistance to this infection.

The tetanus bacteria is found in the intestinal tract of some animals where it does not cause a disease. It is found commonly in soil contaminated by horse and cow manure. Bacteria enter the skin via a puncture or open wound.

Symptoms appear as early as a few days after the injury but can be delayed for as long as several weeks. Tetanus bacteria grow best in tissues where the oxygen level is low. The ideal environment is a deep wound that has sealed over, or one in which there is devitalized tissue heavily contaminated with filth. The bacteria make a toxin that affects the nervous system.

Signs of disease are caused by the neurotoxin. They include spastic contractions and rigid extension of the legs, difficulty opening the mouth and swallowing, retraction of the lips and eyeballs and protrusion of the third eyelid. Contraction of the forehead muscles may cause the ears to stand erect. Muscle spasms are triggered by almost anything that stimulates the dog.

Treatment: Tetanus cannot be treated at home. Fatalities can be avoided by prompt veterinary attention. Tetanus antitoxins, antibiotics, sedatives, intravenous fluids and care of the wound alter the course for the better.

The disease can be prevented by prompt attention to tetanus-prone wounds (see EMERGENCIES: *Wounds*). Since natural resistance is high in dogs, vaccination

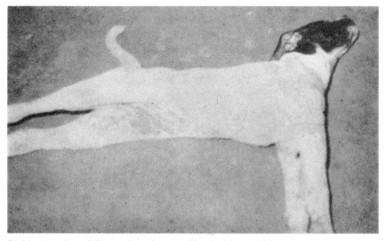

Rigid extension of the neck and extremities in advanced *tetanus*.
(Courtesy American Veterinary Publications)

47

of all dogs is not necessary. Vaccination of herding dogs and those that live around livestock may be indicated.

Tuberculosis

This disease is caused by the *tubercle bacillus*. It affects man and all domestic animals. While there has been a steady decline in the incidence of tuberculosis, it has not been completely wiped out.

Dogs may infect humans and vice versa. The disease is still a problem in cows and other livestock. They may infect the dog also.

Tuberculosis is mainly a lung infection. However, it can affect other organ systems as well. The symptoms depend upon the site of infection. A common finding is low-grade fever with chronic wasting and loss of condition in spite of good care and feeding.

Respiratory tuberculosis causes a chronic cough, labored breathing, shortness of breath and the production of bloody sputum.

Treatment: A typical X ray and the finding of *tubercle bacilli* in sputum or other secretions of the dog make the diagnosis. There are reports of successful treatment in dogs hospitalized over a long period of time and treated with antibiotics. The uncertainty of treatment plus the obvious hazard to human health makes euthanasia the wisest choice.

Bordetella Bronchiseptica

B. Bronchiseptica is commonly isolated from dogs with the kennel cough complex and other respiratory diseases. Experimentally, signs of respiratory illness in dogs have been caused by introducing the bacteria into the respiratory tree. They include cough and nasal discharge. It is quite possible that B.B. is a primary pathogen in some circumstances.

Most cases of B.B. arise in dogs that are recovering from a viral respiratory infection, the bacteria being a secondary invader. Accordingly, it is important to provide a warm, draftfree environment, humidify the atmosphere and avoid stressful activities that might interfere with a smooth recovery from a respiratory illness. The DHLPP shot contains vaccines active against parainfluenza, hepatitis (CAV-2) and distemper: the most common causes of kennel cough complex. Appropriate vaccinations will prevent most infections.

There are two specific bacterins available for the prevention of bordetella bronchiseptica infection. The first is an intranasal vaccine and the second vaccine is given as a shot. The intranasal vaccine, which protects against both B.B. and parainfluenza, gives the more immediate and longer-lasting immunity, but is somewhat more difficult to administer. The injectable vaccine protects against B.B., parainfluenza, distemper, hepatitis (CAV-2) and parvovirus.

Puppies living in areas where B.B. is prevalent can be vaccinated with the intranasal bacterin at two to four weeks of age. Normally the bacterin is given at eight to twelve weeks. A single intranasal dose (puppies and adults) is good for one year.

The injectable bacterin must be given twice—two to four weeks apart. The first injection usually is given at six to eight weeks of age.

It is important to follow the manufacturer's recommendations in regard to dosage and frequency of administration.

Salmonellosis

A number of bacteria of the salmonella species are capable of producing illness in dogs.

Salmonella are resistant to environmental factors and remain alive for many months or years in soil and manure. In dogs, the disease usually is acquired from eating raw or commercially contaminated foods but may be acquired from eating manure. Puppies and young adults are most susceptible, as are dogs housed in crowded unsanitary surroundings whose natural resistance has been weakened by a virus infection, malnutrition or some other stress.

Signs of infection are those of a gastroenteritis with a bloody, foul-smelling stool. Fever, loss of appetite and depression occur. Dehydration develops from vomiting and diarrhea. Bacteria carried in the bloodstream can cause abscesses in the liver, kidneys, lungs and uterus. The acute illness lasts four to ten days, but chronic diarrhea may persist for a month. Dogs that recover may become asymptomatic carriers. The bacteria they shed in their feces can produce active infection in domestic animals and man.

Treatment: Obtain a stool culture and sensitivity. This confirms the diagnosis and helps to select the antibiotic most effective against the specific strain. Many strains are sensitive to chloramphenicol and trimethoprim. It is important to administer fluid therapy to correct dehydration.

Campylobacteriosis

Campylobacteriosis is a disease characterized by acute diarrhea in puppies and kittens. It can occur in kennel dogs and strays, most often in individuals that are poorly cared for and suffering from other intestinal infections.

The bacteria is acquired by ingesting contaminated water or feces. It can survive for two to five weeks in water or milk. House flies are known to be a vector.

The incubation period is from one to seven days. Signs include diarrhea with a watery stool that contains mucus and blood. Vomiting sometimes occurs. The disease usually runs its course in seven to ten days.

Treatment: Treat mild diarrhea as described in the chapter DIGESTIVE SYSTEM. For the more severely affected individual, prevent dehydration with appropriate fluid replacement. Keep the dog warm and dry in a stressfree environment. Antibiotics should be administered. Erythromycin is the drug of choice.

Public Health Considerations: Campylobacteriosis is a more frequent cause of diarrhea in humans than salmonellosis. The enteritis can be quite devastating, especially in debilitated people who suffer from major underlying illnesses such as alcoholism, cirrhosis, diabetes and valvular heart disease, and those who take immunosuppressive drugs. Most cases are thought to arise from contact with newly acquired kittens or puppies suffering from diarrhea. It is important to take the proper precautions when handling sick dogs with diarrhea.

Coliobacillosis

Coliobacillosis is an intestinal disease caused by the bacteria *E. coli*, a normal resident of the gastrointestinal tract in dogs and humans. There are some strains of *E. coli* not normally part of the resident flora. When ingested, these strains are capable of causing an acute diarrhea.

In dogs of all ages a concurrent viral infection of the intestinal tract can permit *E. coli* to become pathogenic and produce a fatal illness.

E. coli can be a problem in newborn puppies under a week of age. If the dam's colostrum does not provide adequate immunity against *E coli*, or if there is a breakdown in the lining of the intestine, bacteria can enter the bloodstream and produce a toxin. Puppies exhibit weakness, depressed sensorium, cyanosis, hypothermia and death (see PEDIATRICS: *Puppy Septicemia*).

Treatment: The acutely ill individual should be hospitalized for intensive veterinary management. It is important to maintain strict sanitary precautions when handling infected secretions.

Tularemia

Tularemia is an uncommon disease in dogs caused by the bacteria *Francisella tularensis*. It is a naturally occurring disease in wild animals, especially rodents and rabbits. Ticks are known to transmit the bacteria. Dogs (and cats) acquire the disease by eating the carcasses of infected animals, or by the bite of an infected tick. The bacteria has been known to penetrate the skin. In humans, tularemia is an occupational hazard for those who handle rabbit meat and pelts. Cats that acquire tularemia can transmit the disease to humans through contaminated teeth and claws. Dogs do not transmit the disease directly to humans, but they can disseminate the infected tick.

In dogs the illness is characterized by ulcerated skin lesions at the site of entrance of the bacteria (direct penetration of the skin or bite of the tick), swollen lymph nodes, pneumonia and weakness of the rear legs. The bacteria passes into the bloodstream and spreads to the lungs, liver, lymph nodes and spleen.

Treatment: Antibiotics are the treatment of choice. Tetracycline, chloramphenicol, streptomycin and gentamicin are effective.

Lyme Disease

Lyme disease is a tick-borne illness caused by the bacteria (spirochete) *Borrelia burgdorferi*. It is now regarded as the most common tick-borne disease in the United States.

The disease was first recognized in 1975 after an outbreak of acute arthritis in several rural communities in southeastern Connecticut including the town of Lyme. It has been found in wooded locations in other coastal northeastern and

Middle Atlantic states, much of Wisconsin and Minnesota, coastal and wooded areas of California and southeastern Oregon, Colorado and parts of the Rocky Mountains.

The white-tailed deer and the white-footed mouse are the reservoir for the disease, but a wide variety of wild and domestic animals and birds can harbor the infection. Lyme disease typically occurs from May through August, peaking in the month of July.

The disease in dogs is typified by the sudden onset of lameness caused by tender swollen joints that are painful to the touch. The dog appears weak and runs a fever. The lameness may last a few days but can recur for several months. Serological blood tests will confirm the diagnosis.

Treatment: Antibiotics are effective. Ampicillin, erythromycin or tetracycline are the drugs of choice. A vaccine is available for the prevention of disease in dogs.

Public Health Considerations: Dogs do not transmit the disease to humans, although they can disseminate the tick vector.

In humans, a red macule appears at the site of the tick bite three to twenty days later. The macule expands to a size of four to eight inches and assumes a round or elliptical appearance with a red border clearing at the center. Symptoms thereafter include fever, chills, fatigue, headache and backache, stiff neck and swollen lymph nodes.

Antibiotic treatment of the early signs shortens the course and seems to prevent complications. It is important to maintain a high index of suspicion for Lyme disease and consult a physician early in the course of this febrile illness.

CANINE VIRAL DISEASES

Distemper

Distemper is a highly contagious disease that is caused by a virus similar to the germ that causes measles in people. Worldwide, it is the leading cause of infectious disease deaths in dogs.

The distemper virus can live for many years in a frozen state. During spring, virus protected by freezing temperatures thaws out. Perhaps this accounts for the higher incidence of distemper during spring months.

Distemper is most common in unvaccinated puppies three to eight months of age. These pups have lost the protection of maternal antibodies. Older unvaccinated dogs can acquire the disease as well.

Among infected dogs, about half show little in the way of illness. In others the disease is severe. The overall condition of the dog has a lot to do with how sick the dog gets. The disease is more severe in poorly nourished and ill-kept dogs.

The distemper virus has a special affinity for attacking epithelial cells. These are the cells that line the surfaces of the body including the skin, conjunctival membranes of the eye, breathing tubes and mucus membranes of the intestinal tract. The brain is also affected.

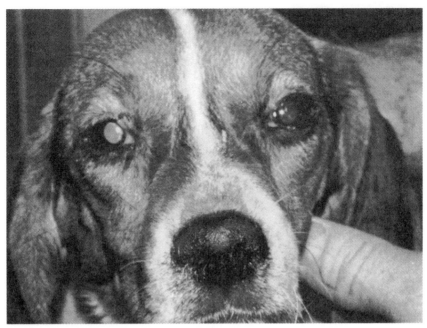

Dryness and chapping of the skin of the nose are early signs of nasal irritation. This dog was coming down with distemper. (Note the cataract in the right eye.)

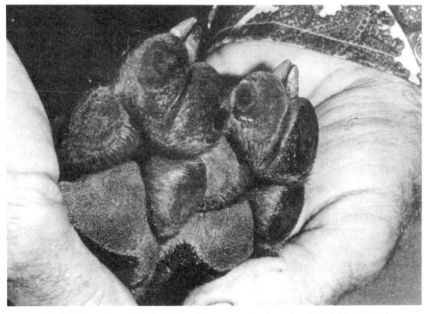

Calluslike pads on the foot of a dog recovering from *hard-pad (distemper)*.

The disease takes a variety of forms. Secondary infections and complications are common. They are sometimes the cause of death.

Typically, the signs of first-stage distemper appear three to fifteen days after exposure.

First stage. The disease begins with a fever of 103 to 105 degrees F, loss of appetite, listlessness and a watery discharge from the eyes and nose. This symptom complex may be mistaken for a "cold," but dogs do not catch colds as people do. Therefore the signs should not be taken lightly.

Within a few days, the discharge changes from watery to thick, yellow and sticky. This is an important indicator of the fact that your dog is suffering from distempter. The nose and eye discharge is accompanied by a pronounced dry cough. Pus blisters may appear on the abdomen. Diarrhea is a frequent problem and can cause severe dehydration.

During the next one to two weeks, the dog continues to run a fever but appears to get better for a day or two, then seems to get worse. The course of first-stage distemper is up and down. The outcome will depend upon whether there is a step-wise improvement or gradual worsening.

Second stage. Two or three weeks after the onset of the disease some dogs develop signs of brain involvement, which begin as brief attacks of slobbering, head shaking and chewing movements as if these were a bad taste in the mouth. Later, epilepticlike seizures can occur. The dog runs around in circles, falls over and kicks all four feet wildly. Afterward the dog may appear confused, even shy away from the owner or wander about aimlessly. These are signs of *encephalitis*.

Another sign of brain involvement is *chorea*, characterized by rhythmic jerks or twitches that affect any part of the body but are more common in the head. They are first seen when the dog is relaxed or sleeping. Later they become continuous day and night. Pain accompanies the chorea and dogs whine and cry, especially at night. Should the dog recover, the jerking continues for life but tends to be less severe as time passes.

Dogs with brain involvement usually do not survive.

Hard-pad is a form of distemper in which the virus attacks the skin of the feet and nose, causing a thick hornylike skin to form on the nose, and calluslike pads to form on the feet. It begins about fifteen days after the onset of the infection. At one time hard-pad and encephalitis were thought to be diseases separate from distemper. They are now recognized as the results of different manifestations of the distemper virus.

Treatment: Because of the complexity of the disease, treatment should be under veterinary supervision.

There is no antibiotic effective against the virus of distemper. Antibiotics are indicated, however, to avoid secondary bacterial complications. Intravenous fluids are employed to correct dehydration. Diarrhea should be controlled with appropriate drugs. Anticonvulsants and sedatives help to manage seizures.

The success of treatment depends upon how soon the owner realizes the dog is sick and seeks professional help, and the dog's ability to respond to the viral infection.

Prevention: Distemper vaccinations must be kept current in all dogs (see *Vaccination Schedule*).

Brood bitches should be given a booster vaccination before they are bred. This assures that their pups will be protected by a high maternal antibody level.

The use of distemper antiserum is no longer recommended.

Herpes Virus in Puppies

Herpes infection is caused by a contagious virus that attacks puppies at one to three weeks of age. The onset is sudden. The principal sign is a tight, painfully distended abdomen in puppies that cry continuously. Nothing seems to relieve their distress. After a brief illness lasting about twenty-four hours they usually succumb.

The disease is discussed in the PEDIATRICS chapter.

Infectious Canine Hepatitis (CAV-1)

Infectious canine hepatitis (Canine Adenovirus–1) is a highly contagious viral disease transmitted only to dogs. It should not be confused with hepatitis in man. Primarily it affects the liver, kidneys and lining of the blood vessels.

Infectious canine hepatitis presents a variety of signs and symptoms that range from those of a mild or subclinical infection at one extreme to a rapidly fatal infection at the other. At times it is difficult to distinguish the disease from distemper.

A few days after a dog is exposed, virus multiplies in the dog's tissues and is shed in its stool, saliva and urine. At this stage the disease is most contagious. It is spread to other dogs coming into contact with the sick dog or its urine, stool and saliva. Convalescent dogs, and those that have recovered, may shed virus in the urine, sometimes for months.

The most severe cases occur in puppies during the first few months of life; but dogs of all ages are susceptible.

In the *fatal fulminating* form the dog suddenly becomes ill, develops bloody diarrhea, collapses and dies. Puppies may die suddenly without obvious illness.

In the *acute form* the dog runs a fever that may reach 106 degrees F. The dog passes bloody diarrhea, may vomit blood and refuses to eat. Movement is painful. The dog may show a "tucked-up" belly, which is caused by painful swelling of the liver. Light may hurt the dog's eyes so that they squint and tear. Tonsillitis, bleeding beneath the gums and under the skin and yellowing of the whites of the eyes (jaundice) may occur.

In *mild or subclinical cases* the dog simply appears lethargic or below a normally good condition. There is a loss of appetite. A blood test may help make the diagnosis.

After the acute symptoms have subsided, about 25 percent of dogs develop a characteristic clouding of the cornea of one or both eyes. It is called *blue eye*. In most dogs it clears spontaneously in a few days. If it persists, it should be treated by a veterinarian. Rarely does the eye remain permanently clouded.

54

Blue eye can occur after vaccination against infectious hepatitis if the vaccine contains CAV-1 instead of CAV-2. This happens to only a small percentage of dogs. To learn more about blue eye, see the chapter on EYES.

Treatment: Infectious hepatitis usually is recognized by the typical clinical picture. It is confirmed by blood tests. Acute cases should be hospitalized for intensive veterinary care.

The disease can be prevented by proper vaccination. These vaccinations must be kept current in all dogs (see *Vaccination Schedule*).

Rabies

Rabies is a fatal disease that occurs in nearly all warm-blooded animals, although rarely among rodents. In the United States, vaccination programs for dogs and other domestic animals have been remarkably effective. They have all but eliminated the risk of rabies in both pets and their owners. The number of human rabies cases has declined to less than five cases per year. The major wildlife reservoir for rabies is now the skunk, which accounts for about 40 percent of cases. However raccoons, bats, foxes and other wild carnivores can serve as a reservoir for the disease, thereby accounting for sporadic cases.

Any strange animal that allows you to approach it without running away from you is acting abnormally. Do not pet or handle such an animal. Rabies should be suspected. *However, the only definite determination of rabies is through autopsy.*

Outside the United States, the main source of infection for humans remains a bite from an infected dog or cat. In India, for example, a country that lacks an effective rabies control program, it is estimated that 15,000 people die each year of rabies. Travelers to countries where rabies is endemic should be alert to the risk of dog bites.

The rabies virus, which is present in infected saliva, usually enters at the site of a bite. Saliva on an open wound or mucus membrane also constitutes exposure to rabies. Animals suspected of having rabies should be handled with great care—preferably not at all!

The average incubation period in dogs is three to eight weeks, but can be as short as a week or as long as a year. The virus travels to the brain along nerve networks. The further the bite is from the brain, the longer the incubation period. The virus then travels back along nerves to the mouth where it enters the saliva.

The signs and symptoms of rabies are caused by encephalitis (inflammation of the brain). The first signs are quite subtle and consist of personality changes. Affectionate and sociable pets may become irritable and aggressive. Shy and less outgoing pets may become overly affectionate. Soon the animal becomes withdrawn and stares off into space. The animal will avoid light, which hurts the eyes (photophobia), and will seek seclusion. Finally, the animal will resist handling. Fever, vomiting and diarrhea are common.

There are two characteristic forms of encephalitis. One is the so-called furious form and the other is the paralytic form. A rabid animal may show signs of one or a combination of both forms.

The *furious* form is the "mad dog" type of rabies. Here the animal becomes

55

frenzied and vicious, attacking anything that moves. The muscles of the face are in spasm, drawing the lips back to expose the teeth. When running free, the animal shows no fear and snaps and bites at any animal along the way.

In the *paralytic* form the muscles of the head become paralyzed, causing the mouth to drop open and the tongue to hang out. The swallowing muscles become paralyzed, which causes drooling, coughing spells and pawing at the mouth. As encephalitis progresses, the animal loses control of movement, staggers about, collapses and is unable to get up.

Once symptoms develop, the disease in dogs and humans is invariably fatal.

Public Health Considerations: The World Health Organization has established certain guidelines for practitioners to follow in the appropriate management of people who are exposed to a potentially rabid animal. The treatment schedule depends upon the nature of the exposure (lick, bite), severity of the injury and the condition of the animal at the time of exposure and during a subsequent observation period of ten days. When an animal is killed or dies during confinement, its brain is removed and sent to a laboratory equipped to diagnose rabies from special antibody studies.

If there is the slightest possibility that a dog or cat is rabid, and if there has been any sort of human contact, *impound the animal immediately and consult your physician and veterinarian.* This holds true even if the animal is known to be vaccinated for rabies.

As an alternative, in the cases of a wild animal or feral dog or cat whose owner is unknown, the animal can be killed immediately. Should it escape, there is no way to prove the animal was not rabid, and post-exposure rabies vaccines may have to be given.

Guide to Post-exposure Rabies Prophylaxis. It is of utmost importance to promptly cleanse all animal bites and scratches, washing them thoroughly with soap and water. Studies in animals have shown that local wound cleansing greatly reduces the risk of rabies.

The introduction of inactivated vaccines grown in human diploid cell cultures in 1980 has improved the effectiveness (and safety) of post-exposure vaccination. When vaccination is indicated, it should begin as soon as possible after the exposure. Vaccination is not effective once the early signs of rabies are present.

Pre-exposure Immunization. Preventive vaccinations are available for high-risk groups including veterinarians, animal handlers, cave explorers and laboratory workers.

Treatment: There is *no* effective treatment for dogs. Be sure your pet is vaccinated at three to four months of age. Then follow the procedure of your veterinarian to keep vaccinations current.

Infectious Tracheobronchitis (Kennel Cough)

This is a highly contagious disease of dogs that spreads rapidly through a kennel. A harsh dry cough is the characteristic sign of the illness. The cough may persist for many weeks and become a chronic problem due to replacement of the virus by secondary bacterial invaders. Chronic bronchitis is a common sequel to kennel cough.

A number of viruses have been implicated in the kennel cough complex. They include adenovirus types 1 and 2, herpes virus in the adult and parainfluenza virus. Immunization of your dog with hepatitis vaccine (as found in the DHLPP shot) protects against adenovirus. Parainfluenza vaccine (CPI) protects against canine parainfluenza virus.

To learn more about tracheobronchitis, see the RESPIRATORY SYSTEM chapter.

Canine Parvovirus (CPV)

Canine parvovirus has a special affinity for attacking rapidly reproducing cells—such as those lining the gastrointestinal tract, bone marrow, lymph nodes and heart. The virus, which is highly contagious, is transmitted from one dog to another via contaminated droplets and feces. It can be carried on the dog's hair and feet, as well as on contaminated cages, shoes and other objects. Dogs of all ages are affected, but the highest mortality occurs among puppies less than five months of age. Two main syndromes are recognized:

Diarrhea Syndrome (Enteritis): After an incubation period of seven to fourteen days, the first signs are severe depression with loss of appetite, followed by vomiting. The dog appears to be in extreme pain, with a tucked-up abdomen. Within twenty-four hours a high fever develops (up to 106 degrees F) and a profuse diarrhea that is frequently bloody. Mouth inflammation (stomatitis) can occur. Almost no other canine disease produces such devastating symptoms.

Cardiac Syndrome (Myocarditis): This form of CPV affects the muscle of the heart, especially in puppies less than three months of age. Puppies with myocarditis stop nursing, cry out and gasp for breath. Death can occur suddenly or in a few days. Puppies that recover sometimes develop a chronic form of congestive heart failure that leads to death in weeks or months.

Treatment: Success of treatment is variable, depending on the form and severity of CPV infection as well as the age of the dog. Note that in puppies between six and twenty weeks of age there is a one- to four-week interval when they are susceptible to infection despite diligent vaccination. This is because declining maternal antibody levels are no longer protective but still interfere with the "take" of the vaccine.

Treatment of CPV includes fluid and electrolyte replacement, medication to control diarrhea and vomiting and administration of broad spectrum antibiotics to prevent secondary bacterial infections. In all but mild cases, hospitalization for intensive management is essential. Dogs that recover are immune to the disease.

The quarters of an infected dog should be cleaned and thoroughly disinfected. This is an extremely hardy virus that resists most household cleaners. The best disinfectant is Clorox (one part to thirty parts of water).

CPV can be prevented by an appropriate vaccination schedule. Parvovirus vaccinations must be kept current in all dogs (see *Vaccinations*).

Canine Coronavirus

This disease was first recognized in 1971 when it was found to be a cause of infectious enteritis in dogs. The distribution of the disease is worldwide. While the virus affects dogs of all ages, it is particularly devastating to young puppies and individuals that have been subjected to environmental stress and concurrent infection, especially parvovirus.

The disease is transmitted by contact with infected oral and fecal secretions. Signs and symptoms can vary from inapparent infection (the usual situation) to rapid death. Outbreaks typically occur in a kennel of dogs.

The early signs are depression and a loss of appetite, followed by vomiting that may contain blood. Fever is not common. A moderate to severe diarrhea ensues. Characteristically, the stool is yellow-orange in color, foul-smelling, watery and sometimes bloody. Dehydration, loss of weight and death can occur. Dogs that appear to recover may suffer a relapse three to four weeks later.

Treatment: It is the same as that for parvovirus. Antibiotics usually are not indicated because of the mild nature of most infections.

Prevention: Killed virus vaccines are available for the prevention of coronavirus infection (see *Coronavirus Vaccine*). Vaccination is recommended for dogs that have frequent contact with other dogs, such as show dogs, or dogs

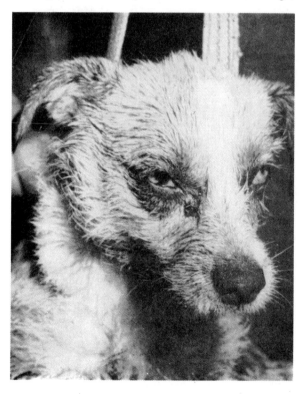

The eyes of a *rabid* dog, showing divergent gaze, protrusion of the nictitating membrane, and pasty ocular discharges.
—Courtesy American Veterinary Publications

living in a kennel where new dogs are moving in and out. If one dog in a household or kennel becomes infected, all dogs should be vaccinated.

FUNGUS DISEASES

Fungus diseases may be divided into two groups. In the first, the fungus affects just the skin or mucus membranes. Examples are ringworm and yeast stomatitis. They are discussed in chapter 4. In the second, the disease can be widespread, in which case it is called *systemic*.

Systemic fungal diseases are not common in the dog. They tend to occur in chronically ill or poorly nourished animals. Prolonged treatment with steroids and/or antibiotics can change an animal's pattern of resistance and allow a fungus infection to establish itself. Occasionally, a dog in good health can come down with one of the systemic fungal diseases.

Nocardiosis, histoplasmosis, blastomycosis and coccidioidomycosis are diseases caused by fungi that live in soil and organic material. Spores, which resist heat and live for long periods without water, gain entrance through the respiratory system or through the skin at the site of a puncture. Respiratory signs resemble those of tuberculosis. They are chronic cough, recurrent bouts of pneumonia, difficulty in breathing, weight loss, muscle wasting and lethargy. Up and down fever may be present.

Fungal diseases are difficult to recognize and treat. X-rays, biopsies and fungus cultures are used to make the diagnosis in systemic cases. A fungus infection should be suspected when an unexplained illness fails to respond to a full course of antibiotics.

Systemic fungus infections do not respond to conventional antibiotics and require intensive veterinary management. Most fungi that cause disease in dogs also can cause illness in man. When the disease is systemic, euthanasia is often recommended.

The following systemic fungal diseases can occur in the dog.

Nocardiosis, Actinomycosis, Cryptococcosis

These are respiratory or skin infections occurring in dogs often under a year of age. They also affect the lymph nodes, brain, kidney and other organs. Large tumorous masses that discharge a material that looks like sulfa granules can appear on the legs or body.

Histoplasmosis

This is a disease caused by a fungus found in the central United States near the Great Lakes, the Appalachian Mountains and the valleys of the Mississippi, Ohio and St. Lawrence rivers. Spores are found in soil contaminated by the dung of chickens and other birds, or bats. In the majority of dogs the signs are those of a mild respiratory illness. There is a systemic form that attacks lymph nodes, the small intestine and other organs. The principal signs are fever, weight loss, muscle wasting, enlargement of the tonsils and a prolonged diarrhea that may become bloody.

Do not kennel dogs in chicken coops, caves or other places where birds and bats roost.

Blastomycosis

This disease is found in the same geographic distribution as histoplasmosis. The skin form is characterized by nodules and abscesses that ulcerate and drain. The systemic form is similar to histoplasmosis. The disease is difficult to treat and presents a hazard to human health.

Coccidioidomycosis

In most dogs this is a mild respiratory infection, but the systemic form can spread to virtually all organs of the body. It is found in dry, dusty parts of the southwestern United States and in California. This is not the same disease as coccidiosis, which is caused by a protozoan. The signs of systemic illness resemble those of histoplasmosis.

PROTOZOAN DISEASES

Protozoans are one-celled animals. They are not visible to the naked eye but may be seen under the microscope. A fresh stool specimen is required to find the parasites. They are responsible for seven major infectious diseases in dogs, as discussed below.

The life cycle of protozoans is complicated. Basically, infection usually results from the ingestion of the cyst form (oocyst). Cysts invade the lining of the bowel where they mature into adult forms and are shed in the feces. Under favorable conditions they develop into the infective form.

Coccidiosis

This is a common protozoan disease found usually in young dogs, although adult dogs are susceptible. It is especially severe in litters of nursing puppies. It is a serious problem in the southern United States but can occur in the northern states. Usually it occurs in connection with filth, overcrowding, poor sanitation and the housing of dogs in cold, damp quarters.

Puppies can acquire the infection from contaminated premises, or from their mother if she is a carrier. When kennel sanitation is poor, puppies reinfect themselves from their own feces. The disease spreads rapidly through a kennel.

Five to seven days after the ingestion of oocysts, infective cysts appear in the feces. The entire cycle is complete in a week. The first signs can be a mild diarrhea that progresses until the feces become mucuslike and tinged with blood. There is loss of appetite, weakness, dehydration and anemia. Rarely this is accompanied by a cough, runny nose and a discharge from the eyes—much like distemper.

Coccidia can be found in the stools of puppies without causing problems until some stress factor such as an outbreak of roundworms or shipping reduces their resistance. Dogs that recover can become carriers. They remain in good health but can suffer relapses when afflicted with some other disease, such as distemper. Carriers and dogs with active infection can be identified by finding adult oocysts in a microscopic slide of fresh stool.

Treatment: Stop the diarrhea with a Neomycin-Kaopectate antidiarrheal preparation. A severely dehydrated or anemic dog may need to be hospitalized for fluid replacement and blood.

Supportive treatment is important since in most cases the acute phase of the illness lasts a few days, perhaps ten days, and is followed by recovery in uncomplicated cases. Sulfonamides and antibiotics have been used to treat coccidiosis. Response is slow once the signs of disease are apparent.

Currently a drug called amprolium, used in the treatment of this disease in poultry, is the agent of choice. It is effective against only one stage in the life cycle of the protozoan. Therefore, it must be continued until all protozoan that reach this stage are destroyed. Mix it with the dog's food or water at a rate of 50 to 100 mg/lb body weight per day. This eliminates oocysts from the stools in seven to ten days. Amprolium is a thiamine (vitamin B_1) antagonist. It should not be used for longer than ten days because puppies can develop a vitamin B_1 deficiency. In kennels where coccidiosis is a problem, amprolium is used on all six-week-old puppies before they are sold or shipped.

Known carriers should be isolated and treated. At the same time their quarters and runs should be washed down daily with *boiling* water to destroy oocysts. Otherwise they will reinfect themselves.

Toxoplasmosis

This protozoan disease affects all animals including man. Cats by far are the more common source of the infection, but the disease can occur in the dog. The mode of transmission in dogs appears to be caused by the ingestion of oocysts in contaminated soil, or the eating of wild game or uncooked meat. Transmission through the placenta from mother to offspring is possible.

Toxoplasmosis often is asymptomatic. When symptomatic, it affects the brain, lymphatic system and lungs. Young puppies with toxoplasmosis may show signs of pneumonia, hepatitis and encephalitis. Serological blood tests are necessary to confirm the diagnosis.

About half the human adult population shows serological evidence of having been exposed in the past. The disease is a real hazard to human health when a pregnant woman without prior immunity is exposed to the disease. Birth defects, largely involving the central nervous system, do occur.

Oocysts are not immediately infective in fresh animal feces. It takes one to three days under ideal conditions of warm temperature and high humidity for oocysts to sporulate. Once sporulated, they become infective. Sporulated oocysts can survive in the environment for months and years. Contact with areas contaminated by feces, particularly cat feces, carries a risk of human infection, e.g., sand boxes, garden soil, litter boxes. Daily cleaning and disinfection of litter boxes greatly reduce the risk of human infection. Pregnant women should take extreme measures to avoid contact with fecal material from cats.

Treatment: This disease is difficult to recognize. Effective medications are available for the dog but should be used under veterinary supervision.

Public health measures in regard to cats are ineffective because cats roam freely and hunt raw meat. It is easier to control the disease in dogs. They can be fenced and supervised.

A blood test can be requested to see if an animal has acquired immunity through piror exposure. A pet with an immune antibody level is safer than one without.

Trichomoniasis

This is a protozoan infection caused by a species of trichomonas often associated with a mucoid (and occasionally bloody) diarrhea in puppies. Commonly it is found in accordance with poor kennel sanitation. Prolonged infection leads to weak, debilitated, stunted puppies with rough hair coat. The diagnosis is made by finding the protozoan cysts in fresh stool smears.

Treatment: The infection responds well to Flagyl.

Giardiasis

This illness is caused by a protozoan of the *Giardia* species. The disease in dogs has received little recognition in the past, although it is growing steadily more common. Outbreaks of waterborne diarrheal disease in humans are becoming more common in the United States, and giardiasis is the most frequent cause.

Most giardial infections in dogs are asymptomatic; but when giardia does cause infection, usually it is immature dogs that are affected. The principal sign is diarrhea, occasionally mixed with mucus and blood. Diagnosis is made by finding the protozoan in saline smears of fresh stool, or by finding characteristic cysts in the stools. Smears from rectal swabs are satisfactory for this purpose. However, a negative smear does not exclude the diagnosis; infected dogs can shed the cysts intermittently. It takes negative smears for three consecutive days to rule out the diagnosis.

Treatment: Giardiasis responds well to Flagyl (metronidazole). It should not be used in pregnant bitches because it can cause fetal damage. Other drugs are available.

Public Health Considerations: Outbreaks of giardiasis in family groups have been traced to a newly acquired puppy that was shedding infective cysts. All dogs (and cats) infected with giardiasis, and all asymptomatic carriers, should be treated to prevent transmission of the disease to their owners.

Prevent fecal contamination of food. Water from private wells contaminated with giardiasis, and water from untreated municipal water systems, should be boiled, filtered or treated with disinfectants approved for potable water. Consult your public health department for more information and to assure that adequate, but safe, concentrations of disinfectants are being used.

Canine Babesiosis (Nantucket Disease)

This illness is caused by a protozoan that destroys red blood cells causing a hemolytic anemia. It is a tick-borne disease. The main reservoirs of infection are rodents and wild and domestic dogs. In humans, babesiosis is called Nantucket disease because most cases of this febrile illness, accompanied by drenching sweats and muscle and joint pains, have been reported in the United States from Nantucket Island and nearby Martha's Vineyard. The disease also is found in tropical and subtropical regions around the world.

In dogs, most infections are inapparent or subclinical, becoming manifest when the animal is stressed. Characteristic signs are anemia, fever, enlargement of spleen and liver and changes in blood chemistries because of interference with bone marrow and liver function.

The diagnosis depends upon finding the protozoan in peripheral blood smears or by antibody tests on the dog's serum.

Babesiosis is transmitted by the common brown dog tick. It is best prevented by keeping your dog free of ticks. To learn how to control ticks on your dog, see *Ticks* and *Insecticides* in the chapter SKIN.

Medications effective against canine babesiosis are available through your veterinarian.

Canine Hepatozoonosis

This protozoan disease also is transmitted by the brown dog tick. It is limited geographically to the Texas Gulf coast and to southern Louisiana. It usually occurs in dogs that are immunosuppressed or younger than four months of age.

The initial signs are diarrhea (often bloody), followed by intermittent fever and severe loss of weight and condition. Treatment has not been successful. The disease is best prevented by control of ticks as discussed above for *Canine Babesiosis*.

Canine Trypanosomiasis (Chagas' Disease)

Chagas' disease, also called American trypanosomiasis, is caused by the protozoan *T. cruzi*. Only a few cases have been reported, principally in Texas and California. Raccoons, opossums, armadillos, rats, cats and dogs serve as the principal reservoir.

Dogs (and humans) acquire the disease from a family of insects called "kissing bugs," so named because they come out of cracks at night and bite the face of sleepers. Infection principally occurs through contamination of bites with the insect's feces.

The disease in dogs attacks the heat muscle causing heart arrhythmias and congestive heart failure. Sudden death is common.

Chagas' disease in dogs does not respond well to drugs. Since this is an often fatal disease that can be transmitted to humans, euthanasia is recommended. It is important to take utmost precautions and avoid contact with infected animals, their blood and discharges.

RICKETTSIAL DISEASES

Rickettsiae are small parasites about the size of bacteria that live within cells. The majority are maintained in nature by a cycle that involves an insect vector and an animal reservoir. Infection of dogs and humans usually is unimportant in perpetuation of the rickettsial species, as man and dog are not the natural reservoirs for further spread of infection.

Canine Ehrlichiosis

Canine ehrlichiosis is a noncontagious acute and chronic infection caused by the organism *E. canis* and transmitted by the bite of a brown dog tick. It is seen most often in the Southern states. The tick acquires the organism by feeding on an infected dog. A wide variety of wild and domestic animals serve as the reservoir.

The *acute* phase of the illness is often mild or inapparent. When symptoms do occur, they include fever, loss of appetite, eye and nasal discharges, swelling of the limbs and occasionally signs of brain involvement (see NERVOUS SYSTEM: *Brain Infection*). Such symptoms are difficult to tell apart from Rocky Mountain spotted fever, Lyme disease and canine distemper.

Most dogs recover from the acute illness in one to two weeks but remain persistently infected. Others develop chronic disease one to six months later. Generally these individuals are immunosuppressed owing to coexistent diseases. In addition, there appears to be a predilection for chronic disease to occur in German Shepherds.

In the *chronic* phase of the illness the disease attacks the bone marrow and immune system. Weight loss, anemia, bleeding tendencies (especially nosebleeds), signs of sepsis and organ system failure occur. These dogs will die despite treatment.

The diagnosis is suspected by finding brown dog ticks on a sick dog in an area where the disease is endemic. It can be confirmed by blood tests.

Treatment: A tetracycline antibiotic is highly effective against rickettsiae and should be given for at least two weeks. Improvement in the acute phase begins within twenty-four to forty-eight hours. Supportive treatment includes intravenous fluids and blood transfusions.

Prevention: Canine ehrlichiosis can be prevented by giving low-dose daily tetracycline to dogs that are at high risk for exposure. Tick control, in the form of premises spraying and dipping, is important (see *Insect Parasites* and *Premises Control* in the SKIN chapter). Repeat monthly.

Rocky Mountain Spotted Fever

Rocky Mountain spotted fever is a rickettsial disease transmitted by several tick species. Most cases occur in the southeastern United States and west to Oklahoma. The Rocky Mountain area, where the disease was first discovered at the turn of the century, now accounts for only 3 percent of human cases. Unlike canine ehrlichiosis, Rocky Mountain spotted fever has a strict seasonal occurrence—spring through early fall.

Many species of small mammals serve as a reservoir. Infected adult ticks transmit the disease to dogs during attachment and feeding. The dog is not a natural reservoir but is capable of disseminating the tick. Therefore, an infected dog is not an immediate danger to people, although the blood and discharges from an infected dog should be handled with strict hygienic precautions.

As with canine erhlichiosis, most infections in dogs are inapparent. In others, especially the Siberian Husky, the infection can be severe or rapidly fatal.

The signs of acute infection in dogs include listlessness, conjunctivitis, depression, high fever, loss of appetite, cough, difficult breathing, swelling of the legs, joint and muscle pains, vomiting and diarrhea. Discharge from the nose and eyes may be mucopurulent. Central nervous system signs include staggering gait, altered mental state and seizures. These signs are like those of canine distemper, which may be the first diagnosis that comes to mind.

As the disease progresses, the dog demonstrates a hemorrhagic syndrome similar to that seen with canine erhlichiosis. Various bleeding disorders include nosebleeds, hemorrhages beneath the skin and passage of blood in urine and stools. This can lead to shock, multiple organ failure and death. The hemorrhagic syndrome occurs one to two weeks after onset of the acute illness.

Rocky Mountain spotted fever should be suspected in a sick dog with a history of tick infestation during spring through fall. The diagnosis, which is difficult, is best achieved by blood tests. Generally such tests are available only through state veterinary laboratories or veterinary schools in Rocky Mountain spotted fever endemic areas.

Treatment: A tetracycline is the drug of choice. It should be started as soon as the diagnosis is considered while awaiting the results of the blood tests. Dogs with acute Rocky Mountain spotted fever will respond dramatically in one to two days. Continue the antibiotic for two to three weeks. Supportive treatment and prevention is the same as that for canine erhlichiosis.

Canine Salmon Poisoning Disease

This is a highly fatal rickettsial disease of dogs and wild canids that requires the presence of several intermediate hosts, including snails, flukes, fish and mammals. Humans are *not* affected.

Dogs acquire the infection when they eat raw freshwater or ocean salmon having rickettsial organisms encysted in their tissues.

Since the first intermediate host is a small snail found only in streams along the coasts of Washington, Oregon and California, this disease has a limited geographic distribution.

The incubation period after the ingestion of infected fish is five to seven days. Illness begins with high fever, loss of appetite and depression. Vomiting and diarrhea may occur. These signs are like those of canine distemper and parvovirus disease, which may be the initial considerations. However, a history of eating raw fish will suggest the diagnosis of salmon poisoning.

Treatment: In untreated dogs, death occurs in seven to ten days. The illness responds well to a number of antibiotics including tetracycline, penicillin and chloromycetin. Supportive treatment with intravenous fluids and blood transfusions (for hemorrhagic diarrhea) might be required.

Prevention: Feed only thoroughly cooked fish or fish that has been frozen for twenty-four hours.

4

Skin

SKIN DISEASE is a common problem in dogs, and the condition of the skin can often tell you a great deal about your dog's general health.

Unlike the skin of people, your dog's skin is thinner and more sensitive to injury. It is easily damaged by careless or rough handling with the wrong kind of grooming equipment, and once the surface of the skin is broken and disturbed by trauma or some sort of skin disorder, the condition tends to spread rather easily and becomes a major problem to the dog and the owner.

The outer skin layer is the *epidermis*. It is thick and tough over the nose and foot pads and is thin and most susceptible to injury in the crease of the groin and beneath the arms.

The next layer inward is the *dermis*. It gives rise to the *skin appendages*, which include the hair follicles, sebaceous glands and toenails.

In humans, the skin is well supplied with sweat glands. *Dogs do not have sweat glands*, except for those found in the dermis of the foot pads. The sebaceous glands are important in that they secrete an oil that coats the hair and waterproofs the coat, allowing it to shed water. Water-going breeds depend upon skin oils to waterproof their coats. Skin oil is influenced by hormone levels in the blood. Large amounts of circulating estrogen reduce oil production, while small amounts of androgen increase it.

The color of your dog's skin may vary from pink to light brown, or it may be dark with patches of black. The dark pigment is called melanin and is produced by cells in the skin called melanocytes.

COAT CARE

Growing a Coat

The growth of a dog's coat is controlled by a number of factors. Some dogs carry a more abundant or more stylish coat.

Dog hair, unlike scalp hair found in people, does not grow continuously. Dog hair grows in cycles. It grows for a short period, then rests. Then it dies and is shed before the cycle begins again. The coat of the average dog takes about 130 days to grow, but there is wide variation. The Afghan, for example, grows its coat for about eighteen months before shedding.

Too much estrogen in the system may slow growth of the coat hair. Too little thyroid hormone in the system often impairs the growth, texture and luster of a dog's coat. Ill health, a run-down condition, hormone imbalance, vitamin deficiency or parasites on the dog or within the dog's system may cause the coat to be too thin and brittle. If you suspect that your dog's coat is below par, see your veterinarian for a general checkup.

Environmental factors have a definite influence on the thickness and abundance of a dog's coat. Dogs living outdoors continuously in cold weather grow a heavy coat for insulation and protection. Some additional fat in the diet is indicated in winter to build up the subcutaneous layer of fat and provide more warmth for dogs living outdoors. Bacon grease can be added to the diet, as this also improves palatability and encourages appetite. Alternately, feed natural corn oil, which is well tolerated by the digestive tract and adds calories. Give about one or two teaspoonsful a day to the average-sized dog.

Nutritional supplements, reported to build coat and improve skin health and hair sheen, are of questionable value in the healthy well-nourished dog.

Shedding

Most dogs shed or "blow" their coats at least once a year. Bitches sometimes blow their coats after heat, during pregnancy or after nursing.

Some dogs have a double coat composed of a long outercoat of guard hair and an undercoat of soft woolly hair. When a dog with a double coat begins to shed, the appearance can be quite alarming and at first suggest a skin disease. This is because the inner coat is shed in a mosaic or patchy fashion giving rise to a moth-eaten look. However, this is perfectly normal. Dogs do not shed their coats evenly or in waves.

Coat loss is occasionally precipitated by stress, illness, pregnancy and changes in hormone levels. Stressful conditions causing hair to drop out first appear on the body and flanks where hair grows the fastest.

Many people believe that it is the seasonal change in temperature that governs when a dog sheds its coat. In fact, shedding is influenced more by changes in surrounding light. The more exposure to light, the greater the shedding. This is why house dogs, exposed to long hours of artificial light, seem to shed excessively.

When shedding begins, remove as much of the dead hair as possible by daily brushing, or in breeds with thick double coats, by a bath that first loosens the dead hair and then makes it easier to remove. Dead hair next to the skin is irritating. It leads to an itch-scratch cycle that damages the skin and causes further problems.

AVOIDING COAT AND SKIN PROBLEMS

Grooming

Brushing a few minutes each day will help to keep your dog free of skin and hair problems. Establish a routine and try to adhere to it. If grooming a puppy, keep the sessions brief and make it a pleasurable experience. If your dog grows to dislike the basic routine, a simple procedure is made most difficult.

Grooming tools that are especially useful are listed below. Your choice will depend upon the breed of dog and the nature of the coat.

- *Grooming Table*. Solid with a nonslippery surface, the correct height is such that you can work on your dog comfortably without having to bend.
- *Nail Clippers*. We prefer those that have two cutting edges.
- *Comb*. Buy a metal dog comb with smooth round teeth especially designed to avoid trauma to the skin.
- *Carder*. A square board with a short handle and fine wire teeth that are bent. Insert the teeth into the hair next to the skin; then pull out. A carder is used to remove dead hair and mats. This is similar to a slicker brush.
- *Brush*. A brush with natural bristles, or a soft wire pin brush, is recommended. *Long hair* is usually brushed *against* the grain, *short hair* is brushed *with* the lay of the coat.
- *Hound Glove*. For short-coated breeds, to remove dead hair and polish the coat.
- *Stripping Comb*. Used to pluck dead hair and dress the coat.
- *Toweling*. Used in short-haired breeds to remove loose dead hair. It tends to tangle long hair.
- *File*. For filing the nails to remove sharp edges.

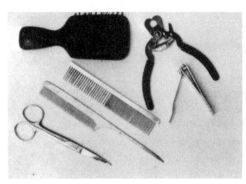 

Grooming and bathing equipment.

When brushing, take care to see that any soft wooly hair behind the ears is completely brushed out, or mats (lumps of fur) will form if neglected. To remove mats, use sharp scissors and cut carefully into the fur ball away from the skin in narrow strips. Pull them out gently with your fingers. Slide a comb under the mat and cut on top to protect the skin.

Groom under the ear flaps after your dog has been in tall grass, weeds and brush. Plant matter can enter the ear canals by first clinging to the hair surrounding the outer openings. To remove dirt and debris, see EARS: *Cleaning the Ears*.

Routine inspection of the teeth will reveal any buildup of tartar or calculus. To learn how to remove calculus, see ORAL CAVITY: *Care of Your Dog's Teeth*.

When the toenails are not worn down through activity, they must be filed or trimmed. Pay special attention to the *dewclaws*. Since these claws do not touch the ground, they will grow back into the pads.

Before clipping the nails, be sure to identify the pink part, or quick. Do not cut into the quick, as it contains nerves and blood vessels. If the nail bleeds, keep pressure over it with a cotton ball. The blood will clot in a few minutes. If it doesn't, a styptic used for shaving can be applied.

Inspection of the anal sacs may disclose a buildup of secretions. To care for the anal sacs, see DIGESTIVE SYSTEM: *Anal Glands or Sacs*.

There are several books that go into considerable detail about grooming for the show ring. *How to Trim, Groom and Show Your Dog* (Howell Book House) is a good one. Most breed books provide information on special grooming requirements.

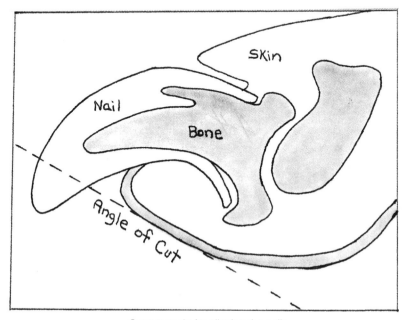

Correct angle for clipping the nails.

Bathing

Overbathing can remove natural oils that are essential to the health of your dog's coat. Guidelines on bathing vary widely among dogs with different coat types.

In general, dogs with *undercoats*, such as the German Shepherd and Great Pyrenees, are best bathed in spring and fall. At other times they can be kept clean with a dry shampoo and brushing.

Dogs with *long, silky coats*, such as the Afghan, may not need frequent baths. Spaniels, on the other hand, can be bathed every six weeks.

Curly- and *woolly-coated* breeds, such as the Poodle and Bedlington, may need to be bathed every four to six weeks and should be brushed every day.

Smooth-coated breeds, such as the Beagle and Doberman, should be bathed only when necessary. Maintain the coat by brushing to a shine with a hand towel or hound glove.

Wire-coated breeds, including the Welsh Terrier and Airedale, usually are bathed every eight weeks.

It may not be necessary to bathe before every dog show. If the dog is about to shed, the bath may hasten the process. However, if a coat is badly stained or has a strong odor, when it appears lumpy in spite of a thorough brushing, the only solution is a complete bath.

How to Give Your Dog a Bath

First, brush out the coat and remove any knots or mats. Matted hair tends to "set" when wet. Plug the ears with cotton. Instill ointment into the eyes to prevent soap burn. A drop of mineral oil in each eye works well (see EYES: *Applying Eye Medicine.*)

The next question is what shampoo to use. Most human shampoos are on the acid side. This is because human skin is more acid than a dog's. Some human shampoos are on the alkaline side and may be suitable. Coconut oil shampoo is safe to use on dogs. In general, it is best to use a good commercial dog shampoo. Lysol and household disinfectants *should not be used* for washing your dog. They are absorbed through the skin and can cause death.

Next, wet your dog thoroughly, using a nozzle and spray. Then lather and rinse the head carefully, keeping soap and water out of eyes and ears. After the whole dog has been lathered and rinsed, relather and rerinse legs, feet and other areas of stubborn stain.

The secret of getting a dog clean while preserving a healthy skin is to rinse repeatedly until all soap and residue has been removed from its coat. Use a spray hose and nozzle. Soap left behind dulls the coat and irritates the skin.

Special rinses are often recommended to bring out the coat for show purposes. Do not use vinegar, lemon or bleaches. They are either too acidic or too basic and will damage the coat and skin. Adding Alpha-Keri bath oil to the final rinse gives luster to the coat. Use one teaspoonful per quart of water.

Now dry the coat gently with towels, or, if the dog doesn't object to it, use an air comb. Remember that a coat takes several hours to dry and your dog should be kept indoors in cold weather to prevent chilling.

When bathing, rinse the dog thoroughly to remove soap and residue from the coat.

(Joyce Stannard)

Dogs with oily coats are prone to collect dirt. A method of dry cleaning the coat between baths is desirable. A number of products have been used successfully as dry shampoos. Calcium carbonate, talcum or baby powder, fuller's earth and cornstarch are all effective. They can be used frequently without danger of removing essential oils or damaging the coat and skin.

Remove excess powder with a soft bristle brush. Start at the bottom and brush against the lay of the hair all the way down to the skin. If you plan to show the dog, you must remove all traces of powder from the coat before you enter the ring. If the judge finds artificial substances, your dog will be dismissed from the show ring.

Special Bath Problems

Skunk Oil: Skunk odor can be removed by soaking the coat in tomato juice and then giving the dog a bath. Alternately, make up a dilute solution of ammonia in water. Use it as a rinse and follow it with a complete bath.

Tar: Trim away excess coat containing tar when feasible. Soak the tarry stains in vegetable oil overnight. Then give your dog a complete bath. Do not use petroleum solvents such as gasoline, kerosene or turpentine; they are extremely harmful to the skin.

WHAT TO DO IF YOUR DOG HAS A SKIN PROBLEM

If your dog begins to scratch all the time, or licks, paws, bites the skin and rubs up against things to relieve discomfort, then you are faced with an *itchy skin disorder* and should attempt to determine the cause. See Table I.

There is another group of skin conditions that have to do with the appearance of the coat and hair. These diseases do not cause much discomfort—at least not at first. *Hair loss* is the main sign. It can appear as impaired growth of new hair, or you may notice patchy loss of hair from certain parts of the body. In general, hair loss caused by hormonal influences are *symmetrical*, while those caused by parasites and other external causes are *asymmetrical*. At times you may notice that the coat is coarse and brittle, dull and lifeless. To determine the possible cause, see Table IIa and IIb.

Your dog has *pyoderma* if you see pus and other signs of infection on or beneath the skin. Pyoderma is characterized by finding cellulitis, papules, pustules, boils and abscesses. See Table III.

There is another class of skin diseases that is characterized by the finding of *blebs*. Blebs, also called *vesicles*, are blisters that contain clear fluid. Large ones are called *bullae*. All tend to progress to skin erosions and ulcers through rubbing, biting and scratching. Look for these changes to begin on the face, nose, muzzle and ears. These are the *autoimmune skin diseases*. See Table IV.

During the course of grooming, playing with or handling your dog, you may discover a *lump or bump* on or beneath the skin. To learn what it might be, see Table V.

If you suspect that your dog is suffering from a skin ailment, conduct a thorough examination of the skin and coat. On short-coated dogs, run a fine-toothed metal comb against the lay of the hair to expose the skin. On long-coated dogs, use a pin brush. In many cases a typical finding makes the diagnosis obvious.

Unfortunately, this is not always the case. The diagnosis of a specific skin disease in dogs can be difficult. Early signs are not easy to detect in heavy-coated dogs. The picture is often complicated by secondary trauma to the skin caused by biting and scratching. Scabs, crusts, scales, erosions and ulcerations are all secondary skin problems usually caused by self-inflicted trauma. History becomes important in trying to decide what could have caused the problem in the first place.

Facts such as age, sex, breed, changes in activity or diet, contact with other animals, emotional states, exposure to skin irritants and environmental influences then become important points to consider.

The Diagnosis of Skin Disease
Table I

Itchy Skin Disorders

Scabies (*Sarcoptic Mange*): The most common cause of *intense* itching. Small red spots like insect bites on the skin of the ears, elbows and hocks. Identify mites. *Typical crusty ear tips.*

Walking Dandruff (*Cheyletiella Mange*): Puppies two to twelve weeks. *Dry flakes* over the neck and back. Mild itching.

Fleas: Itching and scratching along the back, around the tail and hindquarters. Fleas and/or black and white gritty specks in the hair (flea feces and eggs). *Fleas very mobile*.

Lice: Found in poorly kept dogs with matted coats. *Not common*. Look for lice or nits beneath mats. May have bald spots.

Ticks: Large insects fasten onto the skin. *Blood ticks* may swell to pea-size. Cause irritation at the site of the bite. Can be difficult to remove intact. Often found beneath ear flaps and where hair is thin.

Damp Hay Itch (*Pelodera*): Severe itch caused by a worm larva. *Must have contact with damp marsh hay*.

Inhalation Allergy (*Canine Atopy*): Severe itching, face-rubbing and licking at paws (hay fever–type symptoms). Often begins at the same time each year (*seasonal pollens*). Certain breeds more susceptible.

Flea Allergy Dermatitis: Follows flea infestation. Pimplelike rash over the head of the tail, back of rear legs and inner thighs. *Scratching continues after fleas have been killed*.

Contact Dermatitis: Itching and skin irritation *at site of contact* with chemical, detergent, paint, dye, etc. Usually affects the feet and hairless parts of the body.

Allergic Contact Dermatitis: Requires *repeated or continuous contact* with allergen (i.e., flea collar). Rash may spread beyond area of contact.

Food Allergy Dermatitis: *Nonseasonal itching* with reddened skin, papules, pustules and wheals. Found over the rump, abdomen and back of the legs. Skin becomes thickened and dark.

Lick Sores (*Acral Pruritic Dermatitis*): Mainly in large, short-coated individuals. Starts with licking at wrist or ankle.

Fly-bite Dermatitis: Painful bites at tips of erect ears and bent surfaces of floppy ears. Bites become scabbed, crusty-black and bleed easily. See EARS.

The Diagnosis of Skin Disease
Table IIa

Disorders in Which Hair Is Lost or Grows Poorly: Hormone-Related Disorders

---

Thyroid Deficiency (*Hypothyroidism*): Males and females. *Coat is thin and scanty*. Hair is brittle and coarse and falls out easily. Tends to involve the body and neck. Skin is thick, sometimes darker.

Cortisone Excess (*Adrenal Gland Hyperfunction*): Can be caused by prolonged medication with steroids. Males and females. *Hair lost in symmetrical pattern*, especially over the trunk and body. Skin is thin. Does not involve the head and neck.

Estrogen Excess (*Hyperestrinism*): Mainly in females. *Hair has greasy feel*, falls out along flanks and abdomen. Buildup of wax in ears. In males, consider a testicle tumor, especially with a retained testicle. Loss of hair in genital area. Nipples enlarge. Dry skin and brittle hair.

Estrogen Deficiency (*Hypoestrinism*): Mainly in spayed females. *Scanty hair growth* (thin coat). Skin is smooth and soft, like a baby's skin.

The Diagnosis of Skin Disease
Table IIb

Disorders in Which Hair Is Lost or Grows Poorly:
Other Disorders

Zinc Responsive Dermatosis: Crusty, scaly skin with hair loss over the face, nose, elbows and hocks. Cracked feet. Caused by zinc deficiency. *Arctic breeds* most susceptible.

Acanthosis Nigrans: Hair loss begins in *armpit folds*. Black, thick, greasy, rancid-smelling skin. *Mainly in Dachshunds.*

Color Mutant Alopecia (*Blue Doberman Syndrome*): Dry, thin, brittle hair over the body, giving a moth-eaten look. Papules and pustules appear on involved skin. Has a genetic basis in blue- and fawn-colored Dobermans. Can affect other breeds.

Seborrhea: *Dry type*: similiar to dandruff. *Greasy type*: hair and skin is oily; yellow brown greasy scales on skin. *Hair loss in circular patches*, resembles ringworm. Rancid odor.

Collie Nose (*Nasal Solar Dermatitis*): Sunburn-type reaction affects lightly pigmented nose; *mainly in Collies and Shelties*. Loss of hair at junction of nose and muzzle. Can lead to severe ulceration. See NOSE.

Ringworm (*Fungus Infection*): Scaly, crusty or red circular patches one-half inch to two inches in size with hair loss at center and *red margin* at periphery of ring. Affects all parts of coat. Looks healthy unless complicated by scabs and crusts. Some cases involve a large area with hair loss.

Demodectic Mange (two forms):
Localized—Moth-eaten look due to hair loss around eyelids, mouth and front legs. Patches about one inch in diameter, fewer than five in number. *Dogs and bitches less than one year old.*
Generalized—Progression of the above. *Numerous patches enlarge and coalesce.* Severe skin problem complicated by *pyoderma*. Affects dogs of all ages, primarily young purebreds.

Calluses (Elbow Sores): *Gray, hairless, wrinkled pads of skin* usually over elbow but can occur over any bony pressure point from lying on hard surface.

The Diagnosis of Skin Disease
Table III

Painful Skin Disorders with Drainage of Pus (Pyoderma)

Puppy Dermatitis (*Impetigo and Acne*): Puppies under 12 months. Not painful.
Impetigo—Pus-filled blisters or thin brown crusts on hairless skin of abdomen, then groin.
Acne—Purplish red bumps (pustules) on chin and lower lip.

Hair Pore Infections (*Folliculitis*): Dogs of all ages, Schnauzers in particular. *Pimplelike bumps* or blackheads *along the back* and elsewhere. In severe cases, draining sinus tracts and hair loss.

Skin Wrinkle Infection (*Skin Fold Pyoderma*): Macerated *inflamed skin with a foul odor in characteristic locations*: lip fold, nose fold, vulvar fold, tail fold and between toes.

Hot Spots (*Acute Moist Dermatitis*): Mainly in heavy-coated dogs. Rapidly advancing *painful* inflamed patches of skin covered with a *wet surface exudate of pus*, from which *hair is lost*. Skin is irritated from many causes. Disease progresses through self-maceration.

Cellulitis and Abscesses:
 Cellulitis—Painful, hot, inflamed skin. Caused by wound infections, foreign bodies, breaks in the skin.
 Abscesses—Pockets of pus beneath the skin. Painful swelling that comes to a head and drains.

Puppy Strangles (*Juvenile Pyoderma*): Puppies under 4 months. *Sudden painful swelling of lips, eyelids, ears and face.* Draining sores, crusts and sinus tracts.

Mycetomas: Painful swellings beneath skin of legs and feet, which drains pus through sinus tracts.

The Diagnosis of Skin Disease
Table IV

Autoimmune Skin Diseases

Pemphigus: Four types of pemphigus occur in dogs.

 Pemphigus foliaceus—Blebs, blisters and pustules, followed by erosions, crusts, scaling and hair loss. Depigmentation seen in late stages. First appears on *face, nose and muzzle*; can become generalized. Crusts frequently adhere to underlying skin and hair.

 Pemphigus erythematosus—Same as above but *restricted* to face, nose, muzzle and ears.

 Pemphigus vulgaris—Same as pemphigus foliaceus but *limited to oral cavity* (stomatitis) and other places where skin and mucus membranes join.

 Pemphigus vegetans—Flat-topped pustules involving skin folds. Heals with *wartlike growths.*

Bullous Pemphigoid: Similar to pemphigus vulgaris but may become generalized.

Lupus Erythematosus: Two types of lupus occur in dogs.
 Systemic lupus erythematosus—Skin involvement similar to pemphigus foliaceus. First sign of disease may be wandering lameness. Can involve foot pads.

 Discoid lupus erythematosus—Limited to the face. *Nasal ulceration and depigmentation* are characteristic.

Toxic Epidermal Necrolysis (TEN): *Painful* ulcerative skin disease. Blebs and erosion involve the skin, mucus membranes and foot pads.

Erythema Multiforme: Acute eruption of skin and mucus membranes. Often caused by drug reaction. *Target-like* eruptions with red rims and blanching at center are characteristic.

Cold Aggultinin Disease: Requires cold exposure. Involves skin of the ears, tip of tail, nose, paws and scrotum. Skin becomes *black and crusted.* Later separates, exposing raw surfaces.

Cutaneous Vasculitis: Pemphiguslike disease usually *limited to ear flaps*; occasionally affects mouth and foot pads.

Nodular Panniculitis: Multiple lumps, like marbles beneath the skin, appear over the back and along the sides of the body. Lumps open and drain, then heal by scarring.

The Diagnosis of Skin Disease
Table V

Lumps or Bumps on or Beneath the Skin

These diseases are discussed in the chapter TUMORS AND CANCERS:

Papillomas and Warts: Grow out from the skin and look like warts or pieces of chewing gum stuck to the skin. Can occur in the mouth. Not painful.

Hematomas: Collections of blood beneath skin, especially of the ears. Caused by trauma.

Tender Knots: Frequently found at the site of a shot or vaccination. Resolve spontaneously. Often painful.

Cysts: Smooth lumps beneath skin. May grow slowly. Can discharge cheesy material. Become infected. Otherwise not painful.

When a Lump May Be a Cancer:
Rapid enlargement; appears hard and fixed to surrounding tissue; any lump growing from bone; a lump that starts to bleed; a mole that begins to spread and/or ulcerate; unexplained open sore that does not heal, especially on feet or legs; any lump in the breast. *Note: Only way to tell for sure is to biopsy the lump.*

ITCHY SKIN DISORDERS

Insect Parasites

Scabies (Sarcoptic Mange)

This disease is caused by a microscopic spiderlike insect called a mite. The diagnosis must be made by examining skin scrapings under a microscope, or in difficult cases by a skin biopsy (searching for mites).

Probably no other skin disease will cause your dog to scratch and bite at himself with such intensity. The intense itching is caused by the female mites tunneling a few millimeters under the skin to lay their eggs. Mite eggs hatch in three to ten days. The immature mites develop into adults and begin to lay eggs of their own. This whole cycle takes seventeen to twenty-one days.

Signs: These mites prefer the skin of the ears, elbows, hocks and face. Early hair loss and crusts are often seen in these areas. You may also notice small red bumps that itch. They are insect bites. Crusty ear tips, along with an intense itching, make the diagnosis almost certain. If you rub the edge of your dog's ear between your fingers, the dog will begin to scratch on that side.

Later, because of scratching, rubbing and biting at the itch, the skin breaks down, allowing serum to seep out. One sees scabs, crusts and even patches of hair loss. In the final stages the skin becomes thick and darkly pigmented.

If your dog has scabies, you may notice itching of your skin at the belt line. The mites have transferred to you. However, mites do not live over three weeks on human skin. The problem is self-limited if the dog is treated.

Treatment: Clip scabies-affected areas on long-haired dogs and bathe the entire animal in one of the insecticide dips (see *Insecticides*). Dips active against sarcoptic mange mites are Lime-sulphur and Paramite. At least three dips are

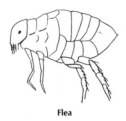

Flea

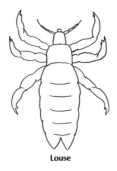

Louse

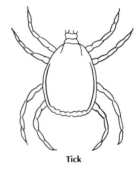

Tick

Flea. Louse. Tick.   (Rose Floyd)

required at intervals of ten days each. A fourth dip may be needed to catch late hatching eggs.

Dandruff shampoos such as Seleen are useful. They can be employed between insecticide dips to loosen scales.

Cortisone relieves severe itching. Infected sores from self-mutilation should be medicated with a topical antibiotic ointment (Neosporin or Triple Antibiotic).

Walking Dandruff (Cheyletiella Mange)

This type of mange occurs primarily in puppies. It is highly contagious. It is caused by a large reddish mite that tends to infest kennels. The mite lives on the surface of the skin and dies in a short time when off the host. Suspect this if you find a heavy dandruff over the top of the neck and back. Itching is mild.

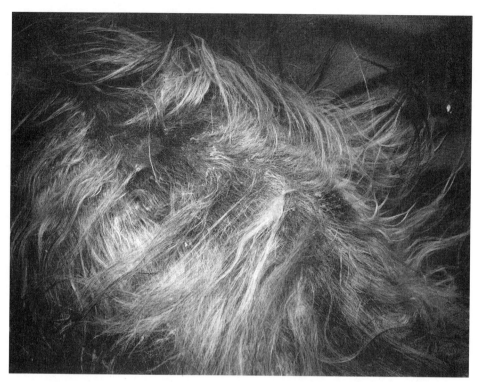

Cheyetiella Mange: Note the heavy dandruff deposits over the top of the neck and back.

The diagnosis is made by finding the mite on the puppy or in dandruff scrapings collected on paper and examined under a magnifying glass.

Treatment: All infected animals should be treated with an insecticide dip once a week for three to four weeks. Control is easily achieved by using the same methods as described for scabies. The kennel should be treated with an insecticide (see *Premises Control*). Dichlorvos fly strips aid in the control of these mites.

Fleas

The ordinary cat flea (*C. felis*) is the leading cause of skin problems in the dog. All dogs are affected except those living at higher elevations. Fleas do not live above 5000 feet. They occur year-round in pets living indoors.

Fleas survive by feeding on blood. In many dogs the bites cause only a mild itch, but a heavy infestation can cause severe anemia and even death. Fleas are also an intermediate host of the dog tapeworm. Some dogs experience a marked hypersensitivity reaction to the saliva of the flea (see *Flea Allergy Dermatitis*).

Signs: Flea infestation can be diagnosed by finding fleas on the dog or by seeing salt-and-pepperlike, black and white grains about the size of sand grains in the coat. These particles are flea feces and flea eggs. Fecal material is made up of digested blood. When brushed onto a wet paper, it turns a reddish brown.

Look for fleas on your dog's back and around the tail and hindquarters. They are sometimes found in the groin. Itching is most severe in these areas.

The adult flea is a small dark brown insect that can be seen with the naked eye. Although the flea has no wings and cannot fly, it does have powerful back legs and can jump great distances. Fleas move through the hair rapidly and are difficult to catch. Ticks and lice move slowly and are easier to pick off.

An effective flea control strategy requires an understanding of the life cycle of the flea.

Life Cycle: In order to flourish and reproduce, fleas need a warm, humid environment. The higher the temperature and humidity, the more efficient they become. Fleas mate on the skin of the dog. The female can lay 2000 eggs in her lifetime. The eggs falls off and incubate beneath furniture and in carpets, cracks and bedding. In a few days the eggs hatch into larvae, which feed on local debris. The larvae spin a cocoon and go into a pupal stage. Under ideal conditions (65 to 80 degrees F, 70 percent humidity), adult fleas can appear in two to three weeks—or they can remain in the pupal stage for several months. After they hatch, fleas search for a host. If one isn't found right away, they can live for four to twelve months without eating.

At any time, about 1 percent of the flea population is made up of adult fleas, while 99 percent remain in the invisible egg, larval and pupal stages. Therefore, to control fleas on your dog, *it is most important that you destroy the large reservoir of fleas on the premises.* Precede with both steps at the same time.

Control of fleas on the dog: A number of insecticide products are available for killing fleas on the dog, but there are differences in their application and effectiveness.

Mild flea *shampoos*, such as Fleavol, and *powders*, such as Diryl, remove fleas; but their effect is short-lasting and you will find it difficult to get adequate concentrations over the whole animal. In addition, success is limited by their lack of residual effect.

Sprays are used most often. They come in pressurized cans (the "hiss" may frighten some dogs) and trigger-activated bottles. Water-based sprays are less expensive but don't penetrate the coat as well as alcohol-based sprays. In general, sprays work best on dogs with short coats.

The best sprays are those with a good knock-down effect, a good residual effect, repellent properties and low toxicity. Pyrethrins have a good knock-down action; organophosphates, carbamates (Sevin) and synergized natural pyrethrins possess good residual effect. Repellent action can be supplied by MGK 11 or MGK 326. Read the label to determine the product's composition. Sprays suitable for use on the dog include Flair, Clinicare Pet Spray, Pestisol R Spray, Secto-O-Spray.

Shampoos, powders and sprays should be used once or twice a week.

Insecticide *dips* are the most effective means of ridding your dog of fleas. A good dip should contain the same properties as a good spray. Suitable ones include Adams Flea-off Dip, Spectro-D Dip, Kem Dip, Paramite and Dermaton. Dips should be utilized every two weeks until the dog is free of fleas by close inspection (see *Dipping*). Between dips, spray short-haired dogs and powder long-haired dogs once or twice a week. One week after the last dip, put on a flea collar and change it according to the manufacturer's recommendations.

Before using an insecticide preparation, be sure to read the section on *Insecticides* to prevent toxic reactions.

Systemic agents: The orally administered Proban (cythioate) and the topically applied Pro-Spot (fenthion) are two organophosphate insecticide drugs that enter the bloodstream and poison the flea when it takes a blood meal. Their efficacy is limited by the ability of a female flea to lay a number of viable eggs before she dies. Best results are obtained when the dog is started on the medication in early spring and kept on the drug until the first frost.

Proban has been implicated in human poisonings when the drug was accidently ingested by people. Pro-Spot must be applied to the skin of the back between the shoulders to prevent the dog from licking it off and getting a toxic reaction. *Use these products only according to the manufacturer's recommendations.*

Flea collars and *medallions* aid in flea control but cannot be relied upon to eradicate all fleas. Most flea collars contain dichlorvos, which vaporizes and surrounds the dog. If the dog sleeps outside, or in front of an air register, the collar will not be effective. Change every two months or as recommended by the manufacturer. *Dog collars should not be used on cats.*

Occasionally a dog is found to be sensitive to the chemicals in a flea collar and develops a skin allergy (see *Contact and Allergic Contact Dermatitis*). This can sometimes be prevented by airing the collar for twenty-four hours before putting it on. A collar should fit loose enough so that you can get two or three fingers between it and your dog's neck.

CAUTION: Do not permit your dog to eat or chew any flea collar or medallion. It contains toxic chemicals. Flea collars impregnated with dichlorvos should be removed one week before deworming with Task (dichlorvos) and should not be put back on until one week after deworming. Otherwise the additive effects of the insecticide in the flea collar and in the worm medication could be harmful to your dog.

Control of fleas on the premises: With a heavy flea infestation you may want to use the services of a professional exterminator. Your veterinarian can recommend a good one.

A most important step in the indoor control of fleas involves a thorough cleansing of the household. For more information, see *Premises Control.*

Insecticides for indoor flea control are delivered via sprays and foggers. *Sprays* suitable for use in the house include Sect-A-Cide Surface Spray and Siphotrol Premises Spray (contains methoprene). Methoprene is a new, safe and highly effective environmental flea-growth regulator that prevents maturation of larvae and pupae into adult fleas.

Foggers usually contain organophospates but may contain permethrins or synergized natural pyrethrins. Some contain methoprene. One disadvantage of foggers is that they tend to settle on the tops of carpets. Flea larvae and pupae, however, burrow deep into the nap. Foggers also may not settle beneath furniture because of uneven convection. To offset these disadvantages, spray first with a surface product before activating the fogger.

Foggers suitable for use in the house include Siphotrol Plus II Fogger (contains methoprene) and Spectro CF Insecticide Fogger. For maintenance and control, repeat applications every eight to twelve weeks.

Outdoor control before spraying or dusting involves the removal of all organic debris by mowing, raking and discarding the debris. When applying sprays or dusts, give special attention to favorite resting places such as beneath the porch, in the garage, the dog house and the family car. Where the dog is likely to have direct contact with the chemical, use an insecticide suitable for indoor application.

Insecticides effective in outdoor control include malathion, Sevin (5% dust), Vet-Kem Yard and Kennel Spray Concentrate and Siphotrol Plus II House Treatment (contains methoprene).

Lice (Pediculosis)

Lice are not very common. They occur primarily in dogs that are run-down and poorly kept. Lice are often found beneath matted hair and around the ears, head, neck, shoulders and anal area.

The usual picture is intense itching. Because of the constant irritation, bare spots may be seen where the hair has been rubbed off.

There are two types of lice. *Biting lice* feed on skin scales. *Sucking lice* feed on the dog's blood and can cause a severe anemia.

Adult lice are pale-colored insects about two to three millimeters long. They lay eggs called nits, which look like white grains of sand and are found attached to the hairs. They are difficult to brush off. Nits may look something like dandruff (seborrhea); but dogs with seborrhea do not itch as they do with lice. Inspection with a magnifying glass makes differentiation easy, as nits are well-formed rounded eggs attached to hair shafts.

Treatment: Lice do not show much resistance to insecticides and do not live long off the dog. They can be killed by giving a thorough bath followed by an insecticide dip effective against fleas. Three to four dips must be given at ten-day intervals. In between, dust the dog with a 5% Sevin powder (see *Insecticides*).

Infected bedding should be destroyed and the dog's sleeping quarters disinfected (see *Premises Control*). Severely anemic dogs may require a blood transfusion or a buildup with vitamins, iron and a high-protein diet.

Ticks

Ticks have a complicated life cycle. It involves three hosts including wild and domestic animals and man. The adult tick fastens onto the dog. The male tick is a small flat insect about the size of a match head. A "blood" tick is a female tick feeding on the dog. She may swell up to the size of a pea. Males and females mate at this time, and the female feeds on the host. When you see a puffed-up tick, look for a small male tick nearby.

There are several species of ticks that live on the dog. The brown dog tick

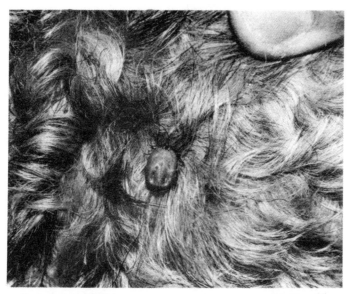

Engorged female tick.   (J. Clawson)

is the most common. All are capable of transmitting diseases. Rocky Mountain spotted fever, canine ehrlichiosis, canine babesiosis, canine hepatozoonosis, tularemia and Lyme disease are some of the illnesses transmitted by ticks. Ticks are capable of secreting a toxin that causes paralysis in dogs (see NERVOUS SYSTEM: *Tick Paralysis*).

Ticks are usually found on the ears, neck, head and between the toes. A dog might be found with hundreds of ticks all over the body. To learn how to treat ticks on your dog's ear, see EARS.

Treatment: If your dog has only a few ticks, the easiest thing to do is to remove them. First kill the tick by applying alcohol, gin, ether or fingernail polish directly to the tick by means of a cotton-tipped applicator. After a few moments, grasp the dead tick as close to the skin as possible with tweezers and apply steady traction until it releases its hold. The blood of ticks can carry diseases dangerous to people. Therefore, do not crush or squeeze a tick with your bare fingers.

If the head remains fixed to the skin, there is no need for concern. In most cases this causes only a local reaction that clears up in a few days. Only rarely does a tick bite become infected.

If your dog has numerous ticks, you will have to resort to a commercial insecticide preparation such as 4% malathion powder, or a dip such as Paramite or Kem Dip. Before using one of these preparations, read the section on *Insecticides*. With heavy infestations, multiple dips are required. Dip once every week for four to six weeks. Be sure to treat the dog's sleeping quarters (see *Premises Control*).

For outdoor control, cut down tall grass, weeds and brush. Spray or dust with Toxaphene or Dieldrin. Use these products with caution. They are toxic to pets.

Damp Hay Itch *(Pelodera Dermatitis)*

This disease is caused by the larvae of a threadlike worm found on damp marsh hay. The larvae burrow into the skin of the dog's chest, abdomen and feet, causing raised pimplelike bumps. Later, you may see raw crusted and inflamed areas where the dog has scratched and infected its skin.

The disease is found in outdoor dogs, especially when damp marsh hay is used for bedding. The diagnosis is made by examining skin scrapings under the microscope.

Treatment: Kill worm larvae by dipping your dog in an insecticide solution such as Dermaton or Paramite once a week until free from itching. Bathe infected areas with a mild soap such as pHisoHex; then apply a topical ointment (Neosporin) three times a day. Change the bedding from hay to cedar shavings, cloth or paper shreds. Spray sleeping quarters (see *Insecticides*).

Lick Sores (Acral Pruritic Dermatitis)

In this condition a sore at the ankle or wrist are caused by a constant licking at that spot. It is called a "boredom" sore because it occurs in dogs left alone for long periods. It is most common in dogs who are middle-aged and therefore less active, especially bird dogs, Labradors, Danes, Dobermans and other large short-coated breeds.

As the dog licks at the wrist or ankle, hair is rubbed off. The surface of the skin gets red and shiny-looking and begins to itch. This leads to further maceration, which continues the cycle. Eventually the skin becomes raised,

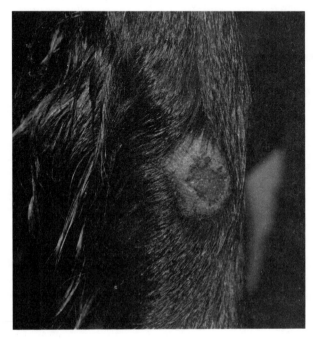

Lick sores are caused by boredom.

thick, hard and insensitive to pressure. However it remains fresh-looking from constant cleaning.

Treatment: The most important consideration is to relieve the boredom. Topical cortisone relieves the itching but will probably be licked off. Cortisone can also be administered by injection directly into the sore. In stubborn cases X-ray treatment and cobra-venom injections have been tried.

Insecticides

Insecticides are used as powders, sprays, dusts and dips for the elimination of insects on the dog. They are also used to disinfect bedding, houses, kennels, runs, gardens, garages and other spots where a dog might reinfect itself by coming into contact with the adult insect or its intermediate forms.

A discussion of insecticides used in flea control is discussed above (see *Fleas*).

Insecticides are poisons!

Before using an insecticide preparation, be sure to read and follow the directions of the manufacturer. This will prevent accidental poisonings from improper exposure.

There are three classes of insecticides in current use. In order of increasing toxicity they are: *pyrethroids* (natural and synthetic pyrethrins), *organophosphates* (dichlorvos, also called Task; Ronnel, also called Ectoral) and *methylcarbamates* (Diryl, Sevin). Pyrethroids are much less toxic than the other two on a milligram per pound weight basis. Pyrethroids and pyrethrins are incorporated into numerous products for control of insect parasites on the host, in the house and on the premises.

Commercial preparations for powdering, spraying and dipping your dog are available through many pet stores and agricultural supply outlets for control of fleas, lice, mites, ticks and other parasites. They all contain insecticides of the classes listed above.

When you purchase one of these products, be sure that it is made *especially for dogs*. Preparations manufactured for sheep and livestock can irritate the skin of dogs and even cause death.

Be sure *not* to use an insecticide preparation on a dog that is taking Proban or Pro-Spot to control fleas without first discussing this with your veterinarian.

An insecticide overdose could cause your dog to twitch at the mouth, foam, collapse, convulse and fall into a coma. Other signs of insecticide toxicity are diarrhea, asthmatic wheezing, staggering gait, muscle twitching and jerking.

If you think your dog might be suffering from an insecticide reaction, give a warm soapy water bath to remove residual compounds from the coat and keep your dog quiet. Contact your veterinarian.

Dipping

The object of a dip is to rid your dog of insect parasites. Choose a dip that is recommended by your veterinarian, or if you decide to wash your dog with a commercial preparation, check the label to be sure that it is effective against the insect in question (see *Insect Parasites*).

CAUTION: Some worm medicines contain insecticides. If your dog has just been wormed, there could be a sudden buildup of chemicals in the system from powdering, dipping or spraying with an insecticide. Check with your veterinarian before applying an insecticide to a dog who has been wormed within one week.

Before dipping, wash your dog with a gentle commercial dog shampoo. Remove excess water from the coat to prevent dilution of the dip. Then rinse thoroughly with an insecticide dip made up according to the directions on the package. Apply eye ointment and plug the ears with cotton so you can treat the head and ears.

Most insecticide dips have to be repeated three or four times at intervals of seven to ten days, depending on the insect in question and the severity of the infestation.

Premises Control

The object of premises control is to prevent reinfection by ridding the environment of insects, eggs, larvae and other intermediate stages.

Treat all animals in contact with your dog or living quarters.

Destroy infected bedding and scrub your dog's quarters with a strong household disinfectant. A thorough housecleaning that includes vacuuming of carpets, spraying of furniture, application of insecticide to corners and cracks will help to eliminate the insect and its eggs and larvae. This usually has to be done two or three times.

Floors should be mopped, giving special attention to cracks and crevices where organic debris and eggs accumulate. With a severe infestation, steam cleaning of carpets is highly effective in killing eggs and larvae. Insecticides can be used in the water of the steam cleaner. Specific products are now available where you rent the cleaner. Vacuum bags should be discarded immediately after use. All infected human bedding must be washed and dried on maximum heat setting. With a heavy infestation, it is sometimes better to enlist the services of a professional exterminator. Your veterinarian can recommend a good one.

Insect bombs such as Vet Fog can be used safely in closed spaces. Remove all pets and read instructions carefully. Some insecticide dips can be used as sprays on gardens, lawns and kennels. Use according to the recommendations of the manufacturer.

Dichlorvos fly strips kill fleas by a vapor blanket if properly placed. Attach a strip three to four feet above the dog's bed. In a dog house, attach half the strip to the inside of the roof and half beneath the floor.

A dog's sleeping quarters should receive at least two treatments spaced two weeks apart. Eggs and cocoons are resistant to insecticides and can remain dormant for several months.

Sevin is an insecticide powder that can be bought inexpensively from garden and agricultural supply stores. It comes in different concentrations. Be sure to purchase the *5% dust*. It can be used safely in kennel runs and dog houses, and on lawns and shrubs. It won't hurt your dog if powder gets on the coat. Dust liberally in and around sleeping quarters, kennels and dog houses using a shaker can. Force dust into crevices and cracks. Sevin is effective against fleas, ants and lice. It is partially effective against ticks.

ALLERGIES

An allergic reaction is an unwanted side effect caused by the *immune system*. In the chapter INFECTIOUS DISEASES: *Antibodies and Immunity* is a further discussion of this system.

A dog can be allergic to various substances such as pollens, molds, house dust, insect bites, certain foods, drugs and chemicals. Exposure to them triggers a reaction, usually typified by itching, sneezing, coughing, tearing, vomiting or diarrhea.

In order to be allergic to something in food or the environment, a dog must be exposed to it at least twice. What the dog is allergic to is called the *allergen*. The way in which the body responds to that allergen is called a *hypersensitivity reaction*. About 10 percent of dogs overreact to allergens and are called *atopic*. The condition is hereditary.

There are two kinds of hypersensitivity reaction. The *immediate type* occurs within minutes of exposure and often produces hives and itching. The *delayed reaction* produces itching hours or days afterward. *Anaphylactic shock* is an example of the immediate type. Emergency treatment is discussed in DRUGS AND MEDICATIONS: *Injections*.

Canine allergy is a major causes of skin disease in dogs.

Hives (Itching, Urticaria)

Hives is an allergic reaction characterized by the sudden appearance of raised, circular, itchy wheals on the skin, especially around the face. The hair sticks out in little patches. Frequently you will see swelling of the eyelids. Hives usually appear within thirty minutes of exposure and disappear within twenty-four hours.

Insect bites are a common cause of hives. Hives can occur after a vaccination. Penicillin and tetracycline can produce hives. Hives can appear after eating spoiled meat. Topical insecticides and soaps are other causes.

Hives that come and go usually are caused by something in the dog's diet.

Treatment: Identify the allergic cause, when possible, and prevent further exposure. When a food allergen is suspected, change your dog's diet (see *Food Hypersensitivity*). You can give a dose of Milk of Magnesia right away to speed removal of the food from the intestinal tract. When hives appear shortly after a shampoo or a use of a topical insecticide, give the dog a bath.

Hives usually respond well to antihistamines such as Benadryl. Give Benadryl at a dose of one to two milligrams per pound body weight every eight hours. Cortisone may be indicated to control a severe case of hives. Use it under veterinary supervision.

Inhalant Allergy (Canine Atopic Dermatitis)

If your dog starts to scratch about the same time each year, the cause maybe a skin allergy brought on by breathing pollens. This is called canine atopy. It is similar to hay fever in humans.

Severe itching is the leading sign. It is often accompanied by licking at a runny nose, rubbing an itchy face on the carpet, sneezing, watering of the eyes and lapping at the paws (look for characteristic brownish stains on the feet). Areas where hair has been rubbed off may be found beneath the arms and along the flanks. The skin is red and scratched. It sometimes feels warmer than normal. In a small percentage of cases you may notice droplets of water on the skin.

Canine atopy usually begins in dogs one to three years of age. There is a hereditary basis. Commonly it is found in Wirehaired Fox Terriers, West Highland White Terriers, Dalmatians and Poodles, but all breeds are susceptible.

Signs appear initially in August and September (the ragweed season). Later, other pollens begin to influence the picture: tree pollens in March and April; then grass pollens in May, June and early July. Finally, the dog starts to react to wool, house dust, molds, feathers, kapok and other allergens. With prolonged exposure and multiple allergens, the condition becomes a year-round problem.

In order to determine whether an inhalation allergy exists, your veterinarian

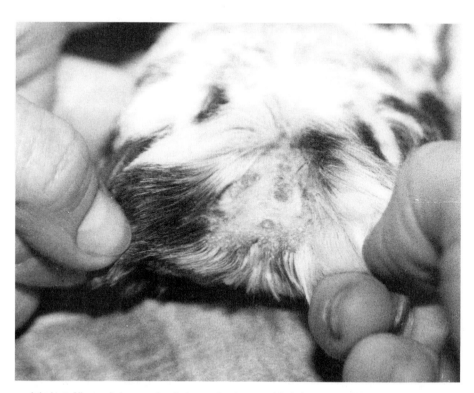

Inhalant Allergy: Itchy papules between the toes and hair loss caused by lapping at paw; occurred every spring and reponded to cortisone.

may wish to hospitalize your dog and see if the condition gets better. If the symptoms come back when the dog goes home, you can be quite certain your dog is allergic to something in the immediate environment. Skin tests with various allergens help to identify the cause. New serological blood tests (called RAST tests) are used in special circumstances.

Canine atopy can be confused with flea allergy, contact dermatitis and sarcoptic and demodectic mange.

Treatment: Try to keep your dog away from the allergen. If just feathers or kapok, this may be possible. However, the atopic dog usually is allergic to many different allergens and it is not feasible to hide from them all. It may be possible for your veterinarian to give a course of injections to desensitize the dog.

Cortisone is effective and helps to control symptoms. It should be used under medical supervision.

Food Hypersensitivity (Allergy)

Food allergy is an uncommon itchy skin reaction of the immediate and delayed type that occurs *nonseasonally* in dogs of all ages. Allergies can develop to meats, milk, eggs, fish, cereal grains, potatoes, soybeans and other substances in the diet. A dog must have had prior exposure to the offending food in order to become allergic to it. Most often he has been on the same diet for months or years.

Along with the itching you may see papules, pustules and skin wheals. They appear over the rump, abdomen and backs of the legs. Initially the skin appears reddened. In time it becomes thick and darkly pigmented. The rash is not specific. Since food allergies are not as common, the dog is often thought to be suffering from a contact or allergic contact dermatitis.

Treatment: The diagnosis is made by placing the dog for eight weeks on a "hypoallergenic" diet such as lamb or mutton and rice. Prior exposure to this trial diet is unlikely. Strict precautions require that the dog drink only distilled water, fast for the first forty-eight hours and take no medications.

The diagnosis is confirmed if the itching subsides and the skin rash improves. Various foods are added one by one until the offending allergen is identified by finding that it exacerbates the itching.

Flea Allergy Dermatitis

A certain percentage of dogs are allergic to the saliva in flea bites and break out in a rash. This is a hypersensitivity reaction of both the immediate and delayed types: itching occurs even after fleas have been eliminated. It is characterized by red pimplelike bumps and severe itching over the base of the tail, back of the rear legs and inner thighs. The pimples may become crusted and infected. Dogs often scoot or back up against something to rub against. After a time, the skin gets thick and pigmented. Hair is lost. If fleas go undetected, itching becomes generalized.

Treatment: Kill fleas with dips and insecticides (see *Fleas*). Cortisone

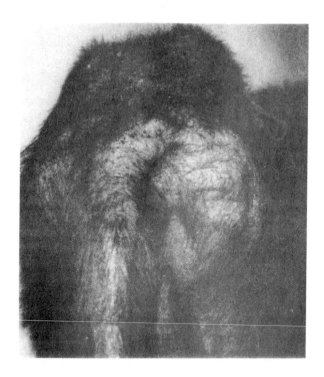

Skin changes on the hindquarters of this dog are caused by hypersensitivity to flea saliva *(flea allergy dermatitis).*

blocks the allergic reaction and relieves the itching. Use it only with veterinary supervision. Treat sores with a topical antibiotic ointment (Neocort).

Contact and Allergic Contact Dermatitis

Contact dermatitis and allergic contact dermatitis are two separate conditions discussed together because they produce similar-looking reactions. Both are caused by contact with a chemical. Whereas all dogs coming into contact with irritating chemicals develop a skin reaction, there are some chemicals that cause a reaction only in dogs that are allergic to them. A dog will not break out with an allergic dermatitis unless exposed to the allergen repeatedly.

A contact dermatitis of either type causes itchy red bumps along with redness and inflammation of the skin. You may notice moist weepy spots, crusts, blisters, ulcerations and pus.

Common contact *irritants* are acids and alkalis, insecticides, detergents, solvents, soaps and petroleum by-products.

Common contact *allergens* are flea powders and collars, poison ivy and poison oak, plastic and rubber dishes and dyes found in indoor-outdoor carpets.

You will find contact dermatitis of both types on the feet, chin, abdomen, groin and scrotum (hairless parts likely to come in contact with chemicals). Since dogs lie on their hocks and stifles, these areas are affected, too.

Flea collar allergy causes local itching and redness followed by loss of hair, skin ulceration and crust formation beneath the collar (see *Fleas*). This condition may spread to other areas.

Food dish dermatitis affects the nose.

Skin disease easily mistaken for contact and allergic contact dermatitis are canine atopy, ringworm and seborrhea.

Treatment: First identify the skin allergen causing the problem and then keep your dog away from it. Treat infected areas with an appropriate antibiotic. Cortisone is of value because it stops the itching, biting and scratching. Use it only under a veterinarian's supervision.

DISORDERS IN WHICH HAIR IS LOST OR GROWS POORLY

The outstanding sign of these nonirritative skin disorders is skin change without itch or pain. The exception is the dog whose primary disease has been complicated by a secondary infection of the skin (see *Pyoderma*).

Hormone-induced skin diseases usually are seen in dogs over five years of age but are not common. They develop slowly, progress gradually and can be a lifetime problem.

Characteristically, hormone disorders cause symmetrical changes over the body, one side being the mirror image of the other. The typical features are first loss of hair, and then darkening of the skin. The diagnosis is difficult, the response to treatment is slow and professional help is required for diagnosis and long-term therapy.

Thyroid Deficiency (Hypothyroidism)

*Hypo*thyroidism is the result of inadequate output of hormone from the thyroid gland in the neck. Thyroid deficiency causes the coat to become scanty. The hair is coarse and brittle and falls out easily. The skin gets thick, tough and dark in color. The neck and body are most often involved.

Since control of metabolism is under the influence of the thyroid, a deficiency of hormone slows down the production of energy. In the dog, the signs of thyroid deficiency are lethargy, obesity, drooping of the eyelids, mental dullness and irregular heat cycles. These signs develop gradually and may take months to become evident. A dog with a mild thyroid deficiency may show little or no signs of it. You might begin to suspect this only in connection with an infertility problem. Diagnosis requires a thyroid blood test.

Treatment: Hypothyroidism is easy to treat with daily thyroid replacement. It usually is permanent and requires lifetime treatment.

Cortisone Excess (Adrenal Hyperfunction)

Adrenal hyperfunction is caused by overproduction of cortisone by the adrenal glands located on top of the kidney. This is rare.

A dog taking cortisone by mouth or injections after a time will get the same effect as if the adrenal glands were making too much cortisone.

The effect on the coat is loss of hair in a symmetrical pattern over the body with darkening of the underlying skin. The head and neck areas are not affected

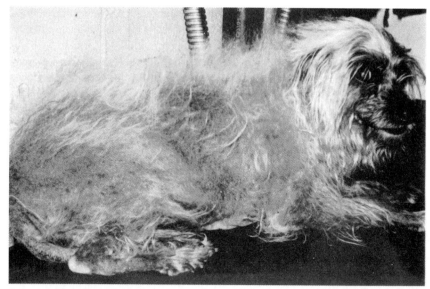

Before treatment of a hormone imbalance *(cortisone excess):* Note loss of hair over the body in a symmetrical pattern.

After treatment the coat looks a lot better.

as they are with thyroid deficiency. This is an important distinguishing factor. Small "blackheads" may be found on the abdomen. There is a potbellied look. Dogs with cortisone excess gain weight and retain fluid.

Treatment: If your dog is getting cortisone by tablet or injection, your veterinarian may want to reduce the dosage or stop the medication. If due to overproduction, a drug can be given to suppress the adrenal glands.

Estrogen Excess (Hyperestrinism)

An excess of female hormone can occur in both males and females. In females it is caused by cystic ovaries that manufacture too much estrogen. Often there is a history of infertility, false pregnancy or enlargement of the nipples and vulva. In the male it can be caused by a tumor of the testicle. Both conditions are rare.

The effect on the skin is to stimulate oil production and cause greasy hair. Wax builds up in the ear canals. Hair falls out along the flanks and abdomen in a symmetrical pattern. The skin in the groin and axilla becomes thickened and tough (like pigskin).

Treatment: The female should be spayed. Males should be castrated.

Estrogen Deficiency (Hypoestrinism)

This is a mild skin condition that occurs in older female dogs spayed as puppies. There is a gradual lack of hair growth over the undersurface of the belly and around the vulva. Later it involves the lower chest and neck. The skin

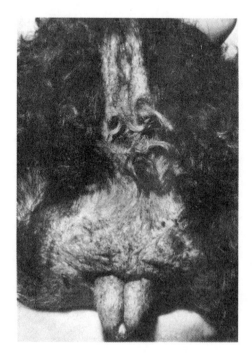

Hyperestrinism: Excess female hormone caused enlargement of the vulva.

becomes soft, smooth and nearly hairless. Females shed very little and do not collect much dirt. They make good house pets.

Treatment: Your female dog will regrow her coat if you give small doses of estrogen over an extended period.

Zinc-Responsive Dermatosis

Zinc is a trace mineral required for normal metabolism including growth of hair and maintenance of the skin. A deficiency of zinc causes thinning of the hair and a scaly crusty dermatitis over the face, most noticeable on the nose, and around the eyes, ears and mouth. Crusts also appear over pressure points such as the elbows and hocks. The feet become callused and crack easily.

A genetic defect causing impaired zinc absorption has been identified in Siberian Huskies, Alaskan Malamutes and Samoyeds. Dogs fed cereal diets deficient in zinc and high in calcium and phytyns or phytic acid (which tie up zinc) can develop similar signs. A closely related condition has been observed with the feeding of dry generic dog foods deficient in zinc.

Treatment: Zinc-responsive dermatosis, irrespective of the cause, responds rapidly to zinc sulfate supplements (220 mg by mouth twice daily until fully recovered). You should expect to see improvement in one week. Switch your dog to a high-quality balanced ration (see PEDIATRICS: *Feeding and Nutrition*). Arctic breeds usually require zinc supplements for life.

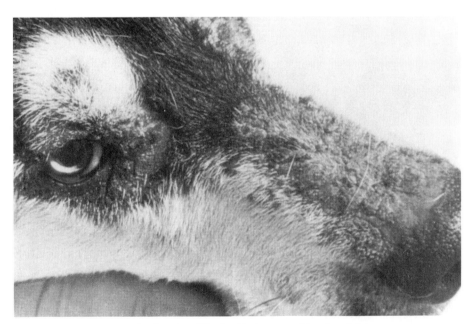

Crusty dermatitis over the face in a Siberian Husky caused by *zinc deficiency.*
(Courtesy Bristol-Myers Squibb).

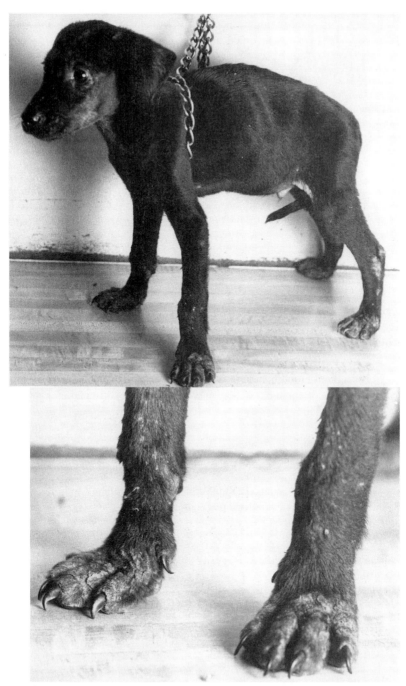

Zinc Responsive Dermatosis: This pup was fed table scraps and generic dog food. Note close-up of feet. A balanced diet corrected the problem.

Acanthosis Nigrans

Acanthosis Nigrans literally means "thickened black skin." The disease affects the armpit folds and those of the groin. It is found most commonly in Dachshunds. The exact cause is unknown.

As the disease progresses you will see an extreme dark black pigmentation and the development of a greasy rancid discharge on the surface of the skin. Bacterial infection is common. Eventually the process may extend over a considerable area, covering the brisket and extending onto and around the legs. This disease causes considerable distress to the dog and the owner.

Treatment: There is no available cure but with continuous management the dog can be kept comfortable. Keep the skin clean with an antiseborrheal shampoo (Seleen) to remove excess oil and bacteria. Cortisone preparations such as Panolog aid in controlling the skin irritation. Weight reduction, to reduce friction in the skin folds, is advisable. Antibiotics are prescribed when the skin is infected.

This condition should be treated by a veterinarian.

Color Mutant Alopecia (Blue Doberman Syndrome)

This hereditary skin disease is seen most often in fawn and blue coated Dobermans, but occasionally is seen in blue Danes, blue Newfoundlands, Chows, Whippets and Italian Greyhounds.

Color mutant Dobermans are born with a healthy hair coat. However, at four to six months of age the coat becomes thin, brittle, dry and takes on a moth-eaten appearance. The skin becomes rough and scaly. Blackheads, papules and pustules appear over the body. Some blue Dobermans may not manifest the disease until they are three years old.

Treatment: There is no cure. Treatment is directed at relieving the surface condition. Immerse the dog in warm water to hydrate its skin and follow with benzoyl peroxide shampooing to remove scales and flush the hair follicles. Repeat as determined by the condition of the skin.

Because color mutant hair coat has a genetic basis, affected individuals should not be used for breeding.

Seborrhea

Two types of seborrhea occur in the dog. The *secondary type* of seborrhea is similar to dandruff. It is flaky and scaly, and easy to lift off the skin. It is usually not a disease in itself. Instead, it is found with other skin diseases such as allergic dermatitis, mange and hormone skin disorders. If your dog has a severe scratching problem and you see dandruff, you probably have not found the cause and should keep looking for it.

The other type of seborrhea is called *primary* seborrhea. Its cause is unknown. Cocker and Springer Spaniels are affected more often than other breeds. Primary seborrhea is associated with excess production of skin oil (sebum). This leads to greasy deposits of yellowish brown scales on the skin and hair, giving the dog a rancid, unpleasant odor. The hair may look as if it had lice nits attached

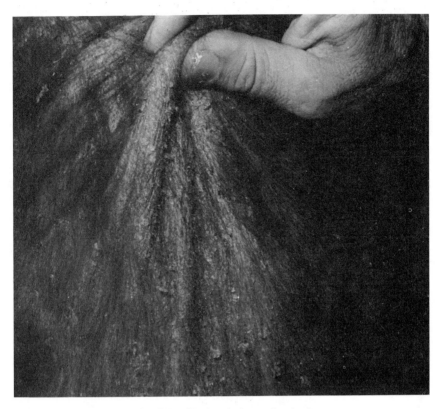

Dry flaky skin *(secondary seborrhea).*

to it. Skin patches may resemble ringworm (distinguished by culture), mange (distinguished by skin scrapings) or hormone imbalance (see *Estrogen Excess*).

The areas frequently involved by primary seborrhea are the elbows, hocks, and hair along the border of the ear. Small circular patches having a pigmented oily center and a red halolike outer rim may occur over the face and chest.

Treatment: Primary seborrhea is incurable but manageable. Sebum-dissolving shampoos (Seleen, Pragmatar, Sebbafon and Sebulex) give good results when used to cleanse the skin of oil and scales. How often to shampoo depends upon the individual case; usually once a week is enough. Leave shampoo on the skin for ten minutes and then rinse well. Creams and ointments (Thiomar cream and Pragmatar ointment) applied to individual skin spots help to keep them in check. Cortisone is used to control itching and redness. Topical and oral antibiotics are used for the treatment of secondary bacterial infection.

Ringworm (Fungus Infection of Skin)

Ringworm is not a worm but a plantlike growth that lives on the surface of the skin. The majority of cases are caused by the fungus *Microsporum canis*.

Ringworm gets its name from its appearance—a rapidly spreading circle having hair loss at the center and a red ring at the margins. This skin disease is

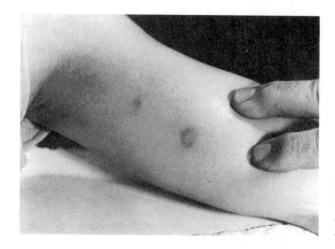

Ringworm is a contagious skin infection. The typical appearance is a round patch with scales at the center and an advancing red ring at the margin.

transmitted to dogs by other animals and man, or to dogs by contact with spores in the soil. Humans can pick up ringworm from dogs and vice versa. Children should avoid handling dogs with ringworm, as they are especially likely to catch the disease. Adults are relatively resistant.

Ringworm grows in circular patches one-half inch to two inches in size. Although simple ringworm is not an itchy condition, scabs and crusts can form, leading to draining sores. Cases do occur in which skin involvement is extensive. Ringworm also invades toenails. When the nails grow out they may be deformed.

Mild cases of ringworm, with just hair loss and local scaliness, often resemble localized demodectic mange or dry seborrhea. A diagnosis of ringworm can be made if the skin glows green under ultraviolet light. This test is positive in only about one half the cases. Microscopic examination of skin scrapings and fungus cultures are more certain.

Treatment: Clip away the infected hair at the margins of the ringworm patch and bathe the skin with Weldol or Betadine shampoo to remove dead scales. One or two small patches can be treated with a fungistatic solution (Tinactin), which can be purchased at a drug store without a prescription. For more extensive involvement, or patches that do not seem to be getting better with topical solutions, your veterinarian may wish to prescribe a drug called griseofulvin (Fulvicin). It is given by mouth in a daily dose of ten to twenty milligrams per pound. It should not be given to pregnant females, as it could be dangerous to unborn puppies. It is also a good idea to give a single large dose (100 milligrams per pound) as a preventative to other animals on the premises that are not infected but may have been exposed. Infected sores should be treated with a topical antibiotic ointment

Demodectic Mange

Signs of demodectic mange are those of hair loss without itch. It occurs among dogs three to twelve months of age and is caused by a tiny mite, *Demodex canis*, too small to be seen without a microscope.

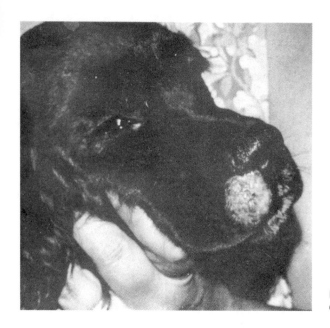

Ringworm on the muzzle of Cocker Spaniel.

Most dogs acquire Demodex mange mites early in life from their mothers. This usually does not cause a problem. All the factors responsible for symptomatic skin disease are not fully understood. It is known that Demodex mites are able to produce a substance that lowers an animal's natural resistance to them, allowing them to multiply on the host. Several kennels have reported that some females have a higher incidence of Demodex mange in their litters than others. This would suggest that in some purebred dogs there is a lowered immunity to the mites.

The disease is more common in short-haired dogs with oily skins. Symptoms appear at puberty. At this time, sebum, which mites feed on, is increasing in amount.

Demodectic mange can take one of two forms:

Localized Form

This occurs in dogs up to one year of age. It begins as thinning of the hair around the eyelids, the lips and corners of the mouth and front legs, giving a moth-eaten appearance. It progresses to patches of hair loss about one inch in diameter (which may be confused with ringworm). If more than five patches are present, the disease could be progressing to the generalized form. After one or two months the hair begins to grow back. In three months most cases are healed.

Treatment: A topical preparation such as Canex or Goodwinol can be used to shorten the course. Many cures attributed to drugs probably are spontaneous recoveries. Watch closely to be sure that localized form is not progressing to the generalized type.

Generalized Form

This starts out as a localized case but instead of improving it gets worse. Numerous patches appear on the head, legs and trunk. The patches coalesce to form large areas of hair loss. Hair follicles become plugged with mites and debris. Skin breaks down to form sores, crusts and draining sinus tracts— presenting a most severe and disabling condition.

Treatment: Treatment is prolonged and response is slow, requiring frequent changes in medication. Cure is not always possible. Recently good results have been reported using an amitraz dip called Mitaban (Upjohn).

Clip away all infected hair to facilitate topical therapy. Wash the whole dog with Betadine shampoo to remove scales and debris. Dip your dog in 10.6 milliliters of Mitaban dissolved in two gallons of water. Allow the dip to dry on the dog. Repeat every two weeks for three dips. Side effects include drowsiness, lethargy, vomiting, diarrhea and uncoordinated movements. Puppies are the most sensitive.

Cultures from infected skin sores will determine the most effective antibiotic. *Cortisone* is *contraindicated* because it may depress the dog's immunity to the mites, making the condition worse.

Generalized demodectic mange should be treated under veterinary supervision.

Calluses (Pressure Sores)

Calluses are gray, hairless, thickened pads of wrinkled skin overlying bony pressure points. They are caused by constant pressure from lying on hard surfaces. The most common site is the elbow, but calluses can occur on the outside of the hocks, the buttocks, and the sides of the legs. They are much more common in heavy dogs and dogs kenneled on cement floors.

If the pressure problem goes unchecked, the surface of the skin breaks down, forming a running sore with serum draining from the hair pores. This becomes a most difficult problem to treat.

Treatment: Provide your dog with a soft sleeping surface to take pressure off the callus and distribute it more evenly. Foam rubber pads or thick rugs can be used. An infected callus should be treated in the same way as an abscess.

PYODERMA (PUS ON OR BENEATH THE SKIN)

Pyoderma is a pus-forming bacterial infection of the skin. Many cases are caused by maceration. When a dog rubs, chews or scratches at a persistent irritant to the skin, it becomes infected. The infection then gets started only because some other problem was there first. This should always be kept in mind. Look for other signs of skin disease before concluding that pyoderma is the *only* problem.

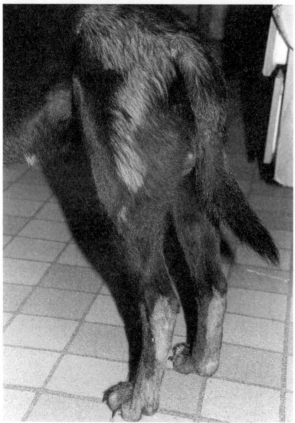

Generalized Demodectic Mange: Large areas of hair loss, skin crusts and sores, involving the head, trunk, legs and feet.

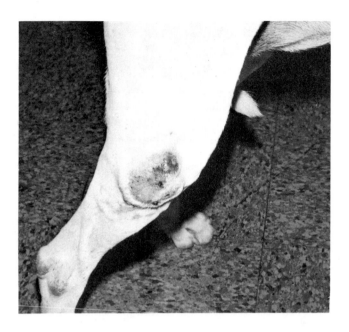

Callus: These pressure sores are caused by lying on hard surfaces such as concrete.

Puppy Dermatitis (Impetigo and Acne)

This is a mild surface skin infection found in young dogs under twelve months of age. There are two types: impetigo and acne.

Impetigo (or milk rash) can be recognized by finding pus-filled blisters first on the hairless parts of the abdomen and then the groin. These rupture easily, leaving thin brown crusts.

Acne is found on the chin and lower lip, or occasionally in the genital area, the perineum and groin. It occurs in puppies three to twelve months of age during sexual development. It is identified by finding purplish red bumps that come to a head and drain pus (like pimples or blackheads). Blockage of skin pores by excess sebum or keratin is a predisposing cause. It is more common among dogs with oily skins.

Treatment: Both infections can be controlled by twice daily cleansing of the skin with a dilute solution of hydrogen peroxide, benzoyl peroxide or surgical soap (pHisoHex), followed by the use of a topical antibiotic. When sebum is a problem, the skin should be cleansed with one of the shampoos described for Seborrhea (itches).

Acne usually clears up as a dog matures. However in certain breeds such as the Doberman, Boxer and Bulldog, the disease can persist. If your dog does not seem to be improving with local care, oral antibiotics may be indicated. See your veterinarian.

Hair Pore Infection (Folliculitis)

In this condition, pimplelike bumps or blackheads are found along the back, the sides of the body and the stifles. It is more common in short-haired dogs and affects dogs of all ages. Some cases are caused by grooming too vigorously, which injures the skin.

Once established, the infection bores down into the hair pores and causes a deep-seated disease in which draining sinus tracts appear and hair is lost in small patches.

A condition called "Schnauzer bumps" is common in Miniature Schnauzers. Dogs suffering from this condition have many large blackheads running down the middle of their backs.

Treatment: Mild cases are treated in the same way as acne. Treatment is sometimes prolonged, requiring the addition of oral antibiotics. Pustules or small abscesses should be left alone. If you squeeze them you might cause the infection to spread deeper into the tissues.

Skin Wrinkle Infection (Skin Fold Pyoderma)

Skin wrinkles and folds provide an ideal location for the growth of bacteria. This infection can present as lip fold pyoderma in spaniels and St. Bernards, as face fold pyoderma in Pekingese, as vulvar fold pyoderma in overweight females and as tail fold pyoderma in Bulldogs (screw tails).

The signs are irritation and inflammation of the skin. The moist skin becomes infected and gives off a foul odor.

Treatment: Relief is obtained by clipping away hair and bathing the skin with a surgical soap (Weldol or pHisoHex). An antibiotic-steroid cream (Panolog)

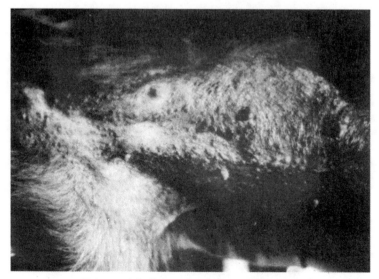

Hair pore infection on the abdomen *(folliculitis)*.

is effective against itching and scratching. Surgical removal of the excess skin is the method of choice when the condition is slow to respond.

Hot Spots (Acute Moist Dermatitis)

A hot spot, *pyotraumatic dermatitis*, is a bacterial skin infection that progresses through self-mutilation. Fleas, ear and anal gland problems, skin irritants, allergies and other factors are probably responsible for initiating the cycle.

Hot spots are warm, painful, swollen patches of skin that exude pus and give off a foul odor. These circular patches appear suddenly and enlarge rapidly, often within a few hours, becoming several inches in size. Hair is lost rapidly. They appear on the neck, ears, chest, back, rump and flanks.

In breeds with a double coat, hot spots are more common just before shedding, particularly in the wet season when dead moist hair is trapped next to the skin.

Treatment: Clip away hair to let in air. Gently cleanse the skin with a surgical soap (pHisoHex or Oxydex) or diluted hydrogen peroxide. Many dogs exhibit considerable pain and may be sedated or tranquilized to facilitate handling and to prevent psychic trauma.

A product called Sulfadene is available at pet stores and works well when applied to the skin. Topical antibiotic-steroid creams (Panolog and Neocort) aid in reducing irritation. Apply them three times a day to achieve good results. Oral antibiotics and steroids may be indicated. Dogs should be prevented from licking

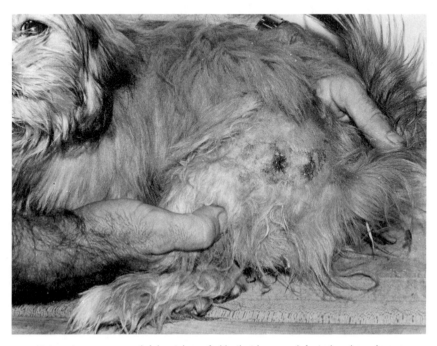

Hot spots are warm painful patches of skin that become infected and exude pus.

and biting at their sores. Use restraints or an Elizabethan collar. Underlying skin problems should be identified and treated along with the hot spots.

Cellulitis and Abscesses

Cellulitis is a bacterial infection that involves the deep layers of the skin. Most cases are initiated by skin trauma. Infection can be avoided in most fresh wounds if they are properly taken care of within the first few hours.

The signs of cellulitis are *pain* (tenderness to pressure), *warmth* (it feels hotter than normal), *firmness* (it's not as soft as it should be) and *change in color* (it appears *redder* than it should be). As the infection spreads out from the wound into the subdermal lymphatic system, you may see red streaks in the skin and be able to feel enlarged lymph glands in the groin, armpit or neck.

A *skin abscess* is a localized pocket of pus beneath the surface of the skin. Pimples, pustules, furuncles and boils are examples. The signs are like those of cellulitis except that an abscess feels like fluid under pressure.

Treatment: Localize a cellulitis by clipping away hair and then apply hot moist packs to assist the natural defenses of the body to surround the infection and make it come to a head. Saline soaks, made up to one teaspoonful of salt in a quart of water, make a suitable poultice. Apply *three* times a day.

Pimples, pustules, furuncles, boils and other small abscesses that do not drain spontaneously need to be lanced with a sterile needle or scalpel. Flush the cavity with Betadine (1%) to keep it open and draining until it heals from below.

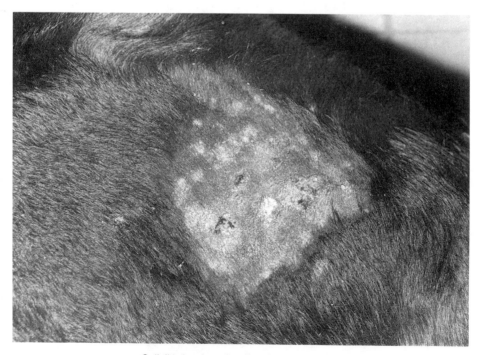

Cellulitis involves the deep layers of the skin.

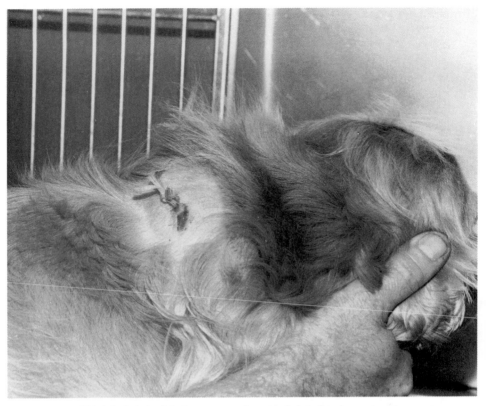

This infected dog bite became an *abscess*. A drain has been placed.

Antibiotics are indicated in the treatment of wound infections, cellulitis and abscesses. Most skin bacteria responds well to penicillin, Keflex, erythromycin or Chloromycetin. Cultures and antibiotic sensitivity tests are indicated to select the drug of choice when the infection is slow to respond.

Foreign bodies (such as splinters) beneath the skin must be removed with forceps, as they are a continuous source of infection.

Puppy Strangles (Juvenile Pyoderma)

Juvenile pyoderma occurs in puppies under four months of age and may affect several puppies in a litter. It can be recognized by a painful swelling of the lips, eyelids, ears and face, along with draining sores, crusts and sinus tracts. The lymph nodes beneath the chin and in the neck swell up; these pups are quite sick and should be seen promptly by a veterinarian.

Although staphylococcal and streptococcal bacteria have been isolated by needle aspiration of lymph nodes, this is the exception rather than the rule. Accordingly, a hypersensitivity reaction to antigens has been postulated as the most probable cause.

Treatment: Your veterinarian will probably want to prescribe moist hot

106

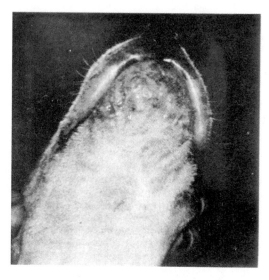

Puppy strangles *(juvenile pyo-derma).*

packs to soften crusts and promote drainage. Treatment includes the use of high doses of corticosteroid. Antibiotics alone are often ineffective.

Do not attempt to express the pus from the sores. This increases the likelihood of scarring.

Mycetomas

A mycetoma is firm swelling beneath the skin caused by a puncture wound in which various soil fungi and bacteria gain entrance and set up infection. The feet and legs are the most common sites. These painful swellings break open and discharge pus through sinus tracts deep in the skin.

Treatment: Complete surgical removal is the treatment of choice for the solitary mycetoma. This is not always possible. Some of the newer antifungal agents (ketoconazole, fluconazole) show promise in treating difficult cases.

AUTOIMMUNE SKIN DISEASES

An autoimmune reaction is the result of a breakdown in the fundamental distinction between self and nonself. For reasons not fully understood, a host identifies some of its own proteins as "foreign" and makes *auto-antibodies* against them. The result is that a disease is actually caused by a host's reaction to its own tissue, thus called an *autoimmune disease.* In INFECTIOUS DISEASES: *Antibodies and Immunity*, there is a discussion of the *normal* functions of the immune system.

The diagnosis and differentiation of the various autoimmune skin diseases based on their clinical appearance and site of skin involvement is difficult at best. Accordingly, an exact diagnosis usually has to be based on laboratory tests that must be performed by your veterinarian or a histopathologist. This involves the study of tissue biopsies under the microscope and the ordering of special tests such as antinuclear antibody (ANA) determinations and immunofluorescence studies of the skin.

The following uncommon skin diseases are being seen and treated in dogs with increasing frequency. This is partly the result of an increased awareness and partly a function of improvements in diagnosis and management.

Pemphigus

Pemphigus is an immune-mediated disease in which auto-antibody is directed against the wall of the skin cell. The cells lose their affinity to each other and separate, forming blebs, vesicles and pustules.

Four types of pemphigus are seen in the dog:

Pemphigus foliaceus is the most common. It occurs in dogs two to seven years of age. The Bearded Collie, Newfoundland, Akita and Schipperke appear to be at greatest risk.

Blebs, blisters and pustules first appear on the face, nose, ears, top of the muzzle and trunk. These blisters rupture, leading to skin erosions, crusts, scaling and hair loss. The crusts frequently adhere to the underlying skin and hair. Areas of depigmentation occur as the disease progresses.

The footpads can become thick and hard. Cracks and ulcers may cause difficulty in walking. In some cases the disease is restricted to the foot pads. Pemphigus foliaceus is a primary consideration for dogs presenting with painful, thickened footpads (see also *Lupus Erythematosus*).

Pemphigus erythematosus is a localized illness with ulcers, crusts, oozing scabs, hair loss and depigmentation restricted to the face, nose, muzzle and ears. This disease is easily confused with *discoid lupus erythematosus.*

Pemphigus vulgaris is a severe disease in which blisters and ulcers form at the junction of the skin and mucus membranes. It involves the mouth and oral cavity, producing an ulcerative stomatitis. The nail beds can be affected with subsequent sloughing of the nails.

Pemphigus vegetans is thought to be a milder form of pemphigus vulgaris. It is the rarest type of pemphigus. It is characterized by flat-topped pustules involving the skin folds of the axillae and groin. Ulcerations heal with wartlike growths instead of normal skin. This is its characteristic feature.

Treatment: Over 50 percent of dogs with pemphigus foliaceus and pemphigus erythematosus can be managed successfully with corticosteroids, often in combination with azathioprine or cyclophosphamide. Long-term treatment is required. Dogs who survive the first year can usually be kept in remission for life. Sunscreen helps to prevent nasal solar dermatitis and ultraviolet injury to exposed depigmented skin.

Pemphigus vulgaris and pemphigus vegetans respond less favorably.

Bullous Pemphigoid

This disease is closely related to pemphigus vulgaris. Eighty percent of cases involve the oral cavity. If it becomes generalized, you will see blisters,

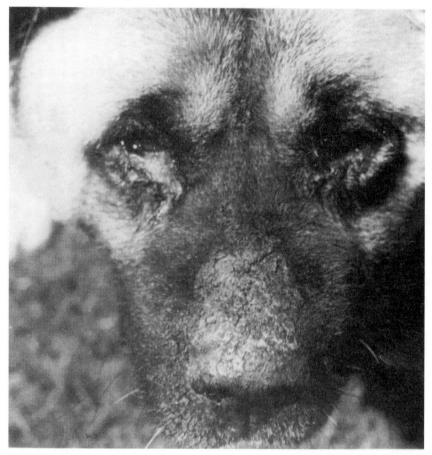

An Akita with *pemphigus foliaceus.*   *(Courtesy Bristol-Myers Squibb)*

bullae and ulcerative erosions affecting the foot pads and the skin of the trunk, groin, axillae and abdomen. Bullous pemphigoid has a predilection for Shetland Sheepdogs and Doberman Pinschers. Treatment is similar to that for pemphigus. In general, the outlook is guarded.

Lupus Erythematosus

Two types of lupus occur in the dog:

Systemic lupus erythematosus is a complex disease affecting multiple organ systems including the skin, kidneys, heart and joints. A stilted gait or wandering lameness may be the first indication.

Skin manifestations include vesicles, pustules, erosions, crusting, oozing and hair loss. This is especially evident about the face and over the nose and muzzle. The oral cavity and mucocutaneous junctions are often involved. The foot pads can become thick and ulcerated with sloughing of the pad.

Secondary bacterial infections are a serious problem in SLE and a prominent cause of death. Intensive treatment of these infections is warranted.

Ulceration and depigmentation of the nose is characteristic of *discoid lupus erythematosus.*
(Courtesy Bristol-Myers Squibb)

Treatment is like that for pemphigus. The outlook for long-term control is guarded.

Discoid lupus erythematosus is the second most common autoimmune skin disease after pemphigus foliaceus. It is thought to be a milder form of SLE and is limited to the face. Ulceration and depigmentation of the nose are the most characteristic findings. In fact, in the absence of other sites of skin involvement, the diagnosis of discoid lupus can be quite certain. Collies, German Shepherds, Siberian Huskies and Shetland Sheepdogs are most often affected.

Treatment of discoid lupus with oral corticosteroids and/or vitamin E is quite successful. In the mildest cases, topical sunscreen and avoidance of sunlight alone may suffice.

Toxic Epidermal Necrolysis (TEN)

TEN is a rare, ulcerative autoimmune disease that appears to be a skin response to various drugs, internal cancers, infections and other bodily illnesses. Blebs, ulcers and erosions affect the skin, mucous membranes and pads of the feet. This skin disease is extremely painful. The dog is severely depressed and refuses to eat.

Treatment involves large doses of corticosteroid. Recovery takes two to three weeks. However, the death rate from secondary complications (or the underlying illness) approaches 30 percent.

110

Erythema Multiforme

Erythema multiforme is an acute eruption of the skin and mucus membranes. Targetlike oval or circular skin eruptions with red rims and blanching at the center are characteristic. There is an association with drugs and staphylococcal folliculitis. Like TEN, it may be secondary to another illness.

Erythema multiforme is rare. Many cases recover spontaneously, especially when a precipitating cause can be found and corrected.

Cold Agglutinin Disease

This uncommon skin disease is caused by an autoimmune reaction triggered by exposure to temperatures below 32 degrees F. Those parts of the body most susceptible to cold exposure and subsequent injury sustain loss of blood flow caused by clumping of blood cells in the capillary circulation. This leads to death of those parts. The resulting gangrenous changes affect the skin of the ear flaps, tip of the tail, nose, paws and scrotum. The skin becomes reddened, cyanotic, black and crusted. Later it separates, exposing raw surfaces.

Treatment: Initially it is like that for frostbite (see EMERGENCIES: *Cold Exposure*). Immunosuppressive drugs are used to prevent further attacks. Avoid exposure to cold weather.

Cutaneous Vasculitis

This rare disease of unknown cause produces a pemphiguslike skin reaction limited in most dogs to the ear flaps. Occasionally it affects the mouth and foot pads. Round or oval areas of reddened skin are followed by ulceration, scarring and deformity of the ears. Treatment is like that for pemphigus.

Nodular Panniculitis

This is an uncommon autoimmune skin disease of unknown cause in which multiple lumps appear over the back and along the sides of the body, much like marbles beneath the skin. They are more easily noticed in short-coated breeds. As the disease progresses, the lumps ulcerate and drain, then heal by scarring. The dog usually runs a fever and appears lethargic.

Biopsy of a nodule confirms the diagnosis. Treatment involves corticosteroids and/or vitamin E. The outlook for long-term control is good.

LUMPS AND BUMPS

Any unexplained lump, bump or open sore on your dog should be checked by your veterinarian. The majority will not be cancerous. However, there is no good way to tell if a growth on or beneath the skin is a cancer until it has been removed and examined under a microscope. Most cancers are painless. So do not delay because your dog does not seem to be feeling much pain.

Benign and malignant tumors of the skin are discussed in the chapter TUMORS AND CANCERS.

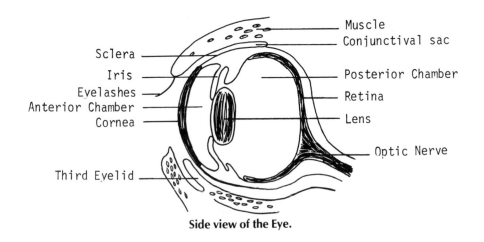

Muscle
Conjunctival sac
Sclera
Iris
Eyelashes
Anterior Chamber
Cornea
Posterior Chamber
Retina
Lens
Optic Nerve
Third Eyelid

Side view of the Eye.

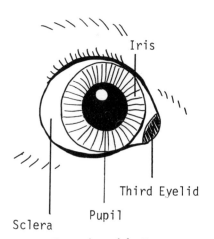

Iris
Third Eyelid
Sclera
Pupil

Front view of the Eye.

Side and front view of the eye.   *(Rose Floyd)*

5

Eyes

HOW A DOG SEES

THE EYE is an organ with several parts, all of which are important to your dog's health and well-being. The eyeball itself is seated in a cushion of fat that protects it in its bony socket. Seven muscles are fixed to the globe. They stabilize the eye and govern its movements.

As you look at the front of your dog's eye, you will see that the surface is rimmed by a narrow margin of white (sclera) much less conspicuous than your own. Most of the eye is pigmented. This pigment is found in the *iris*, a layer of smooth muscle that controls the size of the *pupil*, much as a shutter does a camera. The pupil is located in the center of the iris. Both the iris and the pupil are covered by a layer of thick transparent clear cells, the *cornea*, or window of the eye. The inner eye has two chambers. The *anterior chamber* is found between the cornea and the *lens*; the *posterior chamber*, containing a clear jelly, is the larger central cavity of the eye between the lens and the *retina*.

Light enters the eye by passing first through the cornea and anterior chamber and then through the pupil and the lens. The iris expands and contracts, depending upon the brightness of the light. Light then traverses the posterior chamber and is received by the retina. Here it is converted into nerve impulses that pass via the optic nerve to the brain.

A number of investigators have concluded that dogs are nearsighted and have rather poor visual accommodation. That is, they cannot see things sharply and in focus. We might compare a dog's vision to that of a middle-aged person who wears bifocals. The dog's retina does not have many specialized cells that distinguish colors and instead sees only black and white and various shades of gray (color blind).

On the other hand, dogs have a larger pupil and a wider visual field than humans do and more photoreceptors in the retina for the detection of light. Thus they see very well in the dark. Because of the wide field of vision, they are quite adept at following moving objects. On the whole, dogs are supplied with a type of vision best suited to their needs.

The eyelids are tight folds of skin that support the front of the globe. Actually they do not make contact with the surface of the eye because there is a thin layer of tears between them. On the upper lids eyelashes are always present. They are not present on the lower lids. The borders of the lids should meet when the eye is closed.

Tears serve two functions. First, they cleanse and lubricate the surface of the eyeball. The blink reflex assures that the moisture will be evenly spread out and your dog's eyes will not dry out. Tears also contain immune substances that prevent bacteria from gaining a foothold.

You may have noticed that your dog has a rather prominent layer of tissue (or well-developed membrane) at the inner corner of the eye, resting on the eyeball. This is the third eyelid or haw (*nictitating membrane*). It is an added protective device not found in man. Like a windshield wiper, the third eyelid is capable of sweeping across the surface of the eye, cleansing and lubricating it. In some dogs the third eyelid is more visible than in others. This depends to a

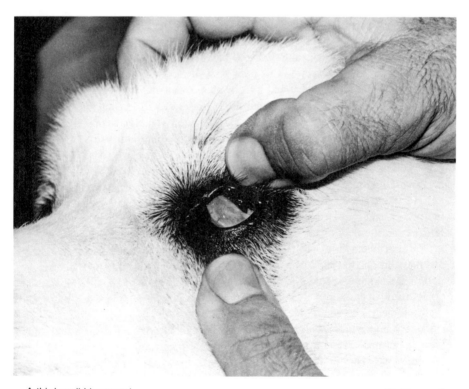

A third eyelid is normal. (J. Clawson)

certain extent upon its size and whether or not it's pigmented. Some breed Standards call for a visible haw; others for it to be scarcely apparent.

When the third eyelid is drawn across the surface of the eye it gives the impression that the eyeball has "rolled back" into its socket. But in fact this is not the case; the eyeball hasn't really moved at all. You can demonstrate this by applying gentle pressure to the globe so as to recess the eye slightly, making the membrane come forward and across.

The *conjunctiva* is a slippery layer of tissue that covers the white of the eye and reflects back to cover the inner surface of the lids. It does not cover the cornea. In certain breeds it may be pigmented or spotted. If you look closely you can see small vessels running through the conjunctiva. It will appear red when the eye is irritated.

Tears are secreted by glands found in the eyelids, in the nictating membrane and in the conjunctiva. A normal accumulation of tears is removed by evaporation. Excess tears are pooled near the nasal corner of the eye and carried via a drainage system to the back of the nose.

WHAT TO DO IF YOUR DOG HAS AN EYE PROBLEM

If your dog has matter in the eye and if the eye waters, if the dog squints, paws at an eye and gives evidence that the eye is painful, then you are faced with an eye problem. The first thing to do is examine the eye to see if you can determine the cause.

How to Examine the Eye

This requires a good light. To examine the eyeball, place one thumb against the skin of the cheek below the eye and the other thumb against the ridge of bone above. Gently draw down on the lower thumb and apply counter traction with the other. Because of the mobility of the skin of a dog's face, the lower lid will sag out and you can look in and see the conjunctival sac and most of the cornea behind it. Reverse the procedure to examine the eye behind the upper lid.

The Foreign Body

One of the most common causes for a foreign body to lodge in a dog's eye (dust, grass seed, dirt and specks of vegetable matter) is because the dog is allowed to ride with its head outside a car window. The first sign is tearing and watering of the affected eye, along with further signs of irritation and blinking and squinting. Examine the eye to see if you can see a piece of foreign material behind the upper and lower lids. If not, the foreign body may be caught behind the third eyelid, in which case most dogs with a painful eye will not allow you to lift it without some form of anesthesia.

If the foreign body can be seen, it can be gently removed with blunt-nosed tweezers, such as those used to pluck eyebrows. Alternately, a cotton-tip swab,

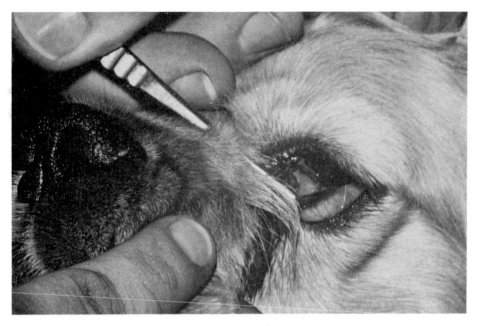

Foreign bodies can be removed with blunt-nosed tweezers.

moistened first, can be used to gently swab the eye. The foreign body may adhere to it. Finally, if there is quite a bit of dirt in the eye, the eye should be irrigated with a saltwater solution (one teaspoonful of salt to a pint of water) by soaking a wad of cotton and squeezing it into the eye.

A foreign body such as a thorn that has penetrated the surface of the eye should be removed by a veterinarian.

If you believe you have successfully removed the foreign particle, finish the job by applying an antibiotic ophthalmic ointment to the eye (Neosporin).

If the dog persists in rubbing the eye after the treatment, the foreign body may still be in the eye, or a corneal abrasion may have occurred. Obtain professional assistance.

Applying Eye Medicine

Pull the lower eyelid down and apply the ointment to the inner surface of the eyelid. Direct application to the eyeball will be resisted by the dog and may be hazardous should the dog jerk its head. Eye drops may be applied directly to the eyeball.

Rub the eyelid gently over the eyeball to disperse the medicine.

When medicating an eye for any reason, *do not* use preparations that are old, out of date or not specifically labeled for *ophthalmologic use*.

Minor eye problems should not be neglected in the hope that they will clear up by themselves. If there is any doubt about the diagnosis, and particularly if the eye has been doctored at home but has shown no improvement in twenty-four hours, call your veterinarian.

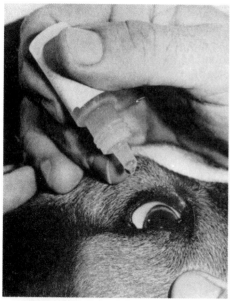 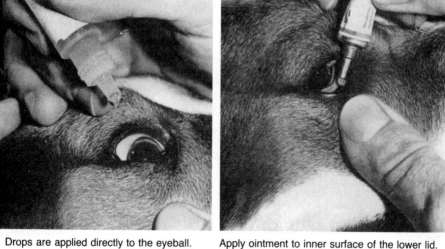

Drops are applied directly to the eyeball.   Apply ointment to inner surface of the lower lid.
(J. Clawson)

Prolonged administration of antibiotics in the eye may lead to fungal infection.

Eye Out of Its Socket (An Emergency)

Prolapse of the eyeball is a common occurrence in dogs with large bulging eyes such as Boston Terriers, Pugs, Pekingese, Maltese and some Spaniels. It is generally caused by bites and other trauma. Struggling with these individuals while attempting to hold and restrain them for any reason can cause the eye to bulge out so far that the eyelids snap behind the eyeball instead of in front of it. This prevents it from returning to the socket.

This is an emergency. Replacement of the eyeball must be accomplished at once. Shortly after the dislocation takes place, swelling behind the eye makes it extremely difficult to manipulate the eye back into its normal position. To replace the eye, lubricate it with vaseline and attempt to lift the eyelids out and over the eyeball while maintaining gentle pressure on the globe with a wad of moist cotton. If the eye cannot be easily replaced, cover it with a wet cloth and seek professional assistance.

Caution: Do not make repeated unsuccessful attempts to manipulate a dislocated eye, as this causes further swelling and inevitably leads to greater eyeball injury.

Other Causes of Eye Displacement

Infections and tumors in the space behind the eyeball push the globe forward so that it bulges out. Tumors are slow-growing and relatively painless.

117

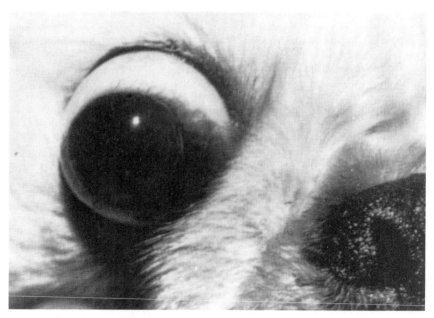

A bulging eye, out of its socket, is an emergency.

Retrobulbar abscess is an extremely painful condition of rapid onset. The head about the eye is usually swollen and exquisitely tender. Dogs with retrobulbar infection experience great pain when attempting to eat, as the muscles of mastication exert pressure on the eyeball when the mouth is opened. These abscesses are treated by incision and drainage.

Hemorrhage behind the eye is seen with head trauma and may occur spontaneously in some of the bleeding disorders. It also causes eye displacement.

EYELIDS

Sudden Swelling (Chemosis)

A sudden swelling of the eyelids may be caused by an allergic reaction. These include insect bites, hives, inhaled irritants and allergens in medications. These lids look fluid-filled and soft. In fact, water has passed out of the circulation into the tissues in response to the allergy. Often dogs rub their muzzles (itching). The condition may be accompanied by hives in which the hair stands out in an erect manner in little patches over the body. Puffy eyelids are seen in skin allergies (see SKIN: *Allergies*).

This is not a serious problem. It is of short duration and improves when the allergic agent is removed. Simple cases may be treated with drops or eye ointment containing a corticosteroid (Neocortef).

Inflamed Eyelids (Blepharitis)

Blepharitis is a name given to a variety of conditions in which the eyelid becomes thick, reddened and inflamed-looking. Usually you will find crusty accumulations and pus adherent to the lid margins. It is seen most often in puppies (see SKIN: *Puppy Strangles*).

Staphylococcal blepharitis is identified by finding small white pimples (abscesses) on the rims of the eyelids. This is caused by a specific bacteria. These abscesses rupture and cause itching and redness. Quite often the glands under the neck enlarge. This condition occurs most commonly in Poodles. It is not a serious problem and can be treated with Neomycin ophthalmic ointment and oral Ampicillin.

Hair Loss Around the Eye (Demodectic Mange)

In young dogs suffering from demodectic mange the hair about the eyelids sometimes falls out, giving a moth-eaten look. When the roots of the hair become secondarily infected with bacteria, a crust forms on the skin. Skin scrapings viewed under the microscope will show the true cause of the problem to be demodectic mites.

Treatment consists of the use of an insecticide (Goodwinol ointment) applied to the infected part three times daily. Be careful not to get any of the mange

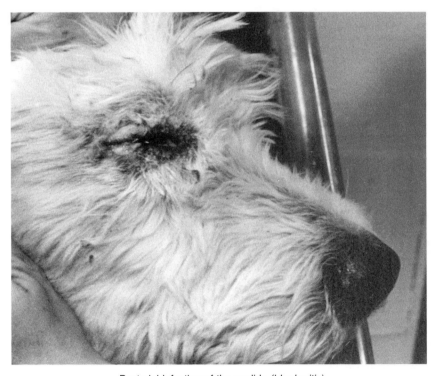

Bacterial infection of the eyelids *(blepharitis)*.

ointment into the eye. As a safeguard, mineral oil should be applied to the eye first.

Ringworm also produces hair loss around the eyes. For more information on ringworm and demodectic mange, see the SKIN chapter.

Stys (Hordeolum)

The eyelid contains numerous glands that open along its margin (*meibomian glands*). They secrete an oil substance that acts as a barrier to the tears, keeping them from overflowing the lids, much as a grease barrier holds back water. Obstruction of the ducts of these glands, or an infection, will result in a swollen, reddened, tender pus pocket on the eyelid. It is referred to as a sty.

A sty may be brought to a head with hot compresses and may rupture spontaneously. In most cases it will need to be punctured with a small sterile needle. Afterward an antibiotic ophthalmic preparation should be applied (Neosporin).

A chronic type of blepharitis involving the meibomian glands occurs in adult dogs. It is difficult to clear up. Treatment involves oral antibiotics, cortisone and hot packs.

Whiteheads (Plugged Meibomian Glands)

Primarily this is a problem among white-coated dogs such as the white Poodle. It is not serious. The main reason for treating it is that it is unsightly. As you look at the rim of the eyelid you will see several large white bumps along the margin. They are caused by an accumulation of glandular secretions. They may be expressed by placing the end of a spoon (bowl) under the eyelid and pressing against the whitehead with your thumb. Infection is usually not a problem. When present, the glands should be expressed and the eye treated with antibiotic eye ointment.

Severe Squinting (Blepharospasm)

Spasms of the muscles around the eye are induced by eye irritation. The irritant causes tightening of the muscles of the eyelid, which rolls the lid against the cornea or conjunctiva. Having once rolled in, the rough margins of the lids and the hairs rub against the eyeball, causing further pain and spasm. Blepharospasm is most often caused by ocular foreign bodies and entropion, but any painful eye condition can cause severe squinting.

Anesthetic drops may be applied to the eyeball to relieve the pain and break the cycle. The relief is temporary unless the inciting factor has been removed.

Eye Irritation from Hairs

There are a number of eye problems in which eye irritation is caused by hair rubbing against the eyeball.

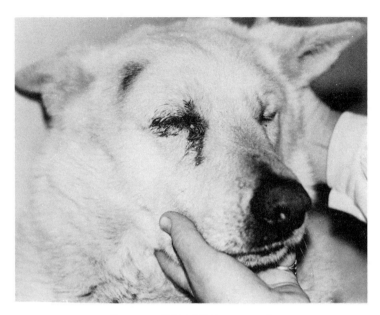

Severe squinting *(blepharospasm)*

Extra Eyelashes (*Distichiasis*)

This is a congenital condition in which an extra row of lashes grows from the lid margins and rubs against the cornea. The irritation may not be severe enough to cause symptoms until the dog is mature. This condition occurs most often in Poodles, Cocker Spaniels and Pekingese—but all breeds can be affected. The hairs may be burned out with an electric needle or removed by surgery.

Facial Hair

This is a condition seen in short-muzzled breeds such as the Pekingese, Shih Tzu, Lhasa Apso and Bulldog in which the hair on the nasal fold grows up against the eyeball. In the Old English Sheepdog, many Terriers and other breeds with long facial hair, it is this hair that falls in against the eye and causes irritation. The offending hairs should be removed by clipping, or in some cases by plucking. Those requiring attention can often be identified because they are stained and discolored by the tears.

Eyelid Rolled Inward (Entropion)

This is the most common congenital defect of the eyelids. It may also be caused by injury or long-standing disease of the lids. Some cases are complicated by blepharospasm.

Breeds commonly affected are the Chow, Irish Setter, Golden Retriever, Chesapeake Bay Retriever, Great Dane, Great Pyrenees, Saint Bernard, Bulldog

Dogs with long hair about the face are subject to eye irritation *(trichiasis).*
(Sydney Wiley)

Ectropion: When the lower eyelids roll out, the eyes are exposed to irritants. *(Sydney Wiley)*

and Shar-pei. Most commonly it affects the lower eyelid. In Bloodhounds and Saint Bernards, and in other breeds with large heads and loose facial skin, entropion can be found in the upper lid as well. The condition requires surgical correction. Of course, dogs whose entropian has been surgically corrected may not be shown.

Eyelid Rolled Outward (Ectropion)

In this condition the lower eyelid rolls out from the face, exposing the eye to irritation. This condition is usually seen in dogs with loose facial skin such as

Entropion: This Shar-Pei's eyelids have been tacked up to prevent further eye injury from rolled-in lashes. The dog may outgrow the entropion.

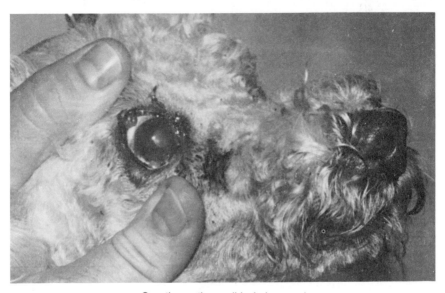

Growths on the eyelids *(adenomas).*

hounds, spaniels and Saint Bernards. It can be seen in older dogs whose facial skin has lost its tone and sags. This is seen temporarily in hunting dogs after a long day in the field. Plastic surgery may be necessary to tighten the lid and protect the eye.

Tumors

The adenoma is the most common tumor of the eyelid. It has a cauliflowerlike appearance and, like most growths of the eyelid, usually is found in the older dog. It should be removed. Otherwise it will continue to grow, irritate the eye and interfere with closing the lids. There are other tumors of the eyelid, some of which are malignant.

THE THIRD EYELID (NICTITATING MEMBRANE)

When the third eyelid is visible over the surface of the eye, it is said to be protruding or prolapsing. A protruding third eyelid can result from one of three causes: sunken eyeball, irritation of the eye or congenital defect.

Congenital prolapse is only important in that the dog has an unsightly appearance. Removal of the eyelid is seldom required.

A sunken eyeball causes the membrane to protrude. This may be the result of malnutrition or prolonged illness in which the fat pad at the back of the eye is reduced in size. Dehydration also gives a sunken eye. The third eyelid may also protrude in order to protect an irritated eye.

A protruding third eyelid gives the "haws," which to dog trainers and handlers is frequently undesirable in that it gives the animal a somewhat haggard look. Most breed Standards require that the haws, if mentioned at all, be scarcely apparent. In Bloodhounds, a visible haw is called for in the breed Standard.

Eversion of the Cartilage

This is a congenital condition among Weimaraners, Great Danes, Golden Retrievers and Saint Bernards. The third eyelid appears to roll back upon itself like a dry leaf. Corneal irritation occurs in some cases. This should be treated surgically.

Cherry Eye

This condition results when the tear gland on the inner surface of the third eyelid enlarges because of infection. As it swells it is forced out from beneath the lid, exposing a red, cherrylike growth at the nasal corner of the eye. It occurs most commonly in Cocker Spaniels, Beagles, Boston Terriers and Bulldogs. Usually it must be removed surgically. A few cases may respond to antibiotics.

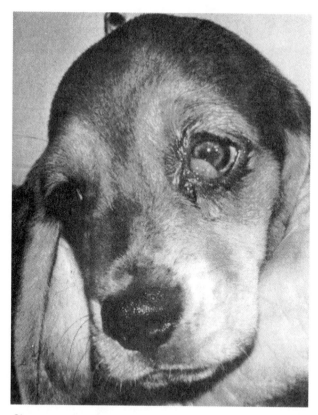

Cherry eye: An infected tear gland on the inner surface of the third eyelid enlarges.

THE OUTER EYE

Conjunctivitis

This is an inflammation of the lining membrane that covers the inner sides of the eyelids and the surface of the eyeball up to the cornea. It is the most common disease of the eye.

Normally the conjunctival membrane is pink (the same color as the inside of the lip). In conjunctivitis the membrane is red. Choking with a leash can produce hemorrhage beneath the conjunctiva, as can some bleeding disorders. These "flame" hemorrhages can be confused with conjunctivitis.

Conjunctivitis usually is accompanied by a discharge from the eye. If the discharge is clear or watery (*serous conjunctivitis*), one of the following may be the cause: foreign bodies, misdirected hairs, physical irritants (such as wind) and various allergens. An allergic conjunctivitis is accompanied by itching. The dog rubs at the eyes.

A discharge from one eye suggests a local infection or foreign body. When both eyes are involved, suspect a contagious disease.

Chronic Purulent Conjunctivitis: The discharge is thick and tenacious. This condition is difficult to clear up.

A discharge that looks like pus and presents a thick, tenacious appearance, often crusting over the eyelids, indicates a bacterial problem (*purulent conjunctivitis*). Cultures may be required to identify the bacteria and to determine the most effective antibiotic for treatment. When this condition persists for a long time it becomes chronic. A deep-seated infection is difficult to clear up. In such cases, one should consider the possibility that the tearing system has been affected, in which case the eye will appear dry (see *Dry Eye*). Repeated cleansing of the eye, correction of any underlying problem and specific antibiotics determined by cultures and sensitivities are the primary approach to this problem.

Treatment: Mild irritative forms of conjunctivitis can be treated at home. The eye should be cleansed with a dilute solution of boric acid made up for ophthalmic use. This can be purchased over-the-counter. Use as is directed for people. You should expect to see definite improvement within twenty-four hours. If not, see a veterinarian. A foreign body or other serious eye disturbance may be present.

Follicular Conjunctivitis

The back side of the nictating membrane and the eyelids enlarge to form a rough cobblestone surface, giving an irritated look to the eye membranes. The eye discharge is mucoid. This type of conjunctivitis is frequently caused by an allergy or an infection. Occasionally, after the inciting factor has been removed,

126

the follicles remain enlarged and the roughened surface of the conjuctiva acts as an irritation to the eye. This roughened surface must be removed by a cauterizing process in which copper sulfate crystals are applied to the affected parts. This causes the tissue to slough. A smooth membrane regenerates.

Conjunctivitis resulting from a fungal or parasitic infection is rare and requires laboratory diagnosis.

Conjunctivitis of the Newborn *(Ophthalmia Neonatorum):* The eyelids of puppies do not open until they are ten to fourteen days old. There is a closed space behind the lids that can become infected if bacteria gain entrance to it via the bloodstream or through a small scratch about the eye. The eyelids look red, swollen and puffy, and there may be a discharge. Any discharge is abnormal.

The eyelids must be pried open to allow the pus to drain out or there may be permanent damage to the forepart of the eye. Once the eyelids have been bluntly separated, pus will drain out in large drops. The eye should be flushed with boric acid eye wash and medicated with antibiotic drops. The eyelids must then be bathed several times a day so that they do not paste shut again. Drops should be applied four times daily.

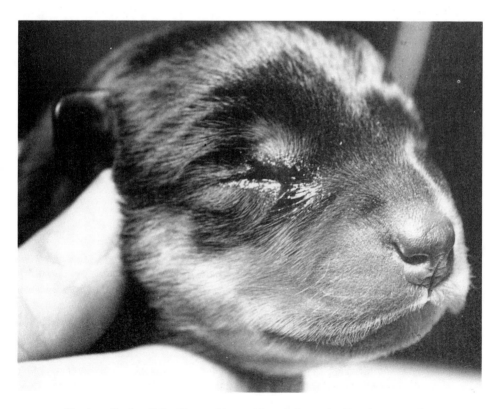

Newborn Conjunctivitis: The eyelids must be pried open to allow the pus to drain.

Episcleritis

Episcleritis can give the eye a red look. It is an inflammation of the sclera, the white part of the eye, adjacent to its junction with the cornea. The cornea becomes cloudy where it joins the sclera. This is a benign condition, thought to be an allergic or hypersensitivity reaction. There is no eye discharge or pain.

Hair Growing from the Eyeball (Dermoid Cyst)

A dermoid cyst usually is noted close to the outer corner of the eye. It contains follicles from which hairs grow. The hair often appears to grow out of the surface of the eye itself. The dermoid is not a malignant tumor, but it should be removed because of the irritating effects of the hairs.

THE TEARING MECHANISM

Tears are made up of three fractions. The *aqueous fraction* is secreted by the lacrimal glands situated around the orbit. An *oily secretion*, produced by the meibomian glands along the margin of the eyelids, acts as a barrier and stops the tears from spilling over or evaporating. Goblet cells in the conjunctival membrane produce *mucin*, a wetting agent, to keep the tears in contact with the eye.

Diseases of the tearing mechanism fall into two separate categories. First is *Dry Eye* (a lack of tears), and second is *Watery Eye* (in which there is an overflow of tears).

Dry Eye (Keratoconjunctivitis Sicca)

The appearance is characteristic. Instead of the bright, glistening sheen and shine that is seen in the normal eye, a dry eye presents a dull lackluster appearance. There is a thick, stringy discharge that is difficult to clear away. Later, as the eye becomes infected, the conjunctiva looks reddened and inflamed. A purulent discharge may complicate the picture.

This disease exists mainly in the older dog, caused by inadequate tear production. This can involve the aqueous fraction (most common), the oily fraction, the mucin fraction or any combination of the above. One of three mechanisms will be responsible:

1. The nerves to the tear glands are at fault. In response to drying and eye irritation, they fail to stimulate the glands in the eyelids to secrete enough tears.

   A branch of the facial nerve innervates the tear glands. It passes through the middle ear. Middle ear infections sometimes damage this branch, affecting the tear glands on that side of the face. The other eye is not affected.

   Another sign of malfunction of this nerve complex is a dry nostril on the same side. The dog will sometimes lick its nose to keep it moist.

Quite often it is this sign, rather than the eye sign, that brings the matter to the owner's attention.

2. The tear glands themselves are at fault. They have been partially or completely destroyed by a chronic conjunctivitis. Canine distemper virus does this to tear glands. Usually the damage is permanent. An immune-mediated destruction of the tear glands occurs with the use of several of the sulfonamide drugs. Other diseases, notably chronic kidney ailments, uterine infections and acute eye inflammations may cause *temporary* depression of tear gland activity.

3. Finally, the tear glands and the nerves are working, but the small ducts that carry the tears from the lacrimal glands into the eye are plugged. Scarring of the lids from long-standing infection (chronic purulent conjunctivitis) is one cause of this.

A combination of the above may be involved in any specific case. In most cases, it is difficult to determine just what was the original cause of the condition.

Dry eye is a serious ailment in the dog. There will be major complications unless the condition is treated in its early stages. The usual complication takes the form of a secondary deep-seated infection that eventually presents the problem of a corneal ulcer.

Treatment: When the primary cause can be identified, treatment is directed at that problem. Conjunctivitis is treated as described elsewhere. Middle ear infections are treated as described in EARS: *The Middle Ear*.

If *sulfa drugs* are being given, they *should be stopped*. Cortisone is used for suspected autoimmune reactions. Cyclosporin eye drops may be available soon with FDA approval. Cyclosporin is an immune-depressant drug showing considerable promise.

Further treatment is directed at re-establishing the flow of tears. It may be possible in certain cases to do this with drugs. At the same time, antibiotics and steroids are used to control infection and inflammation. They should be used under veterinary supervision.

If tears cannot be stimulated, then they will have to be supplied artificially. Artificial tears are available at drug stores, but they have to be used every two hours and are not convenient for some owners. At night, and whenever artificial tears cannot be given regularly, an ointment-based eye preparation is recommended. *Saline drops should not be used* because they remove oily secretions and mucin. This aggravates the problem.

In severe cases an operation may be contemplated. It involves transplanting one of the salivary ducts (from the mouth) up into the corner of the eye. The saliva will then take the place of the tears and keep the eye lubricated.

Watery Eye (Epiphora)

In this category are a great many conditions in which a watery or mucous discharge from the eye overflows the lids and runs down the sides of the face, causing eye stains. There is a constant wetness to the area and the skin may actually become inflamed and secondarily infected, adding to the unsightliness and the dog's discomfort.

Dogs do not experience emotional tearing. They do not cry as people do, so this is not a factor to be considered as one of the causes.

Irritative diseases of the lids, entropion, various forms of conjunctivitis and foreign bodies, as well as corneal ulcers and anterior uveitis, can cause a runny eye. They are discussed in this chapter. All are characterized by excessive tear production in response to a painful eye. Other causes of tearing are discussed below.

Inadequate Tear Drainage (Nasolacrimal Occlusion): A factor to be considered in the dog whose eye has a clear or mucuslike discharge without obvious cause. The problem here is that while tears are secreted in normal amounts, they are not adequately drained away.

Overflow in this situation is caused by an obstruction at some point in the nasolacrimal drainage system. Causes of this are congenital absence of the ducts; congenital narrowing or occlusion of one or both tiny ducts in the eyelids that collect tears at the inner corners of the eye; scarring of these ducts or their openings (for example, after a purulent conjunctivitis); active infection in these ducts or in the main nasolacrimal duct, which causes plugging by cellular debris, and a foreign body (such as a grass seed) anywhere in the system.

The drainage system is first tested to see if it is open by staining the tears with a fluorescein dye. If the dye appears at the nostril, then at least one tear duct is open on that side. Nasolacrimal probes are then inserted into the duct openings and various flushing techniques are used to show the point of obstruction. The flushing often opens the duct and removes the problem. Sometimes a minor operative procedure on an opening is needed to effect a cure. Follow-up treatment includes the use of antibiotics and steroids to reduce inflammation.

Brown Stains in the Corner of the Eye (Poodle Eye)

This is peculiar to certain breeds, most notably the white Poodle. It also afflicts the Maltese, Pomeranian, Pekingese and some of the Toy breeds. The exact cause is unknown in many cases. One theory is that a low-grade infection of the throat, for example a chronic tonsillitis, works its way up into the lacrimal duct and causes scarring. Another theory is that among breeds having a high incidence of the runny eye syndrome, the pooling space at the corner of the eye is too small to collect a lake of tears.

In all dogs having a runny eye syndrome, causes of eye irritation and nasolacrimal duct occlusion should be ruled out before resorting to symptomatic and cosmetic remedies.

Where no underlying disease is found, symptomatic improvement often results after giving the dog broad spectrum antibiotics (tetracycline). If a chronic infection does exist in the pharynx or lacrimal system, the antibiotic treats it, thereby removing a possible cause of obstruction. Tetracycline, which is secreted in the tears after oral administration, also binds that portion of the tears that cause them to stain the face. When the improvement is the result of just the binding action of the drug, the face remains wet but not discolored.

Tetracycline is usually given by mouth for three weeks. Then it is stopped. If the eye stain returns, then long-term administration may be considered. Most owners prefer to add tetracycline in low dose to the dog's food for long-term treatment.

Surgery may be considered as an alternative. The operation removes the gland of the third eyelid (nictating membrane). This makes a better lake at the inner corner of the eye. It also reduces the volume of tears by removing the tear gland in the third eyelid.

Cosmetic Considerations

When a dog with eye stains is made ready for a dog show, the appearance of stains can be improved by clipping the stained hair close to the face. Stain can be removed by bathing it with a dilute solution of hydrogen peroxide (one part to ten parts of water). A minor problem can be improved by a piece of white chalk. All foreign substance must be removed from the hair before the dog is brought into the ring for the judging.

CAUTION: Peroxide must not be allowed to enter the eye. Mineral oil should be instilled first to protect against accidental contact. Do not use chlorine bleaches for eye stain because the fumes are painful and irritating to the eye.

THE CORNEA

The cornea or clear part of the eye is covered by a protective layer of epithelial cells. Most destructive processes affecting the cornea begin with an injury to the eipithelial layer. Any irritative process (such as foreign bodies, misdirected hairs) can cause an epithelial injury. Breeds with bulging eyes (i.e., Pekingese, Maltese, Bostons, Pugs, spaniels) are especially susceptible to corneal injury. Once the continuity of the epithelium has been destroyed, the process either heals spontaneously or progresses to a more serious problem. The outcome will depend upon the magnitude of the injury, how quickly it is recognized and whether the initiating factor has been identified and removed.

Corneal injuries are extremely painful. You will note the dog squints, paws at the eye, avoids light and the eye waters.

Corneal Abrasion

This is an injury to the eye caused by a scratch. Healing usually takes place in twenty-four to forty-eight hours by a process in which the epithelium thins and slides over a small defect. Larger and deeper abrasions require more time.

A corneal abrasion will not heal if a foreign body is imbedded beneath one of the lids. Accordingly, in all but mild cases, an examination for foreign bodies under all three lids should be performed. Early recognition and removal result in

Corneal abrasion on the surface of the right eye.

rapid recovery. Delay leads to a persistent corneal defect (ulcer) or inflammation (keratitis).

Corneal Ulcers

These are serious and must receive prompt attention. Most of them begin as a corneal abrasion. Breeds with a natural bulging or protuberance of the eyeball, especially Pekingese and Boston Terriers, are especially predisposed to foreign bodies, corneal abrasions and injuries caused by the mechanical irritation of skin folds and hair. If the irritation goes unchecked, a corneal ulcer may well develop.

Corneal ulcers are extremely painful and severe squinting is common. Large ulcers are visible to the naked eye as dull spots or depressions on the surface of the cornea. Smaller ones are best seen after the eye has been stained with fluorescein. If the ulcer is deep, that part of the cornea becomes cloudy from uptake of fluid. In three to five days blood vessels begin to grow in from the sides of the cornea in an attempt to repair the damage.

Early treatment is vital to avoid serious complications or even loss of the eye. Atropine eye drops help to relieve pain. Cortisones, which are incorporated into many common eye preparations used in treating conjunctivitis, should not be put into an eye suspected of having sustained a corneal injury. They delay healing and may predispose to rupture.

Rupture of the eye can be anticipated if the cloudy central portion of a deep ulcer begins to clear or the inner lining protrudes like a weak tire. This can be recognized by your veterinarian. It is an emergency. Immediate surgery is necessary to prevent loss of the eye.

Corneal Ulcers in Boxers: A certain kind of corneal ulcer (called indolent or refractory) is found in the Boxer. Occasionally it affects other breeds. The majority occur in spayed females over five years of age. Although the exact

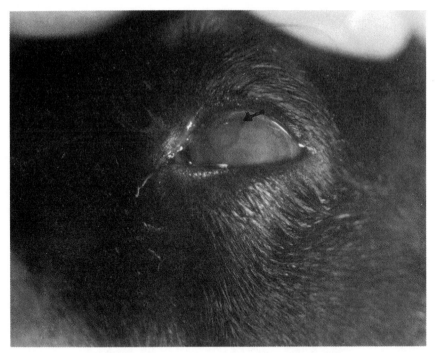

A large *corneal ulceration* of the type often seen in Boxers.

cause is unknown, the epidemiology of the disease suggests that low estrogen levels are a possible factor in its cause. This is a painful problem and treatment is usually prolonged. It involves stripping the poorly adherent corneal epithelium with a cotton-tipped applicator and cauterizing the ulcer with iodine at seven-to-ten-day intervals. If four such treatments are of no aid, then temporary coverage can be provided by suturing the nictating membrane over the surface of the eye.

Cloudy Eye (Keratitis)

Keratitis is an inflammation of the clear part of the eye. There are many different types of keratitis and several causes. All result in loss of transparency of the cornea, which at first appears dull, later hazy, then cloudy and finally milky or relatively opaque. Often a vascular or pigmented layer blocks out light.

Keratitis always is considered serious because it may lead to partial or complete blindness in the eye. All forms of keratitis should be managed by a professional.

Superficial (Surface) Keratitis

This is a sequel to a minor eye injury, such as a corneal abrasion. Since the initial injury is often slight and easily overlooked, there may be a temptation to treat the tearing and discharge as a conjuctivitis. Since this would be a mistake, every effort should be made to distinguish between keratitis and conjunctivitis.

Keratitis is an extremely painful condition accompanied by excessive tearing, squinting and fear of light. Conjunctivitis is characterized by a chronic discharge with very little pain.

Dogs with unchecked superficial keratitis may progress to *ulcerative keratitis*. This is a more advanced condition similar to that described for corneal ulcer. Ulcerative keratitis also is a complication of the dry eye, discussed above.

Infectious Keratitis

This occurs when a corneal injury becomes complicated by infection. A pus or mucuslike discharge runs from the eye. The lids are swollen and mattered. There are several different kinds of bacteria that cause infectious keratitis. Cultures and appropriate antibiotics are indicated.

A fungal keratitis is uncommon. Usually it is caused by prolonged treatment of a chronic eye discharge with antibiotics. The diagnosis is confirmed by cultures. Antibiotics should be stopped and antifungal drugs used instead.

Blue Eye (Interstitial Keratitis)

This is a deep corneal inflammation in which there is a bluish white film seen over the clear part of the eye. It is caused by the virus of infectious hepatitis—either the actual disease itself or after vaccination for the disease with CAV-1. Clinical signs appear ten days after exposure. The eyes begin to water and the dog squints and avoids light. Recovery in a few weeks is the rule.

Vascular or Pigmentary Keratitis

This is a nonulcerative condition of the eye in which there is a growth of blood vessels and/or pigment over the surface of the eye. Deposition of pigment is the end result of unchecked irritation. Any chronic irritation can predispose to this condition. It is most common in the Pekingese. In this breed it is caused by the hair of the nasal skin folds rubbing on the surface of the eye. If not corrected, blindness can result.

When severe enough to obstruct vision, the vascular pigmented membrane should be removed. When the primary irritation is corrected, the cornea often clears.

Pannus

This is a form of corneal inflammation that affects German Shepherd Dogs and their crossbreeds. It involves both eyes. It is characterized by the growth of a membrane across the cornea. The membrane is pink and opaque, being made up of blood vessels, pigment and connective tissue. It may lead to blindness. It usually appears in dogs over two years of age. An inherited predisposition or at least a familial tendency has been suggested. Treatment involves cortisone or cyclosporin eye drops as described for dry eye. Radiation therapy, and in some cases surgery, is also performed.

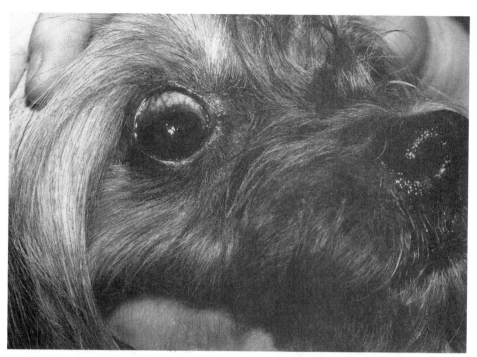

Blood vessels growing on the surface of the eye *(pigmentary keratitis)*, in this case caused by lack of tears *(keratoconjunctiva sicca)*.

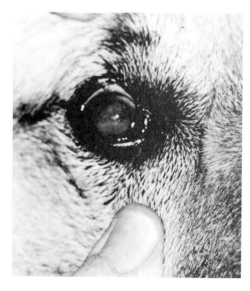

Pannus in a German Shepherd. Note the vascularity on the lower half of the eye.

THE INNER EYE

The Blind Dog

Any condition that prevents light from getting into the eye will impair a dog's sight. Diseases of the cornea (keratitis) and of the lens (cataract) fall into this category. Increased intraocular pressure (glaucoma) is another condition that leads to blindness. Also, any disease that reduces the sensitivity of the retina to light impulses (retinal atrophy), or any disease that affects the optic nerves or the sight center of the brain (trauma), can result in various forms of visual disturbances, including blindness.

Accordingly, most causes of blindness will not be evident on general observation of the eye itself. Ophthalmological studies are required to make an exact diagnosis.

Some signs may suggest that the dog is not seeing as well as before. They are uncertainty of gait (stepping high or with great caution), treading on articles usually avoided, bumping into furniture and carrying the nose close to the ground. Sometimes a dog going blind shows few if any signs of visual impairment.

A blind or nearly blind dog learns very quickly how to avoid collisions. On a leash, the dog learns to use the owner as a "seeing eye" person. We have seen dogs dash down corridors missing objects so adroitly you would be willing to swear that they could see perfectly, yet they were completely blind.

If you wish to confirm your suspicion that your dog is going blind, observe the animal in a strange setting. Place the dog in a darkened room in which the furniture has been rearranged. There should be just enough light so you can see. The dog is then invited to walk about normally. See if the dog moves with confidence or hesitates and collides with the furniture. Afterward, the lights are turned on and the test is repeated.

Shining a bright light into a dog's eye to test for pupillary constriction is an inexact method of determining whether or not the dog sees. The pupil may become smaller simply because of a light reflex. This doesn't tell you whether your dog has the ability to form a visual image in the brain.

After a diagnosis of blindness or irreversible loss of vision has been made, it does not mean the end of a dog's life. The fact is that most dogs, even those with normal eyesight, do not really see very well. To a great extent they rely on their senses of hearing and smell. These senses take over and actually become more acute when their vision begins to go. This makes it far easier for them to get around, sometimes almost normally. One thing that a dog shouldn't do is run free. Actually, all dogs should be enclosed or walked on a leash.

It is important for the owner of a dog to be aware of progressive blindness while the dog still has some sight left. This leaves time for the dog to be taught some basic commands, such as "stop," "stay," "come" and "watch it." It also allows for the dog to remain active and working (as in the case of a gundog) for a longer period. When the dog eventually does go blind, obedience training may be a life saver.

Cataracts

A cataract is a loss of normal transparency of the eye's lens. Any spot on the lens that is opaque, regardless of its size, is technically a cataract. Some cataracts are clearly visible to the naked eye, appearing as white flecks within the eye, or giving a milky gray or bluish white cast to the lens behind the pupil.

Cataracts affect dogs of all ages, but the majority occur in dogs under five years of age.

It is impossible to differentiate hereditary and nonhereditary cataracts solely from the appearance of the lens. Breed predisposition and line history are more suggestive. If you are planning to breed a dog with cataracts, you should consider the possibility of cataracts in the offspring. Hereditary cataracts are most commonly found in Poodles, Cockers, Boston Terriers, Wire Fox Terriers, Siberian Huskys, Golden Retrievers, Old English Sheepdogs and Labrador Retrievers.

Cataracts can develop in diabetic dogs. It is important to recognize the possibility of diabetes before considering cataract extraction. If the diabetes is controlled, the operation is more likely to be successful.

Senile (old age) cataracts are common. Most dogs over eight years of age have some degree of haziness in their lenses. Even when they appear quite opaque, a considerable amount of useful vision may be retained.

A cataract is important only when it causes impaired vision. Blindness can be corrected by removing the lens (cataract extraction). While this restores vision, there is some loss of visual acuity because the lens is not present to focus light

Congenital cataract.

137

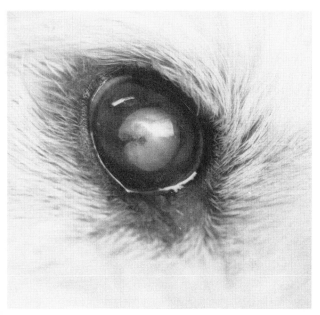

Acquired cataract associated with displacement of the lens into the anterior chamber of the eye.

on the retina. The operation is usually recommended when there is so much visual impairment that the dog has difficulty getting around.

Anterior Uveitis (Soft Eye)

This disease is caused by an inflammation of the iris and the ciliary body that supports the lens. The ciliary body produces the clear fluid that nourishes the structures of the front part of the eye and maintains pressure in the anterior chamber. One of the distinguishing features of anterior uveitis is that the affected eye feels softer than the normal eye. The pupil is small and reacts sluggishly to light. There may be clouding of the anterior chamber.

This is a painful condition, often accompanied by a red eye, severe squinting, fear of light and retraction of the eyeball back into the orbit caused by spasm of the eye muscles.

Anterior uveitis is believed to be the result of a hypersensitivity reaction caused by prior exposure to bacteria. It is often preceded by infections of the cornea (i.e., corneal ulcer) with secondary involvement of the iris and ciliary body. Injuries to the surface of the eye, and penetrating foreign bodies, also can lead to anterior uveitis.

It is of the utmost importance to distinguish anterior uveitis from conjunctivitis, keratitis and glaucoma. Drugs used to treat these conditions are detrimental when used by mistake in anterior uveitis. All three conditions are painful and can produce a red, watery eye.

Treatment: It is directed at correcting the underlying cause as well as treating the uveitis. This requires the care of a professional.

138

Increased Pressure in the Eye (Glaucoma)

This is a serious eye problem in the dog. Usually it leads to partial or total blindness of the eye. Because of an increase in fluid pressure within the eyeball, there is a continuous (although very slow) exchange of fluid between the eyeball and the venous circulation. Anything that upsets this delicate mechanism causes a buildup of pressure. When eye pressure is greater than arterial blood pressure, arterial blood cannot enter the eye to nourish the retina. A sudden buildup leads to acute blindness. A slower, more insidious buildup causes few symptoms, yet the same result. Measurement of intraocular pressure and inspection of the interior of the eye are needed to make the diagnosis.

Glaucoma sometimes occurs as a complication of diseases of the lens or anterior chamber of the eye. This is called *secondary* glaucoma and is distinguished from *primary* (or *congenital*) glaucoma, which occurs without prior disease. Primary glaucoma is seen in Cocker Spaniels, Bassets, Wirehaired Terriers, Poodles and Samoyeds. It has been described in other breeds.

An eye suffering from acute glaucoma is exquisitely painful and has a fixed, blank look because of the hazy and steamy appearance of the cornea and

Uveitis is a painful eye condition with squinting and tearing. The eye feels soft.

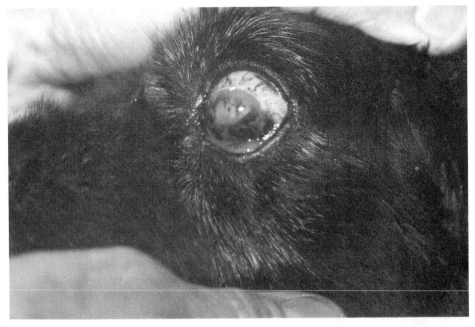

Untreated *glaucoma*. The eye is blind and markedly enlarged. This eye cannot be aided by medication and probably will have to be removed.

dilated pupil. Excessive tearing and squinting often are present. This is a true emergency. Either medical or surgical efforts must be made at once to lower the intraocular pressure.

Chronic glaucoma may be managed for a time with drops and medications. Untreated chronic glaucoma may result in increased size of the eye and protrusion.

Retinal Diseases

The retina is a thin, delicate membrane that lines the back of the eye, and actually is an extension of the optic nerve. There are many diseases of the retina that lead to destruction of the light receptors or cause the retina to become detached from the back of the eye. In these situations the eye loses its ability to interpret the light that gets into it. The visual image may be blurred, or all of the visual field may be blacked out.

The majority of retinal diseases in the dog are inherited. Occasionally, retinitis may be caused by trauma, infection or a vitamin deficiency. Since it is not safe to breed dogs with an inherited defect, it is important to know whether the retinal problem was inherited or acquired. This is best determined by referring the dog to a center in which a highly trained veterinary specialist is available.

At present, the following retinal diseases are well recognized:

Collie Eye Anomaly Syndrome (CEA)

Originally described in the Collie, this syndrome affects Shetland Sheepdogs and other related dogs. The anomalies include retinal degeneration, retinal detachment and cataract. They are not necessarily all present.

CEA may be detected by a qualified professional as early as four to five weeks of age, shortly after the bluish "puppy film" disappears. Sometimes the examination will not disclose retinal degeneration until the dog is one to two years old. Many affected dogs continue to see rather well despite the changes.

Progressive Retinal Atrophy (PRA)

This condition was first discovered in the Irish Setter but now is recognized in a great many other breeds, including Norwegian Elkhounds, Gordon Setters, Toy Poodles, Cocker Spaniels, Samoyeds, Yorkshire Terriers, Giant Schnauzers and Welsh Corgis. It is characterized by degeneration of the cells of the retina, leading eventually to loss of sight.

It is a disease of late onset (five to seven years). It begins with loss of night vision. At this point the dog hesitates to go out at night and won't jump on or off furniture in a darkened room. Later the dog will go up but not down stairs. Other behavioral changes occur. As the name implies, the degenerative changes are progressive but often quite gradual.

Central Progressive Retinal Atrophy (CPRA)

This is a condition closely related to PRA. It affects the pigment cells at the center of the retina. It is recognized in Labradors, Golden Retrievers, Shetland Sheepdogs, Border Collies, Redbone Coon Hounds and others.

The central part of the retina (where the dog sees best) is destroyed initially and therefore the dog with CPRA is unable to see stationary objects well. The dog is able to see moving objects because motion is seen at the *periphery* of the retina.

Inheritance Patterns in Retinal Atrophy

The inheritance of PRA has been thoroughly investigated in the Irish Setter, Norwegian Elkhound and Miniature and Toy Poodle. CEA has been investigated in the Collie. In both cases the disease was found to be the cause of a simple recessive trait. CPRA studies suggest that this may be the case for this disease also.

Accordingly, any dog having one of these defects is capable of transmitting it to any offspring if mated to another dog having the disease (or carrying the recessive trait). For this reason a number of breed clubs, conscientious dog fanciers and breeders have encouraged further research in this area. Many have their breeding stock examined and certified free of congenital eye disease before using them in a breeding program. The Canine Eye Registration Foundation, Inc. (C.E.R.F.) was established in 1974 with the dual purpose of issuing certificates to eligible dogs and collecting statistical data on the incidence of various inherited canine eye diseases. In 1989, the activities of C.E.R.F were combined with those of the Veterinary Medicine Data Bank at Purdue University. For further information, write: V.M.D.B–C.E.R.F., South Campus Courts, Building A, Purdue University, West Lafayette, Indiana. The number to call is (317) 494-8179.

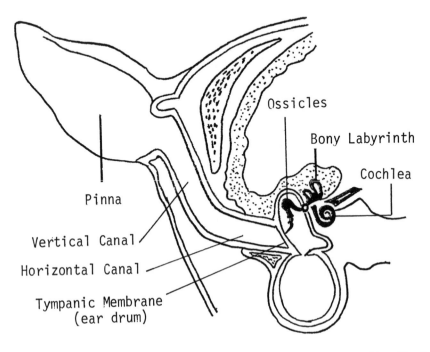

Pinna

Vertical Canal

Horizontal Canal

Tympanic Membrane
(ear drum)

Ossicles

Bony Labyrinth

Cochlea

Anatomy of the ear.   *(Rose Floyd)*

6

Ears

A DOG'S HEARING is one of the best developed senses. Dogs can hear sounds too faint for us to detect and can also hear noises pitched at a much higher frequency. Because their hearing is so sensitive, dogs rely heavily on it to alert to their surroundings.

HOW THE DOG HEARS

Sound, which is really air vibrations, is reflected off the external ear (*pinna*) and enters the comparatively large external ear opening. Vibrations travel down the external auditory canal to the eardrum (*tympanic membrane*). Movements of the eardrum are transmitted to a chain of (three) tiny bones, called the *auditory ossicles*, and then to a fluid filling the bony canals of the inner ear. Within the bony labyrinth lies the *cochlea*, a system of tubes in which fluid waves are translated into nerve impulses. These nerve impulses are conducted to the hearing center of the brain by the *auditory nerve*.

In dogs, ears come in all sizes and shapes—erect, tulip-shaped and flopped-over (drop-ears). The skin on the outside is covered with hair and, like the rest of the dog's body, susceptible to the same diseases. Hair also is present on the inside flap, although more sparsely distributed. The skin on the inside is light pink in color, or in some breeds, spotted. A small amount of light brown waxy secretion in the ear canals is normal.

Ear diseases make up 20 percent of the average practice of veterinary medicine. Most of them involve the ear flap and canal.

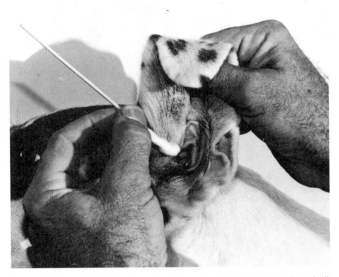

Ears are cleaned with a cotton-tipped applicator soaked in mineral oil.
(J. Clawson)

BASIC EAR CARE

Cleaning the Ears

Most dogs seldom need to have their ears cleaned. Excess cleaning is not desirable because a certain amount of wax is needed to maintain the health of the tissues.

To clean a dirty ear, moisten a cloth with mineral oil and wrap it around your finger. Then insert your finger into the ear canal as far as it will go and gently wipe the surfaces to remove dirt, excess wax and debris. Also clean the skin on the inside of the ear flap.

Folds and crevices that cannot be reached with the cloth can be cleaned with a cotton-tipped applicator, moistened with mineral oil. The ear canal drops vertically a considerable distance before it takes a sharp turn and then continues as the horizontal ear canal, ending at the eardrum. The vertical canal can be swabbed without danger of damaging the eardrum as long as the applicator is held vertically and directed downward. The dog must not be allowed to jerk his head, as the tip of the applicator can then injure the delicate skin lining the sides of the passage.

A dirty ear is usually an indication of an ear problem. It should be watched closely.

How to Avoid Ear Problems

When bathing your dog, see that no water gets into the ears. Prevent by inserting cotton wadding into the ear canals before bathing.

Do not syringe, swab or irrigate your dog's ears with ether, alcohol or other irritating solvents. They are extremely painful and cause swelling of the tissues. Use mineral oil.

Foreign bodies in the ear passages cause irritation and later infection. Frequently, they are caused by plant material that enters the ear by first clinging to hair surrounding the opening of the ear canal. For this reason always groom under the ear flaps, especially after your dog has been running in tall grass, weeds and brush.

Always check the ear flaps after dog fights. Serum and blood make an excellent media for bacterial growth.

When hair beneath the ear flap is thick enough to interfere with air circulation, it should be removed. This reduces the chance of ear infection. A common practice in some grooming parlors is to pluck excess hair out of the ear canals. Serum then oozes from the hair pores. For this reason, ear infections are more frequent among Poodles, Schnauzers and other breeds groomed professionally. When hair has been plucked from the ear to improve air circulation, an antibiotic preparation, as discussed below, should be instilled to prevent this complication.

As an alternative to pulling the hairs out, they can be clipped. In some cases, however, the hair has formed a wad, acting like an obstructing foreign body in the ear; then the hair must be pulled out and the ear medicated (see *Antibiotic Ear Preparations*).

DISEASES OF THE EAR CANAL

Bacterial Infections (*Otitis externa*)

The ear canals of dogs are delicate structures, easily infected. Eighty percent of ear problems occur in the drop-eared breeds. Basically this is a condition of air circulation, since open or erect ears dry out better and provide less favorable conditions for bacteria to grow.

Common predisposing causes are soap, water, wads of hair, mites, allergies and excess wax in the ears. Serum and blood in the canal are excellent bacterial media. Clean, dry ears usually stay healthy.

Signs of an infected ear are tenderness (holding the painful side down), redness and swelling of the skin folds in the canal, purulent discharge and a bad odor.

Acute infections are generally caused by staphylococci. The discharge is a light brown. Chronic ones are generally caused by proteus. The discharge is yellow. There are exceptions. More than one species may be involved, which can complicate treatment.

Bacterial infections that have been allowed to progress for a long time produce extreme reddening and thickening of the ear canal and considerable discomfort and pain. These ears are difficult to cleanse without heavy sedation or an anesthetic. Treatment is prolonged. As a last resort, surgical intervention may be necessary to open the ear, re-establish air circulation and promote adequate drainage. This operation is called a *lateral ear resection* and provides a new external ear opening.

Treatment: The first step in the treatment of an external ear infection is to attempt to determine the cause. Mild cases in which the discharge is not excessive but perhaps associated with a dirty ear or buildup of wax may be treated at home. Clean the ears as described above. Remove crusts with a cotton-tipped applicator. If there is pus, the ear should be flushed with a weak hydrogen peroxide solution (one part in ten) or a surgical soap (Weladol, pHisoHex). When there is excessive wax buildup, a wax dissolving agent such as Squaline or Ceruminex may be needed. Oxydex shampoo is then used to clean the ears. Afterward, dry the ear canal well with cloth or a cotton-tipped applicator and apply one of the antibiotic ear preparations described below.

Antibiotic Ear Preparations

Antibiotics commonly used in the treatment of external ear infections are Panolog (neomycin, nystatin, cortisone), Gentacin Otitic (gentamicin), Tresaderm (neomycin, thiabendazole, cortisone) and Liquichlor (chloramphenicol). Preparations containing cortisone should be used sparingly because of detrimental effects of prolonged usage. Ear preparations should be applied to *cleaned* ear canals twice daily. You should expect to see improvement in two or three days. If not, then consult your veterinarian, as further delay can cause harm. When special cultures are indicated, your dog must be off antibiotics for at least three days, or the cultures may not be positive.

How to Apply Ear Medicines

Some ear ointments come in tubes with long nozzles that are inserted into the vertical canal while holding the nozzle parallel to the dog's head. Restrain your dog so the tip of the tube won't accidently lacerate the thin skin of the ear canal. Squeeze in a small amount of ointment or instill three or four drops of liquid.

As most infections also involve the horizontal ear canal, it is important that the medicine reaches this area, too. With your fingers, rub the cartilage at the base of the ears to disperse the medicine, which makes a squishy sound.

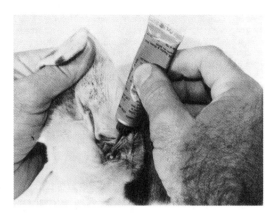

Apply ear medication to the vertical canal. *(J. Clawson)*

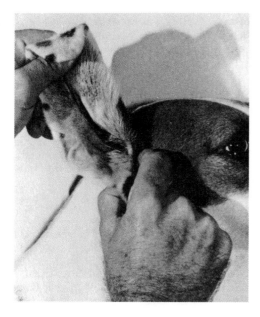

Massage the base of the ear to disperse the medication.   *(J. Clawson)*

The Ear Bandage

As an important step in the treatment of all but minor external ear infections, the ears should be taped over the head to expose the canals to air. This is especially important in dogs with ears that drop down.

The ears are folded over the top of the head with their tips together and held in position by a bridge of adhesive tape. A nylon stocking (or sweater sleeve) is slipped over the head on top of the ears. The covering is kept in place by taping both ends of it to the dog's skin. Be careful not to get the tape too tight around the neck.

Fungus and Yeast Infections

The presence of excess wax and moisture in the ear predisposes to a fungus infection. This is a common cause of external otitis. Secondary fungus or yeast infections frequently occur when long-standing ear infections are treated with antibiotics.

Signs and symptoms are not nearly so pronounced as when the infection is caused by a bacteria. The ear is less inflamed and less painful. The discharge usually is dark, thick, waxy, but not purulent. A *rancid odor* is characteristic.

The treatment is similar to bacterial infections, except that an antifungal agent (nystatin) is used to medicate the ears. Panolog or Tresderm, which contain nystatin, can be used. Yeast and fungal infections tend to recur. Their treatment usually is prolonged.

A condition called *ceruminous otitis* occurs with primary seborrhea. There is a large buildup of oily, yellowish wax in the canal. This provides media for bacteria and yeast. Treatment is lifelong.

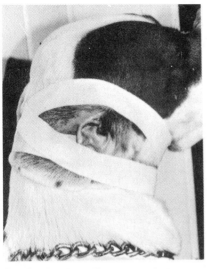

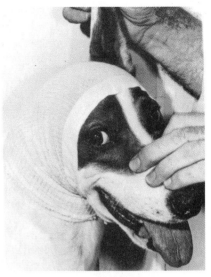

The Ear Bandage: The ears are folded over the head with their tips together and held by a bridge of adhesive tape.   *(J. Clawson)*

A protective stocking is applied if the dog scratches at the dressing.   *(J. Clawson)*

Ear Mites

This disease is caused by tiny bugs that live in the ear canals and feed on skin debris. Mites are the most common cause of an ear infection in a puppy or young dog. Suspect it whenever both of your dog's ears are infected.

The characteristic sign is intense itching (i.e., scratching and violent head-shaking). The ear discharge is reddish brown, or black and waxy, sometimes resembling that of a yeast or fungus infection. To make the diagnosis, remove some ear wax with a cotton-tipped applicator and look at it under a microscope against a dark background. Mites are white specks, about the size of the head of a pin, that move.

At times ear mites leave the ear canals and travel out over the body. They are highly contagious to dogs and cats. If there are other pets in the household, they should be treated.

Treatment: Do not begin treatment until you have identified the mites. Other ear problems can be complicated by using an ear-mite preparation.

Clean the ears as described above. Medicate the ears with a miticide (Canex) twice weekly for three full weeks. As the medication does not destroy eggs, a new crop of mites will reinfect your dog if you stop too soon. Dip your dog in an insecticide, or powder well with flea powder (see SKIN: *Insecticides*). The insecticide kills mites on the surface of the body.

An antibiotic is given if the ear problem is complicated by bacterial infection. Ear preparations containing a miticide, an antibiotic and a steroid (to reduce itching) are available. They include Cerumite, Canex and Tresderm.

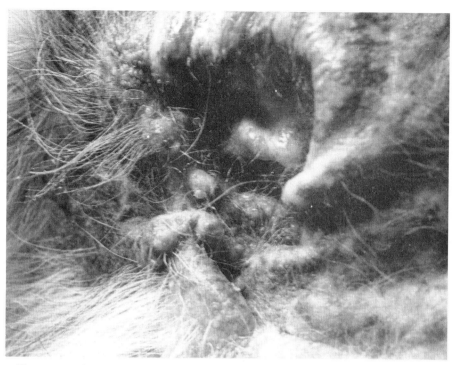

The waxy and greasy appearance of *ceruminous otitis*. Secondary bacterial and fungus infections are common.

Foreign Objects and Ticks in the Ear

Grass seeds are the most common foreign materials in the ear canals. Ears should always be examined after a dog has been running in tall grass. When a foreign body can be seen, it can be removed with a cotton-tipped applicator moistened in mineral oil.

Ticks often adhere to the skin of a dog's ear. If the tick is easily accessible, it can be removed. First kill the tick by applying an insecticide or a substance such as fingernail polish directly to it by means of a cotton-tipped applicator. In a few moments, grasp the dead tick as close to the skin as possible with tweezers and apply steady traction until it releases its hold. The blood of ticks can carry diseases dangerous to people. Therefore, do not crush or squeeze a tick with your bare fingers.

Ticks and foreign bodies can be found deep in the ear canal next to the ear drum. Removal requires an otoscope and an alligator forceps. This is a sensitive area and requires an anesthetic.

Ear Allergies

Allergies are typified by the sudden onset of itching and redness of the skin without discharge. They respond well to steroids (1% hydrocortisone cream).

Because of intense scratching, the dog may traumatize its ears and set the stage for a secondary bacterial infection.

THE EAR FLAP (PINNA)

The pinna is an erect flap of cartilage covered on both sides by a layer of skin and hair. A number of skin diseases involve the ear flaps, especially immune-mediated skin disorders (see SKIN: *Autoimmune Skin Diseases*).

Fly-Bite Dermatitis

Flies attack the face and ears of dogs, sucking blood and inflicting many painful bites over the tips or bent surfaces of the ears. Other flies are attracted. German Shepherd Dogs, Collies and breeds with erect ears are most susceptible.

These bites have a typical appearance. They are scabbed, crusty black and bleed easily.

Treatment: Keep flies away from the ears by applying insect repellant, or axle-grease, to the tips. Tincture of benzoin is also effective. Fly control is recommended. Infected ear tips require special care (see *Ear Fissure*). Antibiotics are indicated if the ear becomes infected.

Frostbite

Frostbite affects the ear tips of dogs left outdoors in severe winter weather, particularly under conditions of high wind and humidity. The treatment of frostbite is discussed in the chapter EMERGENCIES.

A sharp line of demarcation will occur between the devitalized skin and normal skin. Apply antibiotic ointment to raw areas and bandage. You may need

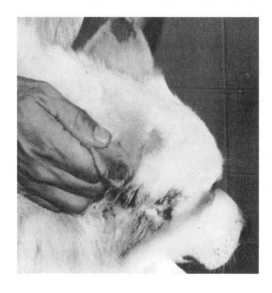

Fly-bite dermatitis affects the ear tips of dogs with erect ears.

to put a protective stocking over the head as shown in the illustration. Change the dressing daily.

Ear Fissure

Ear fissure is found in drop-eared breeds. It results from intense scratching at the ear, along with a violent shaking of the head, which causes the ear tips to snap. The tips of the ears are denuded of hair, irritated-looking and often bloody. In some cases they split, causing a fissure.

The underlying irritation or infection, often an external otitis, which caused the head-shaking, should be sought for and treated along with the ear fissure.

Treatment: Ear tip trauma is treated by applying an ointment containing an antibiotic and a steroid (Panolog) once or twice daily. The dog must be prevented from flapping and snapping its ears. They should be taped over the top of the head and covered with an ear bandage. In severe cases, a fissure may have to be sutured.

Marginal Seborrhea

This condition is caused by a buildup of body oil (sebum) on the hair along the border of the ear. The hair has a greasy feel. When rubbed with a thumbnail, the hair falls out. The cause is unknown.

Treatment: A sebum-dissolving agent, such as Squaline, is used to soften and loosen the greasy material. Liquichlor also is effective. It incorporates Squa-

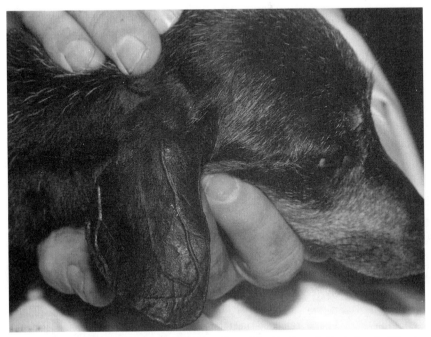

Loss of hair *(alopecia)* of the ear flap is a hereditary defect in Smooth Dachshunds. It begins before a year of age and progresses through life.

line with a topical antibiotic. Apply by massaging it into the affected skin twice daily. Shampoo the ears twice a week with an antiseborrheic shampoo (see SKIN: *Seborrhea*).

Swollen Ear Flap (Ear Hematoma)

Sudden swelling of the ear flap is the result of bleeding into the tissues leading to the formation of blood clot or hematoma. It is caused by violent head-shaking, scratching or rough handling of the ear. It is easily mistaken for an abscess or a growth; but the history of sudden onset eliminates these possibilities.

Treatment: In the absence of known trauma to the ear, predisposing factors (infections, irritations) should be looked for and treated.

Blood should be released from the hematoma to prevent ultimate scarring and deformity of the ear. Removing it with a needle and syringe usually is not effective, as serum accumulates in the space formerly occupied by the blood clot. Surgery, the treatment of choice, involves the removal of a window of skin to provide open and continuous drainage. The ear is then bandaged over the head until it heals.

Ear Mange

Sarcoptic mange, caused by a skin mite, often is first noted over the ear flaps (crusty ear tips). It affects skin over the whole body. It is discussed in the SKIN chapter.

THE MIDDLE EAR

Infection *(Otitis media)*

Middle ear infections are uncommon. Causes are progression of an external otitis (most common), infection from the tonsils or throat, which ascends to the middle ear via the Eustachian tube, and bloodstream infections.

The diagnosis is difficult, often masked by the infection (usually an external otitis) that preceded it. But as the infection begins to involve the middle ear, pain becomes severe. The dog holds the head at an angle with the painful side down and shies away if you attempt to touch the ear.

After the dog has been sedated or anesthetized, the condition usually is recognized by an otoscopic examination that shows perforation or loss of the ear drum.

X rays may show bone involvement. The face may droop on the affected side if one of the nerves that crosses the surface of the eardrum is injured (facial branch). If the other (sympathetic branch) is affected, you will see a triad, which includes a small pupil, protrusion of the third eyelid and retraction of the eyeball into the orbit. This is called *Horner's Syndrome*.

Middle ear infections are serious and can affect balance and hearing. They should be treated by a veterinarian. Surgery may be required.

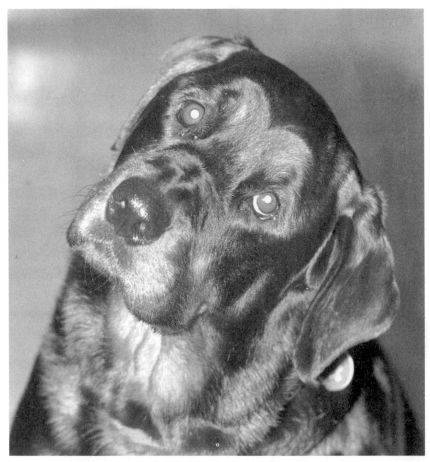

Otitis media involving the left ear. The painful side is tilted down.

THE INNER EAR

Infection *(Otitis interna)*

An inner ear infection is usually preceded by a middle ear infection. Extension to the inner ear should be suspected if the dog vomits or shows signs of *labyrinthitis*. Veterinary management is required.

Labyrinthitis (Dizziness)

Diseases of the middle and inner ear are characterized by *labyrinthitis*, including dizziness, incoordination and loss of balance. The labyrinth, or vestibular apparatus, is a complex organ composed of three semicircular canals, the utricle and saccule (Figure 1). The labyrinth is stimulated by gravity and rotational movements of the head. The purpose of the labyrinth is to maintain correct posture, balance and coordination.

153

Right-sided *facial paralysis* caused by otitis media. The dog is able to move her left ear down. The right ear is paralyzed.

A dog with labyrinthitis will often assume an abnormal posture with a head-tilt toward the affected side, may stagger, circle or lean toward that side and occasionally show rapid jerking movements of the eyeballs (*nystagmus*).

Congenital vestibular syndromes are usually present at birth but may not appear until three months. Signs are not progressive.

The prolonged administration of aminoglycoside antibiotics produces vestibular signs as well as deafness.

Head trauma and brain tumors can produce vestibular signs.

An *idiopathic* vestibular syndrome of unknown cause is common. It is of sudden onset and includes rolling and twisting. Signs disappear in two to three days but head-tilt may persist.

Deafness

Dogs can be born without the ability to hear because of developmental defects in the hearing apparatus. Other forms of congenital deafness can appear later in life. In addition, loss of hearing can be caused by senile changes (old age), infections, trauma, blockage of the ear canal (by wax and debris) and drugs and poisons.

It is sometimes quite difficult to tell if a dog is going deaf. A dog with complete loss of hearing usually exhibits a typical behavior, is difficult to arouse from sleep and is unresponsive to commands. A deaf dog barks less than normal. The voice may be somewhat altered. The ear flaps are not as active as those of a dog with normal hearing. Puppies, in particular, are difficult to test, as they are attentive to so many stimuli. Shouting, clapping the hands loudly when the dog is not looking, blowing a whistle and other attention-getting sounds are used to test a dog's hearing.

A good history is important. A blow to the head, a bout of distemper, history of an ear infection, poisoning or prolonged use of a certain medication—all are telling points.

Senile deafness comes on gradually at about ten years of age. It may not be particularly noticeable unless there is partial loss of vision, too. The dog then becomes less active, moves about more slowly and gives the owner some indication of a problem. Senile deaf dogs often retain some hearing for a high-pitched sound such as a dog whistle. Stamping on the floor also attracts their attention, as they can feel the vibrations.

If the history and physical examination suggest no cause for acquired deafness, it can be assumed that the cause is congenital. Inherited deafness occurs in Dalmatians, Old English Sheepdogs, Cocker Spaniels, Bull Terriers, Sealyham Terriers, Scottish Terriers, Border Collies and Fox Terriers. Undoubtedly it happens to all breeds, but is most common among those having a predominance of white color in their coats, such as Dalmatians and other harlequin-patterned dogs.

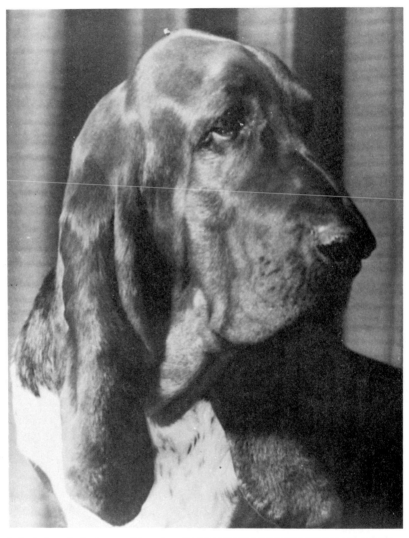

A finely tuned olfactory center makes the Basset Hound a prime example of a dog's superior scenting abilities.

7

Nose

$\mathbf{A}$ DOG'S NOSE is made up of nostrils (nares) and the nasal cavity, which runs the length of the muzzle. The maxillary and frontal sinuses communicate with the nasal cavity. The nasal cavity is divided by a midline partition into two passages, one for each nostril. At the back, these passages open into the throat behind the soft palate.

The nasal cavity is lined by a mucus membrane that is richly supplied by blood vessels and nerves. There are a great many more nerve endings in the nose of a dog than there are in man. They connect with the highly developed olfactory center in the brain. Together these two, the abundant nerve supply and the well-developed center in the brain, account for a dog's scenting ability, which is perhaps one hundred times better than that of humans.

The nasal mucus membrane is extremely sensitive to trauma and bleeds easily when irritated. Instruments should never be poked into the noses of dogs. This causes sneezing and the dog will attempt to jerk back. It is much better to examine the nasal passages after the dog has been given an anesthetic. An otoscope and special forceps are used to remove foreign bodies.

A dog's nose is normally cool and moist. There are no sweat glands in the nose. The moisture is secreted by mucus glands in the lining.

A warm, dry nose suggests a dog has a fever and may be somewhat dehydrated. This is not always the case however. Occasionally, the reverse is true: a sick dog has a runny nose that is cool because of evaporation. If you suspect your dog has a fever, confirm it with a rectal temperature.

Most dogs have darkly pigmented noses, but brown, pink and spotted noses are normal in some dogs.

SIGNS OF NASAL IRRITATION

Runny Nose (Nasal Discharge)

Excited and nervous dogs often show this by secreting a clear watery mucus that accumulates at the tip of the nose. It disappears when the dog relaxes.

A discharge from the nose that persists for several hours indicates a nasal irritation. Common causes are foreign bodies, nasal infections and tumors. To learn about *allergic* nasal discharges, see SKIN: *Allergies*.

Colds

Dogs don't catch "colds" the way people do. If your dog has a runny nose, blobs of mucus in the eyes, a cough and a slight fever, immediately think of a serious condition (one of the canine viral diseases, such as distemper). Call your veterinarian.

Sneezing

One of the first signs of nasal irritation in the dog is sneezing. This is a reflex and results from stimulation of the nerves in the lining of the nasal passages. If the dog sneezes off and on for a few hours, and in between shows no other signs of illness, it is likely that the irritation is not very serious—perhaps dust or pollen in the nose.

Sneezing that persists all day long suggests a more serious irritative process. Check to see if there is less air coming from one of the nostrils. (Hold a mirror in front of the nose and check the vapor condensation.) If one nostril appears to be obstructed, a persistent sneezing problem may be caused by a polyp or tumor on that side.

The sudden onset of frenzied sneezing, along with a discharge from one side of the nose, strongly suggests a foreign body. The dog may paw at the nose and shake its head.

A discharge from both nostrils accompanied by sneezing is typical of canine viral diseases (see *Rhinitis*). Other signs of illness will be present.

Sneezing indicates the irritant involves the front part of the nose. Gagging, snorting and coughing are signs of an irritant in the back, such as food regurgitating up into the nose.

Prolonged sneezing causes swelling and congestion of the nasal membranes. The result is sniffling or a noisy character to the breathing. Nosebleeds can occur after particularly violent bouts of sneezing.

Mouth Breathing

When both air passages are blocked by swollen membranes, the dog breathes through the mouth. This may be obvious only when the dog becomes excited or begins to exercise, at which time the demand for air is increased. This should not be confused with panting, which is normal.

Nosebleed *(Epistaxis)*

Nosebleeds seldom occur spontaneously in dogs as they do in children. They are caused by ulceration or injury to the mucus membrane. Violent sneezing, foreign bodies, tumors that bleed from their surfaces, trauma to the nose and some parasites and bacteria capable of causing erosion of the surface lining can cause a nosebleed.

Treatment: If the cause is not apparent it will need to be determined by veterinary examination. In the meantime, keep the dog as quiet as possible or give a sedative. Ice cubes or packs applied to the bridge of the nose reduce bloody supply and aid in clotting. Do not poke about in the nostrils with nasal packs or instruments, as this only induces sneezing and will be resisted. Most nosebleeds subside rather quickly of their own accord, especially when interference is kept to a minimum.

Reverse Sneezing

This uncommon condition is a cause of alarm because it sounds as though the dog has something caught in the air passages. It is believed to be due to a temporary spasm of the throat muscles. An accumulation of mucus may be involved.

During an attack, the dog violently pulls air in through the nose, producing a loud snorting noise as if something is caught in the nose and the dog is trying to draw it in. The dog is perfectly normal before and after these attacks. There are no ill effects. No treatment is necessary.

Regurgitation through the Nose (Oral-Nasal Fistula)

This is a condition in which food or water regurgitates into the nasal passage when the dog eats or drinks. It usually follows loss of the canine teeth. This results in an opening between the hard palate and the nasal cavity through which water and solids may be regurgitated. Sneezing and a discharge on the affected side are common. The condition is treated by creating a flap of skin from the inside of the lip and suturing it across the defect.

NOSTRILS

Collapsed Nostrils (Stenotic Nares)

This is a birth defect that occurs in short-nosed puppies, such as Pekingese and Bulldogs. The cartilages of the nostrils are too soft. When the pup breathes in, the nostrils collapse, shutting off air. In severe cases the chest is flattened from front to back. There is a nasal discharge that is sometimes watery, foamy and accompanied by snorting. These puppies breathe through their mouths when excited. Because of air lack, they are unthrifty.

Treatment involves removing a portion of the nasal cartilages so as to enlarge the openings.

Collapsed nostrils are common in short-nosed breeds. These dogs snort, sniffle and have a clear, foamy nasal discharge.

Cleft Palate and Harelip

Cleft palate is a birth defect of the nasal and oral cavities. It is associated commonly with harelip. It is caused by a failure of the bones of the palate to form completely. It results in an opening from the oral to the nasal cavity, allowing food and liquid to pass between. Many times it is impossible for the puppy to create enough suction to nurse. Survival then can be accomplished only by hand feeding.

Cleft palate occurs in all breeds but perhaps is most common in Bulldogs, Boston Terriers, Pekingese and Cocker Spaniels. In these breeds the defect is hereditary. *Such dogs should not be used for breeding.*

Harelip can occur by itself or in association with cleft palate. When it occurs by itself, it is caused by an abnormal development of the upper lip. The problem is mainly a cosmetic one.

Cleft palate and harelip can be corrected by plastic surgery.

Nasal Solar Dermatitis (Collie Nose)

This is a weeping, crusting dermatitis that affects Collies, Shetland Sheepdogs and related dogs. It is caused by lack of pigment on the nose and hypersensitivity to sunlight. It requires hereditary predisposition. It is seen most commonly in warm climates, such as in Florida and California.

Prior to onset the skin of the nose appears normal—except for the lack of black pigment. With prolonged exposure to sunlight, the skin next to the nose becomes irritated-looking; then hair is lost. As the irritation continues, serum begins to ooze, forming a crust. With continued exposure, the skin becomes ulcerated.

In advanced cases, the whole surface of the nose becomes ulcerated and the tip itself may disappear, leaving unsightly tissue that bleeds easily. In such cases, a cancer may develop.

Zinc responsive dermatosis, pemphigus foliaceous and *discoid lupus erythematosus* are three skin diseases in which a crusty dermatitis (or blebs, blisters and ulcers) involves the nose, muzzle and face (see the SKIN chapter). Depigmentation occurs as the diseases progress. This distinguishes them from Collie nose, in which lack of pigment is the initiating cause.

Treatment: Prevent further exposure to sunlight. Keep your dog in during the day and take the dog out at night. If this is not feasible, apply sunscreen to prevent ultraviolet injury. This is highly effective. Treat an irritated nose with a skin preparation containing a steroid.

Permanent cure can be accomplished by tattooing the nose with black ink (use a vibrator tattooer). All the nasal skin must be tattooed to protect it from sunlight.

Depigmentation of the Nose

Vitiligo

This name is given to a condition in which there is gradual loss of pigmentation of the nose. (It may extend down to the lips also.) The nose and lips are frequently well pigmented early in life, but gradually the black pigment fades to a chocolate-brown. Although there is no cure known, some dogs may recover on their own.

Snow-Nose

This is a condition in which black pigment on the nose lightens during the winter, then darkens again as summer approaches. It occurs most commonly in white-coated breeds. There appears to be a hereditary predisposition for this condition that runs in certain lines.

Various causes have been suggested. They include cold weather, rubbing the nose in the snow, weak sunlight and lack of iron or vitamins in the diet. As the individual grows older and the cycles repeat themselves, the nose often remains permanently light-colored.

This is not a disease. It is primarily a cosmetic problem. A number of home remedies have been advocated. Success is questionable. Sunscreen, as described for Collie nose, will prevent the complications of nasal solar dermatitis in susceptible individuals.

Plastic Dish Nasal Dermatitis

For want of a better term, this name is given to a form of contact dermatitis that results from eating out of plastic or rubber dishes. It is caused by a hypersensi-

Depigmentation of the nose *(snow nose)* in a white coated dog. This mainly is a cosmetic problem.

tivity of the skin of the nose to the antioxidant found in synthetic rubber products. The nasal skin becomes irritated and inflamed. There is loss of normal pigmentation. The condition can be corrected by feeding from a glass or stainless steel dish.

Nasal Callus (Hyperkeratosis)

In this condition of unknown cause the skin of the nose becomes thickened and rough to the touch. Hornlike projections can appear. The skin is dry. It may develop cracks and fissures that become irritated and infected. Usually there is an associated loss of nasal pigmentation.

Treatment: Excess horny tissue can be trimmed away but callus comes right back. There is no satisfactory cure for it. Treatment is aimed at softening the nasal callus with wet dressings and keeping the nose well lubricated with mineral oil or Vaseline. If infection exists, the area should be treated with a topical antibiotic ointment (neomycin).

A somewhat similar condition occurs as a sequel to canine distemper. The nose becomes thickened, dry and callused. The foot pads also partake of the same process. The disease is called *hard-pad*. As the dog recovers from distemper, his nose often clears up and regains its normal skin texture.

162

THE NASAL CAVITY

Foreign Bodies in the Nose

They include blades of grass, grass seeds and awns, fish bones and wood splinters. The signs are pawing at the nose accompanied by *violent sneezing*— at first continuous and later intermittent. The nose will run (and occasionally bleed) through the involved nostril.

Treatment: A foreign body may be visible close to the opening of the nostril, in which case it can be removed by tweezers. More often it is lodged farther back. If not removed in a short time, it tends to migrate even farther. In such cases it is necessary to give the dog an anesthetic to locate and remove it. Do not poke about in your dog's nose. Nasal membranes are easily damaged.

Following the removal of a foreign body, an antibiotic should be given for two weeks (chloromycetin, tetracycline).

Nasal Infections *(Rhinitis)*

Inflammation of the nasal membranes is called *rhinitis*. The characteristic signs are sneezing and a discharge from the nose. There are several causes:

Allergic

There is abrupt onset of sneezing. It may be seasonal. The discharge is watery. Antihistamines afford relief. Allergic reactions are discussed in the SKIN chapter.

Viral

The sneezing and watery discharge is of sudden onset but usually of short duration. Upper respiratory viruses that cause this problem include herpesvirus, adenovirus and parainfluenza. These viruses produce mild infections. However, damage to the nasal lining often breaks down host resistance and sets the stage for secondary bacterial involvement. To prevent this complication, prophylactic antibiotics are indicated, even though they have no effect on the virus.

Distemper is a more serious problem. There is discharge from the eyes as well as the nose. Both discharges become purulent. Other signs of illness will be present.

Bacterial

Bacterial rhinitis is caused by antecedent viral rhinitis, trauma, nasal tumors, foreign bodies and infected teeth. The presence of a foul-smelling, thick, creamy discharge from the nose suggests bacterial rhinitis. In long-standing cases, suspect a fungus.

Foreign bodies and tumors are associated with a blood-streaked discharge.

Dental infections

The canine and fourth premolar teeth in the upper jaw lie just beneath the nasal passages. Infection of these teeth can progress to the nasal mucosa. Signs are a watery discharge accompanied by sneezing. An abscessed tooth can rupture into the nasal cavity. This produces a bloody discharge and oral-nasal fistula (see *Regurgitation through the Nose*).

Keratoconjunctivitis sicca

A crusty dry discharge occluding one nostril suggests the *Dry Eye* syndrome discussed in the EYES chapter.

Treatment of Nasal Infections

It is directed at finding the underlying cause and treating it along with the nasal discharge. Bacterial rhinitis is treated with appropriate antibiotics. Fungal infections usually respond to one of the newer antifungal agents (ketoconazole, difluconazole).

Tumors and polyps should be removed. Foreign bodies are located and flushed out or removed through an otoscope using alligator forceps. Infected teeth must be extracted.

Inflammation that has become chronic is difficult to clear up. Granulation tissue ("proud flesh") builds up in the nose, causing further blockage and resisting the flow of air. Treatment then requires special cultures and in some cases exploratory surgery. For this reason it is advisable to treat even minor nasal cavity irritations with a penicillin antibiotic such as Amoxicillin to provide a cover and prevent the disease from becoming chronic. Continue for two weeks, or longer if a discharge persists.

Sinusitis

The frontal and maxillary sinuses are extensions of the nasal cavity. They are lined by a mucus membrane similar to that in the nose. Inflammation of this membrane causes sinusitis.

Infections starting in the nasal passages can extend to involve a sinus. Foreign bodies can penetrate a sinus. Roots of teeth that become infected can rupture into a sinus. Tumors can grow in a sinus. These are common causes of sinusitis in the dog.

The infection seldom starts on its own. It is rare for more than one sinus to be involved.

A persistent, chronic, purulent discharge from one nostril, along with sneezing and sniffling, suggests the possibility of an abscessed sinus. The dog should be examined by a veterinarian.

Nasal Polyps and Tumors

A polyp is a growth that begins as an enlargement of one of the mucus glands in the lining of the nose. It is not a cancer. It looks like a cherry on a stalk. Polyps cause symptoms by bleeding and blocking the flow of air through the nostril. They can be removed by your veterinarian.

Benign and malignant tumors are found in the nasal cavity and the sinuses. The leading sign is a discharge through one nostril. They can be removed surgically if they are discovered early and are still small.

Large tumors can make one side of the face protrude more than the other. If they extend behind the eye, the eye will bulge. These tumors are far advanced. Treatment is discouraging.

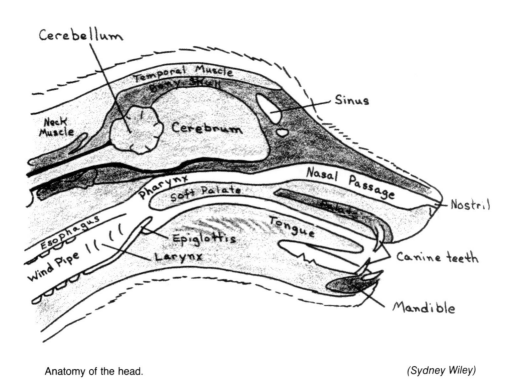

Anatomy of the head.   (Sydney Wiley)

8

Oral Cavity

$\mathbf{T}$HE ORAL CAVITY or mouth of dogs is subdivided into the *vestibule*, the space between the lips and the teeth, and the *oral cavity* itself, which is contained within the dental arches. The mouth is bounded on the front and sides by the lips and cheeks; above, by the hard and soft palate, and below, by the tongue and muscles of the floor of the mouth. Four pairs of salivary glands drain into the mouth.

The saliva of dogs is alkaline and contains antibacterial enzymes. There is a normal flora of bacteria that live in the mouth and keep harmful bacteria from gaining a foothold. These factors serve to make mouth infections in dogs relatively infrequent.

LIPS

Inflammation of the Lips (Cheilitis)

Inflammation of the lips is often caused by periodontal disease and mouth infections. In hunting dogs it may be the result of contact with weeds and brush, causing the lips to become irritated and chapped-looking.

Cheilitis is recognized by serum crusts that form at the junction of the haired parts with the smooth parts of the lip. As the crusts peel off, the area beneath becomes raw, denuded and sensitive to touch. Occasionally inflamed hair follicles or skin glands cause small firm nodules to develop. These nodules may break open and discharge pus.

Treatment: Clean the area with surgical soap (pHisoHex, Weladol) and apply an antibiotic-steroid cream (Panolog) twice daily. When the infection subsides, apply Vaseline to keep the skin of the lips soft and pliable until healing

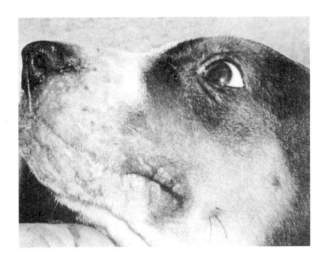

Bacterial infection of the lips
(cheilitis).

is complete. If periodontal disease is present, this should be treated to prevent recurrence.

Lip Fold Pyoderma

In breeds with pendulous lips, such as some hounds, Saint Bernards and Cocker Spaniels, the skin folds on the lower lip that contact the upper fangs are a site of irritation and infection. These skin folds sometimes contain pockets that trap food and saliva, creating a constantly wet environment that favors bacterial growth. When the skin folds are stretched out, a raw, denuded, sensitive surface is seen. The foul odor from the dog's mouth is often the major reason for seeking medical attention.

Treatment: Cleanse the pockets by swabbing them out twice daily with cotton-tipped applicators dipped in peroxide, and apply an antibiotic-steroid cream (Panolog). Clip the hair around the lip fold and keep all affected areas dry and clean. This usually gives a good response. However, the problem may come back when the treatment is stopped. Permanent cure then requires surgical removal of the infected fold of tissue.

Lacerations of the Lips, Mouth and Tongue

The soft tissues of the mouth are common sites for cuts. Some of these are self-inflicted: the dog accidentally biting the lip as we might do to ourselves. Others are caused by the dog picking up and licking sharp objects, such as the top of a food can. Sometimes a canine tooth penetrates the lip and impales itself. One unusual cause of tongue trauma is freezing of the tongue to metal in extremely cold weather. When the tongue pulls free, the mucus membrane on the surface of the tongue strips off, leaving a raw bleeding patch.

Treatment: Bleeding from a mouth injury can be controlled by applying pressure to the cut with a clean gauze dressing or a piece of linen. Minor cuts that have stopped bleeding do not need to be stitched. Suturing of the cut should be considered when the laceration is large, ragged and deep, when the edges gape open, when lip lacerations involve the border of the mouth and when bleeding recurs after the dressing has been removed. When a sore is the result of a mal-positioned tooth, have the tooth removed.

During healing of a cut, cleanse the dog's mouth twice daily with a mild mouth wash such as Scope. Feed a bland diet and avoid kibble, Milk-Bones, knuckle bones and other objects the dog might have to chew.

Burns of the Lips, Mouth and Tongue

Electrical Burns

Electrical burns are almost always caused by chewing on an electric cord. Usually these injuries are limited to the mouth; but if your dog has difficulty breathing, consider the possibility of damage to the lung tissues and seek professional help.

Electrical burns can be quite painful, but in most cases the mucus membranes regenerate and close the defect without surgery. In some cases a gray-appearing membrane develops that eventually becomes ulcerated. Surgical excision of the burn back to healthy tissue is indicated.

Chemical Burns

These are common in the dog. They are caused by lye, phenol, phosphorus, certain acids and alkalies and other corrosive agents. If the substance is swallowed, consider the possibility that your dog's throat is burned—a much more serious problem.

Treatment: Remove poisons from the mouth by sponging and rinsing out with lots of water. Then, if the poison is an alkali, wash the mouth with vinegar or fruit juice; if an acid, use baking soda. For after-care, see *Lacerations* above.

MOUTH

How to Examine the Mouth

Most disorders in your dog's mouth can be identified by a careful inspection of the lips, gums, teeth, palate, throat and the soft tissue of the chin and neck.

Small, movable, nontender nodules beneath the chin, at the angle of the jawbones and below the ear are lymph nodes. When swollen and tender, they indicate a mouth or throat infection. The lips are smooth, with small fingerlike projections along the edge where the skin and mucus membranes meet.

To examine the bite, close your dog's mouth and raise the upper lips while drawing down on the lower lips with your thumb. The bite is determined by seeing how the upper and lower teeth meet (see *Incorrect Bite*). This also gives you the chance to examine the gums and teeth. The gums should be smooth and closely applied to the teeth. The teeth should be firm, healthy-looking and free of dental stain.

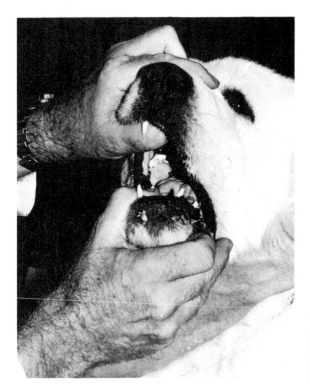

To examine your dog's mouth, place your thumb in the space behind the upper canine tooth and lift up. Pull down on the jaw with your other hand.

If your dog has bad breath, it could be caused by a mouth infection but more often it is the result of poor dental hygiene. Excess plaque and calculus are the leading causes of bad breath.

To open your dog's mouth, place your thumb in the space behind the canine tooth and exert pressure against the roof of the mouth. Pull down on the lower jaw with your other hand. To see beyond the tongue, push down on the back of the tongue with your finger. This allows you to see the tonsils.

Sore Mouth (Stomatitis)

A dog with a sore mouth drools, shakes its head, paws at the face, refuses to eat and shies away when you attempt to look in the mouth. The membranes inside the mouth are reddened, swollen and tender. The gums may bleed when rubbed. The breath has a bad odor. The condition is stomatitis, or inflammation of the mouth.

There are a number of causes, including mouth infections, trauma, vitamin deficiency, kidney disease with uremia, diabetes, leptospirosis, distemper, chemical irritants and corrosive poisons.

A specific type of stomatitis is associated with the autoimmune skin diseases discussed in the SKIN chapter. In these conditions, erosions in the mouth usually appear as well-defined ulcers with scalloped edges. Look for skin changes over the face and other parts of the body.

Treatment: It depends upon finding the underlying cause and correcting it. The common causes of *infectious stomatitis* are listed below.

Trench Mouth (Vincent's Stomatitis)

This is an extremely painful stomatitis caused by a bacterialike germ. It is the most common form of stomatitis in the dog. It is characterized by a beefy-red look to the gums, which bleed easily. There is a characteristic offensive odor from the mouth, usually accompanied by the escape of a brown, purulent, slimy saliva that stains the teeth, muzzle and front legs.

Treatment: Flush the mouth with a weak solution of peroxide (one part in ten several times a day and administer a course of penicillin for at least one week (often three weeks is necessary). Buffered or enteric coated aspirin should be given to control the pain.

Yeast Stomatitis (Thrush)

This is a specific kind of stomatitis usually seen in young dogs after long-term treatment with broad-spectrum antibiotics or steroids, and in dogs whose natural resistance has been weakened by a debilitating disease. You will note that the mucus membranes are covered with soft white patches that coalesce to form a whitish film on the gums and tongue. Painful ulcers are seen as the disease progresses.

Treatment: Feed a soft diet. Large doses of B-complex vitamins are recommended. Antifungal drugs may be needed.

Recurrent Stomatitis

In this condition traumatic ulcers of the mouth occur where jagged, broken or diseased teeth make repeated contact with the mucus lining of the lips, cheeks or gums. A bacteria and a fungus quite commonly are cultured from these ulcers.

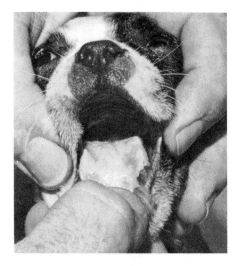

Thrush: The tongue is covered by soft white patches.

Treatment: The teeth should be cleaned. Consider removing those that are diseased. Put your dog on a good home care oral hygiene program (see *Care of Your Dog's Teeth*). Persistent cases require antibiotics.

Warts in the Mouth (Oral Papillomatosis)

Oral papillomas are painless growths in the mouths of young dogs. They are caused by a virus. Initially they are small and pink-looking. Later they become larger, cauliflowerlike, and have a rough, grayish white appearance. There may be just a few, yet in some cases the whole mouth is affected. These warts usually disappear spontaneously in six to twelve weeks. If they don't, surgery can be considered. Once recovered, the dog's system makes antibodies and won't be reinfected.

Foreign Bodies in the Mouth

Common foreign bodies that may be found in the mouth are bone splinters, slivers of wood, sewing needles and pins, porcupine quills, fish hooks and plant awns. They penetrate the lips, gums and palate, become caught between the teeth and get wedged across the roof of the mouth. Foreign bodies in the tongue and throat are discussed elsewhere.

Suspect a foreign body if your dog coughs, gags, licks the lips repeatedly, salivates, shakes the head or paws at the mouth. Sometimes the only signs are a loss of pep, refusal to eat and general unthriftiness associated with bad breath.

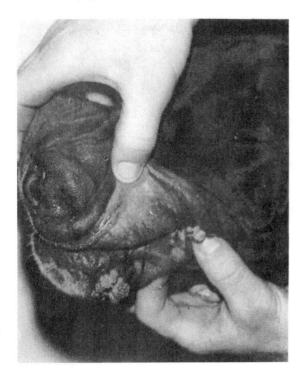

Warts of the mouth are caused by a virus.

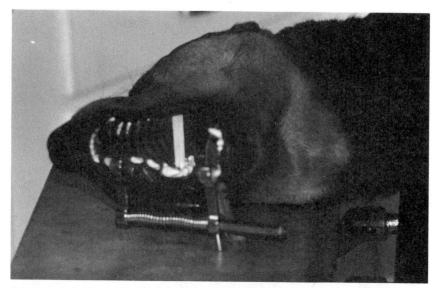

A bone bridging the roof of the mouth. *Impacted foreign bodies* are best removed under anesthesia.

Treatment: Obtain a good light and gently open your dog's mouth. A good look may show the cause of the problem. Direct removal of some foreign bodies is possible, but in an anxious animal suffering from pain, a sedative or anesthetic is necessary.

To remove a fish hook, determine which way the barb is pointing and push it through the soft tissue until it is free. Then cut the shank next to the barb with wire cutters and remove the fishhook in two pieces.

Foreign bodies that have been left in place for a day or longer may cause infection. A broad-spectrum antibiotic is recommended.

Porcupine Quills

Porcupine quills can penetrate the face, nose, lips, oral cavity or skin of the dog. To remove the quills, sedate or tranquilize the dog. Then using a surgical hemostat and needle-nosed pliers, or ordinary pliers if necessary, grasp each quill near the skin and draw it straight out in the long axis of the quill. If the quill breaks off, a fragment will be left behind to work in further, causing a deep-seated infection. Veterinary attention is required. Observe your dog for about one week, looking for signs of infection, abscess formation or deep-seated quills working their way out.

Quills inside the mouth are difficult to remove without first giving an anesthetic.

Growths in the Mouth

Any solid tumor growing in the mouth is a cause for concern. Ninety five percent of mouth growths are cancers. The most common malignant tumors are

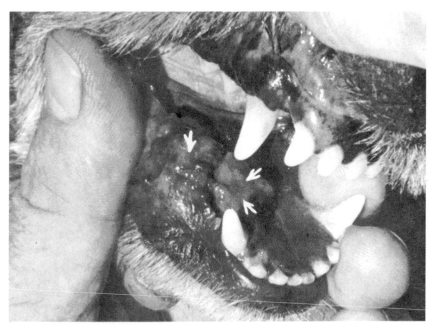

Cancer in the mouth. Note the pigmented growth behind the lower canine tooth.

the fibrosarcoma, malignant melanoma and squamous cell carcinoma. Most mouth cancers occur in older dogs, with Cocker Spaniels and German Shepherds having the highest incidence.

All growths in the mouth should receive immediate professional attention.

TONGUE

Sore Tongue (Glossitis)

A dog with a sore tongue refuses to eat because of the pain. Drooling is common. Inflammation of the tongue occasionally complicates a burn or cut in the mouth. It is also a common feature of stomatitis (see Sore Mouth).

In areas where cockle and sand burrs are prevalent, dogs frequently irritate their tongues while attempting to remove burrs from their feet. Small scratches and puncture wounds of this nature can become infected.

Treatment: If the tongue is infected, give a course of antibiotics (one of the penicillins). If the dog is run-down and in a bad state of nutrition, a vitamin deficiency could be contributing to the sore tongue. Treatment then is directed at building the dog back up with vitamins and a high-protein diet.

Foreign Body in the Tongue

Small plant awns, burrs and splinters can become imbedded on the surface of the tongue. You can remove them with tweezers. Glossitis occurs if the puncture wound becomes infected.

A common place for a foreign body is the underside of the tongue. Confirm this by looking. Sometimes you will see a grapelike swelling, or a draining tract, which means the foreign body has been present for some time. Most of them will need to be removed under anesthesia. A follow-up course of broad-spectrum antibiotic is recommended.

Strangulation of the Tongue

Sudden swelling of the tongue may be caused by strangulation of its blood supply by a rubber band or a piece of string that has become wrapped around it. Gagging and coughing only serve to work it farther to the rear, making it less visible. A careful inspection is necessary to detect and remove the cause of this problem.

GUMS

Healthy gums are firm and pink. The edges are closely applied to the teeth. There is no room for food and debris to get down between them. Pockets alongside the teeth are a source of gum infection and tooth decay.

Pale gums are a sign of ill health (parasites, chronic blood loss and anemia). Bluish gray gums are seen with shock and dehydration.

Gingivitis (Gum Infection)

Dental plaque is the primary cause of gingivitis. Since gum infection is a sign of *periodontitis* and impending tooth decay, it should not be ignored.

If your dog has gingivitis, the first thing you will notice is that gums appear reddened, painful and swollen, and may bleed when rubbed. Next the edges of the gums begin to depart from the sides of the teeth. This causes little pockets

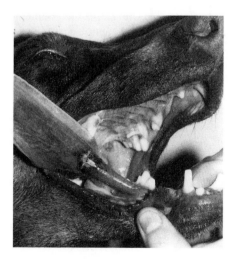

A string from a piece of baloney had wrapped around the tongue, causing *ulceration*. It was not seen until the tongue was raised.

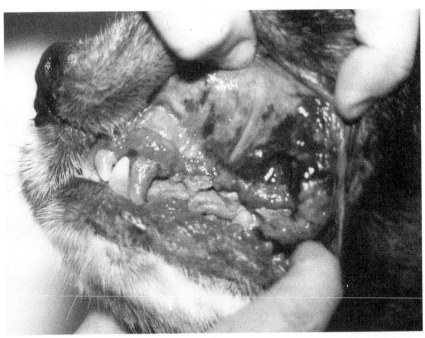

The swollen gums of severe *gingivitis*. Note also the heavy calculus and tartar deposits, indicative of advanced periodontal disease.

and crevices to develop. They trap food and bacteria and cause infection at the gum line. When you press on the sides of the gums, pus may come from below.

The signs of mild gingivitis are bleeding from the gum line (when the gums are rubbed or you brush the dog's teeth) and bad breath. With worsening of the disease the dog may exhibit loss of appetite, difficulty chewing and sometimes drooling.

Treatment: Gingivitis and poor oral hygiene should be treated by brushing the teeth and gums with a 3% hydrogen peroxide solution once a day. Then massage the gums with your finger or a piece of linen, using a gentle circular motion, while pressing on the outside surface of the gums. Continue the program until the gums are healthy looking.

Dental deposits should be broken loose and removed with a dental scaler (see *Care of Your Dog's Teeth*). Sometimes special instruments are needed and the services of a veterinarian will be required. Antibiotics may be necessary to treat infection.

Enlarged Gums (Hypertrophic Gingivitis)

This is a condition in which the gums begin to grow up alongside of (or over) the teeth. As a result they are traumatized, become infected and interfere with good oral hygiene. Collies and the larger breeds seem to be affected most often.

Enlarged gums should be surgically removed.

176

An *epulis* is a form of gingival hypertrophy in which part of the gum enlarges to form a cauliflowerlike mass on a flap of tissue. These noncancerous growths are seen most often in Boxers and Bulldogs. They can interfere with locking of the teeth when the dog's mouth is closed. A large epulis should be removed to promote good oral hygiene.

TEETH

Baby Teeth

The average puppy has twenty-eight *deciduous* (baby) teeth. These are the incisors, canines and premolars. Puppies do not have molars.

With rare exceptions, puppies are born without teeth. The first deciduous teeth begin to appear at three to four weeks of age. They are the canines. Next are the incisors and premolars. The last premolar erupts at about six weeks of age. As a rule, teeth of large breeds erupt more rapidly than those of small breeds.

Teething in Puppies

Puppies begin to acquire permanent teeth at about four to five months of age. During this period, which lasts for about two months, the baby teeth are being shed and replaced by the adult teeth. Teething in puppies may be accompanied by soreness at the mouth and drooling. The puppy may be off feed from time to time, but not enough to affect weight and growth.

The first teeth to be replaced are the incisors, then the canines and premolars. The last molar in the jaw comes in at six to seven months.

Retained Baby Teeth

During teething, the roots of baby teeth are reabsorbed as adult teeth grow out to take their places. Sometimes this does not happen. Toy breeds, in particular, tend to retain their baby teeth as the adult ones erupt. The permanent teeth are then pushed out of alignment. This can cause a bad bite. You may also see what appears as a double set of teeth.

Puppies three to six months of age should be checked from time to time to see that their bite is normal. Also check to see if any baby teeth have been retained. If a baby tooth is still present when an adult tooth has erupted, it should be removed.

Abnormal Number of Teeth

The number of adult teeth in the dog varies according to the breed, but the average is forty-two. Breeds with short faces sometimes have fewer teeth because of shortening of their jaws.

Some dogs carry a mutation for missing teeth. Doberman Pinschers may

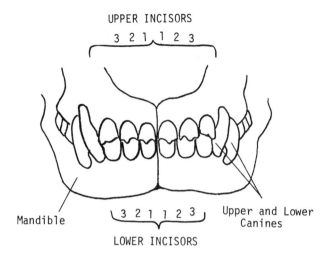

UPPER INCISORS

3 2 1 1 2 3

Mandible

3 2 1 1 2 3

Upper and Lower Canines

LOWER INCISORS

TEETH — FRONT VIEW.

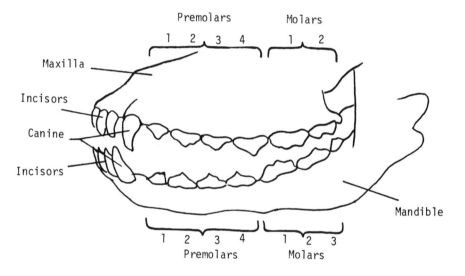

Premolars

Molars

1 2 3 4

1 2

Maxilla

Incisors

Canine

Incisors

Mandible

1 2 3 4

1 2 3

Premolars

Molars

Front and side views of the teeth.

(Rose Floyd)

have fewer premolars than normal. This is considered to be a fault in the show ring, but has little or no effect on the dog's health. Genetic variations of this type usually are hereditary.

Occasionally you may find that your dog has more than the average number of teeth. This occurs most often in spaniels, hounds and Greyhounds. Crowding can cause the teeth to twist or overlap. One or more of the extra *supernumerary* teeth will need to be extracted to make room for the rest.

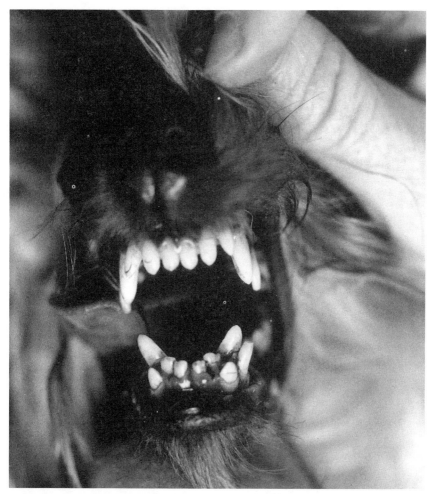

Retained baby teeth can force adult teeth out of alignment, causing malocclusion and gum injury.

Broken Teeth

Broken teeth are common in dogs. They generally occur from catching stones or chewing on kennel fence wire or the bars of cages.

If the fracture involves only the enamel, no treatment is necessary. However, if a tooth fracture (or break in the crown) extends into the dental pulp, restorative dentistry or extraction of the tooth will be necessary to prevent an abscessed root.

Incorrect Bite

A bad bite is a common problem and causes dog breeders more concern than any other mouth abnormality. The ideal bite for most breeds is a *scissors* bite, in which the upper incisors just overlap and touch the lower incisors. In an *even* or *level* bite the incisors meet edge to edge. This is a common bite in dogs but is not considered ideal in many breeds because the edge-to-edge contact causes wear of the teeth.

The type of bite a purebred dog should have is given in the Standard for that breed.

Overshot

In this condition the upper jaw is longer than the lower jaw, so that the teeth overlap without touching. It may also be called a *parrot mouth*. The overshot bite, which occurs in young puppies, may correct itself if the gap is no greater than the head of a wooden match. Most bites are "set" by the time a puppy is ten months old. An overshot bite seldom improves thereafter.

A puppy with an overshot mouth could have a problem when the permanent teeth come in, as they may injure the soft parts of the mouth. These bites should be watched carefully, as extractions may be necessary.

Undershot

This is the reverse of the above, with the lower jaw projecting beyond the upper. It is considered correct in some of the short-faced breeds, including the Bulldog, Boston Terrier and Boxer.

Wry Mouth

This is the worst of the malocclusion problems. In this situation, one side of the jaw grows faster than the other side, twisting the mouth so as to give it a

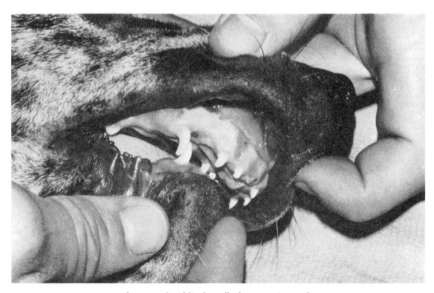

An *overshot* bite is called a parrot mouth.

The *undershot* bite is incorrect for most breeds. Consult your breed Standard.

wry look. This condition can be quite a handicap and leads to difficulty grasping and chewing food.

Treatment of Incorrect Bite

Most bite problems are the results of hereditary influences that control the length of the jaws, so that one grows at a different rate than the other. An overshot mouth in which the upper jaw grows faster is definitely hereditary and may be passed on to some members of the next generation. The undershot mouth *may* be hereditary. Dogs with hereditary dental malocclusion problems should be eliminated from breeding programs.

Bad bites in dogs can be caused by retained baby teeth that interlock in such a way as to block the normal growth of the jaws. When abnormal tooth development is detected early (by twelve weeks), often the problem can be corrected by extraction.

Unstable Jaw

This condition is seen in Pekingese, Chihuahuas and some other Toy breeds. It is caused by persistence of soft cartilage at the point where the lower jaws join together at the front of the chin. (Normally this cartilage becomes calcified, forming bone.) The incisors, whose roots are set in this soft cartilage, become unstable and wobbly. Infection descends to the roots of these teeth and destroys the cartilage. This allows the jawbones to become detached so that each side moves independently. The condition can be treated by removing the diseased teeth, administering antibiotics and stabilizing the joint with wires or screws.

How Dogs' Teeth Tell Their Age

The method of aging a dog by the teeth is a relatively reliable one up to about seven years of age, but individual variations do exist among dogs. They are caused by differences in bites and chewing habits that affect the wear of the teeth.

The cusps of the teeth are the cutting edges. They are best seen on the incisors. The amount of wear on the cusps is used to judge the age of the dog. The incisors (upper and lower) are identified by numbers. These numbers are shown on the drawing Teeth: Front View and Side View, which identifies the incisors in question.

The following generalities are helpful, bearing in mind that individual variations occur:

1½ years	Cusps are worn flat on the lower middle incisors (1). Tartar begins to form on the canines.
2½ years	Cusps are worn flat on the lower intermediate incisors (2). Tartar is quite noticeable on the canines.
3½ years	Cusps are worn flat on the upper middle incisors (1).
4½ years	Cusps are worn flat on the upper intermediate incisors (2).
5 years	Cusps are worn flat on last incisor (3). The canines begin to show wear.
6 years	All the lower incisors are worn flat and the canines appear blunted.

Periodontal Disease and Tooth Decay

Periodontal disease is a term used to describe infections of the teeth and gums. It is one of the most common problems encountered in veterinary practice.

It begins when plaque and calculus are deposited on the teeth near the gum line. This occurs in all dogs living in hard water areas, and will be found to some extent in all dogs over the age of two.

Plaque is a soft, colorless material not easily seen with the naked eye. It consists of organic and inorganic material plus millions of living and growing bacteria.

Calculus or *tartar* is a mixture of calcium phosphate and carbonate with organic material. These calcium salts are soluble in acid but precipitate in the slightly alkaline saliva of the dog. Calculus is yellow or brown in color and produces the characteristic tartar stains. Calculus forms irregular surfaces on the teeth that enhance the deposition of plaque.

The combination of calculus and plaque presents an ideal media for bacterial growth and subsequent infection of the gums (see *Gingivitis*).

The reason why some dogs deposit more plaque and calculus is largely unknown. Certain breeds, such as Poodles and smaller dogs, seem to have a higher incidence. Feeding a soft canned food diet appears to enhance the formation of plaque.

182

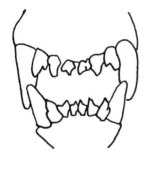

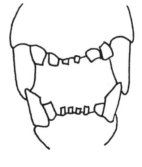

6 Months

*All incisors have
points (cusps)*

2 1/2 Years

*Points worn flat
on lower incisors
(1) and (2)*

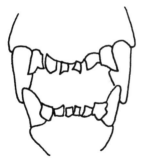

5 Years

*Points worn flat on
all lower incisors*

10 Years

*Points worn flat on
all upper and lower
incisors*

Aging a dog by its teeth.

Periodontitis (Loose Teeth)

Periodontitis develops as a sequel to chronic gingivitis. The teeth are held in their bony sockets by a special kind of connective tissue cement called the *periodontal membrane*. Infection of this membrane and the underlying bone leads to root infection. In time, the teeth begin to loosen and may have to be extracted.

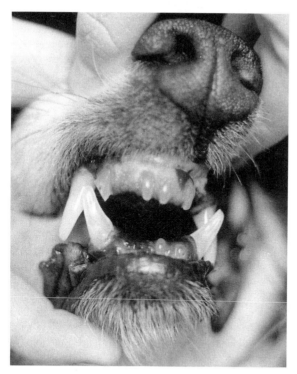

A thirteen-year-old dog. Some incisors are lost and the rest are worn flat.

The signs of periodontitis are like those of gingivitis. An offensive mouth odor may have been present for some time, perhaps even accepted as normal.

Treatment: Follow all the recommendations for gingivitis. In addition, an oral antibiotic should be continued for three weeks.

A surprisingly large number of teeth will reattach themselves to the bone if treatment is started before the condition is too far advanced and extraction becomes necessary. In some instances, severe gingivitis may need to be treated by removing a portion of the diseased gum.

Cavities (Dental Caries)

These are not common in the dog. When present, they occur where plaque accumulates near the root of the tooth instead of the crown (as in humans). Usually the root has been exposed by gum disease. Cavities can lead to root abscesses.

Abscessed Roots

This can involve all teeth, but the ones most often affected are the canines and top fourth premolar. The latter causes a characteristic swelling below the dog's eye. It presents as a recurrent, painful swelling that eventually breaks and drains pus out over the side of the face. Abscessed roots usually are treated by tooth extractions.

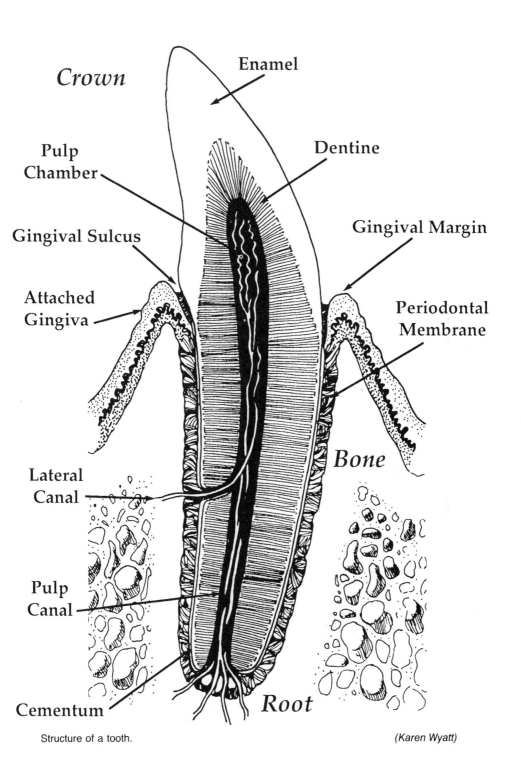

Crown

Enamel

Pulp
Chamber

Dentine

Gingival Sulcus

Gingival Margin

Attached
Gingiva

Periodontal
Membrane

Bone

Lateral
Canal

Pulp
Canal

Cementum

Root

Structure of a tooth.

(Karen Wyatt)

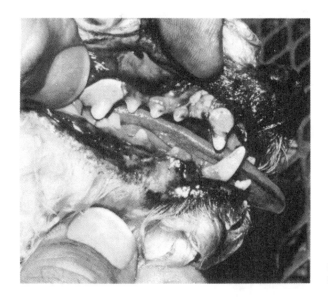

Dental calculus predisposes to gum disease and tooth decay.

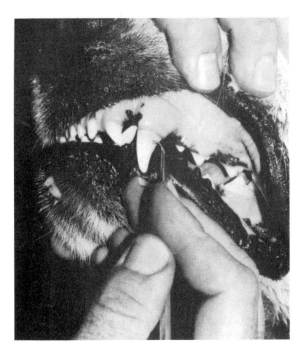

Remove tartar with a dental scraper.
(J. Clawson)

Care of Your Dog's Teeth (Oral Hygiene)

Dogs need special attention given to their teeth in order to prevent gum disease and tooth decay. A program of good oral hygiene is important. You should:

1. Feed kibbled food, Milk-Bones or dog biscuits once a day. Hard foods are abrasive and help to clean the teeth by friction. Avoid "sweets."
2. Give something to chew on at least once or twice a week. Hard nylon bones (not rubber balls) are effective.
3. Remove tartar stains. Moisten a rough cloth and scrub the teeth vigorously, particularly on the outside and next to the gums, where the stains are heaviest. In advanced cases the teeth will have to be scaled and polished. Special dental instruments are needed to break loose particularly thick deposits.
4. Brush teeth and gums twice a week with a toothpaste for dogs (not for people). Use a soft bristled nylon toothbrush with a 45 degree angle at the head. Brush back and forth or in a circular motion only a short distance, pointing the tip of the brush toward the gum line, as you would when brushing your own teeth. Brush all tooth surfaces well. Bleeding may occur with vigorous brushing. This indicates gum disease. Continued daily brushing will usually "tighten" the gums and stop bleeding in one to two weeks. A plaque-retardant toothpaste containing chlorhexidine in a palatable base is available through your veterinarian. This is preferable to using a commercial toothpaste or baking soda in water.

A program of good oral hygiene will increase the life of all dogs' teeth, and help to keep them in good health and condition during later years.

THROAT

Sore Throat (Pharyngitis)

Sore throats are not as common as they are in people. The throat looks red and inflamed. Occasionally a purulent drainage will be seen coating the mucus membrane. Pharyngitis often is associated with a respiratory infection. Symptoms are fever, coughing, gagging, pain on swallowing and loss of appetite.

Treatment: Antibiotics containing penicillin should be given for infection, aspirin for pain. Put your dog on a liquid diet.

Tonsillitis

The tonsils are aggregates of lymphoid tissue, much like lymph glands, which are set at the back of the throat exactly as they are in humans. They may not be visible unless they are inflamed.

Acute tonsillitis is caused by a bacterial infection. It is more common in young dogs of the smaller breeds. Symptoms are similar to those of a sore throat, except that the fever is more pronounced (over 103 degrees F), and the dog appears more ill. The tonsils appear bright red and somewhat swollen. Localized abscesses may be visible as white specs on the surface of the tonsils.

Treatment: Place the dog on a liquid diet and administer a penicillin antibiotic for ten days.

Chronic tonsillitis and tonsillar enlargement are caused by recurrent infections or mechanical irritation from prolonged coughing, retching or regurgitation. Tonsillectomy should be considered for recurrent tonsillitis and when the tonsils interfere with breathing or swallowing. Enlargement alone is not an indication for tonsillectomy.

Foreign Bodies in the Throat (Choking and Gagging)

Dogs choke on small rubber balls and other objects that lodge in the back of their throats and block their windpipes. Bones that lodge sideways in the animal's throat also are a common cause of choking and gagging.

Treatment: If your dog is getting enough air, try to soothe and quiet the animal down. Should a dog panic, the need for air is greater and the situation becomes more of an emergency. Open your dog's mouth and see if you can find the cause of the trouble. If the foreign body cannot be easily removed, do not attempt to remove it yourself. Attempts to remove a stubbornly situated foreign object often cause further damage—or push it farther back. Take your dog to the veterinarian at once.

If the dog has fainted, the object will have to be removed at once to reestablish the airway. Open the mouth. Take hold of the neck in back of the object and apply enough pressure to the throat to keep the object from passing down while you hook it with your fingers. Work it loose as quickly as possible. Then administer artificial respiration.

(**Note:** If the signs are *coughing* and the dog is in respiratory distress, the foreign object may be in the larynx. See RESPIRATORY SYSTEM: *Laryngeal Blockage*).

Prevention: Avoid giving your dog a hard rubber ball to play with. *Don't feed your dog chicken bones or long bones. These splinter easily.*

SALIVARY GLANDS

There are four main pairs of salivary glands that drain into the dog's mouth. Only the parotid gland, located below the dog's ear in back of the cheek, can be felt easily from the outside. The salivary glands secrete an alkaline fluid that lubricates the food and aids in digestion.

Drooling (Hypersalivation)

A common cause of hypersalivation is motion sickness. Apprehension, fear and nervous anxiety also cause an increase in the saliva formation in some dogs.

188

When a dog is drooling excessively and acts irrationally, beware of the possibility of rabies. Other infectious diseases, notably distemper, are associated with drooling. Tranquilizers can cause drooling; so can some poisons (arsenic). A foreign body in the mouth should be considered when there is no apparent cause for the problem. Drooling is associated with painful mouth infections (e.g., stomatitis, gingivitis, glossitis, periodontitis). Dogs with loose pendulous lips, particularly Saint Bernards, Newfoundlands, Great Pyrenees and some Hounds may have a mucoid saliva that hangs in ropes from the corners of the mouth.

Treatment: It depends upon finding the cause and correcting it. In stubborn cases, a drug may be given to slow the flow of saliva or relieve apprehension.

Salivary Gland Infection and Cysts

Salivary gland infections are not common in dogs. When present they are an extension of a mouth infection or an obstruction of one of the salivary gland ducts.

Ducts become blocked by thick secretions, stones or foreign bodies, such as food particles and plant awns. Fluid backs up, ruptures the duct and forms a fluid-filled cyst in the gland (*mucocele*).

Mucoceles can occur in any of the salivary glands, but the one most commonly involved is the submandibular gland. In this location the cyst presents as a large, smooth, rounded swelling in the floor of the mouth on one side of the tongue. This is commonly known as a *ranula* (honey cyst). A less common site is the wall of the pharynx.

Mucoceles can cause problems if they become large enough to interfere with eating, or if they obstruct swallowing or breathing. When a needle is put into the cyst, a thick, mucuslike, honey-colored material is removed. This sometimes effects cure. More often surgery is required.

SWOLLEN HEAD

Head and Neck Abscess

Head and neck swellings that come on suddenly and are accompanied by fever and pain are abscesses. They affect the throat (post-tonsillar and retropharyngeal abscesses), soft tissues beneath the chin (submandibular abscess), side of the face and soft tissues behind the eye (retrobulbar abscess). A retrobulbar abscess causes tearing and protrusion of the eye.

Causes are tonsillitis, sore throat, puncture wounds, mouth infections, abscessed teeth and foreign bodies such as wood splinters, pins, chicken bones and quills that work back from the mouth into the soft tissues.

Head and neck abscesses are exquisitely tender swellings that give a lop-sided look to the head, face or neck. Opening the mouth causes extreme pain in some cases. These individuals refuse to eat and drink.

Treatment: In nearly all cases incision and drainage will be necessary after the abscess becomes fluctuant (soft-feeling). Your veterinarian probably will suggest application of warm saline packs for fifteen minutes four times daily and prescribe an antibiotic.

After incision and drainage, a wick of gauze may be used to keep the edges apart so the wound can heal from the bottom. You may be required to change and dress the wound at home.

Swollen Jaw (Mandibular Osteopathy)

This condition primarily affects young West Highland Whites, Scottish Terriers, Cairn Terriers and Boston Terriers. It recently has been found in Labradors, Great Danes and Doberman Pinschers. A recessive mode of inheritance has been described.

In these animals excess bone material is deposited in the joints of the lower jaw, causing a painful swelling and extreme difficulty in opening the mouth. Drooling and loss of appetite may be the first signs; but when the mouth is forced open, the dog will cry out in pain.

Treatment: The condition has been successfully treated with corticosteroids. Medication must be continued for several months. It must be started before the bone is deposited, or treatment is not effective.

9

Digestive System

THE DIGESTIVE TRACT is a complex system that begins at the mouth and ends at the anus. The lips, teeth, tongue, salivary glands, mouth and pharynx are considered elsewhere. The remaining organs are the esophagus, stomach, duodenum (first part of the small bowel), small intestine, colon, rectum and anus. The organs that aid in the digestion and absorption of foodstuffs are the pancreas, gall bladder and liver.

The esophagus is a muscular tube that carries the food down to the stomach. This is accomplished by rhythmic contractions. The lower esophagus is equipped with a muscular ring; it enters the stomach at an angle. This helps to prevent reflux of foods and liquids back up into the mouth.

Food remains in the stomach for three to six hours. It then passes down through the small intestine and into the colon. Digestive juices in the small intestine break down food into amino acids, fatty acids and short-chain sugars. The end products of digestion are then passed through the wall of the bowel and into the bloodstream. Blood from the intestines flows to the liver. The liver has numerous functions connected with metabolism. Here the materials of the dog's meal are converted into stored energy.

The function of the colon is to remove water and store the waste products until they are eliminated.

Endoscopy (EGD; Colonoscopy)

EGD (*Esophagogastroduodenoscopy*) is a procedure in which a flexible fiberoptic endoscope is inserted through the mouth and passed into the esophagus, stomach and first part of the small intestine (duodenum). *Colonoscopy* is the procedure in which the scope is passed through the anus to examine the rectum

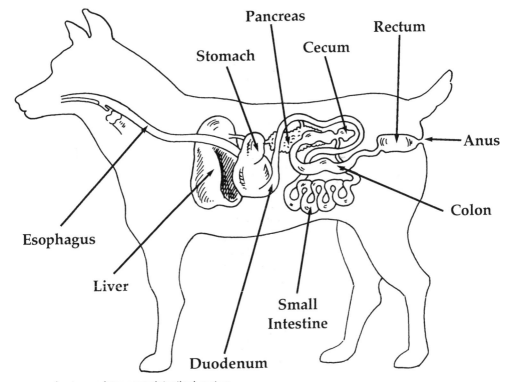

Anatomy of the gastrointestinal system.

and colon. Endoscopy is a good way to diagnose tumors, strictures and ulcers, and remove foreign bodies from the esophagus. It can be performed on small dogs and even cats. Anesthesia is required.

ESOPHAGUS

Regurgitation

A dog that regurgitates food is suffering from blockage of the swallowing tube. *Regurgitation* is the *passive* expulsion of undigested food without conscious effort. It should not be confused with vomiting. *Vomiting* is the *forceful* expulsion of stomach and/or intestinal contents. The material vomited is usually sour smelling, partly digested and stained with yellow bile. Bouts of severe coughing with phlegm and gagging can be mistaken for regurgitation and vomiting. It is important to distinguish between these three conditions because each denotes a disease in a different system.

When regurgitation comes on suddenly, suspect a foreign body. When it occurs from time to time but seems to be getting worse, it can still be caused by a foreign body, as some objects cause a partial blockage that can persist for days. Consider also the possibility of megaesophagus, strictures and growths.

192

If your dog regurgitates immediately after taking a bite or two of food, the block probably is high in the swallowing tube.

Food regurgitated into the nose leads to infection of the nasal passages and nasal discharge. Food regurgitated into the windpipe causes bouts of pneumonia.

Endoscopic examination is helpful in making the diagnosis and planning effective treatment

Painful Swallowing (Dysphagia)

Food can trickle by a partial blockage. Swallowing can be difficult and painful. The dog then does not necessarily regurgitate, but makes repeated attempts to swallow the same mouthful and eats slowly. If a dog doesn't get enough food, there will be noticeable weight loss. As the condition becomes more painful, the dog may stop eating altogether.

Painful swallowing can be associated with mouth infections, dental infections, a sore throat and tonsillitis. In these conditions it is often accompanied by drooling and halitosis.

Swallowing Problems in Puppies

Swallowing problems in puppies are not uncommon. The symptoms are those of regurgitation and dysphagia.

Aortic Arch Anomalies

Retained fetal arteries in the chest can cause regurgitation and dysphagia by producing a stricture around the esophagus. Surgery can correct some of these obstructions.

Megaesophagus (Dilated Esophagus)

In this condition there is enlargement or dilatation of the esophagus, which produces regurgitation, loss of condition and often aspiration pneumonia.

Congenital megaesophagus is the result of improper nerve innervation of the esophagus. This interferes with effective peristalsis and prevents food from passing down into the stomach. In time, the upper esophagus begins to dilate and balloon out. This can be demonstrated by lifting up the puppy's back legs and looking for a bulging out of the esophagus at the side of the neck.

Puppies with megaesophagus begin to show signs shortly after they start eating solid foods. They begin to eat eagerly, but, after a few bites, they back away from the food dish. They often regurgitate small amounts of food, which they eat again. After repeatedly eating the food, it becomes quite liquid and often passes into the stomach. Repeated respiratory infections caused by inhalation of food are common.

Adult-onset megaesophagus can be a late manifestation of congenital megaesophagus, but also can be caused by esophageal foreign bodies, tumors, strictures, neurologic disorders, autoimmune diseases and heavy metal poisoning.

Treatment: A problem can be suspected by the symptoms, but its exact nature can be confirmed only by special studies such as endoscopy or a barium swallow X ray.

In congenital megaesophagus, management is directed at maintaining and improving nutrition. Food and water should be given from a *raised* bowl to promote passage by gravity. Some individuals respond best to a semiliquid or gruel mixture, others to solids. Determine this by trial and error.

Puppies that survive the first few weeks often improve spontaneously. The outlook is less favorable for older dogs with acquired megaesophagus.

Dogs with inherited megaesophagus should not be used for breeding.

Blocked Esophagus

The signs of esophageal obstruction are drooling, difficult and/or painful swallowing, and regurgitation of food. In most cases the dog will be unable to swallow liquids.

Causes are esophageal foreign body, tumor, stricture and megaesophagus.

Foreign Body in the Esophagus

When a dog suddenly becomes distressed, drools and slobbers, swallows painfully or regurgitates food and water, suspect a foreign body lodged in the esophagus. Frequently it is a bone splinter.

A history of regurgitation and difficulty swallowing for several days does not rule out a foreign body.

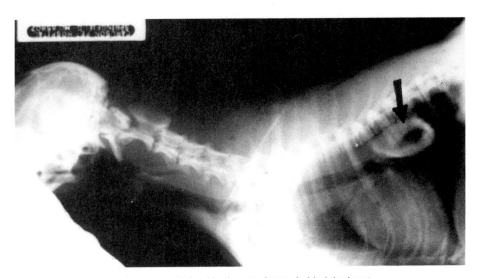

A steak bone lodged in the esophagus behind the heart.

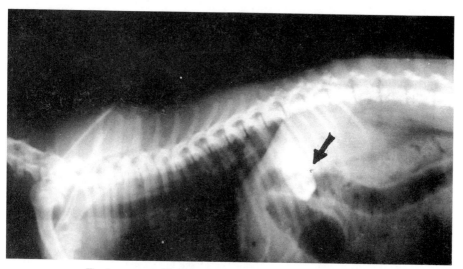

The bone passed into the stomach and was removed surgically.

Treatment: Foreign bodies often can be removed by endoscopy. The animal is given an anesthetic, after which the endoscope is passed through the mouth and directed into the esophagus. The object is visualized through the endoscope and removed with a long forceps.

Difficult foreign bodies and injuries to the esophagus may require surgery.

Stricture

A stricture is a circular scar that follows an injury to the wall of the esophagus. Common causes are foreign bodies, caustic liquids and reflux of stomach acid into the lower esophagus.

Treatment: Most strictures can be treated by stretching (dilatation). This can often be accomplished during endoscopy. Following dilatation, some dogs swallow normally. Others don't; the esophagus above the strictured segment remains enlarged, capable only of weak contractions. These dogs may need surgical removal of the strictured segment.

When a dog has a chronic stricture, overloading the esophagus with large meals aggravates the problem. Feed several small, semisolid meals a day.

Growths

Tumors in the esophagus are not common, but when present, usually are malignant. Growths of the esophagus caused by a worm (*Spirocerca lupi*) do occur, but this is rare.

STOMACH

Vomiting

A number of diseases and upsets in the dog are associated with vomiting. This is one of the most common nonspecific symptoms you are likely to encounter.

All vomiting is the result of stimulation of the vomiting center in the brain. In dogs, the vomiting center is well developed; thus dogs vomit more readily than most other animals. As the need to vomit is perceived, the dog appears anxious. He begins to salivate and makes repeated efforts to swallow.

As the dog starts to vomit, there is simultaneous contraction of the muscles of the stomach and abdominal wall. This leads to an abrupt buildup in intra-abdominal pressure. At the same time the lower esophageal ring relaxes, allowing the stomach contents to travel up the esophagus and out the mouth. With the neck extended, the dog makes a harsh gagging sound.

This sequence should be distinguished from the passive act of regurgitation discussed above.

The most common cause of vomiting in the dog is overeating. Puppies who gobble their food and immediately exercise are likely to vomit. This after-meal vomiting is not serious. It may be caused by feeding puppies from a common food pan (which encourages rapid eating). Separating puppies, or feeding small meals more often, usually eliminates the problem.

The second most common cause of vomiting is eating grass, or some other indigestible material that is irritating to the stomach.

If your dog vomits once or twice, and then appears perfectly normal and has no signs of illness, the condition probably is not serious and requires no special treatment.

Often it is possible to get a clue to your dog's problem by noticing how and what the dog vomits. Types of vomiting that may be serious are discussed below.

Repeated Vomiting

The dog first vomits. Then, continuing to retch, a frothy, clear fluid is brought up. This type of vomiting suggests a stomach irritation. Spoiled food, grass, other indigestibles and certain infectious illnesses (such as gastroenteritis) all cause irritation of the stomach lining (see *Acute Gastritis*).

Sporadic Vomiting

The dog vomits off and on, but not continuously. There is no relationship to meals. Appetite is poor. The dog has a haggard look and shows signs of listlessness and loss of health and glow. You should suspect that your dog is suffering from a disorder of one of the internal organs (kidneys, liver), or has a chronic illness such as a chronic gastritis, a heavy worm infestation or diabetes. A thorough checkup is in order.

Vomiting Blood

Fresh blood in the vomitus indicates a break in the mucus lining somewhere between the mouth and the upper small bowel. Common causes are foreign bodies, tumors and ulcers. Material that looks like coffee grounds is old blood that is partly digested. This usually indicates that the problem lies in the stomach or duodenum. Some cases may be caused by swallowed blood.

When a dog vomits blood, the condition is serious and warrants a trip to the veterinarian.

Fecal Vomiting

If a dog vomits foul material that looks and smells like stool, suspect an obstruction in the intestinal tract. Blunt or penetrating abdominal trauma is another cause of fecal vomiting.

The vomiting associated with intestinal obstruction produces marked dehydration. Professional treatment is required.

Projectile Vomiting

This is a forceful type of vomiting in which the stomach contents are ejected suddenly, often a considerable distance. It is indicative of a complete blockage in the upper gastrointestinal tract. Foreign bodies, hair balls, duodenal ulcers, tumors and strictures are possible causes.

Any condition that causes an increase in intracranial pressure also causes projectile vomiting. This includes brain tumor, encephalitis and blood clots.

Vomiting Foreign Objects

These include bone splinters, rubber balls, pieces of toys, sticks and stones. Occasionally hair balls form a castlike wad, too large to pass out of the stomach. This is called a *bezoar*. Other material may be incorporated into a bezoar.

Puppies with a heavy roundworm infestation occasionally vomit adult worms. These pups should be treated (see *Roundworms*).

Emotional Vomiting

Dogs can vomit when upset, excited or suffering from a phobia (for example, during a thunderstorm). A phobic dog also may drool, whine, paw and tremble.

Remove your dog from the cause of anxiety, if possible, and if necessary, give a tranquilizer.

Motion Sickness

Young dogs often become nauseated and vomit when riding in a car. This is caused by stimulation of the vomiting center in the brain.

Treatment: To prevent motion sickness, give Dramamine by mouth (25 to 50 mg) about one hour before leaving. Don't feed your dog before taking a trip. Dogs travel best on an empty stomach.

If the trip is to be a long one, it may be better to use a tranquilizer. Phenergan (promethazine) is a good one. The dose is 4 mg per pound body weight. *Do not* tranquilize your dog on the day of a dog show.

Most dogs with motion sickness eventually become accustomed to riding in the car and outgrow the problem.

Gastritis (Inflammation of the Stomach)

Gastritis is caused by irritation of the lining of the stomach. The principal sign is vomiting. Gastritis can be of sudden onset (*acute*), or it can come on insidiously and be protracted (*chronic*).

Acute Gastritis

Severe and continuous vomiting comes on suddenly. The most likely cause is an ingested irritant or poison. Grass eating is a common cause of irritant gastritis. Other causes are ingested bones, plastic wrappings, spoiled food, garbage and stools.

Common poisons are antifreeze, fertilizers, plant toxins, crabgrass killers and rat poisons. If any of these are suspected, notify your veterinarian.

When the stomach responds promptly, the foreign material is expelled. Then it is necessary only to rest the stomach and protect it from excess acid.

Treatment: Withhold food and water for twenty-four hours. If your dog appears thirsty, give the dog some ice cubes to *lick*. Administer Pepto-Bismol at a dose of one ml per pound body weight every six hours as long as vomiting continues.

After twenty-four hours start your dog off on a bland diet of boiled rice mixed two parts to one part of hamburger. Boil the hamburger to remove the fat (fat delays stomach emptying). Other bland foods that may be substituted are cottage cheese, baby food and chicken rice soup. Feed small amounts the first twenty-four hours. If well tolerated, advance to a normal diet.

Chronic Gastritis

Dogs with chronic gastritis vomit sporadically (not always after meals), show little appetite, carry a dull hair coat, appear lethargic and lose weight.

The most common cause of chronic gastritis is a steady diet of poor quality or spoiled food. Other causes are persistent grass eating and the ingestion of cellulose, paper and rubber products. Consider also the possibility of hair bezoars. They accumulate in the stomach during springtime shedding from licking and pulling hair out with the teeth.

A condition called *antral pyloric hypertrophy* is an obstructive narrowing of the outlet of the stomach caused by overdevelopment of the muscles in the wall of the pyloric canal. It is like an adult form of pyloric stenosis (see PEDIATRICS). It occurs most often in middle-aged dogs of the smaller breeds. It is characterized by vomiting that occurs three to four hours after eating. Treatment involves surgical removal of the blockage.

Finally, if no obvious cause is apparent, your dog could be suffering from some internal disorder such as kidney failure, and should be examined by your veterinarian.

Treatment: Put your dog on a soft, bland diet as described above. If there is visible improvement advance to a high-quality kibble mix (no fat).

When a smooth object is swallowed (hair, cloth, etc.), and you suspect it might be too large to pass through the lower tract, make your dog vomit it (see EMERGENCIES: *How to Induce Vomiting*).

Other Causes of Upset Stomach

Some dogs apparently are unable to tolerate certain foods or certain brands of commercial dog food. This can be determined by trial and error. Special diets can be prescribed by your veterinarian.

A condition exists in the Bulldog breed in which the stomach does not produce enough acid. It causes symptoms like those of chronic gastritis. It can be treated by supplying the needed acid with meals.

Peptic Ulcers

Stomach ulcers are not common. They usually are caused by drugs and medications—especially non-buffered or uncoated aspirin, the nonsteroidal anti-inflammatory agents such as Ibuprofen, butazolidin and steroids. Most conditions that produce gastritis can also cause ulcers.

Vomiting is the most frequent sign. The vomitus often appears like old "coffee ground" material and occasionally fresh blood. Weight loss and anemia are accompanying features. Diagnosis is made by upper gastrointestinal X rays or by gastroscopy.

Treatment: Discontinue all potential ulcer-producing medications. A number of drugs are available to treat ulcers in dogs. They are the same ones used in people. Veterinary management is required.

Bloat (Gastric Dilatation—Torsion Complex)

This is a veterinary emergency and a life-threatening disease that usually affects dogs in the prime of life. Mortality rates approach 50 percent.

The term *bloat* refers to any of three conditions: acute gastric dilatation, torsion and volvulus.

Bloat, also known as the *overfeeding (or overeating) syndrome*, involves a swelling up of the stomach from gas, fluid or both (*acute gastric dilatation*). Once distended, the stomach may twist abruptly on its long axis. If it does twist, but the twist is 180 degrees or less, it is called a *torsion*. A twist greater than 180 degrees is called a *volvulus*.

There are some interesting facts about bloat:

1. Dogs with bloat nearly always are between four and seven years of age. Two-thirds are males.
2. It usually affects dogs of the larger, deeper-chested breeds: Great Danes, German Shepherds, Saint Bernards, Labrador Retrievers, Irish Wolfhounds, Great Pyrenees, Boxers, Weimaraners, Old English Sheepdogs, Irish Setters, Bloodhounds, Standard Poodles and others of large size (fifty-eight pounds was the average size in one study). It rarely occurs in small breeds.
3. Dogs who bloat tend to eat large quantities of dry kibble.
4. They exercise vigorously after eating, and tend to drink water in large amounts after meals.
5. They may have a history of digestive upsets (gastritis).
6. There may be a familial association with other dogs who have bloated.

If your dog develops a gastric upset that you think may be bloat, it is most important to decide whether this condition is caused by gastric dilatation or torsion of the stomach. A mild gastric dilatation, not complicated by a twist of the stomach and signs of severe distress, is not an acute emergency and can be treated at home. A torsion or volvulus, on the other hand, is a life-and-death situation. It calls for *immediate* veterinary attention.

Acute Gastric Dilatation

The signs are excessive salivation and drooling, extreme restlessness, attempts to vomit and defecate, evidence of abdominal pain (the dog whines and groans when you push on the stomach wall) and abdominal distention. The history is most important. In nearly all cases there is a history of overeating, eating fermented foods, drinking excessively after eating or taking vigorous exercise after a meal (within two to three hours).

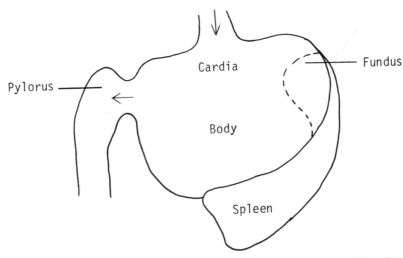

The normal position of the stomach and spleen.   (Rose Floyd)

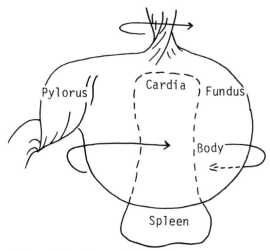

Bloat Syndrome: During volvulus, the gastric twist is greater than 180 degrees. This pinches off the inlet of the stomach and interferes with the blood supply to the stomach and spleen. Relief is imperative. *(Rose Floyd)*

If your dog is able to belch or vomit, quite likely the condition is not caused by a twist. The quickest way to confirm the diagnosis of acute gastric dilatation is to pass a long rubber or plastic stomach tube. As the tube enters the dog's stomach, there is a rush of air from the tube. Swelling in the abdomen subsides. This brings immediate relief.

To pass a stomach tube, insert the tube behind one of the canine teeth and advance it into the throat until the dog begins to swallow. If the dog *gags*, continue to advance the tube. If the dog *coughs*, the tube has entered the windpipe. *Withdraw* the tube a few inches and then advance it. There is little danger of perforating the esophagus with a soft rubber stomach tube.

Treatment: Administer Mylanta by mouth (see DRUGS AND MEDICATIONS:) *How to Give Medications*). The dose for a small dog is six ounces; for a medium-sized dog, eight ounces; for a large dog, twelve ounces. Mylanta is an antacid that contains simethicone (absorbs gas). Walk your dog until you can contact a veterinarian, or until the bloat is relieved.

Torsion or Volvulus

The initial signs are those of acute gastric dilatation except that distress is more marked. The dog breathes rapidly, has cold and pale mouth membranes and may collapse. The shocklike signs are caused by strangulation of the blood supply to the stomach (and spleen).

A gastric tube will not pass into the stomach. Once you have established this, do not attempt to struggle further. This can throw your dog into deeper shock.

Treatment: Rush the dog to a veterinary clinic. If immediate professional help is not available, you may want to relieve pressure in the stomach with a

Before passing a stomach tube, mark the tube by measuring the distance from the nose to the last rib.

large-bore needle inserted through the abdominal wall. This is not without risk. The needle can lacerate the spleen, or fluid can leak out through the hole in the stomach, causing a peritonitis. Despite these risks, relieving pressure can be life-saving.

To insert a needle into your dog's stomach, put the dog in a comfortable position that allows easier breathing. Next determine the highest point just beneath the rib cage where there is a hollow or drumlike sound (find by tapping with your fingers).

You are going to try to put your needle into an air pocket, avoiding fluid that is in the lower part of the stomach. Fluid may plug the needle. Quickly push

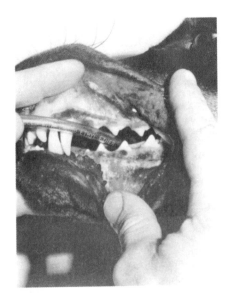

Insert the tube behind one of the canine teeth: advance to the level of the mark.

202

the needle several inches through the belly wall and into the stomach beneath. If done correctly, gas under pressure rushes through the needle. This relieves the condition temporarily, allowing time to get to a veterinarian for definitive treatment.

Surgery is necessary to relieve a torsion or volvulus. The abdomen is opened and the twist is unwound. In some cases the spleen, or a portion of the stomach, must be sacrificed. The chance of a recurrence is about 15 percent. Various surgical procedures are utilized at the time of the initial operation to prevent recurrence.

Prevention: Feed several small meals instead of one large meal. Don't roughhouse with your dog or allow strenuous exercise on a full stomach. The dog should not be allowed to drink water after eating a large meal of dry kibble. These measures may prevent some cases of bloat but they will not prevent all cases.

INTESTINES

Problems in the intestinal tract (small and large bowel) are associated with three common symptoms: *diarrhea, constipation* and the *passage of blood*. They are discussed below.

Diarrhea in *puppies* is discussed in PEDIATRICS.

Diarrhea

Diarrhea is the passage of loose, unformed stools. In most cases there is an increased number of bowel movements. Diarrhea is the most common sign of intestinal disease.

Food in the small intestine takes about eight hours to get to the colon. During this time the bulk of it is absorbed. Eighty percent of water is absorbed in the small bowel. The colon concentrates and stores the waste. At the end, a well-formed stool is evacuated.

Transit time in the intestinal tract can be speeded up for a variety of reasons. When food passes rapidly through the bowel, it is incompletely digested and arrives at the rectum in a liquid state. This results in a large, loose, unformed bowel movement. This mechanism accounts for the majority of acute diarrheas of short duration.

In attempting to narrow the search for the cause of a diarrhea, it is important to decide whether the disease is located in the small intestine or colon. Begin by examining the *color, consistency, odor* and *frequency* of stools, as well as the *condition of the dog*:

Color

Yellow or greenish stool—indicates rapid transit (small bowel).
Black, tarry stool—indicates bleeding in the upper digestive tract.
Bloody stool—red blood or clots indicate bleeding in the colon.

Pasty, light-colored stool—indicates lack of bile (liver disease).

Large, gray, rancid-smelling stool—indicates inadequate digestion or absorption (malabsorption syndrome).

Consistency

Watery stool—indicates small bowel wall irritation (toxins and severe infections).

Foamy stool—suggests a bacterial infection.

Greasy stool—often with oil on the hair around the anus: indicates malabsorption.

Excessive mucus—a glistening or jellylike appearance: indicates colonic origin.

Odor (the more watery the stool, the greater the odor)

Foodlike, or smelling like sour milk—suggests both rapid transit and malabsorption: for example, overfeeding, especially in puppies.

Putrid smelling—suggests an intestinal infection.

Frequency

Several in an hour, each small, with straining—suggests colitis (inflammation of the large bowel).

Three or four times a day, each large—suggests malabsorption or small bowel disorder.

Condition of Dog

Weight loss, malnutrition—suggests small bowel disorder.

Normal appetite, minimal weight loss—suggests large bowel disorder.

Vomiting—small bowel origin, except for colitis.

Common Causes of Diarrhea

Most cases of diarrhea are caused by irritation of the bowel lining from ingested substances or infectious agents, resulting in rapid transit through the small intestine.

Any sudden change in your dog's diet may cause a diarrhea. Dogs get used to water they drink at home. Drinking unfamiliar water may cause a mild intestinal upset. Some dogs are allergic to (or seemingly unable to tolerate) certain foods such as milk, horse meat, eggs and some commercial dog foods.

Dogs on occasion experience diarrhea when they are excited or emotionally upset (for example, at a dog show).

Indiscretions in diet are common causes of diarrhea. Dogs are natural scavengers. They tend to eat a lot of things they can't digest. Some of them are:

204

dead animals, rodents and birds
garbage and decayed food
rich foods, table scraps, gravies, salts, spices and fats
sticks, cloth, grass, paper, etc.
parts of flea collars

Toxic substances causing diarrhea include:

gasoline, kerosene, oil or coal tar derivatives
cleaning fluid, refrigerants
insecticides
bleaches, often in toilet bowls
wild and ornamental plants, toadstools
building materials: cement, lime, paints, caulks
fireworks containing phosphorus

Many of these are equally irritating to the stomach and cause vomiting.

Infectious enteritis can be caused by most of the intestinal parasites; many bacteria and viruses; some protozoans and rickettsia; rarely by fungi. These conditions are discussed in the chapter INFECTIOUS DISEASES.

Treatment: Diarrhea is a symptom, not a disease. The first step is to find and remove the underlying cause, if possible. Diarrhea caused by *overeating* (characterized by several large, bulky, unformed stools per day) is controlled by cutting back the food intake and feeding three meals a day in divided portions. When *unfamiliar drinking water* is the problem, carry an extra supply. When *irritating or toxic substances* have been ingested, an effort should be made to identify the agent, as specific antidotes may be required.

Food Allergies or intolerances respond to removal of the specific food causing the problem (see SKIN: Food Hypersensitivity).

Most cases of diarrhea can be treated at home. Withhold all food for twenty-four to forty-eight hours. If your dog appears thirsty, give a small amount of water or ice cubes to lick. Administer lomotil at a dose of one tablet per twenty-five pounds weight, three times a day. As the dog begins to respond, start an easily digested diet that contains no fats. Diets containing boiled hamburger (one part to two parts of cooked rice; discard the broth), cottage cheese, cooked macaroni or soft-boiled eggs are suitable in small amounts. Prescription diets (Hills i/d) are available through veterinarians. Continue the bland diet for three days, even though the dog seems well.

A diarrhea that persists for more than twenty-four hours, a bloody diarrhea and diarrheas accompanied by vomiting, fever and other signs of toxicity should not be allowed to continue. Consult your veterinarian without delay.

Malabsorption Syndromes

In these disorders the dog does not digest, or does not absorb, food in the small intestines. These conditions are not common. When present, they are caused by pancreatic disease (causing lack of pancreatic enzymes), liver disease (causing lack of bile) or injury to the lining of the intestinal tract from a prior infectious enteritis (causing lack of intestinal enzymes).

Recently a condition called *chronic intestinal bacterial overgrowth* has been identified as a cause of malabsorption in dogs. German Shepherds appear to have the highest incidence. The exact cause is unknown. Loss of intestinal enzymes or adverse affects of bile salts on the intestinal mucosa may contribute to the bacterial overgrowth. The disease often responds to a course of antibiotics.

Dogs with a malabsorption problem are unthrifty and undernourished despite a large appetite. There is a great deal of fat in the stool, giving it a rancid odor. The hair around the anus is oily or greasy.

The exact cause of the malabsorption can usually be determined, but this requires special diagnostic studies. Then the dog can be given the missing substances by mouth with meals. The treatment of pancreatic insufficiency is discussed below.

Colitis

Colitis is inflammation of the large intestine. It is responsible for about half the cases of diarrhea in dogs. There are a number of different types of colitis and numerous causes. Because digestion and absorption of nutrients occur in the small intestine, colitis usually has little effect on the dog's general health and nutrition.

Whipworms are a frequent cause of large bowel diarrhea. Other infectious agents are protozoa, bacteria and fungi.

The *irritable bowel syndrome* describes a colon motility disorder often associated with stress. It accounts for a number of cases of colonic diarrhea. This problem is helped by a high-fiber diet.

Inflammatory bowel diseases are distinguished by the type of cells found in the wall of the colon on biopsy. These diseases have an autoimmune basis. Treatment is prolonged.

Signs of colitis are urgent straining, painful defecation, prolonged squatting, flatulence and the passage of many small stools mixed with blood and mucus. These signs should be distinguished from **constipation**.

Colitis is complicated and requires veterinary diagnosis and management.

Intestinal Obstructions (Blocked Bowel)

The most common cause of intestinal obstruction is a swallowed foreign object. The esophagus in the dog is larger than its small intestine. Accordingly, a dog can swallow an object which can't be passed through the intestinal tract.

The second most common cause is *intussusception*. This term describes a situation in which the bowel telescopes in upon itself, much as a sock pulled inside out. It is most common at the junction between the small and large bowel. As the small bowel inverts into the colon, the lead point travels a considerable distance, ultimately pinching off the bowel passage. Intussusceptions are caused by increased bowel activity (diarrhea). They are most common in puppies and young dogs.

Obstructions also can be caused by tumors, strictures, navel and groin hernias and twists and kinks that become trapped by adhesions.

The signs of intestinal obstruction are vomiting, dehydration and distension of the abdomen. When the blockage is high, projectile vomiting occurs shortly after eating. When low, there is distension of the abdomen and vomiting is less frequent, but when present, it is dark brown and has a fecal odor. A dog with a complete obstruction passes no stool or gas per rectum.

Untreated intestinal obstruction leads to death of the dog. This condition is most urgent when there is interference with the blood supply to the bowel (*strangulation*). This is characterized by a rapid deterioration in the dog's condition, an extremely tender "boardlike" abdomen (to touch) and signs of shock or prostration. Strangulation requires immediate surgical correction. The dead segment of bowel must be removed and the bowel restored by an end-to-end hookup.

Intestinal Foreign Bodies

Obstructions from foreign bodies occur in dogs that eat sticks, stones, cloth, rubber, leather, hides and balls of hair. Passage of these objects can be aided by giving mineral oil. It must not be given to a struggling dog who could accidentally inhale it. It is best to add it to the feed.

If your dog has swallowed bone chips, you might be able to coat them with a substance such as bread or flour paste. This affords the possibility that the chips can pass through without causing harm.

Constipation

A dog who strains repeatedly but is unable to pass stool is constipated. There must be an element of pain, or difficulty in the passage of the stool, to qualify as constipation. Straining also occurs with colitis, bladder infection (cystitis) and diseases of the anus and rectum. The distinction must be made before treating the dog for constipation.

Most healthy dogs have one or two stools a day. This varies with the individual and diet. A day or two without a stool is no cause for alarm.

Establish a daily routine for your dog's elimination. This is especially important for the older dog.

There are many types of constipation in the dog. They are discussed below.

Chronic Constipation

Inappropriate diets are the cause of most chronic constipations. A diet low in residue (fiber) causes small caliber stools. These stools dry out and are difficult to pass. Concentrated high-meat diets produce dark, tenacious, small gummy stools. Owing to their lack of volume and consistency, they also are difficult to pass.

Bone chips are notorious for making the stool hard; they cement together to form rocklike masses in the colon. Other nondigestible substances such as grass, cellulose, paper and cloth can lead to constipation or a *fecal impaction*.

Dogs with impactions often pass blood-tinged or watery brown stool. This might be mistaken for diarrhea. What actually is happening is that liquid stool is being forced around the blockage. If you suspect a fecal impaction, confirm this by digital examination, using a well-lubricated rubber glove.

Older dogs experience reduced bowel activity and weakness of the abdominal muscles. Either condition can lead to prolonged retention and an increase in the hardness of the stool.

Treatment: Attempt to determine the cause of a chronic constipation; remove any predisposing factors to assure long-term success. Don't feed small bones (such as chicken bones) which can fragment. If feeding a high-meat diet, switch to kibble. If already feeding one kibble, switch to another product to see if it makes the stools softer. A prescription diet (such as Hills r/d) works well.

Small, hard stools can be made softer by adding residue to the diet. High residue foods are bran cereal, whole-wheat bread, pumpkin, squash or celery; or you can add unprocessed Miller's bran, one to two tablespoons a day for the average-size dog.

In an old dog with an inactive bowel, soaking the kibble with equal parts of water can help greatly. Let the mixture stand for twenty minutes.

Mild cases of constipation can be treated with a laxative such as mineral oil or Milk of Magnesia. The usual dose of Milk of Magnesia is one-half to two tablespoons a day, depending on the size of the dog. Mineral oil should not be given by mouth because of the danger of aspiration. Add it to the feed once or twice a week at a dose of one teaspoonful per five pounds body weight. Do not give laxatives on a regular basis. Instead, use milk or liver, which have a laxative effect.

A fecal impaction requires an enema. Enemas are given at the rate of one ounce of fluid per ten pounds of body weight. Several kinds are used. Fleet Oil Retention enemas can be purchased over-the-counter. They come in plastic bottles with attached nozzles. Lubricate the nozzle well and insert it into the anal canal.

Tap water enemas are given through a rubber catheter connected to an enema bag. Lubricate the tip and insert it far enough into the anus so that the rectum retains the fluid. Two to three inches usually is far enough. If the dog struggles, the catheter could injure the wall of the rectum. Warm water enemas are particularly good for treating constipation caused by grass eating.

Voluntary Retention

The urge to defecate can be overridden. Puppies learn to do this as they are house-trained. When carried to an extreme, the stools become excessively dry and hard, because of prolonged water absorption by the bowel. Passage then becomes difficult. Dogs left alone in the house are prone to this disorder. Some dogs refuse to go when away from home.

Treatment: Provide opportunity for your dog to go out several times a day. A mild laxative may be indicated when dogs are traveling.

Mechanical Blockage

In older males, an enlarged prostate can bulge into the anal canal, acting as a valve that pinches off the rectum.

Hernias in the rectal area (perineal hernias) weaken the muscular support of the rectum. This interferes with the mechanics of elimination. This diagnosis can be made by observing a bulge alongside the anus. The bulge becomes larger as the dog strains.

Boston Terriers and Bulldogs with screw tails often have a rigid extension of the tail that extends down upon the anal canal, pinching it against the pelvic floor.

Strictures and cancers are other causes of mechanical blockage. Colon cancer is slow-growing and usually does not cause symptoms until quite large. Straining to defecate, the appearance of flat or ribbonlike stools, and the passage of blood with the stool, are characteristic signs. Colonoscopy may be indicated to make the diagnosis.

Treatment: In these cases it is advisable to feed a *low* residue or bland diet, such as Hills i/d. Soak food well with equal parts of water. A stool softener is recommended. Hydrolose and Mucilose, obtained through veterinarians or pet stores, are good ones. Mineral oil lubricates the stool, making it easier to pass.

Constipation associated with the screw tail usually requires surgical correction of the tied-down tail. Surgical removal of an early colon cancer can lead to cure.

Damaged Nerves

A nerve paralysis, usually found with "slipped discs" and malformations of the lower back, results in loss of the urge to defecate. The muscles used to evacuate the bowel also may be paralyzed (see NERVOUS SYSTEM: *Cauda Equina Syndrome*).

Treatment: This bowel condition can be difficult to treat. Enemas and laxatives, along with measures outlined in the treatment of *Chronic Constipation*, above, may be effective.

False Constipation (Pseudoconstipation)

This is a form of voluntary retention caused by inflammation of the anus. It is common in long-haired dogs. Soft stool mats in the hair around the anus, causing a barrier. The skin becomes irritated, tender and infected. Dogs with this problem try to defecate while standing. Other signs are whining, scooting and biting at the rear. The odor is extremely offensive.

Treatment: Dogs with long coats should be groomed around the anus to prevent the buildup of stool. When present, clip away the matted stool to let air get to the skin. If it is weepy-looking, apply a topical antibiotic ointment (Polysporin). Follow the diet recommended for *Mechanical Blockage* above.

Passing Gas (Flatulence)

Dogs that continually pass flatus embarrass or distress their owners. This condition, called flatulence, is caused by eating highly fermentable foods such as onions, beans, cauliflower, cabbage and soybeans, drinking large quantities of milk and swallowing large amounts of air. Diets high in meats predispose to it. Flatulence also occurs with malabsorption syndromes. This is related to incomplete digestion of carbohydrates.

Treatment: Reduce air gulping by feeding free choice or several times a day. Feed a highly digestible diet such as Hills i/d or k/d. Simethicone 40 mg every eight hours helps to absorb gas. If your dog has a robust appetite and passes large amounts of soft stool, check for a malabsorption problem.

Eating Stool (Coprophagia)

Coprophagia is the name given to the habit of eating stools—either the dog's own or another animal's. Some stools have taste appeal to dogs, particularly those containing partially digested food. Once established, the habit is difficult to break.

Do not allow your dog to eat stools, both for aesthetic reasons and because stools are a source of intestinal upset and carry germs and parasites.

Treatment: A poor quality diet may be at fault. Feed high-quality dry kibble as a base, with canned meat supplement not in excess of 25 percent.

Sprinkle a meat tenderizer (such as Adolph's) on the food as an aid in its digestion. A product called Forbid (which is made from alfalfa) works well when added to the diet. When digested, it gives the stool a disagreeable odor and taste.

ANUS AND RECTUM

The signs of anorectal disease are pain on defecation, repeated and ineffective straining to pass stool (*tenesmus*), the passage of bright blood and anal scooting.

Dogs with anorectal pain often try to defecate from a standing position.

Bleeding from the anus or rectum is recognized by the finding of blood on the outside of the stool rather than mixed in with it.

Scooting is a sign of anal itching. It is caused by flea bites, stool adherent to the perianal area and anal sac disease. Less commonly it is caused by roundworms or tapeworm segments.

Proctitis (Sore Bottom)

Inflammation of the anal skin frequently is caused by feces adhering to the hair over the anus.

Irritation of the anorectal canal can be caused by the passage of bone chips and other sharp objects in the feces or by hard dry stool. Repeated bouts of diarrhea (especially in puppies) can cause a proctitis. Insect bites, worms and false constipation are other causes.

The signs of proctitis are scooting, licking and biting at the rear and, in severe cases, straining.

Treatment: An irritated anus can be soothed by applying an ointment such as Vaseline, or one of the hemorrhoidal preparations used by people. Put your dog on a bland diet and feed small amounts more often. For further management, see *False Constipation*.

Protrusion of Anal Tissue (Anal and Rectal Prolapse)

With forceful and prolonged straining, the dog can protrude the lining of the anal canal. This is a *partial* prolapse and is confined to the surface membrane. In severe cases a complete segment of intestine may protrude; it is then called a *complete* prolapse. It can be as long as several inches: the difference is quite evident on examination. Protrusion of anal tissue might be mistaken for hemorrhoids; but for practical purposes, hemorrhoids do not occur in dogs.

Simple anal prolapse is easily treated at home, but depends upon correcting the cause of straining (see *Constipation* and *Diarrhea* above). Apply a topical anesthetic (Benzocaine Ointment) to reduce pain. Treatment is the same as for proctitis.

A complete rectal prolapse can be replaced manually. Clean the tissue and lubricate it with Vaseline. Then gently push it back up through the anus. To prevent recurrence, usually it is necessary for your veterinarian to intake a temporary purse string suture around the anus to hold it in place while healing.

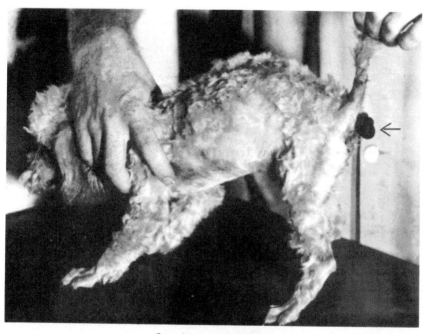

Complete *rectal* prolapse.

Malformation of the Anus
(Imperforate Anus and Rectovaginal Fistula)

In these two conditions found in newborn puppies the anus does not properly develop. When the opening is absent, there is no passage for stool. Abdominal distention appears right after pups start to nurse. When the anus opens into the vagina, stool passes out an intensely irritated vulva. Both conditions require surgical correction if the pup is to survive.

ANAL GLANDS OR SACS

The dog has two anal glands or sacs located at about five and seven o'clock in reference to the circumference of the anus. The openings of the anal sacs are found by drawing down on the skin of the lower part of the anus. By applying a small amount of pressure directly below these openings, fluid can be expressed.

These sacs are sometimes referred to as the "scent" glands. In the skunk they serve a protective purpose. In the dog they appear to be of use in territorial marking, and to enable dogs to identify one another. This probably accounts for the fact that dogs greet each other by sniffing at the other's rear.

The anal sacs normally are emptied by rectal pressure during defecation. The secretion is liquid and brownish. At times it may be thick, yellow or creamy looking.

Anal sacs also are emptied whenever there is sudden contraction of the anal sphincter. This causes a characteristic odor when a dog is upset, frightened

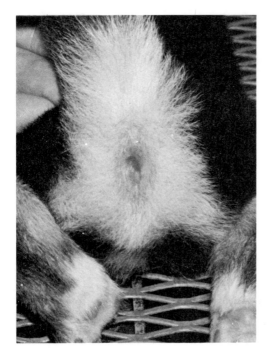

Lack of anal opening in a newborn pup *(imperforate anus)*.

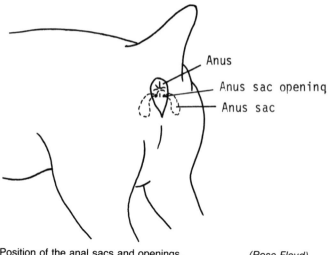

Anus

Anus sac openinq

Anus sac

Position of the anal sacs and openings.   (Rose Floyd)

or under pressure. It is the usual practice in grooming parlors to express the glands before bathing the dog, thus preventing "doggy" odor afterward.

In most dogs it is not necessary to express the glands unless there is some medical reason to do so. However, when frequent odor does pose a problem (for example, in a dog with overactive anal sacs), you can control it by expressing the sacs yourself.

How to Empty the Anal Sacs

Raise the dog's tail and locate the openings of the anal sacs as described above. You can feel the sacs as small, firm lumps in the perianal area at the five and seven o'clock positions. Grasp the perianal skin surrounding the sac with your thumb and forefinger, push in and squeeze together. As the sac empties, a pungent odor is noted. Wipe the secretions away with a damp cloth. If the discharge is bloody or purulent looking, *anal sac infection* is present and you should treat it as described below.

Impaction of Anal Sacs

Impaction of the anal sacs occurs when the sacs fail to empty normally. It is most common in the smaller breeds. Some of the common causes are soft stools (not enough sphincter pressure), small anal sac openings and overactive anal sacs. Secretions become thick and pasty. Anal sac impaction is treated by manual emptying.

Anal Sac Infection (Anal Sacculitis)

This condition complicates impaction. It is recognized by the presence of blood or pus in the secretions. Signs are anal pain and scooting.

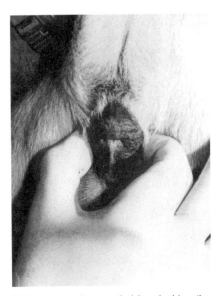

Anal sacs can be emptied by pinching the anal skin between your fingers.

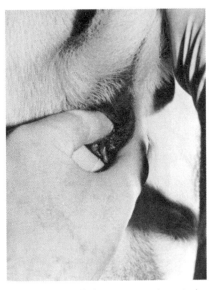

When obstructed, the sacs may have to be expressed with one finger in the anal canal.
(J. Clawson)

Treatment: Empty the anal sacs and instill an antibiotic preparation into the sacs through the duct openings. An antibiotic preparation such as Panolog, which comes in a tube with a small rounded tip at the end, can be used to pack the anal sacs. Insert the tip of the tube into the opening and squeeze. Repeat the packing process in two days. Administer a broad spectrum antibiotic by mouth (chloromycetin or tetracycline).

Anal Sac Abscess

An abscessed anal sac is recognized by the signs of anal infection with swelling at the site of the gland. The swelling is at first red, then later turns a deep purple.

Treatment: An abscess is ready to drain when it becomes fluctuant (soft and fluidlike). At this point it should be lanced so that pus and blood will drain out. The abscess cavity must heal from the bottom out. Keep the edges apart by flushing the cavity twice daily with a dilute peroxide solution. Administer an oral antibiotic. Healing usually is uneventful.

Dogs with recurrent anal gland infections need to have their glands emptied on a regular basis. Surgical removal can be considered.

Perianal Fistulas

Fistulas are open draining tracts and sores in the perianal skin. Usually there is an internal opening in the anorectal canal. They are most common in German Shepherds, but are found in Irish Setters, English Setters, Labradors and other breeds. The symptoms are similar to anal sac abscess, but fistulas are

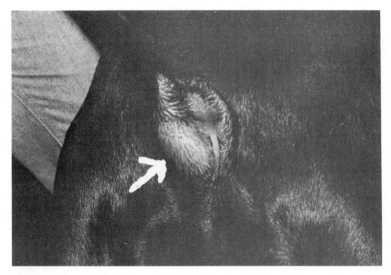

Infected anal sacs produce a tender swelling at the side of the anus *(anal sac abscess). They should be incised and allowed to drain.*

not responsive to simple treatment. Surgical removal by your veterinarian usually is required.

Polyps and Cancer

Polyps are grapelike growths that occur in the rectum and may protrude from the anus. They are not common but when present, they should be removed.

Cancers of the anorectal canal are also not common. They appear as fleshy growths that ulcerate and bleed. When they grow in the rectum, the signs are those of a prolonged proctitis: straining being one of the most common findings.

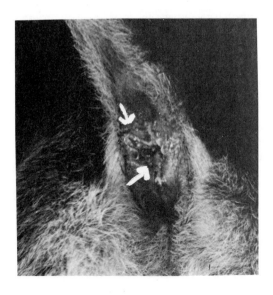

Numerous draining tracts are seen with *perianal fistula.*

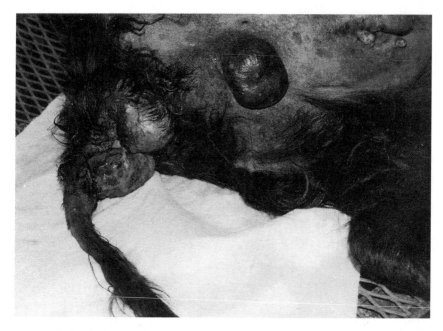

Perianal adenoma, locally advanced with satellite spread to the abdomen.

The diagnosis is made by obtaining a fragment of tissue for microscopic examination.

Perianal Gland Tumor (Adenoma)

This is the most common growth about the anus. It is found principally in male dogs over seven years of age.

These tumors can be recognized by their typical location and appearance. They arise from modified skin glands located around the anus and at the base of the tail. They appear as fleshly, rounded, rubbery growths.

Perianal adenomas grow slowly. As they enlarge, they break through the skin, become secondarily infected, produce pain and interfere with local hygiene. Most of them are not cancers. A few metastasize and end fatally.

Wide local excision is the treatment of choice. Some tumors recur after local removal. Because perianal gland tumors depend upon the male hormone, such recurrences may be held in check by giving estrogens.

Large or ulcerating growths are best treated by a combination of excision and castration.

LIVER

The liver has many vital metabolic functions. They include synthesis of proteins and sugars, removal of wastes from the blood, manufacture of enzymes (including those that cause blood to clot) and detoxification of drugs and poisons.

216

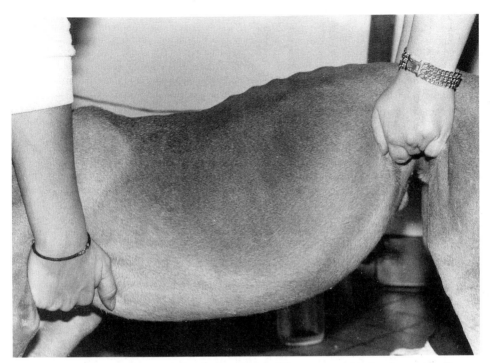
Note the swollen abdomen resulting from *ascites*, in this case caused by heartworm infection.

A common sign of liver disease is *jaundice*, in which bile backs up into the circulation, turning the whites of the eyes yellow and the urine tea-colored.

Ascites is the accumulation of fluid in the abdomen. It is caused by increased venous pressure in the veins that drain into the liver. A dog with ascites has a swollen or bloated look to the abdomen.

Spontaneous bleeding can be a sign of advanced liver disease. Common sites of bleeding are the stomach, intestines and urinary tract. Bruises may appear under the lips and skin.

A dog with impaired liver function appears weak and lethargic, exhibits loss of appetite and weight and may suffer from vomiting and diarrhea, drink excessively and experience pain in the abdomen. Signs of central nervous system involvement in the form of seizures and coma are late manifestations.

A number of diseases, chemicals, drugs and toxins can adversely affect the liver. The liver involvement frequently is just one aspect of a generalized disease such as heartworm infection.

Hepatitis

Inflammation of the liver is called hepatitis. Infectious canine hepatitis and leptospirosis are discussed in the chapter INFECTIOUS DISEASES. The viruses responsible for hepatitis in people may infect the dog. This is just beginning to be investigated.

Chemicals and Drugs

Copper poisoning occurs in the Doberman Pinscher, Bedlington Terrier, West Highland White Terrier and infrequently in other breeds. It is caused by a defect in copper metabolism, which allows toxic amounts of copper to accumulate in the liver. In time this can lead to liver failure and death. Copper poisoning is treated by a low copper diet and medications to remove copper from the system. The disease is inherited. Affected dogs should not be used for breeding.

Chemicals known to induce liver toxicity are carbon tetrachloride, insecticides (chlorinated hydrocarbons such as chlordane and dieldrin) and toxic amounts of lead, phosphorus, selenium, arsenic and iron.

Drugs adversely affecting the liver include some inhaled anesthetic gases, antibiotics, dewormers, diuretics, acetaminophen, anticonvulsants, androgens and steroid preparations. Most of these cause problems only if the recommended dosage is exceeded, or when administered over long periods.

A blockage of the bile ducts by gallstones or liver flukes is not common but becomes a consideration when a dog has jaundice of unknown cause. Metastatic cancer to the liver is another consideration.

Treatment of liver insufficiency depends upon making the diagnosis. This requires hospitalization and a complete workup. Special diagnostic studies (ultrasound, CT scan, liver biopsy) may be needed. Prognosis for recovery is related to the duration and extent of the damage and to whether the cause can be corrected.

PANCREAS

The pancreas has two main functions. The first is to provide digestive enzymes; the second is to make insulin for sugar metabolism.

Pancreatic Insufficiency

Pancreatic enzymes are secreted into the small intestine through the pancreatic duct. A lack of these enzymes causes incomplete digestion of foods in the small bowel and a *malabsorption* syndrome.

The acinar cells in the pancreas are responsible for making digestive enzymes. For unknown reasons, these cells can shrink and stop producing. This condition, called *pancreatic acinar cell atrophy*, is quite prevalent in young German Shepherds but can occur in other breeds at any age. It is the most common cause of malabsorption in dogs. A less common cause is inflamed pancreas, discussed below.

Dogs with pancreatic insufficiency typically have a voracious appetite, pass large, gray cow-pie stools, lose weight and have oily hair around the anus from undigested fat.

Treatment: The single most important step is to feed a *highly digestible diet*. Prescription diets (Hills i/d or k/d) are available through your veterinarian. Simultaneously, the missing enzymes are given by mouth. An antacid, or acid inhibitor such as Tagamet or Zantac, is a useful adjunct. Fat-soluble vitamins should be supplemented. In most cases, lifetime treatment is required.

Diabetes (Diabetes Mellitus)

Sugar diabetes affects all organs. It is the result of inadequate production of insulin by the pancreas. Insulin is secreted directly into the circulation. It acts upon cell membranes, enabling sugar to enter the cells where it is metabolized to form energy.

Without insulin the body can't utilize sugar in the blood. It builds up. Soon there is an excess that the kidneys must get rid of. This results in excessive urination. There is a need to compensate for the fluid loss by drinking lots of water.

Glycosuria is the name given to sugar in the urine. When a urine sugar test is positive, diabetes can be suspected.

Acids (ketones) are formed in the blood of diabetics because of inability to metabolize sugar. High levels lead to a condition called *ketoacidosis*. It is characterized by acetone on the breath (a sweetish odor that smells like nail polish remover), labored rapid breathing and eventually diabetic coma.

In the early stage of diabetes a dog will try to compensate for the inability to metabolize blood sugar by eating more food. Later, with the effects of malnourishment, there is a drop in appetite.

Accordingly, the signs of early diabetes are frequent urination, drinking lots of water, a large appetite and unexplained loss of weight. The laboratory findings are sugar and acetone in the urine, and a high blood sugar.

In more advanced cases there is loss of appetite, vomiting, weakness, ketone breath, dehydration, labored breathing, lethargy and finally coma. Cataracts are common in the diabetic dog.

Treatment: Dietary control and daily injections of insulin can regulate most diabetic dogs, allowing them to lead a normal life. The amount of insulin cannot be predicted on the basis of weight. It must be established for each individual. It is important for success of initial therapy that each dog be hospitalized to determine the daily insulin requirement.

Dietary Management: Obesity greatly reduces tissue responsiveness to insulin and makes diabetes difficult to control. Accordingly, overweight dogs should be put on a diet until they reach their ideal body weight. A prescription diet (Hills r/d) is available for weight reduction.

Daily caloric requirements are determined by the weight and activity of the individual. Once established, the quantity of food can be determined by dividing the daily caloric requirements by the amount of calories per cup or can.

As insulin requirements vary with the diet, it is important that the number of calories your dog takes in be kept constant from day to day. It is equally important to maintain a strict schedule for insulin injections and exercise.

To avoid high levels of blood sugar after eating (*hyperglycemia*), it is best to feed the daily amount at six-hour intervals. Hyperglycemia is much more likely to occur when feeding soft, moist foods because the carbohydrates in these rations are derived from cornstarch, a simple carbohydrate that is rapidly absorbed. Dry and canned foods are less likely to produce hyperglycemia because they contain complex carbohydrates that are absorbed in a more uniform fashion.

As a good alternative, prescription diabetic diets (g/d or w/d) are available from Hills Pet Products. These diets more closely resemble the recommendations for human diabetics.

Your dog's diet may have to be changed from time to time for periods of stress, illness and loss of appetite. Follow your veterinarian's instructions.

Insulin substitutes by mouth (such as those used for people) have been relatively unsuccessful in treating diabetic dogs.

Insulin Overdose

When an overdose of insulin is given, it causes a drop in blood sugar below normal level. This is called *hypoglycemia*. Suspect this if your dog appears confused, disoriented or drowsy, or shivers, staggers about or collapses.

Treatment: If the dog remains conscious and is able to swallow, give it sugar in water, candy, syrup or orange juice. If unable to treat, seek professional help.

Inflamed Pancreas (Acute Pancreatitis)

Sudden swelling of the pancreas typically occurs in dogs two to eleven years of age (the average is six years). Individuals prone to acute pancreatitis are: (a) house pets fed table scraps; (b) those poorly exercised; (c) those that indulge in overeating and (d) overweight spayed females.

In mild cases the signs are obscure and perhaps easily overlooked. There may be loss of appetite, periodic vomiting and diarrhea. The more serious form comes on suddenly as an acute pain in the abdomen with a rigid abdominal wall. The pain is caused by release of digestive enzymes into the abdominal cavity, leading to auto-digestion of surrounding tissues.

If a dog recovers from an acute episode, the pancreas may not return to normal. Instead the dog may acquire diabetes or a malabsorption syndrome secondary to pancreatic insufficiency.

It is important to distinguish between acute pancreatitis and other causes of painful abdomen, such as bloat. Treatment is quite different.

10

Respiratory System

THE DOG'S RESPIRATORY SYSTEM is made up of the nasal passages, throat, voice box, windpipe and bronchial tubes. The latter branch and become progressively smaller until they open into the air sacs. It is here that air exchanges with the blood.

The lungs are composed of the breathing tubes, air sacs and blood vessels.

The ribs and muscles of the chest, along with the diaphragm, function as a bellows, moving air into and out of the lungs.

A dog normally breathes about ten to thirty times a minute at rest. It takes about twice as long to exhale as it does to inhale. Respiratory motion should be smooth, even, unrestrained.

A sustained increase in the rate of breathing at rest, or the presence of coarse breathing, wheezing, rasping, coughing, and bubbling in the chest, indicates an abnormal state.

Bronchoscopy

Bronchoscopy is an endoscopic procedure in which a rigid (or flexible) instrument is inserted into the larynx, trachea and bronchi to view the upper respiratory tract. The procedure does require heavy sedation or general anesthesia.

Bronchoscopy is a useful diagnostic technique in the investigation of chronic cough of unknown cause, hemoptysis (coughing up blood) and pneumonia. It can be used to locate and remove foreign bodies in the upper airways and to remove copious bronchial secretions. Biopsies, washings for cytology and cultures can be obtained through the bronchoscope, thereby making treatment more precise.

ABNORMAL BREATHING

Rapid Breathing

Rapid breathing can be caused by pain, emotional stress, fever and overheating (for example, overexertion or overheated surroundings). Other conditions to consider are shock (reduced circulation, hemorrhage), lung and heart disease (not enough oxygen in the blood) and acid buildup (diabetes, kidney disease). Dehydration caused by prolonged diarrhea and various toxic states will cause the dog to breathe rapidly.

An increased rate of breathing at rest suggests a diseased state and veterinarian examination is necessary.

Panting

Panting is a normal process by which dogs lower their body temperature. This is accomplished by the evaporation of water from the mouth, tongue and lungs, and by the exchange of cooler air for the warm air in the lungs.

When panting is rapid and labored and accompanied by an anxious look, the possibility of heat stroke should be considered (see EMERGENCIES: *Heat Stroke*).

Noisy Breathing

Noisy or stertorous breathing is synonymous with obstructed breathing. It is a loud snorting or snorting sound that originates from the throat.

Elongated Soft Palate

Bulldogs, Pugs, Pekingese, Chows and breeds with "pushed-in" faces frequently show some degree of airway obstruction manifested by mouth breathing, snorting and snoring. These difficulties are more pronounced during exercise and when the dog is hot. They tend to get worse as the dog gets older. In some cases the mouth breathing may be associated with collapsed nostrils.

The problem in the Bulldog breeds is that the palate partially blocks the opening into the voice box. In time, the secondary changes in the voice box lead to attacks of acute airway obstruction (see *Laryngeal Collapse* below). Removal of the soft palate before laryngeal involvement often will give permanent relief.

Croupy Breathing

Croupy breathing, or *stridor*, is a high-pitched wheezing sound produced by air passing through a narrowed voice box. It indicates an acute blockage in the larynx caused by inflammation, foreign body, vocal cord paralysis or tumor. When the onset is sudden, the most likely diagnosis is laryngitis.

Wheezing

A wheeze is a whistling that occurs when a dog forcefully breathes in or out. It indicates narrowing or spasm in the windpipe or bronchial tubes. Tight deep-seated wheezes are best heard with a stethoscope. Causes of wheezing are chronic lung disease, congestive heart failure and tumors or growths in the airways.

Shallow Breathing

Shallow breathing is seen with conditions that restrict the motion of the rib cage. In most cases it is associated with splinting. To avoid the pain of a deep breath, the dog breathes rapidly but less deeply. Pain of pleurisy and rib fracture causes splinting.

Fluid in the chest (blood, pus or serum) produces restricted breathing but without pain.

COUGH

Cough is a reflex that is initiated by an irritant in the air passages. It is a sign common to many diseases that occur in the dog.

A cough may be caused by an infection (virus, bacteria, fungus or parasite), an inhaled irritant such as smoke or chemicals, foreign objects such as grass seeds and food particles, and pressure from tight collars or growths of the air passages. Some coughs are caused by allergies.

The type of cough often suggests its location and probable cause:

- A high, harsh, dry, barking cough is typical of kennel cough (cough without phlegm).
- A moist bubbling cough indicates fluid and phlegm.
- A high, weak, gagging cough associated with swallowing or licking of the lips is characteristic of tonsillitis and sore throat.
- A deep, tight, wheezy cough is heard with chronic and allergic bronchitis.
- A spasm of prolonged coughing, which follows exercise or occurs at night, suggests heart disease.
- A cough that occurs after drinking may be caused by leakage of fluid into the windpipe from faulty closure of the epiglottis.

Coughs are self-perpetuating. Coughing itself irritates the airways, dries out the mucus lining and lowers resistance to infection—leading to further coughing.

Treatment: Only minor coughs of brief duration should be treated without professional assistance. Coughs accompanied by fever, difficulty breathing, discharge from the eyes and nose or other signs of a serious illness require veterinary attention.

It is important to identify and correct any other contributing problem. Air pollutants such as cigarette smoke, aerosol insecticides, house dust and perfumes should be eliminated from the atmosphere. Nose, throat, lung and heart disorders should be treated if present.

A variety of children's cough suppressants are available at drug stores for the treatment of mild coughs. Their purpose is to decrease the frequency and severity of the cough. They do not treat the disease or condition causing it. Therefore, overuse may delay diagnosis and treatment. If you decide to use one of these preparations, the dose for puppies is the same as that for infants. Medium-size dogs should be given a child's dose and large dogs an adult's dose. Administer every four to six hours. (Cough suppressants should not be given to dogs in whom phlegm is being brought up or swallowed. These coughs are clearing unwanted material from the airway.)

VOICE BOX (LARYNX)

The larynx is a short oblong box located in the throat above the windpipe. It is composed of cartilage and contains the vocal cords, which in dogs are large and prominent. A bark is produced when air is forced rapidly out of the lungs through the larynx.

The larynx is the most sensitive cough area in the body. At the top of the larynx is the epiglottis, a leaflike flap that covers it during swallowing, keeping food from going down the windpipe.

Disorders of the larynx give rise to coughing, croupy breathing and hoarseness.

Hoarseness and Loss of Bark (Laryngitis)

Hoarseness and loss of volume of the bark often is caused by excessive barking or coughing (voice strain). It improves with voice rest and treatment of the cough when present. When the condition becomes chronic, vocal cord paralysis or some condition causing narrowing of the voice box should be suspected.

Acute laryngitis in the dog usually is just one aspect of a more extensive process such as tonsillitis or acute tracheobronchitis (see *Kennel Cough*).

Laryngeal Blockage

Laryngospasm

Sudden spasm of the vocal cords may cut off the air supply. The dog becomes frantic in an effort to get air, turns blue at the mouth and collapses. Recovery usually is rapid. Recurrent attacks suggest to many owners a seizure disorder.

Laryngospasm usually is caused by a drop of mucus that falls upon the vocal cords from the soft palate. Thus it is associated with chronic throat irritations.

224

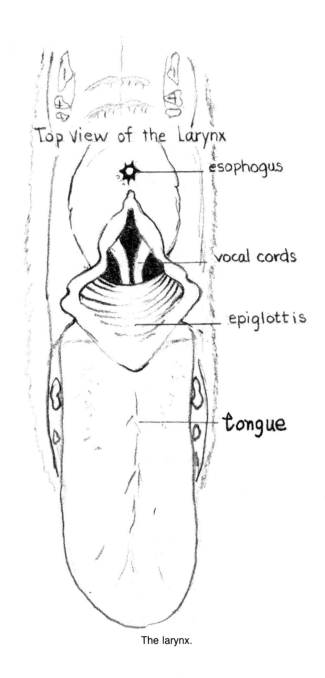

Top View of the Larynx

esophogus

vocal cords

epiglottis

tongue

The larynx.

Foreign Object in the Voice Box

The sudden onset of severe coughing and respiratory distress in a healthy dog suggests a foreign body caught in the larynx. *This is an emergency.* Get your dog to the veterinarian as quickly as possible.

If the dog collapses, not enough air is getting through. Immediately perform the Heimlich maneuver. Lay the dog on its side, place your palms just behind the last rib and give four quick thrusts. The maneuver thrusts the diaphragm upward and produces a forceful exhalation of air. Usually this dislodges the object (commonly it is a large piece of meat). Check the mouth to see if the object has been dislodged; if not, repeat the thrusts.

Foreign bodies caught in the larynx are not common. Most food particles are of little consequence because the resulting cough expels them.

(**Note:** If your dog is choking, gagging and retching, there is probably a foreign body such as a bone, splinter or rubber ball caught in the throat. Open the mouth and see if you can find the cause of the trouble—see ORAL CAVITY: *Throat.*)

Vocal Cord Paralysis

This is an acquired condition in middle-aged and older dogs of the large breeds. It also occurs as a congenital defect in young Siberian Huskies, Bouvier des Flandres and Bull Terriers.

It can be recognized by a characteristic croupy noise during inspiration, or "roaring," as it is sometimes called. It comes on gradually and may appear at first only after strenuous activity or emotional upsets. Sometimes there is a progressive weakening of the bark, or hoarseness, finally ending in a croaky whisper. Later noisy breathing, difficult breathing, reduced exercise tolerance and fainting episodes can occur, especially when the dog is upset or overexcited.

The diagnosis is made by examination of the vocal cords using a laryngoscope. Paralyzed vocal cords come together in the midline and produce a marked narrowing of the air passage.

This condition sometimes can be helped by surgery.

Laryngeal Trauma

Choke chain injuries can fracture the hyoid bone and/or cause compression damage to the nerves of the pharynx and larynx. Dogs with such injuries often breathe normally at rest but show respiratory distress when they exercise. These injuries can be prevented in dogs that lunge on the leash by using a chest halter instead of a collar.

Laryngeal Collapse

This is the final stage of long-standing problems that affect the voice boxes of dogs with an elongated palate or a vocal cord paralysis. At this stage the opening through the larynx is quite small. Any change in the dog's need for air can cause a sudden collapse.

Treatment: If a veterinarian is not immediately available give the dog a mild sedative or tranquilizer and move the dog to humid atmosphere. Humidifiers are helpful, but if one is not available, then steam from a shower can be used. Do not overheat the atmosphere. This can interfere with the dog's cooling mechanism and make matters worse.

226

BREATHING TUBES (TRACHEA AND BRONCHI)

Foreign Bodies in the Windpipe

The sudden onset of severe paroxysmal coughing and respiratory distress suggests aspiration of a foreign body. When the object is lodged low in the airway, the signs may not be so dramatic and the dog may present with recurrent bouts of pneumonia.

Grass seeds and food particles are the most common foreign material of sufficient size to lodge in the windpipe or bronchus when inhaled by the dog. Most of these are quickly coughed up. When the object becomes fixed in the airway, it causes intense irritation and swelling of the passage. Mucus collects below the obstruction and forms an ideal media for bacterial growth and infection.

Lungworms can cause respiratory signs much like those of chronic bronchitis or a bronchial foreign body (see WORMS: *Uncommon Worm Parasites*).

Treatment: Give your dog a mild sedative or tranquilizer to settle the nerves and go to your veterinarian. Cough medicines should be avoided since they serve no purpose and delay treatment. Foreign objects can be located by chest X ray, or located and removed by bronchoscopy.

Persistent foreign bodies can lead to localized dilatation and infection of the breathing tubes (see *Bronchiectasis*).

Collapsed Windpipe (Tracheal Collapse)

Collapse of the cartilages of the windpipe occurs as an acquired (or occasionally congenital) defect in Chihuahuas, Pomeranians, Toy Poodles and other Toy breed dogs, but usually does not cause problems until the dog is mature. Signs are croupy breathing and a honking cough.

Weight control is an important factor in management. Overweight dogs are far more symptomatic, as are those with coexistent heart and lung disease. Medical treatment involves cough suppressants, bronchodilators and antibiotics to treat bacterial infections of the trachea. If not successful, surgery may be required.

| Normal Trachea | Partial Collapse | Complete Collapse |

Collapsed tracheal cartilages lack rigidity and are drawn into the air passages during inhalation.   *(Karen Wyatt)*

227

Kennel Cough (Acute Tracheobronchitis)

Kennel cough is a highly contagious respiratory infection in dogs. Its name comes from the fact that dogs often catch it while boarding at a kennel, where they are exposed to other dogs that either have the disease or are carriers of it. Several viruses and bacteria, alone or in combination, are the causative agents. The most common ones are canine adenovirus 2 (CAV 2), canine parainfluenza virus (CPI) and the bacteria *Bordetella bronchiseptica*. Other bacteria are occasionally found, but only as secondary invaders perpetuating the cough.

While kennel cough is the most common form of tracheobronchitis in dogs, other causes of inflammation of the lining of the upper airway, including distemper and canine infectious hepatitis, should be considered in the differential diagnosis, especially if the dog was not immunized against them.

A *harsh, dry, spastic cough* is the characteristic sign of this illness. Otherwise, the dog looks bright and alert, eats relatively well and seems to maintain an overall good condition. Most cases are mild. Given rest and proper care, these dogs recover in two weeks.

In puppies, kennel cough is a more serious illness. It may be accompanied by nasal congestion. The narrow airways of youngsters are prone to obstruction. Puppies may need intensive support to loosen thick secretions, improve breathing and prevent pneumonia. This is also true of Toy breeds.

Treatment: Dogs suspected of having kennel cough should be isolated so as not to infect others. Be sure to take your dog's temperature every day. A fever indicates a complication.

Rest and proper humidification of the atmosphere are important items in the treatment of bronchitis. Confine your dog in a warm room and use a home vaporizer. A cold-steam vaporizer offers some advantage over a heat vaporizer because it is less likely to cause additional breathing problems because of the heat.

Daily exercise of a moderate nature is beneficial, as it assists in bronchial drainage. Strenuous exercise should be avoided.

Coughing helps to clear the bronchial tree, but excessive spasms of dry, unproductive cough can cause greater irritation and lead to exhaustion. Cough suppressants may be indicated, especially if the dog is unable to rest (see *Cough*).

Antibiotics are used to prevent secondary bacterial invaders and to treat *B. bronchiseptica* when this is suspected. They have no affect on viruses. Ampicillin and chloromycetin may be used.

Vaccines effective against some of the kennel cough viruses are available (see INFECTIOUS DISEASES: *Vaccinations*). They will not prevent all cases.

Chronic bronchitis is a common sequel to kennel cough.

Chronic Bronchitis (Persistent Cough)

A persistent cough of several weeks or months duration suggests the possibility of chronic bronchitis. This problem tends to affect adult dogs of the smaller breeds.

The harsh, dry cough may or may not be productive and is worse with exercise and excitement. With acute exacerbations, coughing episodes may end with retching and expectoration of foamy saliva. Low-grade fever is common. Appetite and condition are well maintained unless the cough is continuous.

Many cases of chronic bronchitis begin as another respiratory infection such as kennel cough. The natural defenses of the respiratory tract are weakened by the primary infection and it is easy for secondary invaders to take over. Because of the persistent cough, the respiratory mucosa is damaged and a cycle is established in which the cough becomes self-perpetuating.

In some cases a careful history reveals an association with dust, cigarette smoke or other environmental irritants in the atmosphere.

Treatment: Eliminate atmospheric pollutants such as dust and cigarette smoke. Minimize stress, fatigue and excitement. It is most important to correct an overweight problem through diet and moderate exercise. Leash walking is good exercise. Use a halter instead of a choke chain to prevent injury to the trachea.

Bronchodilators help to facilitate breathing and reduce respiratory fatigue. Mild tranquilizers and cough suppressants are indicated for a tiring cough.

Acute flare-ups are associated with secondary bacterial infections. The phlegm should be cultured and a specific antibiotic selected by the veterinarian. It should be given for a minimum of ten days.

Although complete recovery is unlikely, most dogs that are well cared for can live comfortably for many years.

Effective treatment of acute respiratory infections helps to prevent this complication.

Asthma (Allergic Bronchitis)

Asthma, or bronchial asthma, is a form of allergy that affects the larger breathing tubes. It is accompanied by cough and wheezing. The wheezing is heard as the dog exhales and usually it is loud enough to be heard with the naked ear.

Pollens are the chief cause of asthmatic attacks (see SKIN: *Allergies*). Repeated bouts can eventually lead to chronic lung disease.

Asthma is uncommon in the dog.

Treatment: Asthmatic dogs should begin to improve in an allergy free atmosphere. Antihistamines can be quite helpful. They have a dilating effect on the airways, reduce irritation and are mildly sedative. Benadryl, Chlor-Trimeton, and Coricidin are effective preparations. They may cause drowsiness. When this occurs, reduce the dose or give the medication less often.

Steroids are sometimes used in the management of the asthmatic dog. They should be administered only under veterinary supervision.

Bronchiectasis

This is the name given to a condition in which one or more of the bronchial tubes becomes dilated and sacklike. The dilatation may be localized, or it can extend down the airways in a cylindrical fashion.

Bronchiectasis usually presents as a complication of persistent airway disease, particularly chronic and allergic bronchitis. Chronic coughing and repeated infections damage the lining of the bronchial tubes, allowing them to increase in diameter.

Localized bronchiectasis can occur below a point of bronchial obstruction caused by an inhaled foreign body or a tumor.

The symptoms are long-standing cough with the production of purulent sputum, periodic fever and loss of weight and condition. Bronchiectasis often will be mistaken for chronic bronchitis. The exact diagnosis requires special X-ray studies or bronchoscopy.

Treatment: When the disease is localized to one segment of the lung, surgical removal is the treatment of choice. If the disease is generalized, the treatment is similar to that for chronic bronchitis.

The dog with bronchiectasis is extremely susceptible to respiratory infections. Without vigorous and often continued antibiotic therapy, the dog will have frequent bouts of pneumonia.

LUNGS

Pneumonia

Pneumonia is an infection of the lungs. Usually it is classified according to its cause: infectious or noninfectious.

Infectious pneumonia is associated with bacteria most often, with viruses such as those of kennel cough and canine distemper, with rickettsia (Rocky Mountain spotted fever, canine ehrlichiosis) and rarely with fungi and parasites.

Primary bacterial pneumonia tends to attack puppies and old dogs. Dogs with persistent infection of the airways, and those who are immune-suppressed or chronically il., are especially prone to a bacterial pneumonia that is secondary to these causes. Fungal pneumonia ordinarily does not occur in dogs unless they are debilitated, on immunosuppressive drugs or taking long-term steroids.

Aspiration pneumonia can occur with chronic regurgitation, loss of consciousness, general anesthesia and forced administration of mineral oil, food or drugs.

Chemical pneumonia can follow smoke damage from fires and the ingestion of hydrocarbons such as gasoline or kerosene.

The general symptoms of pneumonia are high fever, rapid breathing, splinting, cough, fast pulse, rattling and bubbling in the chest. When severe enough to cause oxygen lack, you will notice a blue cast to the conjunctiva of the lower eyelid (cyanosis).

Dogs with pneumonia characteristically sit with their heads extended and elbows turned out to allow for greater expansion of the chest. When lying down, their chest cavity is further restricted. This interferes with air exchange, so they avoid it.

Treatment: Pneumonia is a serious condition and requires confirmation by laboratory diagnosis and chest X-ray.

Until a veterinarian is available, move your dog to warm, dry quarters and humidify the air. Give plenty of water. Treat the fever with buffered or enteric coated aspirin or Tylenol. Do not give cough medicine. Coughing in pneumonia helps to clear the airways.

Most cases of pneumonia respond to vigorous treatment that includes antibiotics specific for the causative agent. Your veterinarian will select an appropriate one based on phlegm culture and sensitivity tests.

Aspiration associated with general anesthesia can be prevented by keeping the stomach empty for twelve hours prior to elective surgery.

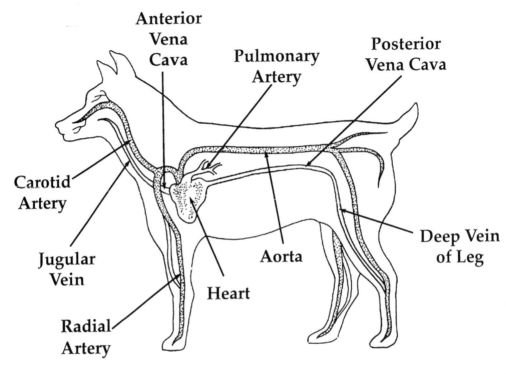

Anterior Vena Cava

Pulmonary Artery

Posterior Vena Cava

Carotid Artery

Jugular Vein

Radial Artery

Heart

Aorta

Deep Vein of Leg

Anatomy of the circulatory system.

(Karen Wyatt)

11

Circulatory System

THE CIRCULATORY SYSTEM is composed of the heart, the blood and the blood vessels.

HEART

The heart is a pump made up of four chambers: the right atrium and right ventricle, and the left atrium and left ventricle. The two sides of the heart are separated by a muscular wall. In the normal heart, blood cannot get from one side to the other without first going through the general circulation, or the pulmonary circulation. Four valves are present. Their function is to keep blood flowing in one direction. When the valves are diseased, blood can leak backward, creating difficulties.

Physiology

Blood, which is pumped out of the left ventricle into the aorta, passes through arteries of progressively smaller caliber until it reaches the capillary beds of the skin, muscles, brain and internal organs. It is conducted back to the heart through veins of progressively larger diameter, finally reaching the right atrium via two large veins called the anterior and posterior *vena cavae*.

The blood then passes into the right ventricle and out into the pulmonary circulation through the pulmonary artery. The pulmonary artery branches into smaller vessels and finally into capillaries (around the air sacs), where gas exchange occurs. From here the blood returns via the pulmonary vein to the ventricles—thus completing the circle.

The beating of the heart is controlled by its own internal nervous system. The force and rate of the heartbeat is influenced by outside nervous and hormonal factors, too. Thus the rate speeds up when the dog exercises, becomes excited, runs fever, is overheated, is in shock—or in any circumstance in which more blood flow to the tissues is needed.

Heart rhythms follow a fixed pattern that can be seen on an electrocardiogram. Whether the heart beats fast or slow, the sequence in which the various muscle fibers contract remains the same. This sequence causes a synchronized beat, allowing both ventricles to empty at the same time. Heart disease can upset this normal pattern, causing arrhythmias.

The arteries and veins also are under nervous and hormonal influences. They can expand or contract to maintain a correct blood pressure.

There are outward physical signs that help to determine if a dog's heart and circulation are working properly. Familiarize yourself with the normal findings so you can recognize abnormal signs if they appear.

Pulse

The pulse, which is a reflection of the heartbeat, is easily detected by feeling the artery located in the groin (femoral artery). With your dog standing or lying on its back, feel along the inside of the thigh where the leg and body are joined. Press with your fingers until you locate the pulsation. Alternately, take the pulse by pressing against the rib cage over the heart. With the dog standing, feel the chest pulse just below the elbow joint. If the heart is enlarged

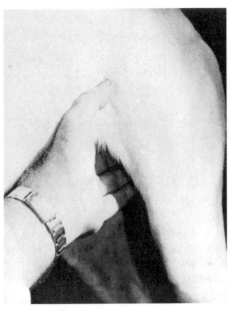
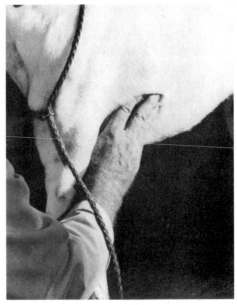

To take your dog's pulse, feel along the inside of one thigh where the leg joins the body. Press with your fingers to locate the pulsation.

Another way to take the pulse is to feel for the heartbeat in back of the left elbow.

(J. Clawson)

234

or diseased, you may be able to detect a buzzing, or vibration, over the chest wall.

The pulse rate, which is the same as the heart rate, can be determined by counting the number of beats in a minute. Most dogs run a rate of 60 to 160 beats per minute at rest. In large dogs it is somewhat slower and in small dogs somewhat faster. It is faster in puppies. Well-conditioned, athletic dogs run a slower pulse (see APPENDIX *Pulse*).

The pulse should be strong, steady and regular. A slight alteration in rate as your dog breathes in and out is normal. An exceedingly fast pulse can indicate anxiety, fever, anemia, blood loss, dehydration, shock, infection, heat stroke or heart (and lung) disease. A very slow pulse can indicate heart disease, pressure on the brain or an advanced morbid condition causing collapse of the circulation.

An erratic, irregular or disordered pulse indicates an arrythmia, which is a serious condition. When untreated, it can cause the heart to fail.

Various drugs your dog might be taking can affect the heart rate and rhythm.

Heart Sounds

Veterinarians use a stethoscope to listen to the heart. You can listen to the heart by placing your ear against the chest. Or you can hold an ordinary drinking glass over the heart and listen through the open end.

The normal heartbeat is divided into two separate sounds. The first is a *LUB*, followed by a slight pause; and then a *DUB*. Put together the sound is *LUB-DUB . . . LUB-DUB . . .* in a steady, regular manner.

When the heart sounds can be heard all over the chest, the heart probably is enlarged. A running together of the sounds, and interrupted rhythm, is abnormal.

Murmurs

Murmurs are caused by a turbulence in the flow of blood through the heart. Serious ones are caused by heart valve disease or birth defects. Anemia can cause a heart murmur.

Not all murmurs are serious. Some are called functional: that is, there is no disease, just a normal degree of turbulence. Your veterinarian can determine whether a murmur is serious or of little consequence.

Thrills

A thrill is caused by turbulence of such a degree that you can feel a buzzing or vibration over the heart. It suggests an obstruction to the flow of blood—for example, a narrowed valve or a hole in the heart. A thrill indicates a heart condition.

Circulation

If you examine the gums or the inner eyelids, you can gain a clue to the adequacy of your dog's circulation. A deep pink color is a sign of good circulation.

The quality of the circulation can be tested by noting the time it takes for the tissue to pink up after the gums have been pressed firmly with a finger. With normal circulation the response is immediate (one second or less). A delay of two seconds suggests poor circulation. When the finger impression remains pale for three seconds or longer, the dog is in shock.

A gray or bluish tinge to the mucus membranes of the lips and tongue is a sign of insufficient oxygen in the blood (cyanosis). It can be seen in heart and lung failure.

CANINE HEART DISEASE

Coronary artery disease, for all intents and purposes, does not occur in dogs.

The major cause of heart disease in dogs is *acquired valvular heart disease*. It is age-related. Other causes of heart disease are birth defects, heartworms and a condition called *cardiomyopathy*.

Congenital Heart Disease (CHD)

Birth defects of the heart account for about 15 percent of cases of heart disease in dogs. They are the most common cause of congestive failure in dogs under a year of age. Older dogs with milder forms of CHD are often asymptomatic, the condition first being discovered on physical examination. There may be a history of fainting (cardiac arrhythmias), low exercise tolerance or stunted growth. Congestive heart failure is a common late sequela.

Almost all forms of congenital heart disease found in people occur in the dog. The most common ones are developmental malformations of the heart valves and septal defects, or holes that connect two of the heart chambers. *Patent ductus arteriosus* is a persistent communication between the aorta and pulmonary artery, which fails to close shortly after birth. Another defect is a marked narrowing of one or more of the major arteries carrying blood from the heart (aortic or pulmonary stenosis). Several defects may occur at the same time.

Most dogs with severe congenital heart defects die in less than a year. However, early detection may allow for surgical correction or medical management, which can prolong life. In dogs there is an hereditary predisposition. Such individuals should not be used for breeding.

Acquired Valvular Heart Disease

This is the most common cause of heart disease in the dog, affecting about one third of dogs over twelve years of age. Changes in the heart valves occur with aging. They undergo degeneration and begin to leak blood backward; this throws an extra strain on the heart muscle.

Occasionally bacteria lodge on the heart valves, forming clumps of infective material containing fibrin and debris. Infected valves become damaged. This condition is called *bacterial endocarditis*. It is less common than chronic valvular degeneration.

A dry, harsh cough is the most common and often the earliest sign of valvular disease. It frequently occurs at night and after exercise.

Many dogs with chronic valvular heart disease remain compensated throughout life and eventually die from other causes. Some develop progressive right- or left-sided congestive heart failure, as described below.

Cardiomyopathy

This is a disease of the heart muscle in which inflammation and scarring cause enlargement of the heart and dilatation of the chambers. Eventually the muscle weakens and the dog develops congestive heart failure.

In most cases the cause is unknown (*idiopathic*), but there appears to be distinct clinical conditions that affect Boxers, Doberman Pinschers, English Cocker Spaniels and dogs of the giant breeds. It occurs most often in young to middle-aged males.

The first indications are those of unexplained lethargy, weight loss, cough, exercise intolerance and shortness of breath. Cardiac arrhythmias may cause fainting. Worsening of weight loss and other signs can occur with surprising rapidity. Acute cardiomyopathy does occur. This is life-threatening.

In a small number of cases there will be an identifiable cause—such as prior infection, hypothyroidism or diabetes. Lyme disease (*Lyme carditis*) is being recognized more frequently as a potential cause of this *secondary* type of myocarditis.

Treatment is difficult and requires intensive veterinary management. Sudden death can occur at any time.

HEART FAILURE

Heart failure may be defined as the inability of the heart to provide adequate circulation to meet the body's needs. It is the end result of weakened heart muscle. It is not a simple condition. The liver, kidneys, lungs and other systems are affected, too, causing a multiple organ-system problem. Most cases represent long-standing conditions that have overstressed or damaged the heart.

When a diseased heart begins to weaken, signs of right- or left-sided failure occur. Symptoms differ. The treatment of heart disease is directed at preventing and treating failure.

Left Heart Failure

When the left ventricle starts to fail, pressure builds up in the pulmonary circulation. The result is lung congestion and accumulation of fluid in the air sacs. In late stages (*pulmonary edema*), dogs cough up a bubbly red fluid and can't get enough oxygen. Aging is the most common predisposing factor in the older dog. In the younger one, it is congenital heart disease (birth defect).

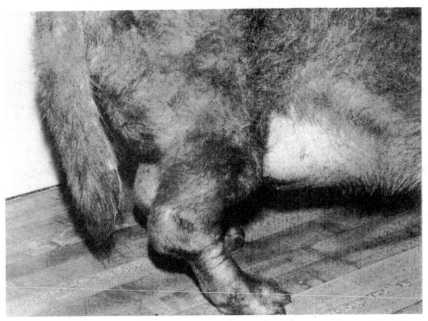

Heart failure, showing swelling of the legs and fluid accumulation beneath the skin.

The early signs of left-sided heart failure are impaired exercise ability and shortness of breath. A hunting dog may tire after an hour or two. As the condition advances, the dog begins to cough when overtaxed by excitement or strenuous exercise. In many cases the cough is first noted at night, about two hours after retiring. You may notice that your dog seems restless and cannot find a comfortable position in which to sleep.

Despite an adequate intake, a dog with heart disease begins to look unthrifty and loses weight and condition. The coat becomes dry and lusterless. The dog's body thins and the muscles over the head waste away, making the bones appear more prominent.

In advanced cases, breathing is labored and the dog assumes a characteristic sitting position with elbows spread apart and head extended to take in more air. The dog may attempt to sleep sitting up. The pulse is rapid, weak, sometimes irregular. A thrill may be felt over the barrel-like chest.

Anxiety and fainting, occurring late in the disease, can be mistaken for a seizure disorder.

Right Heart Failure

When the right heart muscle starts to fail, pressure backs up in the veins, causing congestive heart failure. In advanced cases the gums are gray (*cyanosis*) and the limbs are swollen (*dropsy*).

The early signs of right-sided heart failure are rapid pulse, shortness of breath, loss of pep and intolerance to exercise. In late stages you will observe muscle wasting, enlargement of the liver and spleen and accumulation of fluid in the abdomen (*ascites*), giving a potbellied look. Fluid retention is augmented by the kidneys, which respond to the slowed blood flow by retaining salt and water. You may be able to detect a murmur or thrill.

The most common cause of right heart failure is an already established left-sided heart failure. One of the following—valvular heart disease, heartworms, congenital heart disease, cardiomyopathy or chronic lung disease—usually is at fault.

Treatment of Heart Failure

Treatment of heart failure must be under the supervision of a veterinarian. The first goal of treatment is to remove or correct the underlying cause whenever possible. Congenital heart disease and heartworm infestations are potentially curable if treated in time.

Obesity is a serious complicating factor in all dogs with heart disease. Overweight dogs should be put on a low-calorie diet.

A low-salt diet is of great assistance in treating dogs suffering from congestive heart failure. Most commercial diets contain too much salt. Prescription diets from Hill's Pet Products are available and may be recommended by your veterinarian. Fluid buildup is best managed by the use of diuretics. Potassium supplements may be necessary with the use of diuretics. Vitamin B supplements are indicated in dogs with congestive heart failure.

Restrict activities to those well within your dog's exercise tolerance so as not to overburden the heart.

Various drugs are available that help to increase the force and contraction of the heart, or control arrhythmias. They require veterinary supervision.

These measures can yield substantial results in terms of a more comfortable and more active life for your dog.

HEARTWORMS

Canine heartworm disease, so named because the adult worms live in the right side of the heart, continues to be a common problem. It has been reported in other animals as well—even in man. It is spread by the ordinary mosquito and can be found wherever mosquitoes breed.

Life Cycle

A knowledge of the life cycle of this parasite (*Dirofilaria immitis*) is necessary to understand the rationale for its prevention and treatment.

It requires six to seven months for the worm to complete its cycle.

Infection in the dog begins when larvae from an infective mosquito are deposited in the skin. They burrow into the dog, undergoing several changes in form that eventually lead to the development of small adult worms. This takes three to four months. The worms then make their way into a vein, move to the heart and become sexually mature.

Adult worms can live for about five years in the right side of the heart. As many as 250 worms have been found in a dog. They reach lengths of four to twelve inches. When worms of the opposite sex are present, they mate and the female gives birth to live young called *microfilaria*. Five thousand immature worms can be derived from a single adult female in a day.

Microfilaria must go into a secondary host, the mosquito, to continue their life cycle. While waiting for a mosquito, they can remain alive and viable in the bloodstream of the dog for as long as three years.

When the microfilaria are ingested by a mosquito they develop into infective larvae. In warm (southern) climates this process takes about ten days, but in colder climates it can take as long as forty-eight days. The infective larvae then move to the mouthparts of the mosquito and are ready to infect the new host when the mosquito returns to a dog for a blood meal.

Disease

Adult worms live in the pulmonary arteries and right side of the heart. When the infection rate is low, they will be found in the small pulmonary arteries; when the numbers exceed twenty-five in the average-size dog, they extend into the right ventricle. Numbers greater than fifty frequently result in heartworms being in the right atrium. Less commonly they inhabit the large veins entering the heart, or the veins of the liver.

Heartworms can be carried into the terminal branches of the pulmonary circulation, where they produce clotting of the arteries. This is called *pulmonary thromboembolism*. It can happen by natural migration, or by heartworm treatment when dead or dying worms are carried to the lungs by the bloodstream. This can cause loss of lung function and cardiac failure.

Worms entwined about the heart valves interfere with the mechanics of the heart. In time this extra burden causes right-sided heart failure.

Worms that form clumps in the anterior and posterior vena cavae (or hepatic veins) give rise to a disorder called *vena cava syndrome*. Signs of acute liver failure develop. They include jaundice, blood in the stool, swelling of the abdomen (ascites) and anemia. Collapse and death can occur in two or three days.

Signs: Most infected dogs are asymptomatic. Some dogs can harbor heartworms for several years before showing signs. These signs vary according to the number of worms, duration of infection and immune response of the host. Consequently the disease may be mistaken for another problem.

The most common signs are a soft, deep cough, shortness of breath and intolerance to exercise. After exertion, the cough may be so severe the dog faints. The dog will tire easily, appear unusually weak and listless, lose condition, and may bring up bloody sputum. Weight loss is nearly always present.

As the disease progresses, the dog begins labored breathing at rest. Because of weight loss and increased respiratory effort, the ribs become prominent and the chest starts to bulge.

Congestive heart failure and the vena cava syndrome are signs of advanced disease. Acute pulmonary thromboembolism can lead to collapse and death.

240

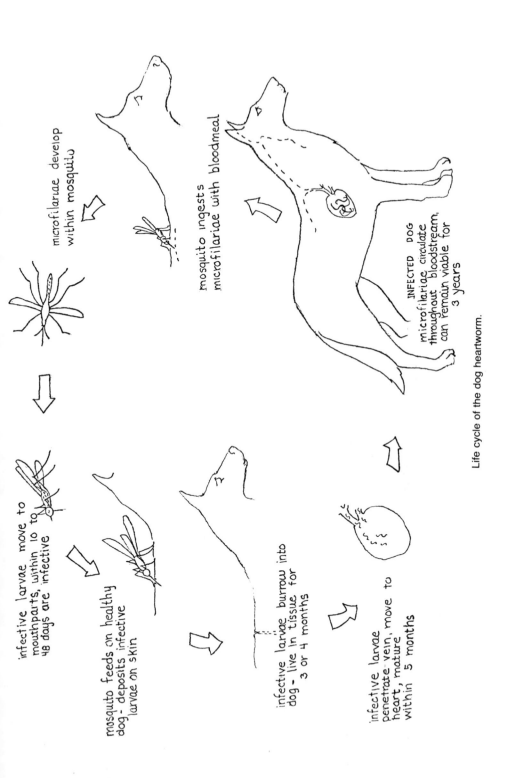

microfilariae develop within mosquito

mosquito ingests microfilariae with bloodmeal

INFECTED DOG
microfilariae circulate throughout bloodstream, can remain viable for 3 years

infective larvae move to mouthparts, within 10 to 48 days are infective

mosquito feeds on healthy dog - deposits infective larvae on skin

infective larvae burrow into dog - live in tissue for 3 or 4 months

infective larvae penetrate vein, move to heart, mature within 5 months

Life cycle of the dog heartworm.

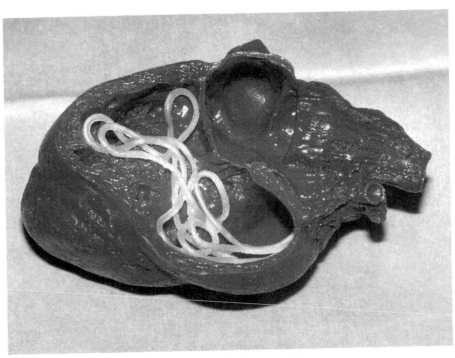

Heartworms in the right ventricle.

Laboratory Diagnosis: The finding of microfilaria in the bloodstream of the dog is an indication of adult worms in the heart.

Various tests are available to detect the characteristic parasites in a sample of blood. However, they are not always 100 percent accurate because:

1. There could be only one sex of worms in the heart—therefore no microfilaria. (Female worms are more resistant to host defenses.)
2. Some dogs make antibodies that destroy the microfilaria, or they may have been destroyed by prior treatment.
3. The adult worms may be sexually immature or too old to reproduce when the blood test is taken—again, no microfilaria.
4. The concentration of microfilaria in the bloodstream may be too small to be detected by the blood test.

It has been estimated that a number of infected dogs do not show circulating microfilaria on a standard blood test. These dogs suffer from what is called *occult* infection. It is now possible to diagnose occult infections by blood tests that detect the adult worms instead of the microfilaria.

There is yet another type of microfilaria that can be present in dogs tested for heartworms. It is called *Dipetalonema*. It is a harmless worm living under the skin of dogs. Its main importance rests in the fact that its microfilaria may be mistaken for those of heartworm.

For the above reasons dogs suspected of having heartworms sometimes require X rays, electrocardiograms, repeat blood tests for microfilaria and occult heartworm tests to establish the diagnosis.

Treatment: Because the treatment is complex and potentially dangerous, it should be undertaken only with veterinary supervision. Before any drugs containing arsenic are started, there should be a careful evaluation to see if your dog is healthy enough to withstand therapy. If the dog has heart failure or liver or kidney insufficiency (from long-standing disease), these should be treated to ensure optimum health.

The first step in ridding your dog of heartworms is to administer an agent to kill the adult worms (*adulticide therapy*). The most effective drug against adult worms continues to be the *thiacetarsamide*. It is administered intravenously in two doses each day for two days. Significant adverse reactions include loss of appetite, cough, vomiting and jaundice. Treatment may have to be suspended if one or more of these side effects is noted.

After thiacetarsamide has been given, the dog must be rested for several weeks to allow the body to absorb the dead worms. If exertion comes too soon, a large mass of dead worms might be dislodged and travel to the lungs, causing acute pulmonary thromboembolism with loss of lung function and cardiac failure. Buffered or coated aspirin before and after treatment seems to reduce this risk, especially in dogs with a heavy burden of worms.

Occasionally adult worms are removed surgically. Surgery is reserved for critically ill dogs—those too sick to take the medication, or having a greater risk of lung complications from dead worms.

The second step is to kill the microfilaria (*filaricide therapy*). Here it is necessary to wait three to six weeks to give your dog time to recover from the effects of killing the adult worms.

Currently two drugs are commonly used (although not approved) for this purpose. They are Ivermectin and Levamisole.

Dogs to be treated with *Ivermectin* are admitted to the hospital in the morning. Ivermectin is given by mouth and the dog is observed for six or eight hours for possible adverse reactions. The more common side effects include listlessness, weakness, stumbling gait, vomiting and diarrhea. Seizures, coma and death can occur, but this is rare. Most reactions are mild, although occasionally a dog will require intravenous fluids and corticosteroids. Shock and death have occurred in Collies and Collie crosses. Ivermectin should not be used in these dogs without further testing.

Dramatic declines in microfilaria counts occur within the first few hours. At three weeks, 90 percent of dogs will be microfilaria-free. At this time the dog should return for a microfilaria concentration blood test. If it is negative, begin prevention therapy as discussed below.

If the concentration test is positive, repeat it in one week to see if the remaining microfilaria have been killed in the interim. If it is still positive, treat again with Ivermectin.

If after a second course of Ivermectin, the concentration test continues to remain positive, then most likely adult heartworms have managed to survive the adulticide therapy. Confirm this with an occult heartworm test.

Levamisole will eliminate 90 percent of microfilaria. It is given in an oral dose of 4.5 to 5.0 mg per pound body weight per day for seven to fourteen days. The most common side effect is vomiting. This can be minimized by giving the drug with a small meal or dividing the daily dose. Levamisole should not be given to a dog that has not recently eaten.

More serious side reactions include lethargy, diarrhea, muscle tremors and stiffness. If these occur, the drug should be stopped.

Perform a microfilaria concentration blood test seven days after treatment. If positive, repeat the treatment for five to seven days. If negative, you still have to wait several weeks and repeat it to be sure there is no recurrence from surviving adult worms. When the second concentration test is negative, begin prevention therapy.

Prevention

It is important that all dogs six months or older be tested for heartworms *before* starting a prevention program. These tests should be repeated semiannually or annually, depending on the prevalence of heartworm in the area.

There are a number of drugs in current use for the prevention of heartworms. They are available through your veterinarian.

Diethylcarbamazine (DEC) has proved to be a very safe drug when given to heartworm-negative dogs. It is given orally on a daily basis. The drug kills the infective larvae before they mature into young adults and migrate to the heart. It does not remain in the bloodstream, which is why it is necessary to keep your dog on it all the time. If you should miss a dose or two, the infective larvae could pass unharmed through the particular stage when they were susceptible to the drug.

Dogs started on (DEC) must be blood-tested to insure that they are microfilaria-free. If microfilaria are found in the blood, the drug should not be given because fatal reactions can occur. Instead, follow the instructions under *Disease: Treatment.*

Assuming that your dog has been tested and found microfilaria-free, administer DEC at a rate of 15 mg per pound body weight per day. Various tablets containing DEC, including Carbam, Filaribits and Nemacide, are available. Consult your veterinarian to determine the appropriate dose for the weight of your dog.

Drugs containing DEC have an extremely bitter taste, difficult to disguise. *Filaribits* is a chewable tablet that combines DEC with a formula for masking the bitter taste. It is well accepted by most dogs.

Interceptor (*milbemycin oxime*) is an orally administered heartworm preventative that, like DEC, can produce shock if the dog has circulating microfilaria. It is essential to clear all microfilaria before using this product. It is given once a month. The dosage is 0.23 mg per pound body weight. It is safe to use in Collies and Collie crosses.

Ivermectin (Heartguard-30) has recently received FDA approval as a heartworm *preventative*. It is given orally once a month. The dose is 1 to 2.5 *micrograms* per pound body weight. Ivermectin's advantages over DEC are that dogs do not need to be free of heartworms for a preventive program to be started, and larvae infecting the dog for as many as two months previously are prevented from developing into adults. One of three tablet sizes is used, depending on the weight of the dog. Adverse drug reactions have been noted in Collies and related crosses. Ivermectin should be avoided in these individuals or used only with veterinary approval.

If you live in an area where mosquitoes are a year-round problem, you should start your puppy on a heartworm preventative program at nine to twelve weeks old and continue giving the drug for the rest of the dog's life. If you live in an area where seasonal considerations make it unnecessary to administer the drug all twelve months, start your dog on the drug one month before the mosquito season and continue it for two months beyond the first frost.

In theory, the best way to prevent heartworms is to keep your dog from being bitten by a mosquito. Unfortunately, mosquito control can never be 100 percent effective.

Areas of most frequent heartworm infestation are along coastal regions where swamps or other bodies of brackish water provide ideal conditions for mosquitoes to breed. Since mosquitoes have a narrow flight range, in many cases spraying areas around kennels can be partially effective.

Dogs can get reasonable protection if kept indoors in the late afternoons and evenings when mosquitoes are feeding.

ANEMIA

Anemia is a deficiency of red blood cells in the circulation. The average life span of red cells in the dog is 110 to 120 days. The purpose of these cells is to carry oxygen to the tissues. Thus the signs of anemia are caused by insufficient oxygen in the blood and tissues.

In adults, anemia exists when the percentage of red cells in whole blood is less than 35 percent by volume. This value is lower in puppies and young dogs. Once anemia is identified, its cause can be determined by other tests.

Causes of Anemia

Anemia can be caused by excessive loss of red blood cells or by inadequate production. In some cases the body produces red cells rapidly, but not fast enough to keep up with the losses. Nutritional iron-deficiency anemia, while common in people, is uncommon in dogs with today's commercially balanced rations. Chronic iron-deficiency anemia is a clear indication that an insidious loss of blood is taking place.

Excessive Blood Loss

Sudden blood loss might be caused by trauma or a major hemorrhage. In such cases the cause is apparent and shock will ensue. Chronic blood loss is less obvious. One should consider a heavy flea infestation, hookworms in young dogs and bleeding from gastrointestinal tumors and ulcers.

Hemolysis

Blood loss can occur through destruction of red cells in the circulation. An immune-mediated anemia is the most frequent cause of hemolysis in dogs. It is seen with drug reactions (rare), canine babesiosis and ehrlichiosis, inherited enzyme defects that shorten the life of red cells, cold agglutinin disease, the feeding of onions and systemic lupus erythematosus. An exact cause of the hemolytic anemia may not be determined.

Clotting Disorders

Most clotting defects are caused by an absence of one of the coagulation factors needed to initiate the clotting sequence. Seven inherited coagulation disorders have been identified in dogs.

Hemophilia is the one most commonly recognized. This is a sex-linked chromosome problem that primarily affects males, although females carry the trait. It occurs in all breeds.

Von Willebrand's disease should be considered in all dogs with demonstrated bleeding tendencies. It is inherited as a nonsex-linked incompletely dominant gene. It has been recognized to date in fifty-four breeds. The Doberman Pinscher has the highest incidence, reported at over 50 percent. Other breeds with high frequency include, in order: the Standard Manchester Terrier, Pembroke Welsh Corgi, Miniature Schnauzer, Scottish Terrier, Standard Poodle, Shetland Sheepdog and Golden Retriever.

In most cases bleeding problems with Von Willebrand's disease are mild or inapparent, and when present, appear to lessen with age. They include prolonged oozing from wounds, nosebleeds, hemorrhage beneath the skin and into the joints and blood in the urine or stools. Bleeding into the joints is especially common with hemophilia.

It has been suggested that all Dobermans should undergo screening for Von Willebrand's disease at eight weeks of age before cropping the ears.

Rat poisons containing anticoagulants can produce spontaneous bleeding into the tissues. The dog may be found dead without apparent cause.

Inadequate Production

Conditions that depress the bone marrow lead to insufficient red-cell production. This is most often associated with chronic diseases, infections and tumors. Other circumstances that may produce bone marrow depression are drugs (estrogens in high doses, e.g., the mismate shot; chloromycetin and butazolidin), kidney failure with uremia, and toxins and poisons.

Signs of Anemia

Signs vary considerably, depending upon the cause. Often they are overshadowed by the signs of a chronic illness, of which anemia is but one of the associated symptoms. In general, anemic dogs lack appetite, lose weight, sleep a great deal and show generalized weakness. The mucus membranes of the gums and tongue are pale instead of bright pink as they should be.

Jaundice with yellow sclera and dark urine suggests hemolysis. Bleeding beneath the skin and mucus membranes indicates a clotting disorder.

With severe anemia, heart murmurs are common. The pulse is rapid and so is the breathing rate. The dog may faint when overexerting. Most of these signs also occur with heart disease, and these two conditions might be easily confused.

Treatment: It is directed at correcting the underlying cause. Anemias require professional diagnosis and management. Acute bleeding episodes in dogs with clotting disorders can be brought under control with blood transfusions and fresh plasma to replace red cells and provide missing factors. Concentrates containing coagulation factors are available.

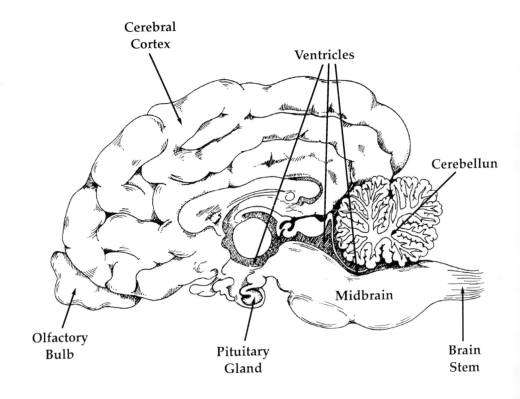

Cerebral
Cortex

Ventricles

Cerebellun

Cerebral
Cortex

Midbrain

Olfactory
Bulb

Pituitary
Gland

Brain
Stem

Cross section of the brain.   *(Karen Wyatt)*

12

Nervous System

$\mathbf{T}$HE *cerebrum* is the largest part of the brain. It is composed of two hemispheres. It is the area of learning, memory, reasoning and judgment. It initiates voluntary action on the part of the dog.

The *cerebellum* also is a bilobed structure. It sits behind the cerebrum and its main function is to integrate the motor pathways of the brain so as to maintain coordination and balance.

In the *midbrain* and brain stem are found centers that control the respiratory rate, the heart rate, the blood pressure and other activities essential to life. At the base of the brain are centers for primitive actions such as hunger, rage, thirst, hormone activity and temperature control. Closely connected to the midbrain and brain stem are the hypothalamus and pituitary gland.

The *spinal cord* passes down a bony canal formed by the arches of the vertebral bodies. The cord sends out nerve roots (thirty-six or thirty-seven pairs) that combine with one another to form the major nerve *plexi*. In turn, these plexi subdivide into the *peripheral nerves*. They carry motor impulses to the muscles and receive sensory input from the skin and deeper structures.

A special set of nerves, called the *cranial nerves* (twelve pair), pass directly from the brain out into the head and neck through special holes in the skull. The optic nerves (to the eyes), the otic nerves (to the ears) and the olfactory nerves (to the scent organs) are examples of cranial nerves.

In the assessment of neurological illness, history is of the greatest importance. Your veterinarian will want to know if your dog has been in an accident. Was there a blow to the head? Was there a history of poisoning? Is the dog taking any drugs? Has there been exposure to other dogs exhibiting signs of illness? When did you first notice the symptoms? Have they progressed? If so, has the progression been rapid or gradual? These all are important points to consider.

To further evaluate a neurological disorder, special tests may be of assistance. They include X-rays, a spinal tap (a procedure in which fluid is removed from the spinal canal and submitted for laboratory analysis) and the EEG (electroencephalogram).

HEAD INJURIES

Head injuries in dogs usually occur from car accidents and falls. Since the brain is not only encased in bone but surrounded by a layer of fluid and suspended in the skull by a system of tough ligaments, it takes a major blow to the head to fracture the skull and injure the brain. Injuries of sufficient magnitude to fracture the skull often are associated with brain lacerations or bleeding into the brain from ruptured blood vessels.

Skull Fractures

Skull fractures can be linear, stellate, depressed, compound (open to the outside) or closed. Fractures at the base of the skull often extend into the ear, orbit, nasal cavity or sinuses, opening pathways for central nervous system infection.

In general, the magnitude of a fracture is an indication of the force and severity of an injury. However, even head injuries without skull fracture can cause severe brain damage.

Brain Injuries

Brain injuries are classified according to the severity of the damage to the brain.

Contusion (Bruising)

This is the most mild sort of injury, in which there is no loss of consciousness. After a blow to the head, the dog remains dazed, wobbly, disoriented—and then clears in a gradual fashion.

Concussion

By definition, a concussion means that the dog was knocked out, or experienced a *brief* loss of consciousness. Upon return to consciousness, the dog exhibits the same signs as contusion.

Brain Swelling or Blood clot

Severe head trauma is associated with swelling of the brain or the formation of a blood clot from ruptured vessels.

Brain swelling, technically called *cerebral edema*, always is associated with a depressed level of consciousness (and often coma). Since the brain is encased in a bony skull, swelling on the brain leads to pressure on the brain stem. As the cerebellum is herniated through the large opening at the base of the skull, the vital centers are in great jeopardy.

Sudden herniation usually leads to death of the dog. The signs of death are no pulse, no effort to breathe, no blink reflex (when you touch the dog's cornea), dilated pupils and a soft eye. Usually it is impossible to tell whether sudden death is caused by head injury or a state of shock from internal bleeding. It is wise to administer cardiopulmonary resuscitation immediately upon suspicion of death (see EMERGENCIES: *Artificial Respiration* and *Heart Massage*).

Cerebral edema also can occur when the brain is deprived of oxygen. Complete interruption of the oxygen circulation for only five minutes can produce fatal brain swelling. This could happen with suffocation, drowning and cardiac arrest.

Blood clots cause localized pressure symptoms. Often one pupil is dilated and will not constrict down when a light is flashed in the eye. A paralysis or weakness may be present on one side of the body. There is a depressed level of consciousness.

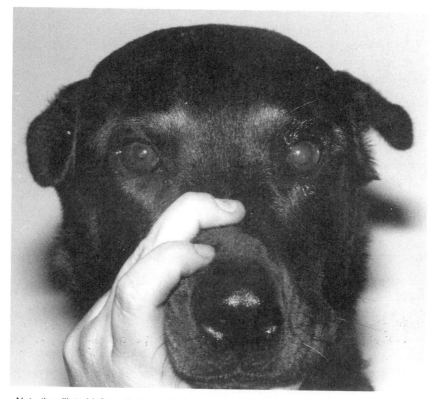

Note the dilated left pupil. It may indicate a blood clot or tumor on that side of the brain.

251

Signs of Increased Intracranial Pressure

Following a blow to the head, or a period of oxygen deprivation, you should watch your dog for signs of brain swelling or the development of a blood clot. These signs can appear anytime during the first twenty-four hours.

The most important thing to observe is the level of your dog's consciousness. An *alert* dog is in no danger. A *stuporous* dog is sleepy but still responds to the owner. A *semicomatose* dog is somnolent but can still be aroused. A *comatose* dog cannot be aroused. After a physical or emotional stress, dogs tend to sleep as the excitement wears off. Awaken your dog every two hours for the first twenty-four hours to check the level of consciousness.

Other signs to look for are:

Slight Pressure on the Brain. The dog is alert but may show weakness on one side. Breathing is normal. The pupils remain small and constrict when a light is flashed in the eyes.

Moderate Pressure on the Brain. The dog may be difficult to arouse and breathing is rapid and shallow. There is generalized weakness. Eye movements and pupils are normal.

Severe Pressure on the Brain. The dog is in a coma. All four legs are rigid, then become flaccid. Breathing is gasping or irregular. Pupils are dilated and don't react to light. The heart rate is slowed. Eye movement is slight or absent.

All signs of increased pressure are serious. Even slight pressure suggests that symptoms are evolving. Notify your veterinarian without delay. Early treatment greatly influences the prognosis for successful recovery.

Treatment of Head Injuries

Treatment of shock and bleeding takes precedence over management of the head injury. If possible, stabilize all fractures before transporting the dog (see MUSCULOSKELETAL SYSTEM: *Broken Bone*).

Handle an injured dog with great care and gentleness. Pain and fright deepen the level of shock. Wrap the dog in a blanket for warmth. This also helps to restrain a dog who is unconscious but may wake up. Carry the dog with the head lower than the feet to avoid aspiration in case of vomiting. Give nothing by mouth. Transport to the nearest veterinary clinic.

Cerebral edema is treated with steroids, diuretics (mannitol, Lasix) or dimethyl sulfoxide (DMSO) to reduce brain swelling. An expanding blood clot (as suggested by localizing neurologic signs) may need to be surgically evacuated. This often leads to cure.

Severely depressed and open skull fractures require surgical cleansing and removal of devitalized bone, or elevation and replacement of a depressed fragment. Antibiotics are indicated to prevent infection. Uncomplicated skull fractures can be observed.

The outlook following head trauma depends upon the severity of the injury and whether treatment is successful. When coma persists for more than twenty-four hours, the outlook is poor. However, if the dog shows steady improvement throughout the first week, the outlook is good.

Dogs that recover from brain injuries may exhibit permanent effects, including seizures, head tilt and partial blindness.

BRAIN DISEASES

Brain Infection (Encephalitis)

Encephalitis is inflammation of the brain. Symptoms are produced either by the destructive effects of the infectious agent or by secondary brain swelling. They include lethargy, fever, confusion, behavioral and personality changes (especially aggression), loss of coordination, staggering gait, stupor, seizures and coma.

Viruses that produce encephalitis include those of rabies, distemper, herpesvirus and canine parvovirus. *Rabies* is of the greatest concern to dog owners. Fortunately, with present-day vaccination programs this disease is uncommon in dogs. *Herpes* and *parvovirus* tend to produce encephalitis in newborn puppies; cerebellar symptoms predominate. In *distemper*, signs of encephalitis appear two to three weeks after onset of the disease.

Postvaccination encephalitis is an uncommon complication that follows the use of modified live virus vaccines. It appears to be a hypersensitivity reaction to the virus antigen or to a substance in the vaccine. It was more common when rabies vaccines were first derived from brain tissue.

Bacteria also can produce encephalitis. Most of them gain entrance to the brain via the bloodstream or by direct extension from infections in the sinuses, nasal passages, eyes, head and neck. Fungal brain infections (*cryptococcosis, blastomycosis, histoplasmosis*) are rare causes of encephalitis, as is the protozoan infection *toxoplasmosis*.

Tick-borne rickettsial diseases, notably *Rocky Mountain spotted fever* and *canine ehrlichiosis*, are being recognized more frequently as causes of encephalitis in dogs. Spinal cord involvement is possible. Rickettsia are extremely sensitive to tetracycline. Although acute signs of illness disappear in twenty-four to forty-eight hours, neurological signs may persist for weeks or even for life.

Pug encephalitis is a chronic progressive disease of unknown cause, although a familial tendency has been described. It is not responsive to medical management.

Meningitis is an infection of the lining of the brain and spinal canal. A blood-borne bacteria is the usual cause. *Aseptic meningitis*, however, is of unknown cause. It tends to affect puppies of the medium and large breeds.

Treatment: This is directed at the cause of the primary disease. In acute illness, corticosteroids are used to reduce swelling of the brain. Antibiotics are used to treat infections.

Granulomatous Meningoencephalomyelitis (GME)

GME is a central nervous system disease of unknown cause, although similarities between GME and both viral and allergic encephalitis suggest that GME may represent a hypersensitivity response to some (as yet unknown) infectious agent. The disease has a worldwide distribution and is more common than initially suspected. Eighty percent of cases occur in middle-aged Toy breed dogs, of which 30 percent are Poodles.

GME can present as a diffuse disseminated brain disease or as a focal disease. An ocular form, affecting the nerves of the eye, also occurs.

The acute *disseminated* disease is of sudden onset, progresses over one to eight weeks and is characterized by loss of coordination, stumbling, falling, head tilt, circling, nerve paralysis, seizures and coma.

The *focal* disease acts like a tumor or space-occupying mass in the brain. Behavioral and personality changes may be the first indication. This form becomes disseminated and progresses over three to six months.

The *ocular* form is characterized by the sudden onset of partial or complete blindness with a fixed, dilated pupil. This is the least common form of GME. It progresses over many months.

GME can be suspected when a Toy dog, Poodle or terrier inexplicably develops a sudden plethora of neurological signs that progress rapidly. Spinal tap and analysis of cerebrospinal fluid help to confirm the diagnosis.

Treatment: Corticosteroids afford some relief by slowing the progress of GME. Improvement may last for several months, but a downhill course is inevitable.

Brain Tumors

Brain tumors are not common in dogs. They tend to occur in dogs over five years of age. The highest incidence is found in short-nosed, large-domed breeds such as the Boxer, Bulldog and Boston Terrier.

Signs of brain tumor come on gradually and are dependent on the location of the tumor and its rate of growth. Diagnosis requires neurologic examination and special studies. In selected cases surgical removal may be possible, especially with a benign tumor. Chemotherapy and radiation therapy for malignant brain tumors have not proven to be efficacious in dogs.

HEREDITARY DISEASES

Hereditary diseases of the nervous system are not common. Most of them have a familial basis. Affected individuals should not be used for breeding.

Hereditary Myopathy (Muscular Dystrophy)

This is a disease caused by a deficiency of a certain type of muscle fiber. It occurs only in Labrador Retriever puppies in the first year of life.

The signs are those of muscle weakness with a marked decrease in exercise tolerance. A pup may have difficulty holding its head erect, "do a bunny hop" when running and collapse after brief exertion. There is loss of muscle mass in the neck and forequarters. Exposure to cold greatly exacerbates the symptoms.

The disease often stabilizes or improves at six to twelve months of age. It is important to warm your dog quickly if exposed to cold weather.

Degenerative Myelopathy (DM)

DM is an immune-mediated degenerative disease of the spinal cord that appears to have a familial basis. It occurs primarily in middle-aged German Shepherds and Labrador Retrievers.

Signs are those of a slowly progressive weakness or paralysis of the hind limbs, along with an unsteady gait suggesting hip dysplasia. The toenails on the hind feet may show abnormal wear from dragging on hard surfaces.

Treatment: Vitamin E (2000 units per day) and high-potency B-complex vitamins can be given for their anti-inflammatory effects. Corticosteroids are indicated. Reports indicate that aminocaproic acid (EACA), 500 milligrams every eight hours, helps to control the degenerative process. All three drugs are recommended. Success is most likely when treatment is started early in the disease.

Sensory Neuropathy

There are a number of uncommon diseases in which sensory nerves undergo degeneration. With loss of sensation, an affected dog does not feel the position of a limb, is unable to move it correctly to prevent stumbling and won't withdraw it from a painful stimulus.

Neuropathy in German Shorthaired and English Pointers

Signs are first noted at three to five months of age. The dog begins to lick and bite at the paws, which become swollen, reddened, ulcerated and eventually mutilated. Loss of sensation can extend up the limb and involve the trunk.

Dachshund Sensory Neuropathy

This disease occurs in Longhaired Dachshund puppies and is inherited as an autosomal recessive. It is characterized by loss of sensation over the entire body, urinary incontinence and uncoordinated gait. Self-mutilation of the penis may be the first sign.

Progressive Axonopathy in Boxers

This is a rare disease that begins in the first few months of life and progresses slowly. It is inherited as an autosomal recessive. The first indication is a clumsy gait, followed by fine body tremors and bobbing of the head. Later the gait problems become more pronounced.

A similar disease, called *Giant Axonal Neuropathy*, has been described in German Shepherds.

There is no cure for the sensory neuropathies, but because of its slow progress many dogs can live comfortably for several years. They may need to be muzzled to prevent self-injury.

Hypomyelination Diseases

In these diseases the substance *myelin*, which forms a sheath around nerve fibers, does not reach complete development at birth. The result is that nerve conduction is slower than normal. This affects coordinated muscle action.

The characteristic sign is muscle tremors involving the limbs, trunk, head and eyes of newborn puppies. The tremors get worse with activity and disappear with sleep. Severely afflicted puppies show uncoordinated body movements and may be unable to stand.

Hereditary hypomyelination diseases occur as specific inheritance patterns in Chow Chows, Weimaraners, Samoyeds and Bernese Mountain Dogs. Hypomyelination called the "Shaking Puppy Syndrome", is a sex-linked recessive that principally affects males.

Tremor of White Dogs

The sudden onset of head and body tremor has been noted in adult dogs of smaller breeds having white coat colors, especially Maltese and West Highland White Terriers. Most individuals exhibit no other neurological signs, but the tremor may be severe enough to cause difficulty in standing. The cause is unknown.

There is no cure for hypomyelination diseases. Treatment usually is not necessary in mildly afflicted dogs. Tremor in many Chow Chows and Weimaraners may improve gradually and disappear at one year of age.

Cerebellar Diseases

Cerebellar disorders have been described in numerous breeds. In some cases the cerebellum is malformed at birth; in others, there is progressive loss of function because of degeneration of nerve cells.

These diseases result in loss of balance and uncoordinated body movements such as jerking, stumbling, over-reaching with the paws, falling and various degrees of spasticity. Symptoms often do not occur until a puppy is three to four months of age.

Inherited syndromes of cerebellar degeneration have been described in the following breeds: Kerry Blue Terriers, Gordon Setters, Collies and Border Collies and Bullmastiffs. There is no cure. In some puppies the disease stabilizes and they are able to compensate and remain active.

The enlarged dome of a hydrocephalic puppy.

Hydrocephalus

Hydrocephalus is caused by an excessive accumulation of cerebrospinal fluid in the ventricles of the brain. This compresses the brain against the skull. Hydrocephalus can be caused by trauma, brain infections and tumors, or it can be congenital.

Congenital hydrocephalus is most often found in Toy breeds and may be hereditary. The characteristic enlargement of the dome of the skull may not be noted until the puppy is several months old.

Treatment is directed at reducing the fluid buildup with drugs or surgery.

FITS (SEIZURES, CONVULSIONS)

A seizure is a sudden and uncontrolled burst of activity that may include one of the following: champing and chewing, foaming at the mouth, collapse, jerking of the legs, loss of urine and stool. An altered level of consciousness is followed by a gradual return to normal.

Grand mal seizures are generalized. *Petit mal* seizures are confined to one part of the body; this indicates an acquired disorder.

Some fits are atypical. Instead of the classical convulsion, the dog might exhibit strange and inappropriate behavior such as frenzied barking, sudden blindness or hysteria. The dog may lick or chew at itself, or turn and snap at the owner. This is called a *psychomotor* seizure.

Seizures are caused by a burst of electrical activity within the brain, commonly in one of the cerebral hemispheres. The electrical focus spreads out and involves other parts, including the midbrain.

Seizures can be caused by a *blow* to the head, or by scars from healed brain injuries.

Hypoglycemia (low blood sugar) and *hypocalcemia* (low blood calcium) can produce seizures as well as coma.

A condition in puppies called "worm fits" can be found during heavy infestations with intestinal worms. The exact cause of the seizures is unknown. Perhaps it is the result of low blood sugar or calcium.

Common poisonings that induce seizures are strychnine, antifreeze (ethylene glycol), lead, insecticides (chlorinated hydrocarbons, organophosphates) and rat poisons. Organophosphates produce seizures that are preceded by drooling and muscle twitching. History of exposure to an insecticide (i.e., a dip) suggests the diagnosis (see SKIN: *Insecticides*).

Kidney and liver failure are accompanied by the accumulation of toxins in the blood, which can cause seizures and coma.

There are a number of conditions that, while actually not true seizures, can easily be mistaken for them. *Bee stings*, for example, can cause frenzied barking followed by fainting or collapse. Similarly, a dog with a foreign object in the larynx that is unable to get air and turns blue at the mouth and collapses might look like a dog having a convulsion. Recurrent attacks suggest a seizure disorder. This condition is discussed in the chapter RESPIRATORY SYSTEM (see *Foreign Bodies in the Windpipe*). *Heart arrhythmias*, with fainting, often are thought to be seizures.

Narcolepsy is an uncommon condition in which the dog suddenly falls asleep and collapses. It is related to a disorder of the sleep mechanism in the brain. A dog can have one or a hundred such attacks in a day. The attacks may last for a few seconds or up to twenty minutes; they can be reversed by petting the dog or making a loud noise. The cause is unknown. Hereditary factors are suspected.

Anxiety attacks, accompanied by overbreathing (*hyperventilation*), produce jerks and spasms like the start of a fit. Overbreathing removes carbon dioxide from the blood and makes it alkaline. This lowers the serum calcium and leads to the muscle twitching. Hyperventilation sometimes occurs in grooming parlors. Have your dog breathe in a plastic bag for a few minutes to reverse the alkalosis. Valium is indicated in stressful situations to prevent future attacks.

Epilepsy

Epilepsy is a recurrent seizure disorder that may be acquired or congenital. St. Bernards, German Shepherds, Poodles and Beagles have a hereditary predisposition for congenital epilepsy.

Three to four months after a brain concussion, some dogs acquire seizures as a result of scars on the brain.

Post-encephalitic seizures occur three to four weeks after the onset of encephalitis. Distemper, in particular, is characterized by typical attacks that begin with champing, tongue chewing, foaming at the mouth, shaking of the head and blinking of the eyes—then a dazed look, and a return to normal.

To establish a diagnosis of epilepsy, the attacks must be *recurrent* and similar. A typical epileptic seizure has three phases. The first is called the *aura*. It is recognized by the onset of sudden apprehension and restlessness. There may be bizarre behavior, such as sniffing in the corner or snapping the air.

Most grand mal seizures start with champing, chewing, foaming at the mouth, head shaking and eye flickering. During the *rigid* phase the dog collapses, the head is thrown back, and the dog slobbers and twitches at the face. Pupils dilate. As the rigid phase begins to pass, the dog makes running movements with all four legs (paddling) and may lose control of bowels or bladder.

During the *postseizure* phase the dog recovers but remains confused and wobbly. If overstimulated by a loud noise or rough handling, a second seizure can occur.

The first two phases pass quickly (in about three minutes). The postseizure state can persist for several hours. This might give the impression that the seizure was of long duration. However, a true epileptic seizure is over in less than five minutes.

Stimuli that can trigger a seizure are fatigue, excitement, anxiety, bright lights, loud noises, fever, overbreathing and estrus.

Not all epileptic seizures are typical. To help make the diagnosis, your veterinarian probably will ask for a description of the attack, and will want to know if other attacks follow the same pattern.

Treatment: When a seizure starts, stand aside until your dog quiets down, or cover the dog with a blanket. (Don't put your fingers in the mouth or try to wedge something between the teeth.) Then call your veterinarian. As most seizures will be over in a few minutes, it is unlikely that your veterinarian will need to stop it with medications. Your vet may want to examine the dog to determine the cause of the seizure.

Seizures lasting over five minutes (continuous seizures) are dangerous. They must be stopped to prevent permanent brain damage. Valium is given intravenously to stop a continuous seizure.

The complete elimination of seizure activity is not always a realistic goal in treating dogs with recurrent seizure disorders. Dosages and rates of action of anticonvulsant drugs are quite variable. Many drugs, such as Dilantin, used for treating epilepsy in people, are rapidly metabolized in dogs when given in like dosage. Only phenobarbital and primidone (which metabolizes to phenobarbital) have been found to be both safe and efficacious for controlling seizures in dogs. In general, seizures will worsen if not controlled, although young dogs are less likely to have progressive disease than dogs that acquire seizures later in life. The most common causes of treatment failure are inadequate levels of medication and failure to administer the drug as directed. *It is important to work closely with your veterinarian.*

LOSS OF CONSCIOUSNESS (COMA)

Coma is a depressed level of consciousness. It begins with mental depression and confusion, progresses through stupor and ends in complete loss of consciousness. Following a blow to the head, coma can occur without progressing through the earlier stages. Unconscious dogs are not responsive to pain.

Coma is found with a number of ailments. A low blood sugar (*hypoglycemia*) is a common cause of coma. It generally occurs in puppies of the Toy breeds, but adult hunting dogs are susceptible to it also. Hypoglycemia is discussed in the chapter PEDIATRICS.

Coma that appears with *high fever* or *heat stroke* is a grave sign. Vigorous efforts to bring down the fever are needed to prevent permanent brain damage (see EMERGENCIES: *Heat Stroke*). Likewise, coma is ominous when it is associated with severe brain injury, or when it occurs in the late stages of kidney and liver disease.

Another cause of coma, which effects breeds with short coats, is prolonged *chilling*. The dog's temperature is subnormal—below the level on the thermometer. Treatment involves intravenous glucose solutions and slow warming.

A dog transported in the trunk of a car can develop *carbon monoxide poisoning* from the exhaust fumes. The dog may be found unconscious, or at first look normal. When starting to hunt, the oxygen supply is used up and the dog collapses, throws a fit or passes out entirely.

Common poisons that cause coma are ethylene glycol (antifreeze), barbiturates, kerosene, turpentine, arsenic, cyanide, hexachlorophene, lead salts and carbon monoxide. Poisoning is discussed in EMERGENCIES.

Treatment: First determine the level of consciousness and whether the dog is alive. An unconscious dog can inhale its own secretions and strangle on its tongue. Pull out the tongue and clear the airway with your fingers. Lift by the rear legs and set the dog on a table with the head hanging over the side. Wrap the animal in a blanket and go at once to a veterinarian. It is important that the dog be carried on a rigid surface.

If the dog shows no signs of life, begin artificial respiration and heart massage (see EMERGENCIES).

If you think your dog might have a piece of food caught in the airway, administer the Heimlich maneuver as described in the chapter on the RESPIRATORY SYSTEM: *Laryngeal Blockage*.

WEAKNESS OR PARALYSIS

There is a group of uncommon diseases that attack the motor nerves, causing weakness and paralysis, but leave the sensory nerves intact. This distinguishes them from *Sensory Neuropathies*, discussed elsewhere in this chapter. These diseases resemble each other and are difficult to tell apart.

Tick Paralysis

The saliva of some common female wood ticks contains a poison that affects the motor nerves of the dog. Clinical signs usually are associated with a heavy infestation. During forty-eight to seventy-two hours the dog gets progressively weaker. There is no evidence of pain or illness. Sensation to pin prick is normal. In time, the paralysis becomes so severe the dog can't raise its head or move its legs and may die because it cannot breathe.

Treatment: Remove all ticks, especially engorged females (see SKIN: *Ticks*). Dip the dog in an insecticide solution (see SKIN: *Insecticides*). If your dog shows signs of weakness, call your veterinarian.

Botulism

Botulism is a paralysis caused by the endotoxin of a bacteria called *Clostridium botulinum*. It is acquired by eating improperly canned vegetables and meats or spoiled carcasses. Signs are similar to tick paralysis.

Treatment: The disease is often fatal. Antitoxins are available; they may be of aid early in the disease.

Coonhound Paralysis

The exact cause of this disease is unknown. It may be the result of a virus. It is acquired by dogs that have hunted raccoons. The dog may have been bitten or scratched by a raccoon a week or two before the onset of paralysis.

The disease begins as a weakness of the hindquarters and progresses forward until the dog is unable to stand. During this time the dog remains alert and concerned by the incapacity. The paralysis reaches its peak at about ten days. Dogs may recover. Treatment is supportive. Seek veterinary aid.

Myasthenia Gravis

This condition is caused by an abnormality in the biochemistry of the nerve endings of the motor nerves. It is not common. The signs are a generalized weakness that is aggravated by exercise. Weakness is most apparent in the hindquarters. There is trouble getting up when lying down, and a swaying or staggering gait. Diagnosis can be made through special studies. Drugs are available to aid the dog.

Low Potassium (Hypokalemia)

Hypokalemia, or low blood potassium, occurs in dogs that are taking water pills to remove excess fluids from the body. Such dogs can develop a generalized weakness as a result of loss of potassium in the urine. Diagnosis is made by measuring the serum potassium level. Potassium can be given to correct the problem.

SPINAL CORD DISEASES

Spinal cord diseases and injuries are a common cause of neurologic symptoms in dogs. They depend on the severity and location of the problem. There may be weakness, loss of feeling or paralysis of both rear legs or even all four extremities. Spinal cord disorders usually produce bilateral symptoms, while localized brain disorders often produce symptoms on just one side of the body—perhaps the front or rear legs on that side. Injuries to peripheral nerves usually affect just one limb.

Spinal Cord Trauma

Traumatic spinal cord injuries are associated with ruptured discs and vertebral dislocations and fractures caused by automobile accidents and falls. Immediate signs are caused by the force of the injury. Signs that occur several hours later are caused by tissue swelling, bleeding around the cord and interference with its blood supply.

Injuries of this magnitude often cause neck and back fractures. The fracture may be unstable. Flexion and extension of the vertebral column can exacerbate—or actually cause—a spinal cord injury.

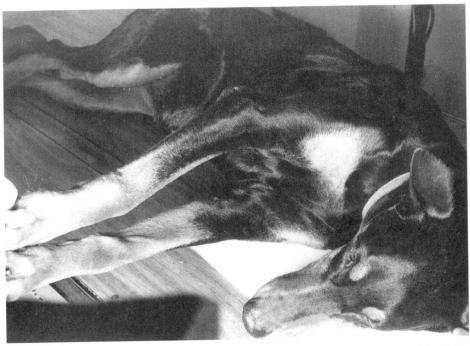

Spinal cord injuries to the midback can produce rigid extension of the front legs and flaccid paralysis of the back legs *(Schiff-Sherrington phenomenon).*

Treatment: A dog with spinal cord trauma may have sustained other life-threatening injuries. These take precedence and require immediate attention (see EMERGENCIES: *Shock*). All dogs unconscious or unable to stand should be considered to have spinal cord injuries and must be handled with great care to protect the spine. At the scene of the accident, move the dog as gently as possible onto a flat surface and transport to the nearest veterinary clinic. A stretcher can be made by folding a blanket over two broom handles. Sliding the dog onto a rug and lifting the corners is a satisfactory means of transporting an injured dog. Your veterinarian may wish to take X-rays before attempting any manipulation.

Mild cord injuries are treated with corticosteroids or diuretics to prevent further swelling at the site of injury. Dogs with severe injuries and those with progressive paralysis may require surgery to decompress the cord or stabilize fractured vertebrae.

A dog with a mild contusion or bruise of the spinal cord may begin to recover in a matter of days. However, if the cord has been severed, it cannot regenerate and paralysis will be permanent.

Infections

Infections of the spinal cord, vertebral bodies and discs are not common. Most are caused by blood-borne bacteria, some by extension of a neighboring abscess related to a gunshot wound or bite. Rarely they are caused by fungal and rickettsial diseases.

Treatment of spinal cord, vertebral body and disc space infections involves the long-term use of antibiotics, preferably selected on the basis of culture and sensitivity tests when material is available. Surgery may be necessary to remove a foreign body, drain an abscess, obtain material for testing or relieve pressure on the spinal cord.

Herniated Disc (Slipped Disc)

Ruptured discs are more common in certain breeds. Dachshunds have twice the incidence of all other breeds. Beagles, Pekingese and mixed breeds are next in frequency.

A disc is a cushion that sits between the vertebral bodies of the spinal column and acts like a shock absorber. It is made up of a rim of tough cartilage that has a gel-like center. When a disc herniates, the whole disc does not "slip" out of position. What happens is that there is a break in the fibrous capsule that allows the inner "nucleus" of the disc to push through the opening and pinch the cord or put pressure on the dorsal nerve roots. The effect is similar to a break in a rubber tire that lets the inner tube bulge out. Herniated discs give rise to pain, weakness, paralysis or loss of sensation. The reason signs are so variable is that a herniation can vary in size and location from animal to animal. Occasionally more than one disc is involved.

The concept that a "slipped" disc can be easily replaced by manipulating the spinal column is based on a misconception that the whole cushion slides in and out of place.

Herniated discs can come on gradually or occur with explosive suddenness. Usually there is a history of trauma, such as jumping off of a sofa. Usually the first sign is pain in the back. The dog assumes a hunched-up position, pants, has a tight abdomen and a look of pain. At the same time, the dog may show weakness and lameness or a wobbly, uncoordinated gait. Sudden disc protrusions in the lower back can produce complete paralysis of the rear legs. These dogs often develop urinary retention and bladder infections.

Disc problems seldom occur in dogs younger than one year of age. About 80 percent occur in the low back between the last thoracic and first two lumbar vertebrae. Most of the remainder occur in the neck.

Dogs with a herniated neck disc carry their heads rigidly, which makes the neck look shorter. Neck discs are extremely painful. Some dogs refuse to lower their heads to eat. They cry out when patted on the head. There may be lameness in the front legs. Complete paralysis of all four legs is rare but does occur.

Treatment: Most disc problems improve without surgery, but the improvement is gradual and depends upon keeping the dog in confinement so that activity won't force more of the disc out and increase pressure on the cord.

For neck and back discs of gradual onset, cage rest for ten days allows the swelling to subside. A neck brace helps to stabilize the cervical spine.

Most dogs will need to be hospitalized. At home they follow their owners and ask to be picked up and carried. Drugs to reduce swelling and inflammation are of value. Strong pain medication usually is contraindicated because it encourages activity.

Explosive discs with paralysis require special care and handling. Dogs should be transported on a flat, hard surface (see *Spinal Cord Trauma*). Often special studies are necessary to locate the exact point of the protrusion. The most useful test is a myelogram, in which a contrast material is injected into the spinal canal to show up the herniation on X rays. Operative intervention may be necessary.

Wobbler Syndrome (Cervical Spondylopathy)

Instability of the neck vertebrae is a relatively common disease in large breeds. The majority of cases occur in Doberman Pinschers four to six years of age, and to a lesser extent Great Danes under eighteen months. The most common spine abnormalities contributing to this syndrome are chronic degenerative disc disease of the last three vertebrae of the neck and partial dislocation (subluxation) of vertebrae when the neck is manipulated or moved.

The leading signs are a slow and progressive loss of coordination in the hind limbs, accompanied by a peculiar, wobbly gait. As the disease progresses, partial paralysis caused by impingement on the spinal cord begins to affect the front legs. Manipulation of the neck is painful and may exacerbate the paralysis.

Since the wobbler syndrome occurs in rapidly growing dogs with long necks, it has been suggested that overnutrition in the form of excess protein, calcium and phosphorus may induce skeletal changes that precipitate the disease. Breed factors and genetic influences may be important. Until more is learned about the exact cause, affected individuals should not be used for breeding.

Treatment: Diagnosis and treatment is like that for herniated disc, discussed above. If not completely successful, surgery to decompress the spinal cord and stabilize the vertebral column can be considered.

Cauda Equina Syndrome

The *cauda equina* is composed of nerves that form the terminal extension of the spinal cord. Injuries to these nerves produce gait disturbances with hindquarter lameness, a limp, paralyzed tail, urinary and/or fecal incontinence caused by paralysis of the bladder and rectum, inability to squat to void and sometimes self-mutilation of the desensitized anal area, tail and hindquarters.

Disorders that produce the cauda equina syndrome in dogs include herniated disc, *spina bifida* (a developmental defect in the closure of the bones in the lower back), disc and spinal cord infections, vertebral canal stenosis and benign and malignant tumors of the cord.

Lumbosacral vertebral canal stenosis is an acquired condition in which there is instability of the lumbosacral spine. There may be a congenital component that produces narrowing of the bony canal. German Shepherds are most often affected.

Treatment: Medical management is like that described for herniated disc, discussed above. It is most successful for dogs with mild symptoms. Surgical decompression and bone fusion is considered for nonresponders and those with severe involvement. Dogs with a paralyzed bladder or rectum are least likely to benefit from surgery.

Bone Spurs (Spondylosis)

Osteophytes are bone spurs that form around intervertebral discs in all breeds as a natural process of aging. Fusion of these osteophytes, called *spondylosis deformans*, restricts motion of the vertebral column and can cause pain. This condition is more pronounced in large dogs.

In most dogs, spondylosis deformans produces few if any symptoms. Dogs with pain and stiffness respond well to analgesics.

On rare occasion, bony spurs can project into the spinal canal or press on nerve routes, causing signs of muscle weakness. In such cases surgery to remove the osteophytes and decompress the spinal cord can be of benefit.

NERVE PALSY (PARALYSIS)

An injury to one of the peripheral nerves results in loss of sensation and motor function in the distribution of that nerve. Common injuries are stretches, tears and lacerations.

Brachial and radial nerve palsies involve one of the front legs. Usually they are caused by an auto accident, during which the leg is jerked backward away from the trunk, stretching the nerves. The leg hangs limp. When paralysis is partial, the dog may be able to stand but stumbles when taking a step.

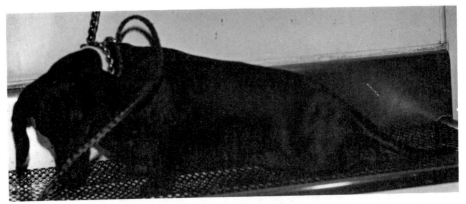

Paralysis in a Dachshund caused by a *herniated back disc*.

Lacerated nerves must be repaired. Stretched nerves often return to normal.

Another cause of temporary nerve paralysis is the injection of an irritating medication into the tissue surrounding a nerve. This problem is infrequent but can be a source of concern. The majority heal spontaneously. The correct procedure for giving injections is described in the chapter DRUGS AND MEDICATIONS.

13

Musculoskeletal System

T HE DOG'S SKELETON is made up of an average of 319 individual bones connected by ligaments and surrounded by muscles. Although the number of bones is roughly the same in all breeds of dog, there is considerable variation in size and shape. This is caused by selective breeding.

The bones of the body are held together by specialized connective tissue called *ligaments*. This union is called an *articulation*, or joint. In some joints a pad of cartilage is interposed between the two surfaces, giving a cushion effect.

Despite the fact that cartilage is tough and resilient, it can be damaged by joint stress and trauma. It is not easily replaced or mended. Once damaged, it may deteriorate, become calcified and act as a foreign body or irritant to the joint surfaces.

Joint position is maintained by ligaments, tendons and a tough fibrous capsule surrounding the joint. These combine to provide stability or tightness to the joint. Joint *laxity*, which is caused by loose ligaments and/or a stretched capsule, predisposes to *subluxation*—a partial or incomplete disolcation of the joint. These joints are subject to chronic injury and later arthritis.

The skeletal anatomys of humans and dogs have much in common, including similar terminology. Because people evolved into two-legged creatures there are some significant differences in terms of angles, lengths and positioning of the bones.

The hock, for example, so prominent on the dog, is actually the hell bone in humans. Whereas people walk on the soles of the feet, the dog walks on the toes. People carry all their weight on the hips; dogs carries 75 percent of their weight on the shoulder joints and front end. This helps to explain why front leg disorders are relatively common in dogs.

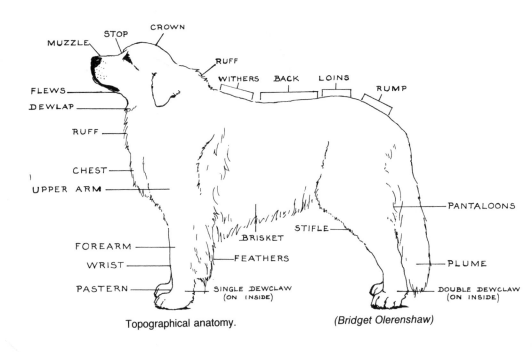

Topographical anatomy. (Bridget Olerenshaw)

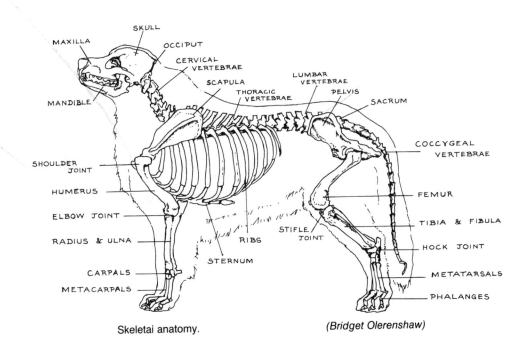

Skeletal anatomy. (Bridget Olerenshaw)

268

Breeders, judges and veterinarians use certain terms to describe a dog's overall structure and composition.

Conformation is the degree with which the various angles and parts of the body agree or harmonize with one another. Standards for purebred dogs describe the ideal conformation for each particular breed. These standards are based to a certain extent upon aesthetic considerations, but they take into account the breed's working purposes, too.

Most breed Standards provide some information as to the desired *angulation*, or slope to the bones of the shoulder, pelvis and limbs. These angles are determined by comparison with imaginary lines drawn horizontally and vertically through the plane of the standing dog.

Another term used to judge the physical attributes of a dog is *soundness*. When applied to the composition of the musculoskeletal system, it means that a sound dog is one in which all the bones and joints are in correct alignment and functioning properly.

BONE AND JOINT PROBLEMS IN GROWING PUPPIES

Growing puppies are especially susceptible to serious injuries to bones and joints caused by improper activity, improper diet and trauma. Injuries can lead to disability or a deviation in the development of the limb.

A puppy (especially of the large breeds) should never be allowed to gain too much weight and should not be encouraged to jump up or walk on hind legs. A pup should also not be made to pull or carry a heavy load.

Secure footing is especially important for dogs. A puppy beginning to walk should be placed on a rug or a rough surface that will help keep the dog's feet under the body. Dogs should not be kenneled on smooth or slick surfaces. House pets should be kept off slippery floors that could cause their legs to slip out from under them.

To learn about metabolic bone disease, and vitamin and mineral supplements for growing puppies, see *Metabolic Bone Disorders* further on in this chapter.

How to Carry a Dog

Injuries to bones and joints can occur from improper handling. Never pick your dog up by the front legs. Heavy dogs must be picked up by placing one arm around the front of the chest and another underneath the stomach or around the back legs. They are then held close to the chest so that if they attempt to squirm they are not easily dropped.

LIMPING (LAMENESS)

A limp is the most common sign of bone or joint disease. However, muscle or nerve damage can produce lameness. It indicates pain or weakness in the involved leg.

Carry an injured dog with one arm around the dog's chest and the other around the back legs. *(J. Clawson)*

Locating which leg is affected can be difficult. A dog often will take weight off a painful leg when standing. When moving, a dog will usually take a shorter step on a painful or weak leg. You may notice that the dog's head ''bobs'' or drops as weight comes down on the affected leg.

Having identified which leg is involved, you should attempt to identify the site and possible cause. First flex and extend all joints to their maximum to ascertain if joint or tendons are involved. Next, carefully feel the leg from the toes up. Attempt to locate a point of tenderness by applying pressure. Having located an area of pain, see if it is produced by movement of a joint, or by local tenderness in a muscle (such as might be caused by a puncture wound or a bruise). Check for swelling and discoloration of the area. With this information, consider the following:

Infected areas are tender, reddened, warm to touch; often they are associated with a break in the skin and progress gradually. Lameness becomes steadily worse. Fever usually is present.

Sprains and strains (of joints, tendons and muscles) are of sudden onset; frequently they show local swelling and discoloration; they gradually improve. Ordinarily the dog has limited use of the leg. Pain is mild. There is no fever.

Fractures and dislocations are associated with severe pain and inability to put weight on the leg. Deformity often is present. Movement of the involved part produces a gritty sound. Tissues are swollen and discolored from bleeding.

Degenerative, congenital and metabolic bone and joint diseases come on gradually. There is no local discoloration. Pain usually is mild and swelling slight.

Weakness or paralysis of one or more legs, in the absence of a history of trauma, suggests that spinal cord disease is the cause of the problem (see NERVOUS SYSTEM).

A firm mass or swelling raises the possibility of a *bone tumor*. Consider this also in a mature dog that begins to limp with no history of injury. Pressure over a tumor often causes varying degrees of pain. Bone tumors are discussed in the chapter TUMORS AND CANCERS.

Bone and joint injuries are discussed below.

INJURIES TO BONES AND JOINTS

Sprains

A sprain is an injury to a joint caused by a sudden stretching or tear of the joint capsule or ligaments. The signs are pain over the joint, swelling of the tissues and limitation of motion leading to temporary lameness.

Cases with severe swelling and/or pain (in which the dog refuses to put weight on the leg) should be examined by a veterinarian to rule out a fracture or dislocation. If the problem does not begin to improve within four days, X rays should be taken.

Treatment: The primary treatment is to *rest the part*. When torn ligaments are suspected, the joint should be immobilized by splinting as described below under broken bone. Ice packs help to keep the swelling down. Add crushed ice to a plastic bag and wrap the limb to hold the bag in place over the injured joint. Apply ice for twenty minutes every hour for the first three hours. *Avoid* pain medication that relieves discomfort and encourages use of the limb.

Tendon Injuries

A tendon may be stretched, partly torn or completely ruptured. An irritated or inflamed tendon is called a *tendinitis*. Strained tendons sometimes follow sudden wrenching or twisting injuries to the limb. In some cases tendinitis follows overuse of the limb (for example, after strenuous field or road work).

The signs of tendinitis are temporary lameness, pain on bearing weight, pain and swelling over the course of the tendon. The tendons of the forepaw (front and back) are affected most often.

Treatment: Rest of the limb is most important. It may be necessary to splint the joint (see *Sprains*). Activity that causes flare-ups should be reduced or stopped. Do not give drugs to relieve pain, since the limp is important in protecting the part from further injury.

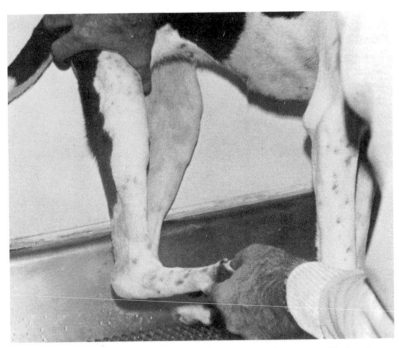

The heel cord tendon *(Achilles)* is the tendon most often ruptured in the dog.

Rupture of the Achilles (heel) tendon, which attaches to the hock joint, can be caused by sudden and extreme flexion. This is the tendon most often severed by dog fights and car accidents. It must be repaired surgically.

Muscle Strain

An injured or torn muscle is caused by: (a) sudden stretching of its fibers; (b) prolonged stress or overexertion; (c) a blow to the muscle. The symptoms are lameness, a knotting-up of the muscle and swelling with tenderness over the injured part.

Treatment: Rest and cold packs are recommended (see *Sprains*).

Dislocated Joint

A strong force is necessary to rupture a joint and displace the bones. Such injuries usually are associated with falls and car accidents. The signs are sudden onset of pain with inability to use the limb; there is an observable deformity (or shortening) when compared to the opposite side.

Subluxations are partial or incomplete dislocations. A severe sprain is the usual inciting cause. Others are of congenital and developmental origin. Subluxations most often affect the hip joint, stifle joint, hock joint, shoulder and elbow.

Treatment: Veterinary examination is necessary to rule out an associated fracture and to replace the joint in its socket. Complete dislocations frequently involve shock and internal bleeding.

Broken Bone (Fracture)

Broken bones are caused by trauma. At times a bone is diseased, which weakens it; then minor trauma can cause a breakage.

Young bones tend to crack (*greenstick fracture*), whereas bones of elderly dogs are brittle and more likely to break completely. Complete breaks are divided into *simple* and *compound*. A simple fracture does not break through the skin. In a compound (open) fracture the bone has made contact with the outside, either because of an open wound that exposes it or because the point has thrust through the skin from the inside. Compound fractures may be associated with bone infection.

Treatment: Many of these injuries are associated with shock, blood loss and injuries to other organs. Control of shock takes precedence over treatment of the fracture.

Suspected fractures should be immobilized to prevent further damage during movement of the dog to a veterinary hospital. Accomplish this by splinting the involved limb. A satisfactory splint is one that crosses the joint above and below the injury. This assures nonmovement of the fractured part.

When a fracture is below the hock or the elbow, immobilize it by folding a magazine around the leg. Then wrap it with roller gauze, a necktie or anything handy. Higher fractures can be immobilized by binding the limb to a padded board or to the body with a many-tailed bandage.

If the fracture is a complete break, your veterinarian probably will want to reduce the fracture and return the ends of the bones to their original position. Reduction is accomplished by pulling on the limb to overcome muscle spasm, which causes shortening. Usually this requires an anesthetic. Once reduced, the position of the bones must be maintained. Splints and casts are effective, especially for greenstick fractures; at times metallic plates and pins are needed. Such complicated fractures require open surgery.

Bone Infection (Osteomyelitis)

A bone infection is a hazard whenever bone is exposed. The most common causes are open fracture and surgical operations on bones and joints. In rare cases it is the result of blood-borne bacteria and fungi; the dog might be suffering from leukemia or some other disease that impairs immunological competence.

The signs of osteomyelitis are lameness, fever, pain, swelling and discharge through a sinus tract connecting the bone to the skin. The diagnosis is confirmed by X-ray.

Treatment: Successful treatment of osteomyelitis presents one of the most difficult problems in veterinary medicine. The causative agent (bacteria, fungi) is first identified; then the dog is placed on appropriate long-term antibiotics. Surgical removal of devitalized bone is often necessary.

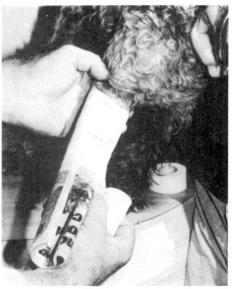

A magazine makes a good contemporary splint for fractures of the front leg below the elbow.
(J. Clawson)

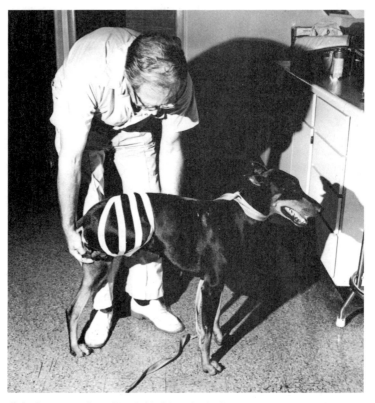

If the leg cannot be splinted, bind it to the body.   *(J. Clawson)*

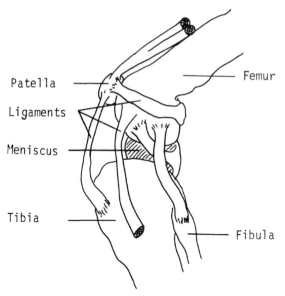

The stifle joint. Ruptured ligaments are common.

(Rose Floyd)

Torn Knee Ligaments (Ruptured Cruciates)

The knee, or stifle joint, is stabilized by two internal ligaments (the cruciates) that cross in the middle of the joint. Rupture of a cruciate is a common serious derangement of the stifle joint. Torn knee ligaments occur in Toy breeds and on occasion in larger breeds.

There might be a history of trauma, but in many cases the presenting sign is just moderate to severe lameness in one or both hind legs. The diagnosis is confirmed by palpating the stifle joint and finding instability.

Treatment: Surgical repair of the torn ligaments is the treatment of choice. When allowed to heal spontaneously, the leg develops scar tissue around the joint capsule, which lessens the degree of mobility. Arthritis occurs later in life.

INHERITED BONE DISEASE

This is a group of bone disorders having a genetic or hereditary basis, despite the fact that only a limited number of offspring may be affected. If, after a careful veterinary examination, one of these conditions is found, do not breed your dog without first discussing it with your veterinarian.

Canine Hip Dysplasia

This is the most common cause of rear-end lameness in the dog. It occurs almost exclusively in the larger breeds—those weighing more than thirty-five

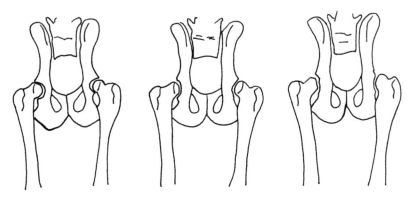

Normal Hips   Moderate Dysplasia   Severe Dysplasia

Hip dysplasia is a moderately heritable condition.

pounds as adults. Dysplastic dogs are born with normal-appearing hips that subsequently undergo progressive structural changes.

The problem lies in the structure of the hip joint. The head of the *femur* (thigh bone) should fit solidly in the *acetabulum* (cup). In hip dysplasia, loose ligaments allow the head to begin to work free. A shallow acetabulum also predisposes to joint laxity. Finally, the mass or tone of the muscles around the joint socket is an important factor.

Tight ligaments, a broad pelvis with a well-cupped acetabulum and a good ratio of muscle mass to size of bone predispose to good hips. The reverse is true of dogs that are likely to develop the disease. Environmental factors, including weight and nutrition of the puppy and rearing practices, figure into the final outcome.

Hip dysplasia is a moderately heritable condition. It is about twice as common among littermates having a dysplastic parent. But *even dogs with normal hips can produce dysplastic pups.* Some dogs with X-ray evidence of severe hip dysplasia show no clinical signs, and the disease goes entirely unsuspected until an X-ray is taken to check for it.

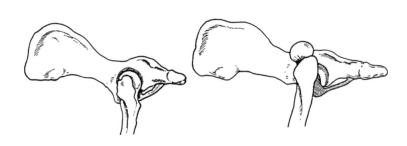

Normal Hip   Severe Dysplasia with
Upward (Dorsal) Dislocation

Upward (dorsal) displacement is the most common type of dislocation in hip dysplasia.

Joint laxity is the earliest sign of hip dysplasia. Therefore, gait abnormalities without obvious lameness and stiffness may precede degenerative joint changes by several months. Often the first signs appear during a time of rapid growth (four to nine months). A puppy might show pain in the hip, walk with a limp or swaying gait, bunny-hop when running and experience difficulty getting up. Pushing down on the rump can cause the pelvis to drop. If you roll the dog on its back, the rear legs may resist being spread into a "frog-leg" position.

Because of joint laxity, there is abnormal wear and tear on the articulating surfaces of the joint. In time this leads to arthritic changes in the dysplastic hip. Pain and limitation of movement frequently parallel the degree of bone deformity (or grade of dysplasia) at the joint.

The diagnosis is made from X-rays of the pelvis and hips. Heavy sedation or general anesthesia may be required.

Canine hip dysplasia is graded according to the severity of joint changes seen on X-ray. Joint laxity and minor remodeling characterize mild dysplasia. Erosion of the joints, subluxation of the hips (moving out of the socket) and arthritic changes characterize moderate dysplasia. In severe dysplasia, the acetabulum is extremely shallow or nearly flat, the femoral head is rough and flattened, subluxation is severe and arthritic changes are marked.

The Orthopedic Foundation for Animals provides a consulting service for purebred dog owners. For a nominal fee, the OFA's panel of expert radiologists will review a properly taken X-ray, and if the conformation of the hips is normal for that breed, certify the dog by assigning an OFA number. Currently, the OFA certifies dogs who are twenty-four months of age or older. For more information, write Orthopedic Foundation for Animals, Inc., University of Missouri, Columbia, Missouri 65211. The number to call is (314) 442-0418.

Treatment: Medical treatment is directed at relieving pain and improving function by giving buffered or enteric coated aspirin or one of the newer synthetic coated aspirin products (but not IBUPROFEN) used in the treatment of degenerative joint disease in humans (see *Arthritis*). Treatment is most effective for dogs with mild to moderate symptoms that exercise and remain active.

Moderate exercise is important, as it encourages muscle mass and helps to support the rear.

Surgical treatment usually is reserved for dogs with more incapacitating symptoms. Four surgical procedures advocated in the treatment of hip dysplasia are: (1) division of the pectineus muscle or tendon, (2) pelvic osteotomy, (3) femoral head ostectomy and (4) total hip replacement. With bilateral hip involvement, surgery is performed on both sides.

Pectineus myotomy or tendenectomy is a relatively simple procedure in which the pectineus tendon or muscle is surgically divided. It often affords temporary relief from pain for many months, but will not prevent the progression of degenerative joint changes. Some orthopedic surgeons believe that the simultaneous division of the adductor magnus muscle provides additional benefit.

Pelvic osteotomy is a recent, more complicated operation in which a new acetabulum is created in a more favorable position. In experienced hands, it has produced good results in about 60 percent of cases. Unlike tendon surgery, osteotomy does appear to retard the progression of joint disease.

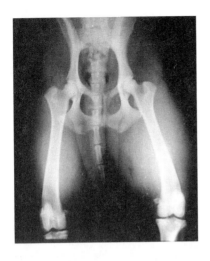

X-ray of normal hips. The femoral heads are well-rounded and fit snug and deep in the sockets.

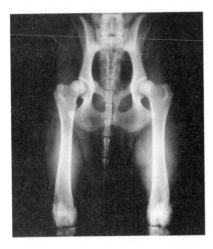

Moderate Dysplasia: Loose hips are wearing the walls of the sockets and flattening the femoral heads.

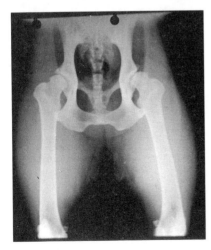

Severe Dysplasia: These loose hips are partially dislocated. Note the bone spurs on the femoral heads and rims of the sockets, indicative of degenerative arthritis.

Removal of the entire head of the femur, called *femoral head ostectomy*, creates a new "false" joint. It is quite effective in relieving intractable hip pain.

Total hip replacement, used in humans for many years, is now being done successfully in dogs. The entire ball-and-socket joint is removed and replaced by a stainless steel joint. Although an effective treatment for advanced hip dysplasia, the cost of the operation has tended to restrict its use.

Statistics compiled by the OFA over a ten-year period show that repeated selection of normal dogs for breeding stock significantly reduces the incidence of hip dysplasia in susceptible bloodlines.

Destruction of the Ball of the Hip (Aseptic Necrosis)

Aseptic necrosis of the head of the femur is caused by impaired blood supply to the ball of the hip. It leads to gradual destruction of the hip joint. Primarily it occurs in young Toy dogs between four and ten months of age. Genetic factors may be involved. In other breeds it can be a sequel to sudden hip dislocation (auto accident).

The signs are severe lameness and refusal to bear weight on the leg. Muscle wasting is pronounced. There is loss of motion at the joint and the leg can be shortened.

Treatment: Surgical removal of the head of the femur gives good results. Anti-inflammatory drugs such as buffered or enteric coated aspirin and Butazolidin can be tried to relieve pain. Spontaneous improvement has been reported.

Slipping Kneecap (Patellar Dislocation, Luxating Patella)

Dislocating kneecap can be inherited or acquired through trauma. It occurs sporadically among Toy breed dogs, although it can be found in large breeds, too.

In dogs the kneecap is a small bone that protects the front of the stifle joint; it is the counterpart of the kneecap in man. It is anchored in place by ligaments, and slides in a groove in the femur.

Conditions that predispose to dislocation of the patella are a shallow groove, weak ligaments and malalignment of the tendons and muscles that straighten the joint. The patella slips inward or outward.

The signs of a slipped kneecap are difficulty straightening the knee, pain in the stifle and a limp. The tip of the hock often points outward and the toes inward (the reverse of cow hocks).

The diagnosis is confirmed by manipulating the stifle joint and pushing the kneecap in and out of position.

Treatment involves surgery to deepen the groove and/or re-align the tendon.

Popping Hock (Laxity of the Hock Joint)

This condition, which may affect one or both hocks, is caused by looseness of supporting structures around the joint. It is more common in large dogs with straight rear-end angulation. Usually it is not painful but can impair the dog's drive and agility. In late stages the joint can become arthritic.

The diagnosis can be suspected by observing the dog in motion, at which time the hock will appear to give, causing an irregular gait. Manipulation of the joint reveals the lax ligaments. The hock slips out of place (either forward or to the side) when the joint is straightened.

Treatment: Early immobilization by splints (or cage rest) may reverse the condition in some young pups. The disease is carried in certain bloodlines. It can be reduced by proper breeding practices.

Elbow Dysplasia

This condition is caused by one or more of the following: un-united anconeal process of the ulna, fragmented medial coronoid process of the elbow joint and un-united medial epicondyle of the humerus. Two separate conditions occur in most large breeds. All three are of developmental origin and produce an incongruent elbow joint that articulates poorly, wears badly and produces degenerative joint disease over a period of months or years. Loose fragments of bone or flaps of cartilage in the elbow joint act as an irritant and abrasive.

Elbow dysplasia is found most often in Golden Retrievers, Labrador Retrievers, Flat-Coated Retrievers, German Shepherds and Basset Hounds, and has been described in other breeds. It is thought to be inherited.

Pups begin to show lameness in the front leg at about six months of age. Some are unable to bear weight; others limp only when trotting. Characteristically, the elbow is held outward from the chest.

Treatment: X-rays taken after five months of age are diagnostic. Removal

The enlarged elbow joints and wide stance of a dog with bilateral *elbow dysplasia.*

of a loose piece of bone (joint mouse) or scrapping of the joint space to remove devitalized cartilage and connective tissue affords some relief. However, this does not change the basic problem of joint incongruity. Degenerative joint disease will occur over time. For further information on the treatment of degenerative joint disease, see *Arthritis*.

The Orthopedic Foundation for Animals will evaluate X-rays for elbow dysplasia as they do for hip dysplasia.

Separation of Joint Cartilage (Osteochondritis Dissecans)

Osteochondritis dissecans (*OCD*) affects dogs of the large rapidly growing breeds between the ages of four and twelve months. It usually is found in the shoulder joints, but rarely it can affect the hocks or stifles.

It is caused by a defect in the cartilage overlying the head of one of the long bones. A puppy that jumps down stairs might sustain such an injury. The tendency for cartilage to be easily damaged may be hereditary. Repeated stress to the joint perpetrates the condition.

The signs are gradual lameness in a young dog of one of the larger breeds. Pain is present on flexing the joint. X-rays may show fragmentation of the joint cartilage or a loose piece of cartilage in the joint.

Treatment: A large piece of cartilage or bone fragment in the joint space causing pain and lameness in a pup four to six months of age is best treated by surgical removal. Often this surgery can be performed through the arthroscope (arthroscopy). Small defects, especially when seen in older pups seven to nine months of age, will often reabsorb with early strict confinement for one month. If lameness returns, then surgery is indicated.

Wandering Lameness (Eosinophilic Panosteitis)

Panosteitis, also called "growing pains" or "wandering lameness," is a disease of puppies between five and twelve months of age. Suspect this diagnosis if your pup suddenly presents with an acute lameness unrelated to trauma. The cause is unknown, but there is a tendency for the disease to run in families. German Shepherds and Doberman Pinchers are affected most commonly.

A characteristic sign is the tendency for pain and lameness to shift from one location to another over a course of several weeks or months. The disease often is accompanied by fever, eosinophils in the white blood count, muscle wasting and unthriftiness. Pressure over the shaft of the affected bone elicits pain. X-rays show the characteristic picture of increased density in a long bone.

Treatment: As the cause is unknown, treatment is directed at the relief of bone pain (see *Arthritis*). Most dogs recover spontaneously, but if severely affected, may never regain full muscle strength and condition.

ARTHRITIS (DEGENERATIVE JOINT DISEASE)

Arthritis is a condition that can affect one or more joints in the dog. In some cases it can be accounted for by a history of wear and tear to the joint. In others it seems to occur with advancing age. Although it can begin in the first half of life, usually signs don't appear until the dog is at least ten years of age.

Large breeds are affected more often than small ones. Heavy dogs, regardless of breed, are more likely to experience symptoms because of the excess stress placed upon their joints.

Rheumatoid arthritis is part of a generalized disease of body connective tissue. This is a rare cause of arthritis in the dog. Predominately it affects small or Toy breeds. The cause is unknown, but an autoimmune basis is suspected.

It is characterized by morning stiffness, shifting lameness and swelling of the smaller joints, particularly the pasterns and hocks. Fever, loss of appetite and lymphadenopathy are accompanying features. Diagnosis is made by joint X rays, laboratory studies and specific serological blood tests. Effective treatment requires the long-term use of corticosteroids and immunosuppressives.

Septic arthritis is caused by bacteria that gain access to the joint space through penetrating wounds, neighboring bone infections or via the bloodstream from a remote focus of infection. Nonsterile injections into the joint are another cause. Treatment requires intravenous antibiotics (or by local infusion if only one joint is involved). This must be continued for several weeks.

Certain infections diseases can produce septic arthritis. Rickettsial arthritis is seen with Rocky Mountain spotted fever and canine ehrlichiosis; spirochetal arthritis with Lyme disease. These are being recognized more frequently. Fungal arthritis is a rare finding in generalized fungus infections. These diseases are discussed in the chapter INFECTIOUS DISEASES.

Autoimmune arthritis is an unusual group of diseases in which an altered immune response is the cause of the disorder. Autoimmunity is discussed in the SKIN chapter.

The most common autoimmune arthritis is called *idiopathic nondeforming arthritis*. It tends to occur in large breeds, particularly German Shepherds and Doberman Pinschers. The signs are intermittent fever, loss of appetite and joint swelling with stiffness and lameness in one or more limbs. The disease responds moderately well to corticosteroids and immunosuppressives.

Joint inflammation can occur as part of a generalized disease process such as lupus erythematosus, chronic inflammatory bowel disease, liver disease or malignant tumor. All of the above are rare causes of canine arthritis.

Drug-induced hypersensitivity reactions involving the joints are being seen more often. Hives and other skin rashes occur along with the arthritis. Antibiotics are the chief offenders.

The most common type of arthritis in dogs is called *osteoarthritis* or *degenerative joint disease*. Dogs with degenerative arthritis experience varying degrees of lameness, stiffness that is worse in the morning (or after getting up from a nap) and pain in the joints. Cold and damp weather increase the severity of pain, stiffness and reluctance to move.

An acute flare-up leads to accentuation of the above symptoms and the development of a swollen tender joint (effusion). A "grating" sensation may be detected when working the joint back and forth.

X-rays show varying degrees of joint space narrowing, joint destruction and remodeling of articular surfaces and compensatory new bone formation in and around the joint.

Treatment of Arthritis: In those cases with a known cause, the treatment is directed at the primary disease. In osteoarthritis, it is directed at relieving joint pain and encouraging moderate activity to prevent stiffness.

Dogs with degenerative joint disease should be given daily periods of rest interspersed with moderate exercise. Exercise is important because this maintains muscle mass, helps to support the joints and prevents weight gain. Overweight dogs should be put on a diet.

Extremes of exercise should be avoided. However, dogs seem to be able to put up with almost any amount of pain for the sheer pleasure of hunting, jogging, playing or hiking with their owners. In general, activities that cause your dog to become noticeably lame should be curtailed or cut back.

Anti-inflammatory drugs are used to relieve pain and encourage moderate activity. Buffered or enteric coated aspirin is perhaps the safest medication to use for this purpose. The dose is five grains per twenty-five pounds body weight. This dose should be given two times a day. Gastrointestinal bleeding is a potential danger, but buffered or enteric coated aspirin does not produce gastric ulcers in dogs nearly as often as aspirin does in humans.

Some of the newer nonsteroidal anti-inflammatory drugs used to treat arthritis in people can be given to dogs; however, their efficacy in dogs has *not* been shown to be superior to that of buffered or enteric coated aspirin, and they are much more likely to cause gastrointestinal bleeding. Indocin also is more likely to cause ulcers in dogs.

Butazolidin (phenylbutazone) has been used to treat dogs with degenerative joint disease. Bone marrow depression can be a serious side effect, especially when used in high doses over a prolonged period of time. Corticosteroids when used for short periods have considerable benefit for the severely arthritic dog. Both of these drugs should be used under veterinary supervision.

Surgical fusion of painful joints, such as the hock or elbow, relieves pain and restores limb movement in selected individuals. Femoral head ostectomy or joint replacement can be helpful in dogs with badly diseased hips (see *Canine Hip Dysplasia*).

METABOLIC BONE DISORDERS

Parathyroid Bone Disease

There are four small glands in the neck of the dog, located in proximity to the thyroid. They are called the *parathyroids*. They secrete a hormone important in calcium and bone metabolism. Too much parathyroid hormone in the system impairs the formation of new bone in young dogs. In the adult dog, it leads to softening and weakening of established bone.

To understand the effects of parathyroid hormone on bone, it is important to know three facts:

1. Low serum calcium stimulates the parathyroid glands to secrete more hormone.

2. Parathyroid hormone restores blood calcium levels by drawing calcium out of the bones.
3. Concentration of calcium and phosphorus in the blood is inversely related: a high blood phosphorus, for example, causes a low blood calcium (and vice versa).

With these facts in mind, it is not difficult to understand the mechanisms of metabolic bone disease caused by calcium or phosphorus imbalance.

Primary Hyperparathyroidism

This condition is caused by a tumor of one of the parathyroid glands. The tumor produces excess hormone. It is rare in the dog.

On X-ray the bone is demineralized, thin and often looks cystic (small holes in the bone). Minor stress can cause a fracture.

Surgical removal of the affected gland is the only possible treatment.

Renal Secondary Hyperparathyroidism

This is the result of long-standing kidney disease, which causes retention of phosphorus in the blood. The high phosphorus concentrations depress the blood calcium that, in turn, stimulates the parathyroid glands to produce excess hormone.

The effects on bone are the same as those of primary hyperparathyroidism, but the symptoms in the dog are usually dominated by the kidney picture (uremia).

Treatment is directed at correcting the kidney problem.

Nutritional Secondary Hyperparathyroidism

This disease is caused by a deficiency of calcium or vitamin D in the diet. It is also caused by an excess of phosphorus. It was common when the unsupplemented "all meat" diet was commercially popular.

Either a deficiency of calcium or an excess of phosphorus has the effect of stimulating the parathyroid glands to secrete more hormone. This depletes the bones of calcium, leading to structural weakness.

Vitamin D deficiency causes the problem because vitamin D is required for calcium to be absorbed from the intestinal tract.

The daily calcium, phosphorus and vitamin D requirements for *growing puppies* are:

Vitamin D : 9 units per pound body weight
Calcium   : 240 mg per pound body weight
Phosphorus: 200 mg per pound body weight

The requirements for adult dogs are exactly one-half of the above.

To achieve a desired calcium/phosphorus ratio of 1.2 to 1, a diet must provide an adequate intake of both minerals. Most commercial foods for adult dogs and growing pups provide adequate concentrations.

Feeding practices that *can* lead to calcium deficiency are unsupplemented high-meat diets, all-vegetable diets, corn bread diets and feeding too many leftover table scraps (especially as they are frequently just vegetables).

In *puppies* and young dogs the signs of skeletal disease are lameness, thriftlessness, bone pain, stunted growth and spontaneous fractures.

In *older* dogs periodontal disease usually is the first sign. It causes thinning of the jaw bones with exposure of the roots of the teeth. The teeth loosen and are expelled.

When unchecked, the condition eventually leads to death.

Treatment: Correct the diet by feeding a good quality, balanced commercial ration, one advertised as supporting normal puppy growth.

Calcium carbonate should be supplemented when, because of advanced periodontal disease or fixed eating habits, the dog will not consume adequate amounts of a balanced kibble ration. Excess calcium should be avoided. Overdosing may make the dog worse.

Vitamins A and D (and trace minerals) should be added, but only to meet normal requirements.

Rickets (Osteomalacia)

Rickets (called osteomalacia in the adult) is caused by a deficiency of vitamin D. Since this vitamin is active in the absorption of calcium and phosphorus from the intestine, these minerals may be deficient also. The disease in the dog is rare. Many cases classified as rickets are probably nutritional secondary hyperparathyroidism.

Signs: There is a characteristic enlargement of the joints where the ribs meet the cartilages of the sternum (rachitic rosary). Bowing of the legs and other growth deformities in the puppy, along with fractures in the adult, are common in severe cases.

Treatment: It is the same as for nutritional secondary hyperparathyroidism.

Hypertrophic Osteodystrophy (HOD)

This disease affects puppies of the large, rapidly growing breeds three to seven months of age. It resembles scurvy in humans, but in dogs the cause is uncertain. (Scurvy is caused by a deficiency of vitamin C.)

Because the dog manufactures vitamin C (in contrast to humans who have to depend on an outside source), it has been suggested that HOD in the dog may be the result of improper synthesis of this vitamin or a defect in its utilization by the tissues.

Vitamin C is needed to make *framework* for bone. In contrast, vitamin D is needed to *mineralize* bone, once formed.

HOD affects the long bones near the joints (wrists and the hocks). These joints become swollen, tender and give rise to lameness. X-rays initially show a "moth-eaten" area in a long bone above the growth plate. Later, too much bone is laid down (hypertrophic osteodystrophy). Impaired growth of bone leads to deformities.

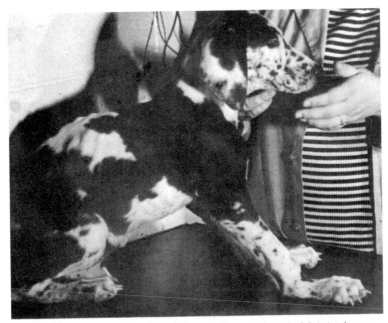

Nutritional deficiency and mineral imbalance can cause the wrist joints to give way.

Some cases classified as HOD probably are caused by improper feeding practices, such as feeding too many calories, giving too much calcium and overdosing with vitamins during the growth period. These practices lead to an X-ray picture identical to hypertrophic osteodystrophy. They should be avoided.

Treatment of HOD involves resting the dog and giving buffered or enteric coated aspirin to control pain and swelling. Most dogs recover spontaneously in one to four weeks. Relapse is uncommon.

Overdosing with Vitamins

Many people think that a rapidly growing puppy needs to have supplemental vitamins and minerals in order to build strong bone. Modern name-brand commercial dog rations, made up for puppy growth and development, supply all the needed vitamins and minerals to sustain normal growth—provided the puppy or young dog eats it well. Vitamins and minerals in excess of those required will not add more bone and substance to the growing animal.

When calcium, phosphorus and vitamin D are given beyond a dog's capacity to use them normally, growth and development can be adversely affected. Overfeeding and overdosing with vitamins, as discussed above, can cause a bone disorder similar to HOD.

Vitamin and calcium supplements might be indicated for rapidly growing pups who are poor eaters. If you own such a dog, discuss this with your veterinarian.

14

Urinary System

THE URINARY TRACT is composed of the kidneys and ureters, bladder, prostate and urethra.

The kidneys are paired organs located on each side of the backbone just behind and below the last ribs. Each kidney has a renal pelvis or funnel that siphons the urine into a ureter. The ureters pass on down to the pelvic brim and empty into the bladder. The passageway that connects the neck of the bladder to the outside is called the urethra. The opening of the urethra is found at the tip of the penis in the male and between the folds of the vulva in the female. In the male, the urethra also serves as a channel for semen.

The function of the kidneys is to regulate the water, mineral and chemical balance of the blood, and to excrete the wastes of metabolism. This is accomplished by *nephrons*, the basic working units of the kidneys. Damage to nephrons leads to renal insufficiency (kidney failure).

Normal urine is yellow and clear. Its color can be altered by the state of hydration of the dog and by certain drugs. Buffered or enteric coated aspirin, for example, turns urine an orange-yellow.

The act of voiding is under the conscious control of the central nervous system. A dog can decide when to void. This is the basis for successful house training. But once the decision to void is reached, the actual mechanism of bladder emptying is carried out by a complicated spinal cord reflex.

To learn more about disorders of the male and female *reproductive* system, see the chapter SEX AND REPRODUCTION.

SIGNS OF URINARY TRACT DISEASES

Most urinary tract disorders are associated with some disturbance in the normal pattern of voiding. The things to look for are:

Painful Urination (Dysuria): Signs are obvious distress during urination with straining, dribbling, licking at the penis or vulva, crying out in pain, voiding frequently in small amounts, squatting but not passing urine after many tries and the passage of mucus, blood clots or bloody urine. Pain and swelling within the lower abdomen suggest an overdistended bladder. These symptoms indicate a disorder of the bladder, urethra or prostate.

Blood in Urine (Hematuria): Blood in the first fraction of urine that clears with voiding indicates a problem in the urethra, penis, prostate, uterus or vagina. Blood which appears at the end of voiding suggests a disease of the bladder or prostate. A uniformly bloody urine is seen with diseases of the kidneys, ureters and bladder. Bleeding without dysuria suggests a kidney or uterine problem.

Excessive Urination (Polyuria): Frequent passage of large volumes of urine suggests kidney disease. The dog compensates by drinking large amounts of water. You may notice this first. Diabetes mellitus is another cause of excessive thirst and urination. Polyuria should be distinguished from *dysuria* (above).

Urinary Incontinence: This is defined as an abnormal pattern of voiding in which there is inappropriate urination. Dribbling, urgency, frequency and bed-wetting are characteristic signs (see *Urinary Incontinency* below).

Because of overlapping symptoms and the fact that more than one organ may be involved at the same time, it is difficult to make an exact diagnosis on the bases of symptoms alone.

In the diagnosis of urinary tract disease, the laboratory can be of considerable help. Routine tests are a urinalysis, which tells your veterinarian whether your dog has a urinary tract infection, and blood chemistries, which provide information about the function of the kidneys.

Additional studies are often indicated. They include urine cultures and X-ray examinations of the abdomen. The intravenous pyelogram is an X-ray examination in which a dye is injected into the circulation. It is excreted by the kidneys and outlines much of the urinary tract.

Cystoscopy is an examination of the interior of the bladder using a lighted instrument. Other selective studies may be performed when indicated. They include surgical exploration and/or biopsy.

KIDNEY DISEASE

Inflammation of the Kidney and Pelvis (Pyelonephritis)

One or both kidneys may be involved by a bacterial infection. Usually this is preceded by an infection lower in the system. There may be a blockage or congenital malformation of the urinary tract. In some cases bacteria gain entrance to the kidney via the bloodstream.

Acute pyelonephritis (days to weeks) begins with fever and pain in the kidney area. A stiff-legged gait and a hunched-up posture are characteristic signs.

The arched back and humped-up posture of a dog suffering from *acute pyelonephritis*.

Pus may appear in the urine. It is often bloody. Disturbances in the normal pattern of voiding are common.

Chronic pyelonephritis (months to years) is an insidious disease. It may be preceded by signs of acute infection but often these are lacking. You may see signs of kidney failure when the disease is of long duration. If chronic pyelonephritis is found before irreversible changes occur in the kidneys (for example, during a periodic health checkup), treatment may prevent complications.

Treatment: The urine should be cultured. Appropriate antibiotics are selected on the basis of bacterial sensitivity. Antibiotics should be continued for four to six weeks in the treatment of all upper urinary tract infections. Relapses are common. It is important to culture the urine once a month for three months, and then every three months for a year. If relapses occur, the dog should be placed on a daily low-dose long-term antibiotic.

Nephritis and Nephrosis

These names are given to certain conditions of the kidneys that cause scarring. When the scarring is caused by leptospira and other bacteria, the viruses of distemper, hepatitis and herpes, some drugs and poisons and certain congenital and familial diseases, the result is a *nephritis*—or *inflammation of the kidneys*.

When it is caused by degenerative changes in the tissues of the kidneys, the condition is called *nephrosis*.

One cause of nephrosis is maldevelopment of the kidneys. It occurs in Lhasa Apsos and Norwegian Elkhounds.

In many cases, the exact cause of nephritis or nephrosis will be unknown. As the disease progresses, the signs and symptoms become those of uremic poisoning or kidney failure.

Kidney Failure (Uremic Poisoning)

Kidney failure may be sudden and acute or chronic and progressive. Acute failure occurs after certain infectious diseases, such as leptospirosis, and during shock and poisoning. Chronic failure is the end result of nephritis and other long-standing diseases.

Azotemia refers to a buildup of nitrogen wastes in the blood (blood urea nitrogen, or BUN, and creatinine). The kidneys concentrate and excrete nitrogen, thus keeping the BUN and creatinine levels within normal.

The kidneys will not make urine and therefore cannot maintain normal blood levels if the blood pressure falls below a threshold critical to perfusion of the kidneys. Accordingly, dehydration, blood loss, shock, congestive heart failure and injuries to the arteries of the kidneys all can cause acute renal insufficiency. Since this happens even though the kidneys are normal, this type of kidney failure is called *prerenal azotemia*. It will improve if the underlying cause is treated promptly.

Nor will the kidneys make urine if the lower urinary tract is blocked by a stone, tumor or infectious process; urine then backs up, shutting off production. This type of kidney failure is called *postrenal azotemia*.

By far the majority of kidney failures are chronic and renal in origin. *Renal azotemia* occurs when 75 percent of kidney function is lost to disease. In consequence, the kidneys cannot concentrate and eliminate waste products, nor can they absorb water and electrolytes back into the system. The result is an obligate urine output much greater than normal and a buildup of metabolic wastes in the blood.

At first you may notice that your dog seems to drink and void a lot more than usual and will want to go outdoors several times a day to void. If confined to the house, the dog will begin to make mistakes—especially at night.

Uremic poisoning: As kidney function continues to deteriorate, the dog will begin to retain more nitrogen, ammonia, acids and other wastes in the blood and tissues. Signs of uremia are apathy and depression, refusal to eat, loss of condition, dry hair coat, a brownish discoloration to the surface of the tongue and an ammonialike odor to the breath. Vomiting, diarrhea and gastrointestinal bleeding can occur. Anemia is common. Terminally, the dog falls into a coma.

A condition called *rubber jaw* occurs with chronic kidney failure. It is caused by prolonged loss of calcium through the kidneys and failure to deposit calcium around the teeth. It is characterized by loosening of the teeth and ulcerations of the mouth and gums.

Treatment: The outlook depends upon the cause of uremia and how much damage has been done to the kidneys over time. A dog suffering from chronic kidney failure still can have many happy months or years of life ahead with

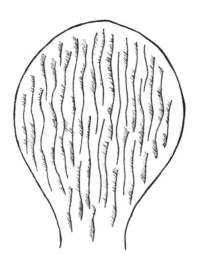

Figure 1
Normal bladder mucosa.
(The mucosa lines the
inside of the bladder).
Drawing by Michelle Bamberger
D.V.M.

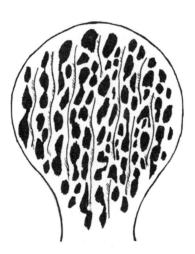

Figure 2
Cystitis. The mucosa
of the bladder is
filled with blood, pus
and bacteria.
Drawing by Michelle Bamberger
D.V.M.

proper treatment. Your veterinarian may wish to make an exact diagnosis by ordering special tests or by exploratory surgery and biopsy. This helps to determine whether the ailment is reversible.

It is important in the management of kidney failure to replace salt lost in the urine by giving sodium chloride tablets by mouth, to feed a high-quality, low-protein diet and to give vitamin supplements to replace vitamins lost by the kidneys.

A recipe for a homemade *low* protein diet is:

¼ lb. lean ground beef
1 hard-boiled egg
2 cups of cooked rice
3 slices of bread (crumbled)
Add balanced vitamin and mineral supplements

Or Hills Prescription Diet k/d can be used for this purpose.

A recipe for a home-made *very low* protein diet is:

2½ cups of cooked rice
1 ounce vegetable oil
1 hard-boiled egg
Add balanced vitamin and mineral supplements

Or Hills Prescription Diet u/d can be used for this purpose.

Water should be available at all times. Some exercise is good for a uremic dog, but stressful activity should be avoided.

DISORDERS OF THE BLADDER, URETHRA AND PROSTATE

In the lower urinary tract there are four basic problems, often interrelated. They are infections, obstructions, stones and urinary incontinence.

Bladder Infection (Cystitis)

Cystitis is a bacterial infection of the lining of the bladder. Infections in the genital tracts of both males and females may precede bouts of cystitis. Females with cystitis may lick at their vulva and have a discharge. Most cases of cystitis are caused by bacteria that gain entrance to the bladder through the urethra. In some cases bacteria gain entrance through the bloodstream or via the kidneys.

The most common signs of cystitis are frequent urination and the passage of blood or traces of blood in the urine. If your dog strains to void or exhibits signs of pain on urination, cystitis or a bladder outlet obstruction may be the cause.

Treatment: Cystitis must be treated promptly to prevent ascending infection and damage to the kidneys.

A urine culture can be taken to determine an appropriate antibiotic combination. An initial attack should be treated for fourteen days and the urine rechecked three to five days later to be sure the infection has cleared. A recurrent attack should be treated for at least three weeks with frequent follow-up urine tests.

Chronic forms of cystitis require the use of urinary antiseptics and/or chemical substances to acidify the urine. Giving one or two teaspoonfuls of table salt a day will cause your dog to drink more water and pass more urine. This helps to flush out the bladder.

Obstructed Bladder (Urinary Retention)

A dog that strains to pass urine, or has obvious difficulty emptying the bladder, is probably suffering from a blockage in the bladder outlet or urethra.

Stones in the bladder or urethra are the most common causes. However, tumors, strictures and infections are at times responsible. Enlargement of the prostate gland is not a common cause of obstruction in the dog, as it is in humans.

A dog with an obstructed bladder is acutely uncomfortable or in dire distress. Males and females often assume a peculiar splay-legged stance while painfully attempting to void. Continuous straining might be confused with constipation. Pressure on the abdomen beneath the pelvis may reveal a swollen, tender bladder, which feels like a large ball in front of the pelvis. With *complete* obstruction, no urine is passed.

A *partial* obstruction can be suspected when the dog begins to dribble, voids frequently, has a weak, splattery stream, but is not in acute distress. A partial obstruction may, with continued irritation, terminate in a complete obstruction.

Treatment: Complete obstruction of the bladder is a medical emergency. A sterile catheter must be inserted into the bladder to provide relief. It should be done by one familiar with the technique and having the necessary equipment. Treatment then is directed at the underlying cause.

Stones

In human beings, stones often are formed in the kidneys. However, in the dog the bladder is the usual location. Some breeds are more likely to form bladder stones than others. They include the Pekingese, Dachshund and Cocker Spaniel. The Dalmatian is the only breed that excretes uric acid of the human type; therefore, it is the only breed that can form uric acid stones.

Most stones in dogs are *struvite* (magnesium ammonium phosphate). They form in an alkaline urine, are associated with diet and with urinary tract infections and have a genetic predisposition. These factors are closely related.

Calcium-containing stones occur much less frequently as do those containing cystine and uric acid.

Bladder stones are of several types. There may be a single large stone that blocks the flow of urine or many small gravelly stones that are voided painfully and cause the dog much distress. Stones in the bladder eventually will cause cystitis, if this is not already present.

Treatment: While most stones form in an alkaline urine, some stones form

Bladder stones.

in an acid urine. It is important to analyze the urine for bacteria and urine acidity—and if possible the stone—to determine the best treatment.

Medical management is directed at dissolving small stones and keeping new ones from forming. Struvite stones are dissolved by acidifying the urine, feeding a diet low in magnesium ammonium phosphate and treating underlying cystitis, if present.

Prescription diets are available through your veterinarian for treating and preventing various types of stones. Large stones must be removed by an operation.

Urinary Incontinence

Incontinent dogs are those that have an abnormal pattern of voiding. They may lose control, void frequently, often dribble and begin to make mistakes in the house. There may be a strong ammonialike odor about the dog or bedding. Skin around the penis or vulva can become scalded.

Most cases of urinary incontinence can be treated, provided that the underlying cause can been determined:

Behavioral Incontinence

The individual squats or lifts a leg and urinates *voluntarily*. Usually the purpose is territorial marking. This can happen when a dog is introduced to a new household. Management is the same as for housebreaking (see *PEDIATRICS: Training and Socialization*).

Bladder Infection

This is an *urge* type of incontinence. The individual squats or lifts a leg and voids *voluntarily*. However, with bladder infection there is an element of pain and frequency. Only a small amount of urine is passed each time. Treatment is discussed above (see Bladder Infection).

Obstructed Bladder

Signs are like those of bladder infection, but because the dog is not able to empty a *full* bladder, the urine leaks out in small amounts and the dog *dribbles*. An overdistended bladder can often be felt by pressing on the abdomen just in front of the pelvis.

Damage to the nerve supply of the bladder (caused by spinal cord disease, ruptured disc, tumor) can result in a large flaccid bladder that contracts poorly, overflows frequently produces dribbling, and gives the impression of an obstructed bladder.

These two conditions can be distinguished by veterinary examination and the passage of a urinary catheter. Drugs can be given to stimulate bladder emptying for neurologic causes. Stones and other causes of mechanical blockage are discussed elsewhere in this chapter.

Hormone Deficiency

In this type of incontinence, which is much like bed-wetting, the individual urinates normally but wets where resting or sleeping.

This problem is seen most often in the older female that has been spayed. It is caused by a deficiency of estrogen. Estrogen is important in maintaining muscle tone of the urethra. Testosterone serves this same purpose in the male. Therefore, older castrated males may exhibit this problem.

Incontinence in spayed females has long been treated with estrogen replacement. Prolonged use does have undesirable effects, which include bone marrow depression, skin problems and attraction of males. Accordingly, other medications may be prescribed.

Testosterone is the treatment of choice for castrated males with hormone-responsive incontinence.

Other Causes

Incontinence present from birth suggests a congenital defect in which the ureter joins the vagina instead of the bladder.

Incontinence shortly after spaying usually is caused by postoperative adhesions. It is correctable by surgery.

Enlarged Prostate

The prostate is an accessory sex gland in males found at the base of the bladder. It partly surrounds the urethra. Prostatic enlargement occurs in many dogs over five years of age, but few show any ill effects from it. Those that do usually are elderly. An enlarging prostate gland usually expands backward into the rectum. But when large enough, it can push forward and exert pressure on the outlet of the bladder, causing changes in the voiding pattern (frequent urination, dribbling and loss of control). This is not common.

The outstanding sign of prostatic enlargement is straining at stool, during which there is obvious pain. The feces may appear flat on one side or ribbonlike. Blockages do occur (fecal impactions). Oddly, one sign of fecal impaction is diarrhea. It is caused by liquid feces forcing its way around a solid lump.

Treatment: It is required only for symptoms. Castration is the treatment of choice. It eliminates the stimulus (testosterone) for prostate enlargement. If this is not an option, low-dose estrogen can be considered. The exact dose is important. Prolonged use can actually cause the prostate gland to enlarge and become cystic. This predisposes to prostatitis.

If your dog is having difficulty emptying the rectum, read the section on constipation, in the chapter DIGESTIVE SYSTEM: *Intestines*.

Cancer of the prostate gland is uncommon in the dog.

Prostatitis

Acute prostatitis is a bacterial infection of the prostate gland. The signs are fever, an arched back or a tucked-up abdomen, pain on urination and difficulty in voiding. Infected-looking secretions may drip from the penis. The disease can become chronic with periodic flare-ups. It is one cause of sterility in the male.

Treatment: Prostatitis should be treated by a veterinarian. Appropriate antibiotics are employed, based on cultures of prostatic secretions. They must be continued for four to six weeks. Castration is often recommended when there is a lack of response to antibiotics.

15

Sex and Reproduction

SEX AND SOCIABILITY

Centuries of selective breeding for qualities that make the dog useful for various purposes have also caused a profound change in the dog's social orientation and sexual responses.

At a time when the wild ancestors of dogs ran in packs, they must have had unlimited opportunity to learn species behavior patterns and establish appropriate roles within their pack hierarchy. But today many dogs seem to be rank amateurs in the mere business of greeting and getting along with members of their own kind. This is especially true where dogs have lived almost exclusively with people and have had little or no opportunity to form social relations with other dogs.

In contrast, wolves, wild cousins of the dog, are extremely affectionate with one another. But in wolf society actual mating enters into the picture only during a short breeding season each spring. In a pack of any size only the dominant male and female are permitted to breed. Others must provide food, stand watch over the litter and assist in the preparation of the den and the guarding of it against enemies. This is the economy of nature that provides for survival of the species.

Early sexual maturity and high fertility in the dog is a direct result of selective breeding. This has brought about physical changes in the dog as well. Dogs develop quickly and attain puberty at an early age. A male may be able to sire puppies at ten months old. Females become sexually mature when they reach their second heat.

Dogs are sexually compliant in the sense that they don't mate for life and are willing to accept a breeding partner chosen for them by their owners. Unlike

297

wolves, they remain firmly attached to their owners, forming less firm bonds with members of their own species.

At times, this can create problems for the dog breeder.

BREEDING

If you plan to breed purebred dogs, it is important to begin with a mental grasp of what it is you are trying to accomplish. The object of any breeding program is to preserve the essential qualities and physical attributes of the breed.

A thorough understanding of the breed Standard is a basic requirement. Beyond the Standard, however, there is an elusive something extra; a certain, almost extrasensory, perception that gives success to those who have it, which others never seem quite able to grasp.

A successful breeder is one who knows desirable traits and is willing to breed for them and try to eliminate undesirable ones. Knowledge of this sort does not come spontaneously. You may be lucky enough to have been born with an eye for a good dog. Still, you need to learn everything you can about your breed, especially the bloodlines from which you plan to choose your stock. Visit as many kennels as you can, talk to their owners and see the tried-and-true producers, the retired dogs and the up-and-coming ones.

You will notice that the successful breeder is the one who sees faults in his or her own dogs as readily as those in a rival's. Perhaps that little "something extra" is the good sense to breed with the *whole* dog in mind—not to put emphasis on any one single attribute at the expense of the overall dog.

Pedigrees are important because they are the means to study the bloodlines and learn the relationships between the various dogs. They are of greatest value when the dogs are known or actually have been seen.

Championships do indicate merit and do give some indication of quality. However, they are not always completely informative as to the overall superiority of the individuals listed. Some championships are won through the accident of less than normal quality in the competition. The opposite is also true—some dogs do not win their titles simply because of lack of exposure.

Count the championships, but also study the patterns of inheritance. Look for qualities that have endured from generation to generation. Familiarize yourself with the individual dogs. This will give you a sound perspective on the assets of the bloodlines in question.

Genetics

Breeding is subject to the chance combination of countless genes. The smallest combination of genes that can determine a hereditary trait is a pair. One gene is inherited from each parent. When two genes combine, the *dominant* gene is the one that determines the trait. A *recessive* gene does not determine a trait unless it is combined with another recessive gene. Other combinations may be *additive*—that is, both genes contribute in part to the expression of the trait.

Unfortunately, most traits that we as breeders are interested in are deter-

298

mined by a great many genetic pairs—which is why dog breeding is an art and not an exact science. Since a dog has thirty-nine pairs of chromosomes and each chromosome contains more than 25,000 genes, the genetic possibilities are almost infinite.

About one out of every hundred puppies born will express a demonstrable congenital defect. Many undesirable hereditary traits are expressed by recessive genes. Such a gene can be carried down through many generations of offspring, causing no problem until it is combined with a like recessive gene. This is why recessive traits cannot be eliminated in one or two generations of careful breeding, and why sporadic hereditary defects are more frequently caused by recessive genes.

In contrast, dominant traits are seen in the first generation of puppies. Breeders easily recognize problems caused by dominant genes. By choosing not to breed such individuals and their offspring, they eliminate those traits from their breeding program.

Undesirable hereditary traits commonly seen by dog owners include: undescended testicles; inguinal and navel hernias; abnormally short or absent tails; canine hip dysplasia and elbow dysplasia; Wobbler's syndrome; malocclusion and incorrect bite; cleft palate and harelip; slipping kneecaps; congenital cataracts; coagulation disorders; congenital deafness; entropion and ectropion; Collie eye and progressive retinal atrophy; behavioral disorders, such as inherited aggression and shyness.

When you breed two dogs with a common ancestor, their litter inherits some of the same genes from each side of the pedigree. This allows for the statistical possibility that genes will "double up" at the same locus. The result is two-fold: first, the expression of traits is more uniform and more predictable, but undesirable recessive genes, if present, may come to the surface, thereby giving rise to problems. Therefore, breeds in which there are only a few foundation animals are more vulnerable to genetic defects. Again, this vulnerability is not direct. It is related to the statistical chance that the foundation animals carry an undesirable recessive gene.

Linebreeding and Inbreeding

Inbreeding is a term usually applied to those matings that are in the order of parent to offspring or brother to sister. Breeding among dogs further removed is *linebreeding*.

Linebreeding is the safest and best method to preserve type and conformation, provided that the foundation dogs are well chosen and one has the judgment and experience to pick the best puppies. Inbreeding, on the other hand, requires a genetically clean stock, a knowledge of the faults and virtues of all the common dogs in the pedigrees for at least three generations and the willingness to cull ruthlessly when it becomes necessary.

Most breeders prefer to avoid inbreeding. Instead, they keep the overall relationship to common dogs rather high by using them several times further back in the pedigree.

A common misconception is that inbreeding causes high-strung, nervous or aggressive dogs. Because two individuals are closely related does not mean that their offspring are going to be unsound. It is the genetic potential in the background of the pair that determines the outcome. A fundamentally sound strain remains fundamentally sound. One that has some unstable dogs in its inbreeding program is likely to have problems.

After having linebred for three or four generations, most breeders have found from experience that it is wise to bring in new blood. The use of a stud from a totally different bloodline may be considered. This produces an *outcrossed* litter and "reshuffles" the genes that have tended to become fixed in a more or less predictable manner through previous linebreeding. Many times, particularly with an overly refined bitch, an outcross will give surprisingly good results. An improvement in the health and vigor of the resulting puppies is apparent from the time they are born. This process is known as "nicking." While the litter will sometimes lack uniformity, nevertheless some very good show dogs have been produced in this manner.

When two strains have nicked successfully, other crosses between them may work as well. Puppies from such matings usually are bred back into one of the two strains, thereby providing a basis for a new line.

One final method is to breed a dog and a bitch that are both of mixed line ancestry. Neither has a linebred background. When using this approach, it is essential that one has a definite goal in mind. One dog may carry an attribute or quality totally lacking in the other. However, breeding strengths to weaknesses in the hope that strengths will win out sometimes is disappointing—too often it is the weaknesses that win out, producing puppies of inferior quality.

The Brood Bitch

Before you decide to breed your female, give careful consideration to the effort and expense that goes into producing a litter of healthy and active puppies. It can be both time-consuming and expensive. You should give consideration to your bitch's overall conformation, disposition and the qualities she will pass along to her puppies.

Another factor to consider is that many purebred puppies cannot be sold locally. This means advertising and the added cost and effort of finding the *right home* in which to place them.

In contrast to a popular belief, *a female does not need to have a litter in order to be psychologically fulfilled.* In fact, a neutered female makes an outstanding house pet. She is able to devote herself exclusively to her human family.

Most breeders do not mate a bitch before her second or third season, at which time she is emotionally mature and able to adjust well to the role of a brood matron.

A prospective brood matron should be kept in top physical condition. An overweight bitch, lacking in exercise tolerance, is difficult to mate and many times will not come into season regularly and may have difficulty in whelping.

Once you decide to mate your female, take her to your veterinarian for a physical checkup. A maiden bitch should be examined to make sure that her

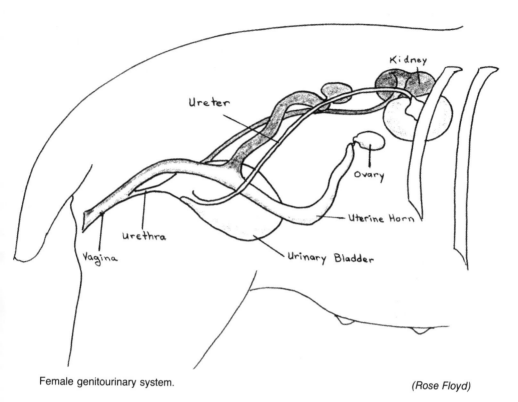

Female genitourinary system.

(Rose Floyd)

vaginal orifice is normal in size. There should be no constricting ring that could prevent normal entry.

Her physical checkup should include a test for heartworms in areas where this is a problem. She should be given a DHLPP booster shot at this time. Because of an increase in the incidence of brucellosis in dogs, a serum agglutination test should always be done before mating. This test is now available in veterinary clinics and can be run from a blood sample in a few minutes.

Particularly if you own a bitch of a breed that averages over thirty-five pounds, ask your veterinarian to X-ray her hips. This should be done after two years of age, if you plan to have her OFA-Certified. *If the X rays show hip dysplasia, do not breed her.* Certification by the OFA or other highly reliable authority is desirable.

Also, before mating, the bitch should be checked for worms. Roundworms are difficult to avoid in puppies. Other parasites, if found, should be vigorously treated. A bitch with an active worm infestation is less likely to whelp healthy, active puppies.

The Stud Dog

Part of the breeding preparation is to choose the stud dog well in advance.

The show record of a prospective stud dog may include a championship, multiple Breed wins, Group placings or even a Best in Show. Unfortunately, not

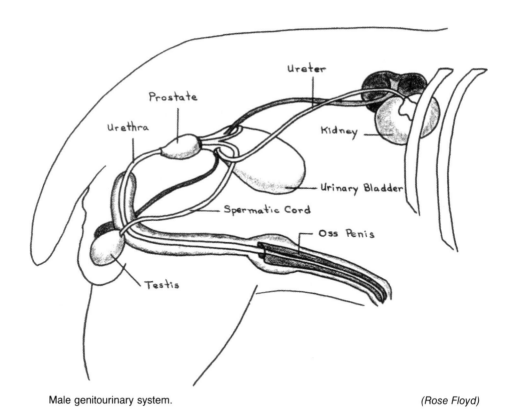

Male genitourinary system. *(Rose Floyd)*

all great show dogs are outstanding producers. By the same token, some of the top producers have not been particularly outstanding in the ring. Therefore, a show record beyond a championship is not a criterion that should greatly influence your decision.

If a stud dog has had a career as a producer, this record becomes a matter of considerable importance. If he has sired the type of dog you like, particularly if several bitches were used, you have strong evidence in favor of his dominance. The number of champions produced is not always as meaningful as you might think. Usually there is a lapse of several years before a mating and a championship. Some of the top producers are often recognized well after they have stopped producing, but their offspring may retain their sire's dominance.

If your bitch came from a show/breeding kennel, it is clearly a good idea to talk to your breeder before making a final decision. Your breeder will be familiar with the strengths and weaknesses that lie behind your bitch. This knowledge can be vitally important in choosing a compatible mate.

Some breeding kennels offer stud service. If you have an outstanding bitch from that bloodline, you may give serious thought to using a stud from that same strain to reinforce the best qualities in your bitch.

It is the responsibility of the breeder (the owner of the bitch) to come to a clear understanding with the owner of the stud dog concerning the breeding terms. Usually a stud fee is paid at the time of the mating, or the stud owner may agree to take "pick of the litter," which is a puppy of the stud owner's

302

choosing. The age of the puppy should be agreed upon. If the bitch does not conceive, a return service is usually offered at no extra charge. However, this is not obligatory. Terms vary with the circumstances and policies of the kennel. If these are in writing, there will be no misunderstandings at a later date.

A stud should be kept in top physical condition with regular exercise, routine health checkups and a sound diet. Excessive weight is a severe handicap to a stud dog. He could be too heavy to mount a bitch. A poorly kept or run-down dog is unsatisfactory.

Before a dog is offered as stud to the public, a brucellosis slide test should be made to establish that he is free of this disease. Brucellosis, once introduced into a kennel, can cause widespread sterility and the ruin of an outstanding breeding program.

Stud dogs should also be X-rayed for hip dysplasia. *Dogs with hip dysplasia should not be offered at stud.* Certification by **OFA** or some other highly reliable source is desirable. (See MUSCULOSKELETAL SYSTEM: *Canine Hip Dysplasia*.)

A male may be used at stud after he is over one year of age. If an older dog is not a known producer, a sperm count is desirable. A culture of the prostatic secretions should be done if the fertility is low. A chronic infection often can be treated.

Before your dog is used at stud for the first time, check to be sure he has no problem that could interfere with successful mating. Some males have a long flexible forepart to the penis. If it bends backward it could make intromission impossible. If this is the case, he will have to be bred by artificial insemination.

Push the prepuce back to make sure that the penis is able to extend normally. A retained fold of skin (frenulum) may prevent protrusion of the penis. When present, it can be cut easily.

Red pimplelike bumps or growths on the penis should receive veterinary attention. Lacerations and erosions tend to bleed when the dog has an erection. During intercourse, blood if mixed with semen reduces the motility of the sperm.

Other abnormalities are a stricture foreskin, an infection beneath the sheath, abnormal or undescended testicles and a discharge from the urethra. To learn more about these conditions, see *Diseases of the Male Genital Tract* elsewhere in this chapter. If one of these is present, the dog should be examined and treated by a veterinarian before mating.

The Estrous Cycle (Heat Cycle)

The *estrous* cycle (heat cycle) is the entire process of proestrus, estrus, metestrus and anestrus.

As the most common cause of unsuccessful mating is breeding at the wrong time of the heat cycle, a thorough understanding of this cycle is important.

Most females come into heat at six month intervals. As a general rule, heat lasts twenty-one days, as reckoned from the first sign of vaginal bleeding. It ends when the female refuses to stand for the male.

The onset of heat (called *proestrus*) lasts six to nine days. It is signaled by a dark bloody discharge and firm swelling of the vulva. It is during this stage that the female begins to attract the male, who is able to detect chemical sub-

Proestrus: Note swelling and enlargement of the vulva. Check for bleeding with a tissue.

stances, called *pheromones*, discharged from her vulva and excreted in her urine. During this preovulatory phase in the heat cycle, the female will not accept the male. If mating is attempted she will jump away, sit down, growl or snap at the male to drive him away. Occasionally she may be willing to mount the male a day or two before she is receptive to his advances.

The second phase of the estrous cycle is called *estrus* or *standing heat*. It is the time during which the female is receptive. It usually occurs about two days before she ovulates. At this time she begins to flirt with the male, raises her tail and flags it to the side, lifts her pelvis and presents her vulva when touched in the rear. The vulva softens and the discharge becomes watermelon-colored or pinkish. A microscopic examination of the vaginal secretions at this time (*vaginal cytology*) will show a marked reduction in the number of red cells. A few white cells will be seen. Also, there are changes in the appearance of the surface cells of the vaginal lining. These changes enable a veterinarian to determine whether the bitch is ready to be bred.

There is another test for ovulation that utilizes a paper strip to test the mucous from the cervix of the uterus. This is the same sugar test tape used by diabetics to check for sugar in the urine. The test is based on the fact that sugar appears in the mucus of the cervix when the bitch begins to ovulate. Insert the paper strip into the vagina near the cervix and leave it for one minute. Then remove it and read the color. A negative sugar test suggests that the bitch is not ovulating. However, a positive test may be a false positive if a vaginal infection is present. This test is not as predictable as vaginal cytology.

The third phase in the reproductive cycle is called *metestrus*. It begins when the female refuses to stand for the male and lasts through the period of uterine repair (about 60 to 105 days). After a bitch has gone into heat once, her breasts and vulva will remain slightly larger than before.

The fourth phase of the reproductive cycle, called *anestrus*, is a period of reproductive rest. It lasts 100 to 150 days.

The heat period usually comes every six to eight months. However, some bitches go into heat every four months and others only once a year. Several factors, such as the time of year, hereditary tendencies and emotional states, have a bearing. Some of these are discussed below (see *Infertility*).

Hormonal Influences During Estrus (Pituitary and Ovarian)

The heat cycle begins when the **pituitary gland** releases FSH (follicle stimulating hormone), which causes the ovaries to grow the egg follicles and begin to make estrogen. Under the influence of another pituitary hormone called LH (luteinizing hormone), the egg follicle ruptures and releases eggs into the Fallopian tubes.

When progesterone (for example, in the birth control pill Ovaban) is given during the *first three days* of proestrus, it blocks the release of pituitary FSH and aborts the heat cycle.

Testosterone, which blocks the release of LH, will prevent heat if given *before* the first signs of proestrus.

To learn more about the use of hormones as contraceptives, see *Birth Control* in this chapter.

Estrogen from the **ovary** causes the vulva to become swollen and turgid. It also effects the lining of the uterus and begins the discharge. These are the first signs that the bitch is going into heat (proestrus).

Some bitches have a very light pinkish to yellow discharge early in proestrus. If you are not sure whether your bitch is going into heat, wipe a Kleenex across her vulva. If you see a pinkish color on the Kleenex, she is in early heat.

As the egg follicles mature, they make less estrogen and begin to produce progesterone. This hormone makes the vulva soft and pliable, making intromission possible. These vulvar changes occur late in proestrus or early in estrus.

After the eggs have been shed from the ovary, they must mature in the female for seventy-two hours before they can combine with the sperm. Sperm, on the other hand, can survive in the female for up to seven days. Fertilization occurs in the Fallopian tubes, which lead from the ovary to the uterus. Fertilized eggs implant in the uterus on the fourteenth to eighteenth day. An important function of progesterone is to prepare the lining of the uterus to receive the fertilized eggs. Such preparation can be blocked by giving an injection of estrogen *within seven days of mating* (see *Accidental Pregnancy*).

The egg follicle now becomes a small cystic structure called the corpus luteum. Its function is to continue to make progesterone and support the pregnancy. Removal of the ovaries, or inadequate output of progesterone from the ovaries during early pregnancy, will result in abortion.

When to Breed

The leading cause of an unsuccessful mating is improper timing. Most dog owners are day-oriented. They attempt to breed on the tenth to the fourteenth day of the heat cycle. Recent advances in the understanding of the reproductive cycle of the female dog indicate that ovulation cannot be accurately predicted just by counting the days of the heat cycle. You may miss the early signs of heat, or your dog may show very little evidence of them. Also, ovulation may occur several days after the female is in standing heat instead of the first or second day. Furthermore, when the eggs have been shed, they must mature for seventy-two hours before they can combine with the sperm. Fortunately, nature provides a safety factor in that sperm are able to survive for up to seven days in the female reproductive system.

There are reports of bitches being bred as early as the fourth day and as late as the twenty-first day of the mating cycle—and yet conceiving a litter. Practically speaking, a certain amount of trial and error is necessary.

Accordingly, many veterinarians recommend that bitches be bred three times: on the second, fourth and sixth day of standing heat. An important indicator is the deportment of the bitch. If she plays coyly, if she flags, if she presents her parts and stands firm—these all are signs that she is ready to be bred. Other signs are softening of the vulva and lightening of the discharge. Vaginal smears taken by your veterinarian may be helpful in determining the optimum mating time.

An experienced stud dog will make his own investigations. A knowledgeable one ignores the bitch until the moment is right.

The Tie

Dogs differ from humans in that they do not have tubes above the prostate (seminal vesicles) to store the sperm. Sperm flows directly into the urethra from the vas deferens and does not mix first with prostatic fluid.

The mechanics of sexual intercourse in the dog also are different from those of human beings. After intromission, a knot at the base of the penis, called the *bulbus glandis*, becomes swollen. It is held by the constrictor muscles of the vagina forming a union between the two animals called the "tie."

During intercourse the first part of the male's ejaculate is clear and contains no sperm. The second part is cloudy and does contain sperm. The final fraction is composed of prostatic fluid. It serves to wash out the urethra and neutralize the acidity of the vagina and propel sperm up into the uterus.

The exact function of the tie in unknown. Perhaps it holds the penis in place while the sperm flow up from the testicles. For a tie to be effective, it must last for at least two to three minutes. Many ties last thirty to forty minutes. Contrary to popular belief, the length of the tie, beyond a few minutes, has little effect upon the likelihood of pregnancy or number of puppies conceived.

If the knot at the base of the penis swells up *before* intromission, the penis may be withdrawn prematurely. Some inexperienced males may have enlargement of their penis before intromission, thus making intromission impossible. These dogs should be taken away from the female until the penis returns to its normal size. For dogs to mate, full erection must take place after intromission.

MATING

Getting Ready

When the bitch is due in season, she should be watched carefully. As soon as she shows color (bleeding from her vulva), the owner of the stud dog should be notified and may want the bitch sent at once. This has the advantage of letting her settle into her new surroundings after a nerve-racking trip. Also, the owner of the stud dog is less likely to miss her ovulation if the bitch arrives in plenty of time.

If the female has a heavy or matted coat, it is a good idea to trim the hair away to expose the vulva.

If the male has long hair on the prepuce or near the head of the penis, it may catch on the penis during erection. When the penis returns, the prepuce may be rolled under, causing a constriction. Accordingly, clip away hair on long-coated dogs before mating.

Normal Mating Procedure

Neither animal should be fed for several hours before the mating. Avoid the heat of day. In summer, bring both dogs into the house or a kennel room where it is relatively cool. Otherwise the bitch should be taken to the enclosure of the stud dog, as the male is more confident and assertive in his own surroundings. If the female is shy and retiring and if the male is strong and assertive, it may be better to take the male to the enclosure of the bitch.

Keep the number of people to a minimum. The fewer distractions the better. Both dogs are introduced to each other on leads. Once it is certain that the bitch is friendly and receptive, the dogs may be let off leash to romp for a short while and perform necessary foreplay. If the stud is disinterested or the female resents the male, it suggests that the bitch is not in standing heat. Separate the dogs and try again in forty-eight hours.

Do not insist that the male attempt to breed an unwilling bitch. This tends to confuse and frighten the female, thereby making future attempts more difficult, if not impossible. A slightly nervous bitch, or one who would rather frolic than get down to the business at hand, may have to be held. *All bitches should be under control throughout mating.* This may require muzzling.

Small dogs can be mated on a table with carpet for good footing. Support the female with a hand under her pelvis.

The procedure for assisting at the mating of larger dogs requires two or three people. The first holds the male on the leash. If the dog mounts at the side or front, that person gently pulls him off and heads him in the right direction, encouraging him to mount at the rear. The second person sits on a stool at the bitch's side. One knee supports the bitch's abdomen. With one arm beneath the bitch, the tip of the tail is drawn in a circle around the outside of her opposite back leg and held. A third person steadies the bitch from in front.

Intromission is a hit-or-miss affair for the male. A cooperative female raises her vulva so that the male can make a straight entry into the vagina. The individual holding the bitch can make matters easier for the male by raising the vulva of the female with a hand placed between her legs.

Young and inexperienced males may become so excited that they ejaculate prior to intromission. This is especially likely to occur if an attempt is made to help the male by taking hold of his penis near the back of the shaft, resulting in erection and ejaculation.

If the bitch is ready to be mated, she will hold her tail to the side and stand quietly for the male while he mounts. As the male begins to penetrate, he will grasp her with his forelegs around the loin and thrust forward, raising her pelvis. At full penetration he will begin to tread up and down instead of thrusting forward. The bulbus glandis swells and is clasped by the vulva. This produces the tie and stimulates the male to ejaculate.

After the tie is accomplished, the male unclasps his forelegs and places both feet on the ground on the side of the bitch. He may lift his hind leg over the back of the bitch so that the two stand back to back. The dogs may remain joined for ten to thirty minutes. It is wise to have someone posted at the head of the bitch to steady her.

Bitches may cry, whine or grunt during a tie. This is not a cause for alarm. The important thing is to be sure that the bitch does not become frightened and begin to struggle and try to pull away from the male. When a dog and bitch separate after a tie, momentarily it can be painful. Be prepared for either one to make a sudden snap.

A mating between a tall dog and a short bitch can present a mechanical problem. The answer is to stand the male in a ditch or breed on a slope to equalize the difference.

Prolonged Tie

One may encounter a situation in which the animals remained tied for an hour or longer. The problem is that the constricting vaginal ring maintains the erection. The blood cannot leave the bulbus glandis and return to the body. As the animals become frustrated and begin to tug against each other, the situation is aggravated. Do not throw water on the dogs or try to pull them apart. They are unable to help themselves. Instead, turn the male so that he mounts the female and then push on his rump to increase the depth of penetration. This relieves the constricting effect of the vaginal ring so that the dogs can slide apart.

Nervous or apprehensive owners communicate this to their dogs. A calm approach is the best. If one dog is a house pet, or if for any other reason the mating is difficult for the owners, the entire matter should be put in the hands of a capable veterinarian.

308

Shy Breeders—Dogs That Won't Mate

The most common cause of sexual reluctance is breeding at the wrong time in the estrous cycle. During proestrus, a male may mount a female but then seem to lose interest. A female may allow a male to mount her, only to sit down or jump away if he begins to thrust. This is normal proestrus behavior. An inexperienced breeder may see it as a sign that mating isn't going to take place.

A timid female that refuses a male may do so out of fear and insecurity. Before coming to this conclusion, check to be sure she is in standing heat. A simple test is to stroke the female's vulva, at home where she is relaxed, and see if she raises her vulva and flags her tail. These signs suggest she is ready for breeding. If she continues to refuse the male, then quite likely the problem is psychological. Psychological factors are much more common than hormonal or physical ones. Try and breed her at home. A tranquilizer may help to relax her.

Some bitches will mate only with a very aggressive male.

A male may become a shy breeder because of unpleasant associations with sex. Many owners will scold or punish their dog if he shows sexual advances toward other dogs or toward people. Thus he believes he will be punished if he attempts mating. Some may have a fear of attempting mating because of prior experiences with an unwilling or aggressive bitch. Others may have been injured during mating because of inadequate restraint of the bitch. Some dogs that have had little association with other dogs relate poorly to them, preferring people. Finally, and least likely of all, a dog may be suffering from a hormone imbalance (see *Impotence* below).

A spoiled female that has been raised as a house pet may be a reluctant breeder (because of inadequate canine association). An extremely submissive female may clamp down her tail and fail to raise her vulva, making intromission impossible. Some females are quite selective and won't mate with a dog they can dominate. A bitch that runs with a certain dog in a kennel may mate willingly with that dog but refuse another. Rarely one encounters a bitch that panics at the approach of a male and throws herself on the ground. This is seen with overly submissive bitches. Tranquilization may be of aid.

Treatment: In the case of the uncooperative bitch, the breeding can still take place if the bitch is restrained and tranquilized, provided that the stud is experienced and aggressive. Because she won't display the usual social signs of sexual readiness, vaginal cytology is indicated to determine the moment of peak fertility.

If for other reasons it appears that the mating might not take place naturally, then one will need to decide whether to let nature take its course and try again later, or proceed at once to artificial insemination (see *Artificial Insemination*). Breeding by A.I. will not spoil a dog or bitch in the future for natural breeding.

To help a male regain self-confidence, let him run with an easygoing bitch that likes to be dominated. An experienced brood matron that is a willing breeder can help a bashful dog build up his ego. Once he has bred a female successfully, generally his problems are over.

If a bitch of outgoing disposition consistently refuses to receive a stud, it is a good idea to have her examined for a vaginal infection or some other disorder that could cause pain during intercourse (see *Diseases of the Female Genital Tract*).

INFERTILITY

When a bitch fails to conceive after successful matings, you may be faced with an infertility problem. This is especially likely to be true if the dogs were bred more than once. Either the stud dog or the female could be at fault.

Fertility Problems in the Male

Infertility in the male can be classified as congenital or acquired.

A stud dog who has never sired a litter should be considered congenitally infertile until proven otherwise. Some causes of congenital infertility are chromosome abnormalities, lack of testicular development (*testicular hypoplasia* or *aplasia*), lack of development of the seminiferous tubules (*ductal aplasia*), undescended testicles and anomalies of the penis and prepuce.

Acquired infertility occurs in a proven stud dog that subsequently becomes infertile. This frequently follows testicular injuries and infections, and may occur as a consequence of diseases of the male genital tract, discussed below. Drug therapy, adrenal gland tumors and immune-mediated orchitis are less common causes.

Hormonal disorders of the pituitary and thyroid gland can cause both congenital and acquired infertility. Hypothyroidism is the most common. It can lower a dog's sperm count as well as his libido.

Retrograde ejaculation is caused by failure of the internal urethral sphincter to contract fully during ejaculation, allowing the sperm to enter the bladder instead of exiting at the penis.

A significant cause of reduced fertility in the male is excessive use. Males used for three consecutive days should be rested for forty-eight hours; or they may be used regularly at forty-eight-hour intervals. When a stud dog is much in demand, a single mating and low fertility may be the cause of a missed pregnancy. Dogs that have not been used at stud for some time may have a low sperm count because of sexual inactivity. During a second mating, forty-eight hours after the first, the quality of semen often is improved.

Prolonged elevated body temperature depresses sperm formation. Some dogs are less fertile in the summer months, especially when the weather is hot and they cannot get cool. A stud dog run down by a chronic illness may take several weeks or months to regain a normal sperm count. An age-related decline in sperm production may exist in some cases.

Treatment: A semen analysis is indicated to see if the sperm are of normal quantity and quality. When sperm are present, often the stud's potency can be improved by treating the underlying problem. A male of marginal fertility should be bred at the peak of female fertility (seventy-two hours after ovulation, as determined by vaginal cytology).

Stress, sexual overuse, thermal damage and temporary injury to the seminiferous tubules are potentially reversible and often improve with a period of sexual rest.

Other problems are more difficult to diagnose and require, in addition to semen analysis, the measurement of pituitary and thyroid hormones, testosterone concentration and biopsy of the testicle. Hormonal manipulation and the use of drugs to correct retrograde ejaculation and immune-mediated orchitis have been of aid in some cases. Genetic and chromosomal abnormalities are rare causes of infertility. They are difficult to diagnose. Such investigations are best carried out at a school of veterinary medicine.

Dogs with congenital infertility and those with acquired infertility that do not produce sperm after three months of treatment usually do not become fertile.

The treatment of infertility caused by diseases of the male genital tract is discussed below.

Impotence

Most cases of impotence are caused by psychological factors. (See *Shy Breeders—Dogs That Won't Mate*.)

The male sex drive is under the influence of testosterone, which is produced by the male gonads. Rarely impotence is caused by failure of the testicles to produce enough hormone. Semen analysis is not a test for the male hormone because the cells that make the sperm are not the same ones that make testosterone. A fertile male can be impotent and a sterile male can be quite able and willing to mate a bitch.

An estrogen-producing tumor of the testicles can cause both impotency and lack of sperm. Other signs are feminization of the dog. He loses his masculine appearance, becomes plump, may develop enlarged nipples and attract other male dogs. Usually this tumor develops in an undescended testicle. Such dogs should be watched carefully for a swelling in the scrotum that could indicate a growth.

Treatment: Impotency resulting from hormonal rather than behavioral causes is difficult to diagnose and treat. Some dogs may respond to the administration of testosterone when given before breeding. Unfortunately, the dose that stimulates the male libido also depresses sperm production. It must be used with caution. Consult your veterinarian.

Fertility Problems in the Female

Fertility problems in females fall into two categories: those with abnormal heat cycles, and those in whom the heat cycle is normal but some other cause of infertility exists.

Infertility with a Normal Heat Cycle

The leading cause of infertility in the female is infection in the uterus or reproductive tract (see *Chronic Endometritis*).

Vaginal stricture can prevent intromission and cause failure to tie. Surgery or artificial insemination will be required for successful pregnancy.

Uterine tumors and blocks in the Fallopian tubes can prevent the union of egg and sperm.

Other causes are abnormal genes and chromosomes, which are difficult to diagnose and treat.

Abnormal Heat Cycles

The *interestrous interval* is the time between one heat cycle and the next. In the average bitch this interval is five to nine months. Abnormal heat cycles can be associated with a shortened or prolonged interestrous interval.

Additional estrous problems are staying in heat too long and not coming into heat at all.

Abnormal interestrous intervals: Often a bitch's heat cycle is irregular, being either longer or shorter than normal. Some bitches, for unknown reasons, come into heat every four months and others once a year. Females that are slow to come into heat often will do so when kenneled and allowed to run with a male for three to four months.

Occasionally a bitch will skip a heat period. This is not uncommon. Young bitches frequently have irregular, frequent or silent heat periods. Generally these cycles become regular by two to three years of age.

One cause of a shortened interestrous interval is "split" or "false" heat. It can be recognized by two heat cycles coming close together. In the first cycle the bitch apparently goes into heat with vulvar swelling, vaginal bleeding and attraction of the male. However, because of a deficiency of luteinizing hormone, the ovaries do not produce egg follicles. The bitch does not ovulate and goes out of heat.

During the second heat cycle, which occurs two to twelve weeks later, a normal hormonal sequence generally takes place. This "true" or final heat is typically fertile. Split heats usually are seen in young bitches. They are not worrisome and do not influence future fertility.

Prolonged interestrous intervals (ten to twelve months) are common in older bitches. As a bitch grows older, her heat cycles become less frequent and in some cases are not accompanied by ovulation. This is not cause for concern.

Any major medical problem can delay estrous. Hypothyroidism is the most common medical cause. Other indications of hypothyroidism may or may not be present. The diagnosis is confirmed by blood tests. This condition is treated by giving thyroid hormone. Hypothyroidism is also the cause for absent heat.

Prolonged heat: This occurs when a bitch stays in heat over twenty-one days. This is abnormal. Cystic ovaries (ovaries that produce excess estrogen) keep dogs in heat for several weeks or months and may require surgery.

Infection of the uterus can give signs similar to prolonged heat in that a discharge is seen, but the female is not receptive to the male. When there is prolongation of heat, the bitch should be examined by a veterinarian to see what is causing the problem.

Absent heat: Heat will not occur if there is a low estrogen level. This condition, called *hypoestronism*, is not common. It is caused by failure of the ovaries to develop to sexual maturity. Owing to estrogen deficiency, the breasts and vulva remain small and underdeveloped.

Many cases thought to be lack of heat are really a "silent" type of heat, which is not noticed because of scant or absent bleeding. Some females are quite fastidious and lick themselves clean. If you are not familiar with the normal size of the bitch's vulva, you may not notice the swelling. Close examination once or twice a week is a good way to recognize mild enlargement of the vulva or a slightly bloody discharge. Another way is to expose the bitch to a male once a week and observe her behavior.

One cause for a failure to cycle is when the ovaries have been removed by hysterectomy. This is a consideration when the history of the bitch is unknown. A scar will be visible in the midline below the umbilicus.

If your bitch does not go into heat by eighteen months of age, you should have her examined by a veterinarian.

Induction of Estrus

One approach to the bitch with absent or abnormal heat cycles is to induce estrus and ovulation with hormone injections. The most successful drugs currently available for this purpose are pregnant mare serum (PMS) and human chorionic gonadotropin (HCG). Various treatment programs have been employed, including pretreatment with estrogen.

None of these programs are consistently successful, but conception rates of 60 percent are possible, especially if the bitch does not have a potential disorder in the pituitary gland or ovaries, and if vaginal cytology is used to determine when to begin breeding. Breeding (or artificial insemination) should continue on an alternate-day basis until the bitch goes out of heat.

Brucellosis

Brucellosis is a major cause of infertility in males and females (see INFECTIOUS DISEASES). One mode of transmission is by venereal contact. Another is by contact with the products of conception or vaginal discharge of an infected female that has aborted. Because of an increasing incidence of brucellosis in dogs in the United States, a blood test should be done on both the bitch and stud dog before mating. This test is available in veterinary clinics and can be run from a blood sample in a few minutes.

Diseases of the Male Genital Tract

There are several disorders of the male genital system that can lead to mating problems or infertility. Orchitis, balanoposthitis, phimosis, paraphimosis, undescended testicles and prostatitis are the most common ones.

Examination of the prostate gland and evaluation of the quality of the semen are two examinations that must be done by a specialist. They are indicated when a fertility problem exists or when there are indications of prostatic infection. Prostatitis is discussed in the chapter URINARY SYSTEM.

Infection of the Prepuce and Head of the Penis (Balanoposthitis)

A small amount of white or yellowish discharge from the prepuce is present in nearly all mature males. An excessive purulent discharge is associated with overt infection. Awns or pieces of straw can get caught beneath the foreskin of the male and cause irritation of the skin of the penis, followed by infection and abscess of the sheath. These infections are called *balanoposthitis*.

If your dog begins to lick himself excessively and has a purulent, foul-smelling discharge from the prepuce, probably he is suffering from balanoposthitis. This condition also may be caused by prolonged sexual intercourse. Such infections can be transmitted to the female during mating.

Treatment: First, clip away the coat hair on or near the foreskin. Push back the foreskin to expose the head of the penis. Wash the area thoroughly with surgical soap and apply an antibiotic ointment. If your dog will not allow you to retract the foreskin, use a syringe and flush the sheath with dilute hydrogen peroxide solution twice daily. Then infuse Panolog or Furacin ointment. Repeat until all signs of discharge and inflammation are gone.

For persistent cases, flush the sheath with an astringent solution made up of 5% tannic acid and 5% salicylic acid mixed with two parts of propylene glycol and continue the treatment for four days.

Strictured Foreskin—Penis Can't Protrude (Phimosis)

Here the opening of the sheath is too small to let the penis extend. The opening may be so small that urine can escape only in small drops. Some cases result from infection. Many are caused by a congenital abnormality—puppies are born that way. Several male puppies in a litter may be so affected.

If the condition is caused by an infection of the sheath, treatment of the sheath infection may correct the phimosis as well. If it is because of a congenital abnormality, a surgical operation is required.

Penis That Can't Retract (Paraphimosis)

In this condition the penis is unable to return to its original position inside the sheath. The sheath may serve as a constricting band around the shaft of the penis, cutting off the blood supply. A predisposing cause is long hair on the skin of the sheath that causes the foreskin to roll under when the penis is partly retracted, often following mating. It can be prevented by cutting the long hairs from around the foreskin prior to breeding. Check your male after using him at stud to be sure that the penis has returned to its sheath.

Treatment: The penis should be returned to its normal position as quickly as possible in order to prevent permanent damage. Apply ice packs to reduce

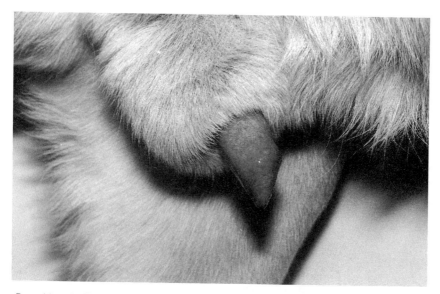

Paraphimosis: The penis is unable to retract. This condition is most common after mating.

swelling. Push the prepuce backward on the shaft of the penis, rolling it out so the hairs are not caught. Lubricate the surface of the penis with mineral oil or olive oil. With one hand, gently draw the head of the penis forward while squeezing it so as to reduce the swelling. With the other hand, slide the prepuce forward. If these measures are not immediately successful, notify your veterinarian.

In most cases the skin of the penis is severely irritated, and it will be necessary to flush the sheath twice daily with an antiseptic solution as described under the treatment of balanoposthitis.

Undescended Testicles

Testicles usually descend before birth. In some dogs the testicle may descend as late as five to six months of age. If a testicle can be felt one time but not at another, there is no need for concern. Testicles can retract back up into the groin when a puppy is cold, excited or actively playing. Both testicles should be fully descended before six months of age. Consult your veterinarian if they have not come down by that time.

The testicles should be of similar size and feel rather firm. Since much of the testicle size is the result of sperm-producing tissue, soft or small testicles in the sexually mature dog are likely to be deficient in sperm.

Monorchid dogs, those with only one testicle in the scrotum, may be fertile. However, they should not be used as stud because the condition is inherited. *Cryptorchid* dogs, those with no testicles in the scrotum, are sterile.

Treatment: Hormone injections have been used to stimulate testicular descent in puppies. Results are questionable.

If the testicles do not seem well developed at one year of age, ask your veterinarian to do a semen analysis.

315

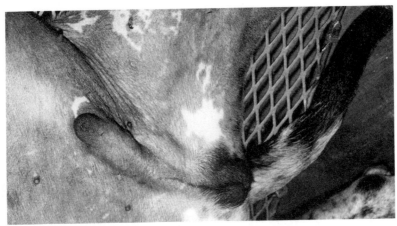

Undescended testicle on the right side.

Orchitis (Inflammation of the Testicle)

Swelling and inflammation of one or both testicles can be caused by trauma (dog bites, shotgun wounds, blows), injury to the skin of the scrotum (frostbite, weed burns, chemical and thermal burns) and the spread of infection from elsewhere in the genitourinary tract (cystitis, prostatitis, balanoposthitis). The vas deferens serves as a conduit to carry bacteria back to the testes from the urethra.

The distemper virus and the bacteria causing brucellosis can attack and destroy the testicles. Injuries or infections of the testicle are the most common causes of male infertility.

The signs of orchitis are swelling and pain in the testicle. The testicle becomes enlarged and hard. Your dog probably will not allow you to handle him. His gait is spread-legged with his belly tucked up. He sits most of the time, especially on a cool surface.

Later the diseased testicle shrinks and becomes small and firm.

Treatment: Minor scrotal injuries should be cleaned and salved with an antibiotic ointment. Orchitis should be treated by a veterinarian. Cultures and specific antibiotics are indicated.

Diseases of the Female Genital Tract

Diseases of the female genital system may be divided into those affecting the vagina (vaginitis, vaginal prolapse) and those affecting the uterus (chronic endometritis and pyometra). All adversely affect fertility and the health of the female.

Vaginal Infection

Bacterial infection of the vagina often spreads to the urinary tract, causing burning on urination and increased frequency. It may ascend into the uterus, causing a chronic endometritis.

The main sign is a vaginal discharge and staining of the hair about the vulva. This is not always seen because many bitches lick themselves clean. If your bitch seems to lick herself excessively, suspect vaginitis.

Your veterinarian may want to do a vaginal examination to confirm the diagnosis and rule out a chronic endometritis. A bitch with vaginitis should not be bred until the infection has been treated. Infected vaginal secretions are spermicidal. More important, there is a danger of infecting the male.

Juvenile vaginitis is seen in puppies six to twelve weeks of age. The signs are vaginal discharge along with painful urination.

Treatment: Administer a Betadine vaginal douche twice daily for seven days and accompany it with an oral antibiotic. An appropriate antibiotic can be selected on the basis of cultures and sensitivities. Treat urinary tract infection if present.

Vaginitis in puppies is difficult to clear up. Flush the vagina twice daily with neomycin solution or Massengill douche. Estrogen tablets, prescribed by your veterinarian, are of help in difficult cases. Most puppies with juvenile vaginitis clear up once they go into heat for the first time.

Protrusion of the Vagina (Vaginal Prolapse)

This condition occurs during heat. It is seen in Boxers and St. Bernards most commonly. It results from a very marked estrogen-induced swelling of the vagina. When the vagina no longer can be contained, it protrudes out through the vulva, resulting in severe irritation.

Vaginal prolapse tends to recur in subsequent heats. It is very difficult to breed a dog with this condition even by artificial insemination.

Treatment: Sometimes the vagina can be pushed back into place and held with sutures. This is not always possible. One treatment is to administer Ovaban, which has a progesterone-like effect, and takes the bitch out of heat. Treat irritated vaginal surface with antibiotic salve or ointment.

Chronic Endometritis

This is a low-grade infection of the uterus caused by bacteria that ascend upward from the vagina. Its main concern is that it is the leading cause of infertility in the female. During estrus the vulva of the bitch becomes quite enlarged. At the same time the protective plug of mucus is discharged from the cervix, opening the route to bacterial invasion of the lining of the uterus. Vaginitis is a predisposing cause.

Suspect the possibility of chronic endometritis when your bitch refuses to accept the male; when she is bred at the right time but fails to conceive, especially on two successive heat cycles, and when she delivers stillborn puppies or puppies that sicken and die within the first few days.

The disease is difficult to diagnose and requires the use of appropriate smears and cultures taken from the cervix or the uterus during proestrus.

Treatment: Antibiotics are started seven days prior to breeding and continued throughout until seven days after the mating. Bacterial culture and sensitivities indicate the drug of choice.

Abscess of the Uterus (Pyometra)

Pyometra is a life-threatening disease of the uterus that occurs most commonly in females over six years of age. It is believed to be caused by a hormonal imbalance. The earlier birth control injections (Promone), which contained large amounts of progesterone, were found to cause pyometra and were taken off the market.

Pyometra appears one to twelve weeks after the bitch goes out of heat. A bitch with pyometra refuses to eat, appears depressed and lethargic, drinks a great deal and urinates frequently. Often there is abdominal enlargement. A low-grade fever, or a normal (even subnormal) temperature, may exist. The condition is due to an abscessed uterus.

In the *open* type, the cervix relaxes, releasing a large amount of pus that resembles tomato soup. In the *closed* type, pus collects in the uterus. An enlarged uterus may be felt as a painful swelling in the lower abdomen.

Treatment: In order to save the life of the bitch, a veterinarian should be called at once. Hysterectomy is the treatment of choice. It is much better to do this operation on a nontoxic dog.

Rarely it may be possible to preserve the uterus in a valuable breeding bitch by scraping out the infection and giving antibiotics and hormones.

A disease similar to pyometra, acute metritis, occurs in the postpartum bitch (see PREGNANCY AND WHELPING: *Postpartum Problems*).

ARTIFICIAL INSEMINATION

This is a technique whereby semen is collected from the male and introduced into the reproductive tract of the female. When properly performed, it is as successful as actual mating. Unfortunately, artificial insemination is often used as a last resort, when it is too late in the heat cycle for the bitch to conceive.

Artificial insemination has its widest application when natural mating is contraindicated or impossible. Usually this is for psychological or anatomical reasons, or fear of transmitting disease.

Techniques to freeze and preserve canine semen have met with some success, as has use of chilled semen, and it is entirely possible that these techniques will alter the future of dog breeding.

In the United States the **American Kennel Club** has definite regulations concerning the registration of dogs produced by artificial insemination. If you plan to register your litter, check first with your veterinarian and the **AKC**.

Equipment

A minimal amount of sterile equipment is required. The semen may be deposited directly into a 10 cc hypodermic syringe from which the plunger has been removed; or a rubber conical sheath for use as an artificial vagina can be obtained from a veterinarian. Attached is a glass tube to hold the semen.

An ordinary red rubber catheter, which fits the end of the syringe, is used to deposit the semen up into the vagina. All equipment used to collect and handle

318

the semen *must be sterilized*. It should be handled in such a manner as to prevent contamination of the sample by bacteria.

Sterilize the equipment by boiling it in water for thirty minutes. Do not use chemicals or detergents, as even traces of chemicals can kill sperm.

Collecting the Semen

Sperm die of cold shock if the temperature of the sample is allowed to drop. Always collect the ejaculate indoors and warm the receptacle by holding it next to your body or encircling it with the palm of your hand. Semen should not be kept less than a few degrees below body temperature.

The male dog should be at ease in the surroundings and familiar with his handler. Some males will not achieve or maintain an erection unless they can mount a female. In others, semen can be collected without the presence of a female in heat.

Clean the prepuce with pHisoHex to remove loose hair or debris that might contaminate the sample. Stimulate erection by massaging the sheath in the area of the head of the penis, gradually working backward to the bulbus glandis at the base. As erection progresses, the end of the penis will protrude from the sheath. Once the penis becomes erect, encircle the base of the penis with your thumb and forefinger behind the bulbus glandis and maintain a constricting pressure. Then draw the penis downward and backward, directing the end of it toward the collection container. Avoid repeated contact between the head of the

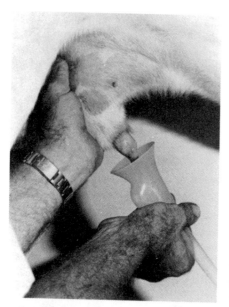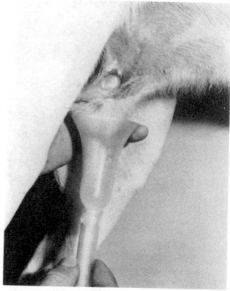

Collecting the Semen: Once the penis becomes erect, encircle the base of the penis with your thumb and forefinger behind the bulb and maintain a constricting pressure. As the dog begins to ejaculate, draw the penis down and back, directing it toward the collection container.

(J. Clawson)

319

penis and the container, as this may lead to loss of erection. The container is grasped tightly in the opposite hand and held into position to collect the ejaculate.

As ejaculation begins, you may notice that your dog makes vigorous thrusting motions that last for a moment or two and are followed by pulsations.

The first fraction of the ejaculate varies from a few drops to one or two milliliters in volume. The second part is milky and contains the sperm. It measures one to four milliliters in volume. The third part is prostatic fluid. It varies in volume from five to twenty milliliters depending on the length of the ejaculation time. Only a small portion of this third fraction usually is collected for artificial insemination. The erection subsides when pressure on the penis is released.

A suitable semen sample will contain five to twenty milliliters of fluid. If it appears bloody, green or discolored, it should not be used for insemination until an infection has been ruled out.

If you use some other collection container, transfer the semen sample to a glass or plastic hypodermic syringe, taking care not to injure the sample by bubbling air through it while replacing the plunger. Connect the sterile catheter to the end of the syringe. Prewarm syringe and catheter to prevent cold shock to semen. All equipment must be sterile, clean and dry.

Inseminating the Bitch

The procedure for inseminating the bitch is quite simple. The leash of the female should be tied securely to a post or doorknob. An assistant straddles the female and lifts her rear feet off the ground by taking hold of her legs above the hocks. Another person introduces the red rubber catheter into her vagina.

When positioning the catheter, care must be taken to avoid a blind pouch

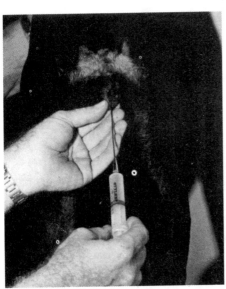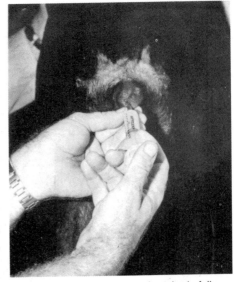

Inseminating the Female: Direct the tube along the top of the vagina. When the tube is fully inserted, slowly empty the syringe.

(J. Clawson)

320

in the lower half of the vagina. Spread the vulva and insert the catheter along the *top* of the vagina, directing it first upward and then forward. If the catheter won't pass easily, put on a sterile glove and insert your finger into the vagina and guide the tube over the brim of the pelvis above the finger. The insemination tube should go in four to nine inches (depending upon the size of the bitch), thereby putting the tip in close proximity to the cervix of the uterus. Slowly empty the syringe. Hold the lips of the vulva tightly around the tube to prevent loss of semen. Remove the tube and massage the vulva.

The hindquarters should be elevated for six minutes to retain the semen. Keep the bitch quiet for the next two hours.

FALSE PREGNANCY (PSEUDOCYESIS)

False pregnancy is a common condition in which a nonpregnant female thinks she is pregnant. She exhibits all the behavioral and physical signs and symptoms associated with a true pregnancy. Physical signs suggest that it is caused by an excess of progesterone. However, progesterone levels in false-pregnant females are the same as those for normal females.

False pregnancy occurs about six to ten weeks after estrus. The signs are an increase in the amount of body fat, particularly in the abdomen. Often the breasts enlarge and secrete a clear or brownish fluid or milk. Some females make a nest and experience abdominal cramps like labor. Some show a mothering instinct and become attached to small toys and other objects that are puppy substitutes. Others vomit off and on, become depressed, and a few develop diarrhea.

Occasionally, the false-pregnant bitch appears to exhibit severe uterine cramps. Caking of the breasts is not unusual and is another source of discomfort.

Treatment: Mild cases require no treatment. The female begins to return to her normal condition in twelve weeks or less. Bitches with uterine cramps can be given the birth control pill Ovaban in a dose of 1 mg per pound of body weight for eight days. This will often relieve discomfort. Your veterinarian may also wish to prescribe testosterone and/or diethylstilbestrol (DES). For caked breasts, see PREGNANCY AND WHELPING: *Postpartum Problems.*

A false-pregnant female is likely to have other false pregnancies. It may be a good idea to have her spayed.

ACCIDENTAL PREGNANCY

Accidental pregnancies do occur. Male dogs are remarkably adept at getting to a female in heat. Ordinary measures, such as confining a female behind chain-link fencing, are no guarantee that she won't be reached by an amorous male.

Once you are certain that your female is in heat, keep her indoors or on a leash. *Do not let her out of your sight.* Female dogs must be isolated throughout the entire estrous cycle, which begins with the first show of color and continues for at least three weeks.

If your female has been bred, there are two alternatives to an unwanted litter. One is a hysterectomy. This can be performed during the early stages of pregnancy without added risk to the female. During the later stages of pregnancy, hysterectomy is a more formidable undertaking.

The second alternative is to prevent the pregnancy by means of an injection of estradiol cypionate (ECP), known as the "mismating shot." This hormone works by preventing implantation of the fertilized ova into the wall of the uterus.

Currently ECP is not FDA-approved for mismating injections because of potentially serious side effects. The greatest danger is from severe and even fatal bone marrow depression. Under no circumstances should more than one injection of ECP be given during one estrous cycle. Other problems associated with the mismating shot are an increased risk of pyometra, risk of cystic ovaries and the prolongation of heat for about ten days.

If you choose this method, take your bitch to a veterinarian as soon as possible. The injection *must* be given within *seven* days of impregnation. A mismating shot usually has no adverse affect on future fertility.

BIRTH CONTROL

There are two methods to prevent conception in the female dog. They are surgery (ovariohysterectomy or tubal ligation) and birth control drugs.

Chlorophyll tablets, which you can purchase from your veterinarian or pet stores, may help to mask the odor of a female in heat but are not effective as a birth control measure.

The two operations used to sterilize the male are castration and vasectomy. These are not soley effective as population control measures, as another male can fertilize a bitch in heat.

Spaying (Ovariohysterectomy)

The most effective method for preventing pregnancy is to have a bitch spayed. In this operation the uterus, tubes and ovaries are removed.

Some people have heard that when a female is spayed she becomes fat or lethargic. A bitch that becomes fat is getting too much to eat. Many people forget that a grown dog needs less food than a puppy. Since a bitch often is spayed at the end of her puppyhood, if she gets too much to eat and puts on weight, the tendency is to blame the operation.

Another misconception is that a bitch needs to have a litter to be fulfilled. Dogs are people-oriented. They seek human companionship and look to their owners for personal fulfillment.

There are certain health benefits to ovariohysterectomy. You do not have to worry about pyometra. A spayed bitch is less likely to get breast cancer. Finally, there is no messy heat to go through twice a year.

The best time to spay most females is after they are six months of age and before they go into their first heat. At this time the operation is easy to perform and there is less chance of complications.

After you have made arrangements to have your female spayed, be sure to withhold food and water on the evening prior to surgery. This operation is done under general anesthesia. A full stomach could result in vomiting and aspiration during induction of anesthesia. Check with your veterinarian concerning other special instructions or precautions to be taken before and after the operation.

Tubal Ligation

In this operation the Fallopian tubes are ligated to prevent eggs from getting from the ovaries to the uterus. It has nearly the same risks as ovariohysterectomy and is only slightly less expensive in most veterinary clinics. It won't stop the bitch from going into heat and attracting the male and does not have the health benefits of ovariohysterectomy. Most veterinarians recommend ovariohysterectomy when an operation is to be performed for sterilization purposes.

The Pill (Ovaban)

Dogs are more sensitive to the progesterone component of birth control pills than are women. In the past a long-lasting progesterone was used to prevent estrus. The drug was found to cause pyometra in a certain number of cases. It was withdrawn from the market.

Currently, Ovaban is the only birth control pill approved for use in the dog in the United States. It is believed to work by suppressing the pituitary output of follicle stimulating hormone (see *Hormonal Influences During Estrus*).

Ovaban is a prescription item that is safe and effective when used according to the recommendations of a veterinarian. A veterinary examination is advisable to rule out diseases of the uterus, breast tumors and diabetes mellitus before starting the pill. If any of these are present, the pill should not be used.

To *prevent heat* start the pill at the first signs of proestrus (within the *first three days* of the heat cycle) and continue it for eight days. This will take your bitch out of heat. Heat will be postponed two to nine months. Your veterinarian must be sure she is in proestrus.

To *postpone heat* (i.e., for a hunting trip, pleasure trip or dog show) start the pill at least one week before you plan to leave and continue it for thirty-two days. It must be started at least one week before proestrus.

CAUTION: You must adhere to a strict time schedule. Always confine your bitch during the first eight days of heat. You could have missed the first signs of proestrus and started the drug too late, thereby failing to stop estrus. In the event that an unplanned mating does take place and your dog has not been on Ovaban for three full days, stop the pill and decide whether to treat for *Accidental Pregnancy*. If mating occurs after three days, complete the course. She will not become pregnant.

The first heat cycle in puppy bitches is frequently unreliable. To insure proper drug performance, Ovaban should not be given until the second heat. It should not be administered to pregnant females, as it is harmful to puppies in utero.

Bitches taking Ovaban may become hungry or lazy, gain weight, experience personality changes or show breast enlargement. These changes return to normal when the drug is stopped.

Prolonged administration in rare cases may cause an infection of the uterus (pyometra). Accordingly, the drug should not be used to postpone heat or to take a bitch out of heat for more than two consecutive heat cycles without a rest.

Liquid Contraceptive (Cheque)

Mibolerone, also called Cheque, is a liquid birth control preparation containing testosterone that you can obtain from your veterinarian. Although the drug has a high safety factor, not enough information currently is available as to its effect on future fertility in bitches. Accordingly, it is recommended only for bitches that will never be used for breeding. It prevents ovulation by blocking the effects of pituitary luteinizing hormone (see *Hormonal Influences During Estrus*).

Your veterinarian will recommend an appropriate dose. Drops are given *daily* by mouth, as described in the chapter DRUGS AND MEDICATIONS), or they can be mixed directly with the food. Start Cheque at least thirty days before your bitch goes into heat. Masculinization, vaginal discharge, excessive tearing and a musky body odor occasionally are seen. In most cases, the side effects last only as long as the drug is given.

CAUTION: If the bitch goes into heat within the first thirty days, the drug may not be effective. It definitely will not prevent pregnancy if started after proestrus.

Discontinue Cheque after twenty-four months of continuous use.

Male Castration

Castration is an operation in which both testicles are removed. When the male is castrated after sexual maturity, his sex drive may be normal even though he is unable to get a bitch pregnant—but this is unusual. When a dog is castrated before puberty, sexual urges do not develop. However, castration before puberty is not recommended. It has an adverse effect on the development of bone, stature and secondary sex traits of the male dog.

Castration sometimes is advised to tone down an overly boisterous or aggressive male, or one that continuously urinates in the house or is otherwise obtrusive and unmanageable. Unfortunately, overindulgent owners (not male hormones) are often at fault. The dog must be shown its place in the household hierarchy. Obedience training is a good idea. Ask your veterinarian about other steps to modify unruly behavior.

Castration may be indicated for medical reasons. It is recommended in some cases of testicular disease, chronic prostatitis and perianal adenomas.

Vasectomy

Bilateral vasectomy is the treatment of choice when sterilization *alone* is the reason for surgery. In this operation a segment of the right and left vas deferens is removed. These tubes transport the sperm from the testicles to the urethra. The operation does not disturb the hormone functions of the testes.

Vasectomized dogs have normal sexual responses, can breed and mate with a bitch, but are not fertile. The operation can be done at any time in the life of the dog without adversely affecting growth and development.

A well–conditioned bitch and a well–prepared owner are the best insurance policy for a healthy litter.

(Artist—Jan Walker)

16

Pregnancy and Whelping

PREGNANCY

GESTATION (pregnancy) is the period from conception to birth. As determined from the day of first successful mating, it averages sixty-three days. Puppies born on the fifty-ninth or sixty-sixth day fall within the normal range. However, if the bitch whelps *before* the fifty-seventh day, the puppies will probably be too young to survive.

Determining Pregnancy

Many bitches, especially those of the larger or barrel-chested breeds, carry their litters well up under their rib cage. It is not always possible to tell whether they are pregnant. False pregnancy, which is more common than most people realize, can complicate matters.

The uterus in dogs is a Y-shaped organ with a horn on each side. The puppies are carried in the uterine horns. A veterinarian can tell by palpation whether a bitch is pregnant by twenty-seven days after the last breeding. At this stage, the puppies are no bigger than the size of a walnut.

The technique for palpating puppies is to have your bitch stand. Place one hand on either side of the lower abdomen. By pressing with your fingers you may be able to detect several small firm lumps, which are the puppies growing in the horns of the uterus. Unless you are experienced in palpating the pregnant uterus, a negative palpation does not rule out a pregnancy. From thirty-five to fifty-five days the uterus is fluid-filled and palpation is not reliable.

Ultrasonography is a safe technique that does not employ X-ray and is

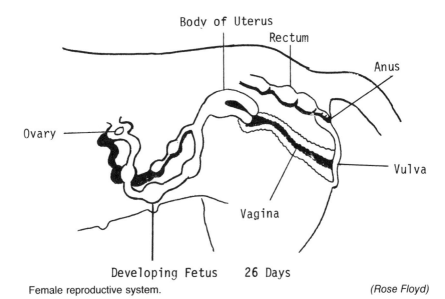

Body of Uterus

Rectum

Anus

Ovary

Vulva

Vagina

Developing Fetus   26 Days

Female reproductive system.   *(Rose Floyd)*

capable of visualizing fetuses in the uterus throughout pregnancy, beginning on the twenty-first day postbreeding.

By forty days of gestation one can see a darkening and enlargement of the nipples. At this time, too, the breasts enlarge, and as the time of birth approaches, a milky fluid may be expressed from the nipples. Other signs of pregnancy are weight gain, increased appetite, an enlarging abdominal girth and sometimes morning sickness.

There is no blood or urine test for pregnancy in dogs as there is in people. X ray of the abdomen can be done after forty-five days from the last breeding but should be reserved for those situations in which it is absolutely necessary to confirm pregnancy. It should be avoided in early pregnancy.

Morning Sickness

Dogs, like humans, can suffer from morning sickness. Usually this happens during the third to fourth week of pregnancy. It is caused by hormonal changes, plus stretching and distention of the uterus. You may notice that your bitch appears a little depressed. She may be off her feed or vomit from time to time. Morning sickness lasts only a few days. Unless you are unusually attentive, you may not even notice it.

Treatment: If your female seems to be suffering from morning sickness, feed her several meals spaced throughout the day. Your veterinarian may want to prescribe a drug to relax her uterus. Vitamins B and C may be given.

Prenatal Checkups

Before you breed your bitch it is a good idea for your veterinarian to see if she has any physical abnormalities that should be treated, and to find out if there is a problem that might prevent normal mating or delivery.

Be sure to have her checked for periodontitis and dental infections. Bacteria from the bitch's mouth can be passed onto newborn puppies during biting of the umbilical cord. This is one cause of serious navel infections.

Two to three weeks prior to her due date, have her thoroughly checked over again. Your veterinarian will want to discuss with you the normal delivery procedures, alert you to the signs of impending problems and give you instructions for care of the newborn.

Be sure to ask where you can get help (emergency service) if needed after hours.

Care and Feeding During Pregnancy

A pregnant bitch should be lean and well-conditioned, neither run-down nor depleted from an earlier litter nor allowed to become fat. Her eyes should be bright and alert, coat shiny and gums a healthy bright red. Routine daily exercise of a moderate nature is advisable. However, pregnant bitches should not climb fences, roughhouse with other dogs, leap down flights of stairs or engage in other violent pursuits.

During the first four weeks of pregnancy, feed your bitch her usual daily ration of high-protein kibble. Protein requirements begin to *increase* during the second half of pregnancy. Increase her ration by one-half with an eye to keeping her trim. Excessive weight gain should be avoided at all costs. An overnourished bitch is apt to carry fat puppies, which may make labor difficult. At this time many breeders switch to puppy kibble, which, ounce for ounce, is higher in protein. Commercial rations are formulated so that if dogs eat the amount they need, they get all the nutrients they require. If you add meat or some other protein supplement to such a diet, your bitch may be getting less of the other things she needs, including fats and carbohydrates. Supplements and vitamins are not required unless a bitch is below par from an earlier litter or recovering from an illness. Follow the advice of your veterinarian.

A bitch's appetite may decrease a week or two before she delivers. At this time her abdomen is crowded with puppies. It is better to feed several smaller meals instead of one large one.

Many drugs cannot be given during pregnancy. They include some of the flea and insecticide preparations, dewormers and certain hormones and antibiotics. Live virus vaccine should not be given to pregnant females because of the risks of abortion and congenital malformations. Check with your veterinarian before starting a pregnant female on a medication.

Whelping Preparations

Bitches should deliver at home where they feel secure. They are easily upset by strange people and unfamiliar surroundings. This can delay and arrest labor. The whelping quarters should be located in a quiet, out-of-the way spot, free from comings and goings.

The best place to whelp bitches and deliver puppies is in a whelping box. An adequate box for a large dog is at least four-by-five feet in size. A box two-by-three feet in size is sufficient for the Toy breeds. The sides should be tall enough to keep puppies from crawling out but not too high for the dam to step over. One side can be made shorter than the others. This side can be replaced by a taller board when the puppies are older. The sides should not be nailed to the floorboard. Instead they should be held in grooves made by nailing one-by-two-inch molding around the margins. The sides are then joined together and held in place by hook-and-eye latches. The floor is much easier to clean when the sides can be removed.

A ledge around the inside of the box, a few inches from the floor, should be made by nailing three-to-six-inch wide boards to all four sides. Puppies will crawl under these ledges instinctively and are protected from being accidentally smothered or sat on by the mother.

Several layers of clean newspaper are laid on the bottom of the box to absorb moisture and odor. However, newspapers are not a suitable surface for puppies to crawl and walk on, as they are slick and offer little traction for their feet. Heavy towels, mattress pads, indoor-outdoor carpeting or any other surface that gives good traction and is disposable or washable is suitable and should be used on top of the newspapers. Disposable baby diapers are excellent for Toy breed puppies. Small puppies should never be placed in deep loose bedding, such as straw, which might obstruct their breathing or be inhaled.

The whelping quarters should be clean, dry, draftfree and warm. When puppies are born, the floor temperature should be kept at 85 degrees F for the first seven days of life. It can be reduced 5 degrees F weekly when the puppies are seven days old, and then progressively reduced to 70 degrees F by the time the litter is six to eight weeks old. Keep a constant check on the temperature with a thermometer on the floor of the box.

If the temperature in the whelping room cannot be maintained with the existing heating system, additional heat may be supplied by using 250 watt infra-red heat bulbs, either suspended above the floor of the litter box or mounted in photographer's floodlight reflectors (or plant lights). Be sure to leave an area of the box out of the direct source of heat so the mother can rest in a cooler area when she wants to.

The bitch should be introduced to the whelping box about two weeks before she is due and required to sleep in it. By the time she whelps she will understand that she is to do so in the box and not in her owner's bed.

Other whelping accessories include a small box with a hot water bottle or heating pad at the bottom of it to place puppies in while others are being born (be sure to cover with a towel, as it is easy to burn puppies by direct contact with a heating pad), a bulb syringe to aspirate secretions from the mouths of the newborns, artery forceps to clamp a bleeding cord, dental floss or cotton threads for ties and an antiseptic, such as iodine, to apply to the umbilical stumps. Scissors, clean laundered towels and plenty of fresh newspapers complete the whelping equipment.

One week before your female is due to deliver, clip away any long hair over her breasts and around her vulva. If she is a long-coated breed, trim the back of her thighs.

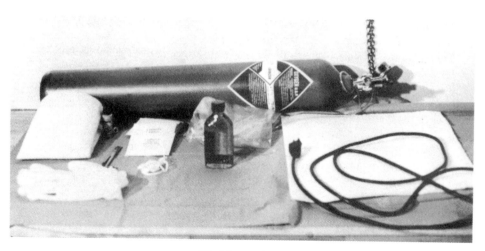

Whelping equipment.

WHELPING

Signs of Delivery

Twelve to twenty-four hours before your bitch is due to give birth she may exhibit a loss of appetite and increased restlessness. Often she rummages in closets, digs a nest in the garden and goes about in a flurry of activity, which is the ritual of making her nest.

Eight to twelve hours before delivery her rectal temperature drops from a normal of 101 degrees to 99 degrees F or below. This two-degree drop in temperature can be missed. A normal temperature does not mean she will not whelp in a few hours.

Labor and Delivery

There are three stages of labor. In the first stage the cervix dilates, opening the birth canal. In the second stage the puppies are delivered. In the third stage the afterbirth is delivered. Bitches may lie down to deliver or stand and squat.

The first stage begins with uncomfortable involuntary uterine contractions manifested by rapid panting, uneasiness or perhaps vomiting. Vomiting is a normal reflex and should not be taken as a sign of distress. On one side of the uterus a horn contracts and expels a puppy into the body of the uterus. Then the uterus contracts and pushes the presenting part of the puppy against the cervix, which causes the cervix to dilate. At complete dilation the dam begins to strain and the puppy slides into the vagina.

This signals the onset of the second stage of labor. The water bag around the puppy can be seen bulging between the lips of the vulva. It serves to lubricate the passageway. If the uterus applies enough pressure to break the water bag, a straw-colored fluid is passed. Then a puppy should be delivered in a few minutes.

After the head is delivered, the rest of the puppy slides out easily. Instinctively the mother removes the fetal membranes, severs the umbilical cord and begins to lick and clean the puppy. No attempt should be made to interfere with maternal care. This is an important part of the mother-puppy bond. She is learning that this is her puppy and she must take care of it. If she appears rough it is only because she is trying to stimulate breathing and blood circulation.

If the dam is occupied with another puppy and forgets to remove the amniotic sac, you should be prepared to step in and strip away the fetal membranes so that the puppy can breathe (see *Helping a Puppy Breathe*).

A placenta follows in a few minutes of the birth of each puppy. The dam will try to eat some or all of the placentas. Some breeders believe the bitch needs the afterbirth because it contains hormones that aid normal labor and stimulate milk production. Others believe it upsets the digestive tract. It is n ʌ essential that the bitch consume the afterbirths. You may wish to limit the number or let nature take its course. The important thing is to count the placentas, since a retained placenta can cause a serious postnatal infection (see *Acute Metritis*).

Bitches sever the umbilical cord by *shredding* it. If the cord is cut too cleanly or too close to the puppy's navel it may continue to bleed. You should be prepared to clamp or pinch off the cord and tie a thread around the stump. The stump should be cauterized with iodine or some other suitable disinfectant.

The next puppy will be born from the opposite uterine horn. When it is about to appear, remove the first puppy and place it in a box warmed to 85 degrees F with a hot water bottle. This prevents chilling or temperature shock, which is a leading cause of newborn puppy deaths.

In between births put the puppies on the nipples. Their sucking action brings on the colostrum, first milk of the dam, which contains the all-important maternal antibodies.

Puppies can be born as close to each other as every fifteen minutes or as far apart as every two hours. An average time of delivery for four to six puppies is six to eight hours, but a large litter can take considerably longer. Although puppies usually appear at regular intervals, it is not a cause of concern if a puppy does not arrive for one or two hours. If the interval is longer than this or if the bitch appears to be continuously straining and in distress, then something is wrong (see *When to Call the Veterinarian* below).

Assisting the Normal Delivery

When labor is going well, it is best not to attempt to aid the bitch, as she knows by instinct how to whelp her puppies and take care of them. But on occasion a large puppy gets stuck in the vaginal canal. The head or presenting part appears during a forceful contraction, then slips back inside when the bitch relaxes. At this point it is wise to step in quickly and complete the delivery. Once a puppy moves out of the uterus down into the vaginal canal, oxygen from the bitch gets cut off. Delivery must proceed rapidly.

It is not difficult to complete a partial delivery if the following steps are taken:

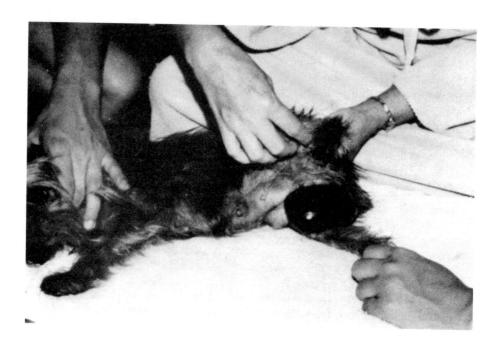

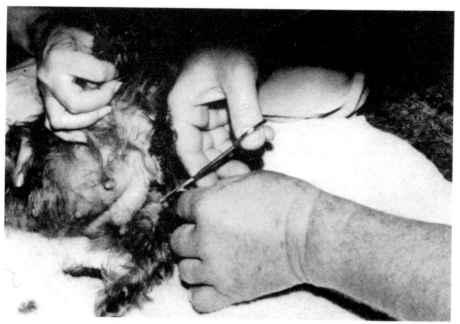

Birth of Puppies: The water bag around the puppy can be seen bulging through the vulva.

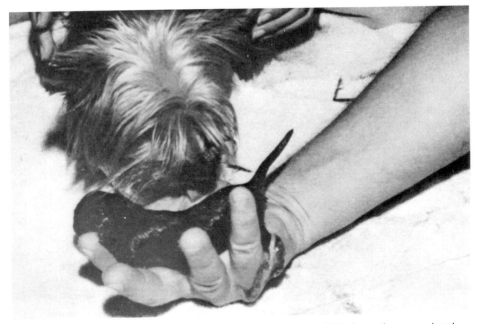
Present the puppy to the dam to lick and cuddle. This helps to establish the mother-puppy bond.

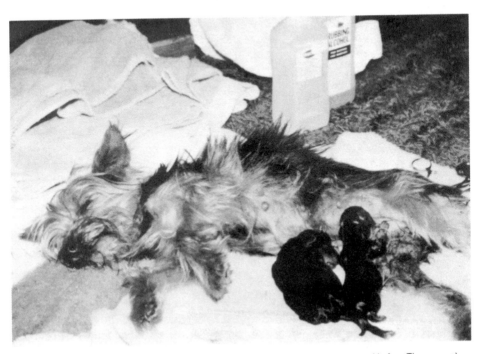
Puppies can be allowed to nurse between deliveries. *(JoAnn Thompson)*

As the presenting part appears at the vaginal opening, apply pressure on the perineum just below the anus and push down to keep the puppy from slipping back into the mother. Next, slide the lips of the vulva over the head of the puppy. Once this is accomplished the lips hold the puppy in place, giving you a chance to get another grip. Now grip the skin of the puppy with a clean piece of cloth behind the neck or along the back and draw the puppy out. Apply forceful contraction only to the skin, not to the legs or head, as this can cause damage to a joint. Often it is helpful to rotate the puppy first one way and then another, especially when something seems to be stuck. The birth canal usually is wider one way than the other. If these measures are not immediately successful, proceed as described under *Canine Obstetrics*.

After your bitch has delivered the last puppy, your veterinarian should examine her to be sure there are no retained puppies or placentas, and may administer an injection to clear the uterus. The injection also stimulates the letting down of milk.

PROLONGED LABOR (DYSTOCIA—DIFFICULT LABOR)

The elongation of any phase of labor is called *dystocia*. It is caused by either a birth canal that is too narrow in relation to the size of the presenting part (*mechanical blockage*), or by failure to develop enough strength to expel the fetus (*uterine inertia*). Often these two are related, a difficult birth being followed by arrested labor because of uterine muscle fatigue.

Dystocia is much more common in older brood bitches and those allowed to become too fat. This is why it is so important to keep your female trim and in top condition.

A less common cause of mechanical blockage is a narrow pelvis.

An abnormal presentation can occur at any time but is much more likely to arrest labor in the overweight, poorly conditioned female. Normally, puppies come down the birth canal nose-first, with their backs along the top of the vagina and their feet at the bottom. The rump-first position, called the *breech*, occurs so often that it may be inaccurate to classify it as a malpresentation. Usually it causes problems only when it occurs in the first puppy. When the head is bent forward, or to the side, the pup may get caught in the birth canal. Uncommonly, the pelvis of the puppy hangs up in the pelvic outlet of the bitch.

Uterine inertia is an important cause of ineffectual labor. Mechanical factors can cause the uterus to become overdistended with stretched-out fibers and therefore lose the power of contraction. Among these factors are a single large puppy in a small uterus, a very large litter and *hydrops amnion*, a condition in which there is too much amniotic fluid.

Uterine inertia can be caused by emotional upsets. Sudden anxiety induces a form of hysteria that stops normal labor. This is why it is important to whelp a bitch where she is at ease and familiar with her surroundings, away from casual spectators and other nerve-racking influences.

Some cases of inertia, called *primary*, seem to be caused by a deficiency of oxytocin (a hormone produced by the pituitary gland) or calcium, or both. The uterus may respond to injections of oxytocin, which stimulate stronger contractions. Intravenous calcium may also be given.

Oxytocin is contraindicated when:

1. There is mechanical blockage (e.g., too large a puppy for the size of the birth canal).
2. The dam is mouth-breathing (indicates she is in distress).
3. There is prolonged straining for two to three hours without progress (indicates uterine muscle fatigue).
4. The uterus is vigorously contracting (additional stimulus is not necessary).

Oxytocin should be used only by a veterinarian, as it can lead to rupture of the uterus.

When to Call the Veterinarian

It is certainly better to call your veterinarian on a "false alarm," even if only to gain reassurance, than to delay in the hope that in time the situation will correct itself without help. Often the problem can be dealt with rather simply if attended to at once. However, the same problem, when neglected, becomes complicated—often leading to an emergency operation.

Something may be wrong when:

a. A bitch goes into labor (serious straining) and does not deliver a puppy within two hours. Purposeful straining indicates a puppy is partly in the birth canal. It is a mistake to wait four or six hours, as the mother is now exhausted and normal deliver may not be possible even when the cause is removed.
b. The bitch passes dark green or bloody fluid *before* delivery of the first puppy. This indicates separation of the placenta from the wall of the uterus, which means that the puppy is not getting oxygen from the mother. After the first puppy, green or bloody fluid is normal.
c. The membranes rupture and a puppy is not delivered in thirty minutes. The passage of yellow fluid means rupture of the water bag (amniotic sac) surrounding the puppy.
d. Labor stops and there are signs of restlessness, anxiety, weakness or fatigue. Puppies come fifteen minutes to two hours apart. Over three hours between puppies may be a sign of trouble.

Canine Obstetrics

If it is impossible to get prompt veterinary help or if the water bag breaks and the puppy is stuck in the birth canal, there are ways to assist in delivering the puppy.

Clean the outside of the vulva with soap and water. Put on a pair of sterile gloves and lubricate your finger with pHisoHex, K-Y Jelly or Vaseline. Before

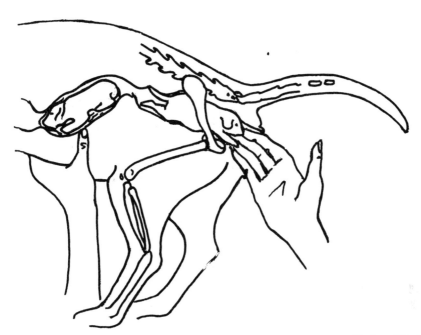

Normally, puppies are delivered head first.   *(Sydney Wiley)*

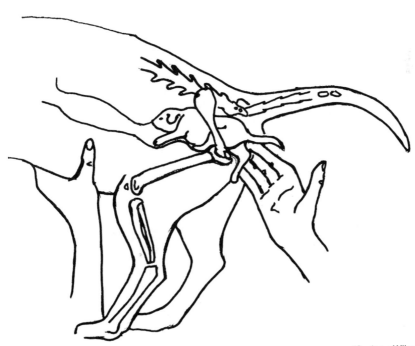

The breech presentation is common in the dog.   *(Sydney Wiley)*

inserting your finger into the vagina, be careful not to contaminate your gloves with stool from the anus.

Place one hand under the abdomen in front of the pelvis of the dam and feel for the puppy. Raise the puppy up into position aligned with the birth canal. With your other hand, slip a finger into the vagina and feel for a head, tail or leg. When the *head is deviated* and will not pass through the outlet of the pelvis, insert a finger into the puppy's mouth and gently turn the head, guiding it into the birth canal.

When the puppy is coming as a *breech* (rump first), hold the puppy at the pelvic outlet as described. With the vaginal finger, hook first one leg and then the other, slipping them down over the narrow place until the pelvis and legs appear at the vulva.

If the mother has been *unable to deliver a large puppy coming normally*, insert a gloved finger into the vagina alongside the puppy until you can feel the front legs at the elbows. Hook them and pull them through individually.

Once the puppy is in the lower part of the birth canal, it should be delivered without further delay. To stimulate a forceful push by the mother, gently stretch the vaginal opening. If you can see the puppy at the mouth of the vagina appearing and disappearing with straining, grip the pup *with a clean piece of cloth* and pull out as described under *Assisting the Normal Delivery*. Time is of the essence—particularly when the puppy is a breech. It is better to take hold and pull out the puppy even at the risk of injury or death since that puppy, and perhaps the others, will die if something is not done.

Sometimes the blockage is caused by a retained placenta. Hook it with your fingers and grasp it with a sterile cloth. Maintain gentle traction until it passes out of the vagina.

When the uterus becomes exhausted and stops contracting, it is difficult to correct a malposition without instruments. Only those experienced in the use of instruments should attempt this feat, as the risk of uterine rupture is considerable. Caesarean section often is indicated. When the puppy comes sideways, usually it is not possible to correct the problem short of a Caesarean section.

Helping a Puppy Breathe

When a puppy is born surrounded by the amniotic sac, it should be removed within thirty seconds in order to allow the puppy to breathe. If the bitch fails to do this, you should tear open the sac and remove it, starting at the mouth and working backward over the body. Aspirate the secretions from the mouth with a bulb syringe. Rub the puppy briskly with a soft towel.

An alternate method of clearing the secretions is to hold the puppy in your hands while supporting the head. Then swing the pup in a downward arc, stopping abruptly when the nose is pointing to the floor. This helps to expel water from the nostrils. Present the puppy to the mother for her to lick, sniff and cuddle.

After a difficult delivery, a puppy may be too weak or too flaccid to breathe on its own. Squeeze the chest gently from side to side and then from front to back. If the puppy still will not breathe, place your mouth over the mouth and nostrils and breathe out gently until you see the chest expand. Do not exhale too

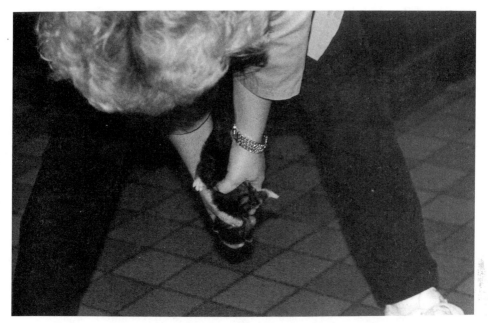
Swing the puppy down to clear secretions from the nostrils.

forcefully as this can rupture the lungs. Then remove your mouth to allow the puppy to exhale. Repeat this several times until the puppy is breathing and crying.

CAESAREAN SECTION

Caesarean section is the procedure of choice for any type of arrested labor that cannot be relieved by drugs or obstetrical manipulation. Most veterinarians feel that after twenty-four hours of unproductive labor, Caesarean section is indicated. It is indicated sooner for a mechanical blockage that cannot be rapidly corrected. The decision ultimately rests with the veterinarian. Consideration will be given to the condition of the dam, length of labor, how many puppies can be delivered by instruments (usually not more than two because of subsequent swelling of the birth canal induced by the instruments), the size of the puppies in relationship to the pelvic outlet, failure to respond to injections of oxytocin and whether the vaginal canal has become dry.

Because of their anatomical makeup, certain breeds—such as the Bulldog, Chihuahua, Pekingese, Toy Poodle and Boston Terrier—are prone to whelping difficulties and Caesarean section may be indicated as an elective procedure as soon as the cervix dilates. If you own one of these breeds, discuss this possibility with your veterinarian.

Caesarean section is an operation done under general anesthesia in the veterinary hospital. The risk to a young, healthy dam is not great. However, when labor has been unduly prolonged, when toxicity is present, when the puppies are dead and beginning to decompose or when uterine rupture occurs,

339

then the risks become significant. Usually a bitch is awake and stable and able to nurse the puppies at home within three hours of the operation.

If a bitch has a Caesarean section, she may or may not require a section with her next litter. This depends upon the reason for the first one. Many bitches who have had one Caesarean section are able to have normal vaginal deliveries the next time they become pregnant.

POSTPARTUM CARE OF THE DAM

Twelve to twenty-four hours after your bitch delivers, ask your veterinarian to examine her and check her milk for color, consistency and quality. (If the milk is thick, stringy, yellowish or discolored it may be infected). Palpation and/ or X rays of the uterus rule out a retained puppy. Many veterinarians prescribe an injection of oxytocin to aid in letting down milk and involution of the uterus.

During the first week, take the mother's temperature at least once a day. A temperature of 103 degrees F or higher indicates a problem (retained placenta, acute metritis, mastitis).

A greenish discharge is normal for the first twelve to twenty-four hours. It is followed by a variable amount of reddish-tinged to serosanguinous discharge, which lasts two to three weeks. A green, brownish or serosanguinous discharge that lasts over twenty-one days signifies something is wrong (uterine subinvolution).

Feeding During Lactation

During lactation a bitch's caloric requirements increase by 25 percent per week. By the fourth week, twice the prewhelping amount is required. At this time it is particularly important to be sure that your dam is getting enough to eat. Otherwise, she will quickly lose weight and fail to produce enough milk to satisfy the puppies.

Feed a good commercial adult kibble preparation. (Some veterinarians suggest using a puppy chow). Name-brand dog foods are formulated to meet the National Research Council's recommendations for nutritionally complete diets. They provide protein, fat and carbohydrate, along with vitamins and minerals, in correct balance. They are quite suitable for a lactating dam—who *eats the required amount.* By the second or third week, a nursing dam eats three times the normal daily ration—or three full meals spaced throughout the day. Many veterinarians recommend supplementing the kibble base with canned meat or cottage cheese in the following proportions: 80 percent kibble to 20 percent canned meat or cottage cheese. If this ratio is exceeded a correct balance will not be obtained.

Some bitches are likely to have inadequate calcium during nursing. A balanced vitamin-mineral supplement, such as Pet-Cal, is most beneficial when used during lactation. *Follow the manufacturer's recommendations in regard to dosage.*

Tense, overactive bitches, or those with a big litter, may require extra

When litters are large, the pups may have to be supplemented. *(Sydney Wiley)*

energy. Add three tablespoons vegetable oil to each pound of dry dog food. Give vitamin B supplements to dams with a marginal milk supply.

POSTPARTUM PROBLEMS

Problems that can affect the dam following delivery are acute metritis, mastitis, caked breasts and milk fever. A few bitches have problems accepting their puppies because of emotional upsets and psychological blocks.

Acute Metritis (Infected Uterus)

Acute metritis is an infection that spreads upward through the birth canal during delivery or immediately afterward. It affects the lining of the uterus. It is most likely to occur when part of the placenta has been retained. Some cases are caused by a retained fetus that has become mummified. Other cases are caused by contamination of the birth canal by unsterile instruments and fingers during delivery. A difficult or prolonged labor and a pre-existing vaginitis are other predisposing causes.

Chronic endometritis and *abscess of the uterus* are other uterine infections that may be confused with acute postpartum metritis. They are discussed under SEX AND REPRODUCTION: *Diseases of the Female Genital Tract*.

Most cases of inflamed uterus can be anticipated and prevented by a postpartum checkup. A veterinarian often will want to clean the uterus with an injection of oxytocin. Vaginitis should be treated as soon as it is diagnosed, preferably before heat and certainly before labor and delivery.

A dam with acute metritis is depressed, hangs her head, refuses to eat, has a temperature of 103 to 105 degrees F and may cease to care for her puppies or keep the nest clean.

There is a heavy, dark, bloody greenish or tomato-souplike discharge that appears two to seven days after whelping. It should not be confused with the normal greenish discharge that disappears during the first twelve to twenty-four hours, or the light reddish, serosanguinous discharge that lasts two to three weeks. A normal discharge is not accompanied by high fever, excessive thirst or other signs of toxicity such as vomiting and diarrhea.

Treatment: Acute metritis is a life-threatening illness. A veterinarian should be consulted immediately to save the life of the dam. Usually puppies will have to be taken off the mother and reared by hand (see PEDIATRICS: *Raising Puppies by Hand*), as she will be too sick to take care of them. Her milk may be toxic.

Mastitis

The two breast conditions affecting the nursing dam are caked breasts and acute mastitis. One often leads to the other.

Caked Breasts (Galactostasis)

This is a form of mastitis caused by too much milk in a breast gland, either because of overproduction or because the breast is not being adequately suckled by the puppies. A deformed nipple may be at fault. Caking of the breasts can occur during false pregnancy where there are no puppies to remove the milk.

Affected glands, usually the two hind ones, are swollen, painful, warm and hard. Litmus paper may be used to test the acidity of the milk. Normal canine breast milk should test to a pH of 6.0 to 6.5 (colostrum often tests to a pH of 7.0). Milk (not colostrum) which tests to a pH of 7.0 is infected and will make puppies sick. Milk from simple caking of the breasts tests to a normal pH and is okay for puppies to suckle. If the pH is 7.0, see *Acute Septic Mastitis* below.

Treatment: Withhold food from the bitch for 24 hours and limit the size of feedings for the next three days. Massage the caked gland twice a day with camphorated oil, apply cold packs, and express the gland to draw out some of the coagulated and caked milk. This also stimulates lactation.

Bromocryptine (Parlodel) can be given to dry up the breasts if there is no further need for nursing. Diuretics may help to reduce the swelling. Buffered or enteric coated aspirin should be given to relieve pain.

Severely caked breasts may become infected, leading to an *acute septic mastitis*. Watch for signs as described below.

Acute Septic Mastitis (Breast Infection or Abscess)

This infection of one or more of the mammary glands is caused by bacteria that get into the breast tissue during nursing from a scratch or puncture wound. Some cases are blood borne (See *Acute Metritis*).

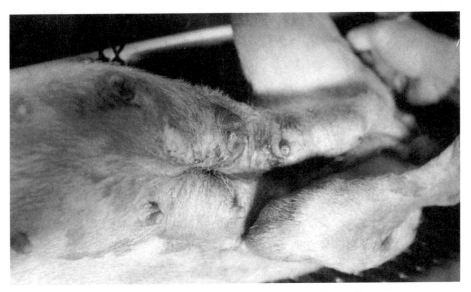

The inflamed breast of a dam with *acute septic mastitis*.

When the puppies are two to three weeks old, their nails should be trimmed once a week to keep them from scratching the skin of the dam. A mammary gland with acute mastitis is swollen, extremely painful and usually reddish blue in appearance. Milk may be blood-tinged, thin, yellowish or stringlike. In some cases, the milk will look normal yet will test to a pH of 7.0 or greater.

Mothers with acute mastitis refuse to eat, appear listless, are restless and run a high fever (which suggests abscess formation).

Puppies should be prevented from nursing at an infected breast since they can come down with a fatal infection themselves.

Treatment: Acute mastitis should be treated by a veterinarian. Routine measures include the use of appropriate antibiotics and gentle massage of the glands three or four times a day with camphorated oil followed by application of hot packs.

The nipple of an infected gland can be taped so that the puppies can't nurse on it. If more than one gland is involved, or if the dam is quite toxic, it is advisable to remove the puppies altogether and raise them by hand. If they are three weeks of age, they can be weaned. Bind the breasts using a many-tailed abdominal bandage (see EMERGENCIES: *Wounds*).

When milk from an infected breast returns to a normal appearance and tests to a pH of less than 7.0, the puppies can nurse. The procedure for drying up the breasts is explained in PEDIATRICS: *Weaning*.

Milk Fever (Eclampsia, Puerperal Tetany)

Eclampsia is caused by an upset in the calcium regulatory mechanism that leads to a low calcium level in the blood. It is called milk fever because it often occurs during the first four weeks of lactation, but can occur as early as twenty days before whelping and as late as forty-five days after whelping. During this time there is a drain on calcium stores in the body. Primarily this is a disease of small dogs with large litters, especially Toys.

Low serum calcium levels cause tetany. The first signs are restlessness, anxiety, rapid breathing and whining. A dam will frequently leave the puppies and begin to pace up and down. Her gait is stiff-legged, uncoordinated and jerky. Her face takes on a pinched look, with the skin pulled back to expose the teeth. As the condition worsens, she falls down on her side, exhibits spasms, kicking all four legs, and salivates profusely.

The temperature often is elevated up to 106 degrees F. This causes more panting, washes out carbon dioxide, raises the pH of the blood and lowers the serum calcium even further. Death can occur from hyperthermia, respiratory depression and subsequent brain damage.

Certain bitches seem predisposed to milk fever. If your bitch is one of the Toy breeds, or has had milk fever in the past, she is likely to have it again. Discuss with your veterinarian the possibility of supplementing the diet with calcium during the last half of pregnancy. However, do not oversupplement with calcium as this can upset regulatory mechanisms and cause further problems.

Treatment: *Puerperal tetany is a real emergency.* Notify your veterinarian at once. Intravenous calcium solutions should be given at the first signs to re-establish normal blood calcium levels. Cardiac arrhythmias can occur when calcium is given too rapidly, so this should be done by a professional.

If the rectal temperature is over 104 degrees F, treat as you would for heat stroke while awaiting the veterinarian's arrival.

Puppies must be taken off the dam for twenty-four hours and given supplemental feedings. Whether to resume nursing after that depends on how well the dam is responding to treatment and also the age of her puppies. If they are three weeks of age, they can be weaned. If the decision is made to allow restricted nursing, the dam should be supplemented with calcium, phosphorus and vitamin D.

Puppies should be put back on the breasts for only a few minutes the first day, gradually allowed to nurse for longer periods over the next three days and returned to a normal schedule by the fifth day. During this time they will need to be supplemented.

Mothers Who Neglect or Injure Their Puppies

To encourage quality mothering, adequate nutrition, absence of complications during whelping and lactation, clean, dry, odorfree surroundings with acceptance of the whelping box and finally a lack of excessive interference and environmental disturbances are most important factors.

Mothers learn to recognize and care for their puppies as they are born, cleaned and begin to nurse. This bond sometimes is not as strong when the puppies are born by Caesarean section. Such mothers can have difficulty in accepting their puppies for the first forty-eight hours. This is less likely to happen when some of the puppies are born before the surgery or when they are put to the nipples before the sedation wears off.

344

A novice mother often has difficulty coping with a litter of squirming puppies for the first few hours. This is understandable. With a little help, she can be shown how to nurse the puppies and keep from stepping on them. Spoiled house pets sometimes will not care for their puppies until they are allowed to regain their former position in the family hierarchy.

Sometimes, due to a hormonal imbalance, the milk does not come down for the first forty-eight hours. During this time the bitch may reject the puppies. Milk can be helped in flow by oxytocin and other hormones. Once the milk comes in the puppies are accepted.

A hypothermic puppy, one whose body temperature has dropped below normal because of sickness or constitutional weakness, instinctively is pushed out of the nest. This is nature's way of culling.

Other causes of puppy rejection are postpartum infections and complications such as milk fever, mastitis and acute metritis. Dams who continue to ignore or reject their puppies sometimes may be helped by tranquilizers. If the problem is caused by maternal infection, then the puppies may have to be removed and reared by hand.

A bitch whelping her first litter should be watched closely. She may accidentally confuse the puppy with the placenta or injure a puppy while attempting to sever the cord and remove the membranes. Breeds with an undershot jaw or a malocclusion problem are particularly prone to this difficulty.

A novice dam may attempt to pick up and carry a puppy to some other nest. Do not allow your bitch to carry puppies, as she may become nervous or upset and bite down too hard. Nest-seeking can be avoided if the dam is introduced to the litter box two weeks before the due date and required to sleep in it.

In other cases, a nervous, possessive or overprotective dam can injure puppies out of emotional upset caused by too much handling of the puppies by children or strange people. It is important not to allow visitors for the first three to four weeks—especially when the bitch is high-strung or not well socialized to people.

The picture of health, these young Bulldog puppies nurse vigorously in an area their mother has worked hard to keep clean.

Patty Rungo

17

Pediatrics

NEWBORN PUPPIES

A HEALTHY NEONATAL PUPPY from birth to three weeks of age is the picture of contentment, sleeping 90 percent of the time and eating about 10 percent. The newborn nurses vigorously and competes for nipples. For the first forty-eight hours, a sleeping newborn's head is curled under the chest. While sleeping, puppies jerk, kick and sometimes whimper. This is called "activated sleep." It is normal. It is the newborn puppy's only means of exercise and helps to develop muscles that will be used later.

A good mother instinctively keeps her nest and puppies clean. By licking the belly and rectum of each pup, she stimulates the elimination reflex.

Physiology

At one day of age puppies have heart rates of 160 beats per minute, breathing rates of ten to eighteen breaths per minute and temperatures that vary from 92 to 97 degrees F. Between two and twenty-one days the heart rate increases to 220 beats per minute and the breathing rate from eighteen to thirty-six breaths per minute. Temperature is 96 to 100 degrees F.

Eyes and ears, which are sealed at birth, start to open at ten to sixteen days. Puppies are sight-and sound-oriented at twenty-five days of age. Usually they will stand at fifteen days of age and begin to walk at twenty-one days. They can control the urge to eliminate at three weeks.

During the first week of life peripheral blood vessels do not have the capacity to constrict or retain heat—nor can a puppy shiver to generate heat by itself. This means that a newborn cannot sustain body temperature and needs an outside source of heat. The mother's body warmth keeps a puppy's temperature between 96 and 100 degrees F. When the dam is away for thirty minutes, in a room at 72 degrees F (well below the recommended level), the neonate's temperature can fall to 94 degrees F or below, quickly chilling the pup, a condition that causes gravely reduced metabolism.

Neonatal puppies have little subcutaneous fat. Energy is supplied through feedings. Reserve energy is supplied almost entirely by glycogen in the liver. The liver is the last organ to grow in size, while the brain is the organ that consumes the most energy. A puppy with a brain too large in proportion to the liver rapidly runs out of energy because of low blood sugar. Accordingly, the weight of the liver must be at least one and a half times the weight of the brain at birth. A liver-brain ratio of two to three is even better. Even if these conditions are met, there is little margin for reserve in the newborn. Potentially low blood sugar must be offset by frequent feeding. A puppy that does not eat frequently, for whatever reason, is heading for trouble.

Kidney function in the newborn is 12 to 25 percent of what it will be later in life. These immature kidneys are unable to concentrate the urine, which means that it is necessary for puppies to excrete large amounts of dilute urine. This obligatory water loss of the kidneys must be offset by sufficient intake of milk, or in the case of puppies raised by hand, by a formula containing adequate amounts of water.

Drugs and medications are not metabolized or excreted as well in newborns as they are in older puppies. The milk of a dam that is on these preparations could contain toxic amounts. Precautions should be taken, as discussed in DRUGS AND MEDICATIONS: *Drugs in Pregnancy and Lactation*.

Why Puppies Die

Thirty percent of puppies die between birth and weaning. Three-fourths of these die in the first two weeks of life. Many puppy deaths undoubtedly are caused by lack of advanced preparation: providing adequate heat in the whelping quarters (which should be clean and dry as well), vaccinating the prospective dam and getting her on a sound feeding program during pregnancy and lactation.

Some deaths are attributable to birth trauma, congenital defects, maternal neglect, something wrong with the milk supply and infectious diseases.

Congenital defects are not a major cause of newborn deaths. But when they do occur they may be lethal. Hemophilia is a clotting disorder that leads to internal bleeding or bleeding from the body openings. Cleft palate, often associated with harelip, prevents effective nursing. Large naval hernias allow prolapse of abdominal organs. Heart defects can be severe enough to lead to circulatory failure. Other disorders may be responsible for mysterious or unexplained deaths.

Cardiopulmonary Syndrome (Circulatory Failure of the Newborn)

This is a shocklike state that occurs in pups under five days of age. After this age pups can respond better to stress, as they are more mature.

Chilling, overheating, impaired breathing and inefficient nursing produce a drop in temperature, heart and breathing rate. These in turn lead to weakness and inability to digest food. If the body temperature drops below 94 degrees F, there is further depression of vital functions. This cycle is progressive and soon becomes irreversible. Early treatment is imperative to avoid death.

Because of immaturity these pups are unable to mount a specific response to specific stress. Whatever the cause of the problem, the symptoms and signs are similar.

At first, pups may salivate excessively, cry and make swallowing movements. Gradually, their crawling and righting ability are lost and they lie on their sides. Heart and breathing rates are slow until the heart rate is forty beats per minute and the breathing rate is four per minute.

Later, poor circulation affects the brain, causing tetanic spasms (rigors), accompanied by breathless periods lasting up to a minute. At this point, the condition is irreversible. Blood in the stool and urine (as a result of circulatory failure) may be noted. Gagging and fluid in the nostril may be noted.

Treatment involves the administration of oxygen, dextrose and slow warming. Adrenalin may be of aid. Veterinary assistance is required.

The Runts

Physically immature puppies are at a distinct disadvantage because of low birth weight and lack of muscle mass and subcutaneous fat. These puppies may be unable to breathe deeply, nurse effectively and maintain body warmth. Their liver-brain ratio may be less than 1.5/ 1. Birth weight may be 25 percent below that of their littermates.

A distressed newborn with *circulatory failure* and terminal seizures. Early rewarming is imperative to prevent this problem.

The most common cause of subnormal birth weight is inadequate nourishment while in the uterus. When all the puppies are undersized, a poorly nourished bitch is the prime consideration. When one or two puppies are below par, most likely the fault is one of placental insufficiency caused by overcrowding, or a disadvantageous placement of a placenta in the wall of the uterus. These puppies are immature on the basis of their development rather than their age. If they are to survive, they must be separated from the dam and raised by hand in an incubator as described elsewhere in this chapter.

Fading Puppies

These puppies are apparently vigorous and healthy at birth, then fail to gain weight, lose strength and vitality and the urge to feed. For want of a better term, the condition is called "Fading Puppy Syndrome." There is no general agreement as to the cause of fading puppies. Some cases may result from immaturity, others from birth defects, environmental stress and maternal factors. The syndrome may be reversible if the cause can be determined and steps taken to correct it.

CARING FOR THE NEWBORN

Newborn puppies are born without the capacity to adapt to environmental stress. With proper care and attention to the special needs of these infants, many unnecessary neonatal deaths can be avoided.

Neonatal puppies do not respond to environmental stress and illness in the same way as do adult dogs; a special approach is needed to monitor the well-being of newborns as soon as they are born. The two crucial aspects to watch closely are the puppies' body temperature and weight. General appearance, heart rate, breathing rate, skin turgor, muscle tone, mobility and body position, sound of their cries and sucking reflex also can provide useful information as to their overall health and vitality. These perimeters are discussed below.

General Appearance and Vitality

Healthy puppies are "round, firm and fully packed." They nurse vigorously and compete for nipples with their littermates. If you insert a finger into their mouths, they have a strong, vigorous suckle. They are warm and plump. The mouth and tongue are wet; the skin has a pink appearance. When pinched, it springs back in a resilient fashion. Pick them up and they stretch and wiggle energetically in your hand. When removed from the dam, they crawl back to her. Newborn puppies "pile," or crawl together for warmth. They seldom cry. Crying indicates that a puppy is cold, hungry or in pain. A sick puppy presents a dramatically different picture. This puppy is limp, cold and hangs like a dishcloth when picked up. When you put a finger into the mouth, this pup pushes it out and shows the same lack of interest in nursing.

Distressed puppies are hyperactive. They crawl about looking for help and fall asleep away from the life-sustaining warmth of their dam and littermates. They rest with their legs splayed apart and their necks bent to the side. Their cry is plaintive and piercing and sometimes goes on for more than twenty minutes.

Body temperature is lower than it should be, often 94 degrees F or below. Breathing rate is often less than ten per minute. Signs of dehydration are lack of moisture in the mouth, a bright pink color to the tongue and mucus membranes of the mouth, loss of muscle tone and weakness. When the skin is pinched, it stays up in a fold instead of springing back. Viral and bacterial infections may produce a diarrhea that becomes profuse as the condition deteriorates. As the pup grows weaker, so does the heart rate and respiration. These puppies often are rejected by the dam that senses they are not going to survive and pushes them out of the pile rather than waste her energies. If this can be reversed, the puppies are treated and the body temperature is brought back to normal, the bitch will accept them back.

Temperature

At birth, a puppy's temperature is the same as that of the dam. Immediately afterward it drops several degrees (how much depends upon the temperature of the room). Within thirty minutes, if the puppy is dry and snuggled close to the dam, the temperature begins to climb back up and soon reaches 94 degrees F. Twenty-four hours later the rectal or core temperature is 95 to 97 degrees F, and steadily increases until at three weeks of age it is 98 to 100 degrees F. A healthy puppy can maintain a temperature 10 to 12 degrees F above the immediate surroundings.

While chilling is the single greatest danger to the infant puppy, the opposite is also true. Overheating and dehydration can produce many problems. The temperature of the whelping box and the area in which the box is kept must be 85 to 90 degrees F during the first week. The five-degree variation depends upon the nature of the hair coat. The construction of a suitable whelping box is described in the chapter SEX AND REPRODUCTION.

Warming a Chilled Puppy

Any puppy whose body temperature is below the normals for its age is a chilled puppy. A chilled puppy must be warmed *gradually*. Rapid warming (for example, by a heating pad) causes dilatation of skin vessels, increased loss of heat, added expenditure of calories and greater need for oxygen. This is detrimental.

The best way to warm a puppy is to tuck the pup down beneath a sweater or jacket next to your skin, letting your own warmth seep into the puppy's system. If body temperature is below 94 degrees F and the pup is weak, warming will take two to three hours. Afterward, the puppy may have to be placed in a homemade incubator (see *Raising Puppies by Hand*).

Never feed formula or allow a cold puppy to nurse. When so chilled, the stomach and small intestines stop working. If a formula is given it will not be digested. The puppy will bloat and perhaps vomit. A chilled puppy can utilize a

5 to 10 percent glucose and water solution (glucose can be purchased at drugstores). Give one milliliter per ounce of body weight every hour, and warm slowly until the pup is warm and wiggling about. If a glucose solution is not available, use honey and water, or as a last resort, use household sugar and water: one teaspoonful per ounce.

Importance of Weight Gain

Puppies should gain one to one and a half grams of weight per day for each pound of anticipated adult weight, and should double their birth weight in eight to ten days. To estimate the adult weight of a puppy, weigh the dam. A steady gain in weight is the best indication that puppies are doing well. Similarly, a puppy that doesn't gain weight should be singled out for special attention. For this reason, puppies should be weighed on a gram scale at birth, at twelve and twenty-four hours, daily for the first two weeks of life and every three days until a month old.

When several puppies in a litter are not gaining weight, you should think of a maternal factor (such as toxic milk, metritis or inadequate milk supply). If the mother is not getting adequate calories, her milk supply will be inadequate to support a large litter. A nursing dam needs two to three times more food than a normal adult dog. The diet must be balanced to meet the needs of lactation. This subject is discussed in PREGNANCY AND WHELPING.

A sudden drop in weight with diarrhea is the cause of water loss. A balanced electrolyte solution is needed. This is the same solution used in correcting dehydration in hand-fed puppies. It is discussed in *Common Feeding Problems*. Puppies dehydrate quickly when they stop nursing. Therefore, dehydration has to be considered a factor whenever a puppy fails to thrive, loses weight, becomes chilled and is too weak to nurse.

When to Supplement

Puppies that gain weight steadily during the first seven days are in no immediate danger. Puppies that experience a weight loss not exceeding 10 percent of birth weight for the first forty-eight hours of life and then begin to gain should be watched closely. Puppies that lose 10 percent or more of their birth weight in the first forty-eight hours and do not begin to gain by seventy-two hours are poor survival prospects. Start supplemental feedings immediately (see *Raising Puppies by Hand*).

If at birth a puppy is 25 percent under the expected birth weight for the breed or the weight of littermates, you can expect high mortality. Place this puppy in an incubator to be raised by hand. Many immature puppies can be saved if their condition is not complicated by diseases or congenital defects.

RAISING PUPPIES BY HAND

A dam could be unable to raise the litter because of postpartum uterine infection or breast infection, toxic milk, eclampsia or inadequate milk supply. In such cases the pups have to be supplemented or hand-fed.

The decision to supplement a puppy is based upon general appearance and vitality, weight at birth and progress in comparison to littermates. As a rule, it is better to step in early and start hand-feeding in borderline cases, and not wait until a puppy is in obvious distress. Depending upon the overall condition of the pup and response to supplement feeding, it may be possible to feed two or three times a day and let the pup remain with the mother. Others must be taken away and raised as orphans. They require intensive care.

If you think a puppy needs supplemental feeding, calculate the total daily requirements (the method is given in *Calculating the Right Formula*) and assume that a nursing puppy eats four times a day. Give one-fourth of the total daily requirement at each feeding.

Accurate record keeping is important at all times, but is absolutely essential when puppies are raised by hand. Weigh them at birth, at eight-hour intervals for four days, daily for the first two weeks of life and then every three days until they reach one month.

Three areas of critical importance are furnishing the right environment, preparing and feeding the right formula and providing the right management. Feeding equipment should be thoroughly cleaned and boiled. Visitors should not be allowed in the nursery. All personnel should wash their hands before handling the puppies—especially if they have been with other dogs. Many diseases, including distemper, can be transmitted to puppies by a person who has recently handled an infective dog.

If the puppies were unable to receive the colostrum, or first milk of the dam, they lack passive immunity and are susceptible to a variety of diseases including distemper. Vaccinations are then given after three weeks of age.

Since chilling is the single greatest danger to the newborn puppy's survival, you will need an incubator.

The Incubator

A satisfactory incubator can be made in a few minutes by dividing a cardboard box into compartments so that each puppy will have a separate pen. These pens are important when puppies are being fed by stomach tube because, having no nipple to suckle, they tend to suckle each other's ears, tails and genitalia. If they are nursed from a bottle they may not need to have separate compartments.

Place a small electric heating pad in the bottom of the incubator. One-fourth of it should lie against the side of the box, and three-fourths on the bottom. This permits puppies to get close to the heat when they are cold and get away from it when hot. Cover the pad with a waterproof material such as plastic or rubber. On top, place a baby diaper that can be changed as often as it becomes soiled. This also gives a means for checking the appearance of each puppy's stool. Another means of providing sufficient warmth is to use overhead heat lights. These may not be as satisfactory as a heating pad.

A thermometer in the incubator monitors the surface temperature. Keep the incubator at 85 to 90 degrees F for the first week. During the second week, reduce it to 80 or 85 degrees F. Thereafter, gradually decrease the temperature so that it is 75 degrees F by the end of the fourth week. Maintain constant warmth and avoid chilling drafts.

Maintain the humidity of the room at about 55 percent. This helps to prevent skin drying and dehydration.

General Care

Keep the puppies clean with a damp cloth. Be sure to cleanse the anal area and skin of the abdomen. A light application of baby oil may be applied to these areas and to the coat to prevent drying of the skin. Change the bedding often to prevent urine scalds. When present, they can be helped by the application of baby powder. If infected, apply a topical antibiotic ointment (Panolog).

For the first ten days, massage the abdomen and perianal area of the puppies after each feeding to stimulate elimination. (This is something the mother would do.) A wad of cotton soaked in warm water works well.

Hand-feeding

This is not the chore it used to be because of the ready availability of artificial bitch's milk available through your veterinarian or a commercial source. It has replaced the need for special formulas, goat's milk and foster mothers.

The composition of various milk sources is shown in the following table:

Average Analysis of Milk in Percent of Dry Matter

	Bitch	Cow	Goat	20% Solids
Dry Matter	22.8	12.4	13	20
Protein	8.1	3.3	3.3	5.8
Fat	9.8	3.8	4.5	6.6
Lactose	3.5	4.7	4.5	8.2
Calcium	0.28	0.12	0.13	0.2
Phosphorus	0.22	0.09	0.11	0.16
Calories/ounce	36	18	21	36

Cow's milk contains only half the number of calories and nutrients needed to rear puppies. Goat's milk has a higher calorie count but is still well below the ideal. Substituting either cow's milk or goat's milk for bitch's milk is similar to diluting bitch's milk by one-half.

Twenty percent solids (formula #3 below) has a composition similar to bitch's milk but contains twice as much lactose. Newborn puppies do not have adequate enzymes with which to break down lactose. This leads to diarrhea.

The addition of three egg yolks and one tablespoon of corn oil to formula #1 increases the protein level and fat level, and raises the total number of calories.

While artificial bitch's milk (such as Esbilac from Borden's) is the most desirable substitute for the bitch's natural milk, in an *emergency* situation one of the following formulas can be used as a temporary substitute. Mix well and refrigerate the unused portions.

Formula #1: 1 cup homogenized milk
3 egg yolks
1 tablespoon corn oil
1 dropper liquid pediatric vitamins

Formula #2: 26.5 ounces of homogenized milk
6.5 ounces of cream (12% fat)
1 teaspoonful bone meal
1 egg yolk
4 grams citric acid
Liquid vitamins to provide 2,000 I.U.
Vitamin A, 500 I.U. Vitamin D

Formula #3: Evaporated milk reconstituted to 20%
solids (1 part warm water to 5 parts evaporated milk)
1 teaspoonful bone meal per pint

These formulas provide thirty-six to thirty-eight calories per ounce, or one to one and one-fourth calories per milliliter of formula.

Artificial bitch's milk comes in both powder and liquid. When reconstituted, it should be prevented from freezing. Follow the directions of the manufacturer with regard to storage. Nutritional cataracts have been reported with the feeding of artificial bitch's milk. This is believed to be caused by a deficiency of the amino acid arginine.

Calculating the Right Formula

The best way to determine how much formula each puppy needs is to weigh the puppy and use a table of caloric requirements. All formulas provide one to one and one-fourth calories per milliliter. It is safe to use as an approximation one calorie per milliliter when computing the amount of formula. Daily requirements according to weight and age are given in the following table:

Age in Weeks	Calories or ml Needed Per Pound Weight Per Day	Number of Feedings Per Day
1	60	4
2	70	3
3	80	3
4	90	3

Divide the total daily requirement by the number of feedings per day in order to get the amount of each feeding.

Example: An eight-ounce puppy during the first week requires thirty calories per day (i.e., one-half of sixty calories per pound per day). Divide by the number of feedings (four), which gives 7 to 8 ml per feeding. If the puppy's weight doubles as expected in ten days, it will weigh about one pound and will require 70 ml per day, or 23 ml per feeding. However, if the puppy cannot take in the required amount in three feedings, then the number of feedings should be increased.

As long as the pup does not cry excessively, gains weight and feels firm to the touch, the diet is meeting the nutritional needs. Gradually increase the amount you are feeding, using the above table as a guide.

How to Give the Formula

Puppies may be fed by spoon or eyedropper, baby nursing bottle or stomach tube.

An *eyedropper* is readily available and may be used as an emergency measure in the absence of a baby nurser or stomach tube. However, puppies can choke when formula is dropped or spooned into their mouths. This can lead to aspiration into the lungs.

The *baby bottle* has the advantage of satisfying the suckling urge but requires that the puppy be strong enough to suck the formula. When using a small doll's bottle or a commercial puppy nurser with a soft nipple, usually you will have to enlarge the hole in the nipple so that the milk will drip out slowly

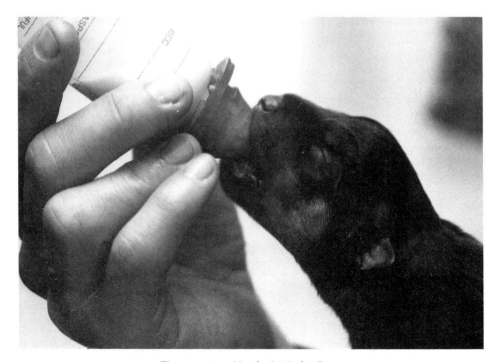

The correct position for bottle feeding.

when the bottle is turned over. Otherwise, the puppy will tire after a few minutes of nursing and will be unable to get enough to eat. However, it is most important that the hole in the nipple be small enough to prevent the milk from coming out too fast, as this will cause the puppy to choke. Warm the formula to about 100 degrees F (slightly warm to the wrist) as you would a baby's bottle.

The correct position for bottle nursing the puppy is to open the mouth with the tip of your finger, insert the nipple and hold the bottle up at 45 degrees. The angle of the bottle is such that air does not get into the puppy's stomach. Keep a slight pull on the bottle to encourage vigorous sucking. With a slow drip, it takes five or more minutes to supply its needs. A bottle-fed puppy will need to be "burped."

Tube feeding has several advantages. It takes about two minutes to complete each feeding. No air is swallowed (no burping required). It insures that a proper amount of formula is administered to each puppy. *It is the only satisfactory method of feeding immature or sick puppies too weak to nurse.*

If too much formula is injected, or if given too rapidly, it can be regurgitated. This can lead to aspiration of formula and pneumonia. The complication can be avoided if care is taken to monitor the weight of the puppy and compute the correct amount. Puppies fed by tube do not get a chance to suckle and must be kept in separate compartments.

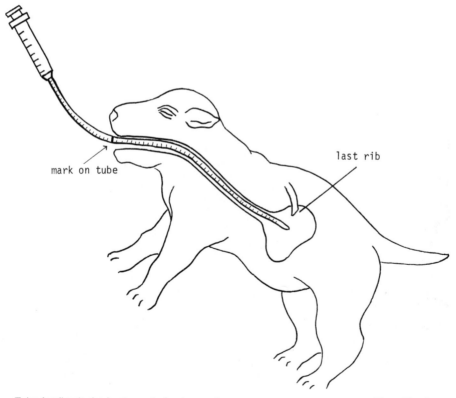

mark on tube

last rib

Tube feeding is the best way to feed a weak puppy.   *(Rose Floyd)*

Tube feeding is not difficult and can be mastered in a few minutes. It requires a soft rubber catheter (size 8 to 10 French, which can be bought at a drugstore), a 10 or 20 cc plastic or glass syringe and a gram scale to calculate the weight of each puppy and monitor progress.

A puppy's stomach is located at the level of the last rib. Measure the tube from the mouth to the last rib and then mark the tube with a piece of tape. Draw the formula into the syringe and warm it to body temperature by placing it in hot water. Moisten the tube with formula, and then open the puppy's mouth and pass the tube slowly over the tongue and into the throat. The tube will be too large to enter the smaller passage of the windpipe, so there is little danger of passing it the wrong way. With steady pressure the puppy will begin to swallow the tube. Pass it to the level of the mark, or until resistance is met. Connect the syringe to the tube and *slowly* inject the formula down the tube into the puppy's stomach.

At about fourteen days of age the windpipe of many puppies will be large enough to accommodate the tube. If the tube goes down the wrong way the puppy will begin to cough and choke. Change to a larger tube; or by now the puppy may be strong enough to suckle from a bottle.

Common Feeding Problems

Common feeding problems are overfeeding and underfeeding. They cause diarrhea or failure to gain weight. If your puppy is putting on weight and seems reasonably happy and content, with a normal stool (firm, yellowish), you can be pretty sure you are feeding the right amount.

Experience indicates that owners are much more likely to overfeed than to underfeed orphaned puppies. The best way to tell about this is to look at the stools. If a puppy is fed four times a day you can expect four to five stools, or about one stool for each feeding.

The first sign of overfeeding is a loose stool. A loose yellow stool indicates a *mild* degree of overfeeding. With *moderate* overfeeding, there is more rapid movement of food through the intestinal tract, indicated by a greenish stool. The color green is caused by unabsorbed bile.

The first step in management is to dilute the formula to half strength (one part water to one part formula). As the stools return to normal, gradually increase the strength of the formula by reducing the amount of water until the formula is back to full strength.

Unchecked overfeeding leads to a depletion of digestive enzymes and causes a grayish diarrheal stool. Eventually, when there is little or no digestion of formula, the stool looks like curdled milk. At this point the puppy is getting no nutrition and is becoming rapidly dehydrated. Treat diarrhea like this by diluting the formula to half of its strength and give 1 to 2 ml of Milk of Magnesia every three hours.

Dehydration is corrected by giving a Ringer's lactate solution mixed half and half with 5% dextrose in water (or use a balanced pediatric electrolyte solution such as Pedialyte). These solutions are available at drugstores or through your veterinarian. Give ½ ml per ounce body weight per hour by bottle or stomach tube. Other supportive measures, such as warming a chilled puppy, are

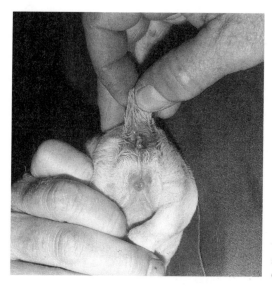

The inflamed anus and grayish stool of a newborn puppy with *unchecked* diarrhea.

indicated. Veterinary administration of electrolyte solution subcutaneously is highly desirable.

All puppies with gray or white stools should be examined by a veterinarian. They may have a neonatal infection.

Puppies that are not getting enough formula cry all day, appear listless and apathetic, gain little or no weight from one feeding to the next and begin to chill. Check the temperature of the incubator. Puppies dehydrate quickly when not getting enough formula. They should respond to appropriate dietary management.

PUPPY DISEASES

Bleeding (Hemorrhagic Syndrome)

A tendency to bleed easily is present in most puppies until three to four days of age. It is caused by lack of prothrombin, a *clotting factor* manufactured by the liver, which depends upon *vitamin K* for its synthesis.

Vitamin K is produced by intestinal bacteria. Since newborns do not have intestinal bacteria for the first few days of life, they depend upon maternally acquired vitamin K to promote clotting. Accordingly, if the dam is poorly nourished or deficient in vitamin K, a hemorrhagic syndrome is more likely to ensue.

The symptoms are those of bleeding from the body openings. Minor degrees of trauma, such as those occurring during whelping and shortly thereafter, may lead to internal hemorrhage. Spontaneous bleeding also occurs. Usually the cause is not discovered until an autopsy.

Treatment: When one puppy bleeds, all the puppies in the litter should be treated with an injection of vitamin K. In kennels where bleeding has been a problem in the past, the administration of vitamin K to bitches during the last weeks of pregnancy will prevent it.

Toxic Milk Syndrome

Mother's milk can be toxic to puppies for a number of reasons. The primary cause is mastitis, an infection of the milk glands. Acute postpartum metritis, an infection of the uterus, also may lead to toxic milk. These conditions are discussed in the chapter PREGNANCY AND WHELPING. In some cases the cause is unknown. Presumably there are toxins in the milk that cause digestive upsets in nursing puppies.

The toxic milk syndrome usually affects puppies at three to fourteen days of age. Puppies appear distressed, cry continually and sometimes drool. Diarrhea and bloating are especially common. The anus often is red and swollen because of the acidity of the stool. One complication of this syndrome is puppy septicemia.

Treatment: Sick bloated puppies should be removed from the nipples and treated for diarrhea and dehydration (see *Raising Puppies by Hand*). Chilled puppies should be warmed and placed in an incubator. If the puppies are well enough to remain with their mother, you can prevent them from nursing by applying a many-tailed bandage around the mother's chest and abdomen, as shown in EMERGENCIES: *Bandaging*. In this way she can clean and care for them.

Navel Infection

An umbilical stump can be the site of an infection. Predisposing causes are dental disease of the dam (she transfers bacteria to the umbilical cord when cutting it), contamination in the whelping box from stool and spilled food and factors that reduce puppies' resistance to disease.

An infected navel looks red and swollen and may drain pus. There is a direct communication to the liver, which makes even a low-grade infection of the stump potentially dangerous. Untreated, the signs of puppy septicemia can appear. Prophylactic iodine should be applied to the navel stump at birth to reduce the likelihood of this complication.

Treatment: Cleanse the navel with a dilute solution of hydrogen peroxide, followed by a pHisoHex wash. Apply a topical antibiotic ointment (Panolog). Oral or intramuscular antibiotics may be indicated. If the infection does not clear up quickly, consult your veterinarian. This disease can be present in other puppies in the litter.

Puppy Septicemia (Blood Poisoning)

Sepsis in infant puppies is caused by infections that spread rapidly and cause signs mainly in the abdomen. They occur in puppies four to forty days old.

The usual port of entry is the digestive tract. Until a puppy is seven days old, bacteria can penetrate the lining of the bowel just as maternal antibodies can. Infected milk is a major cause of infant sepsis. Navel infection is another.

The initial signs are crying, straining and bloating. They are like those of the toxic milk syndrome. As the disease progresses the abdomen becomes rigid and distended, and its skin takes on a dark red or bluish tint. These are signs of

360

a peritonitis. Other signs of infection include weight loss, chilling, weakness and dehydration. Death occurs rapidly.

Treatment: The cause must be discovered at once—otherwise the whole litter can be affected. Sick puppies should be treated for dehydration, diarrhea, chilling. They should be given a broad-spectrum antibiotic (Chloromycetin), removed from the litter box and raised by hand. Septicemia is best managed under veterinary supervision.

Herpes Virus of Puppies

This is an insidious disease. The dam appears healthy, the milk production adequate and the puppies nurse in a normal manner until shortly before their deaths. The early signs are an abrupt cessation of nursing, chilling, painful crying, abdominal distention, loss of coordination and a yellowish green diarrhea. Puppies are in agony and cry out pitifully when their abdominal muscles are in spasms. Nothing seems to relieve their distress. Death occurs in twenty-four hours.

The virus attacks puppies between five and twenty-one days of age. During this time puppies are susceptible to herpes virus because their body temperature is below 98 degrees F: the temperature at which the virus incubates.

Herpes virus causes vaginitis in some bitches. Puppies probably acquire the infection while passing through the birth canal during the whelping process. It can be spread to a litter by an infected dog, or anyone who has first handled an infected dog. Bitches develop immunity and subsequent litters are not affected.

Treatment: There is no vaccine available. Infected puppies raised in incubators that maintain a body temperature of 100 degrees F may survive the disease. The virus does not multiply well at temperatures above 98 degrees F.

Herpes infection should be distinguished from other treatable causes of neonatal infection and from infectious hepatitis (see INFECTIOUS DISEASES). When the illness is caused by herpes virus, an autopsy will show bright red blood spots on the surface of the kidneys (''speckled kidneys''). Recovered puppies frequently develop kidney failure at eight to ten months of age.

Neonatal Isoerythrolysis

This is a rare but acute and often fatal hemolytic anemia of the newborn that begins shortly after puppies ingest colostrum containing antibodies that destroy their red cells.

These antibodies are acquired by the dam as a result of a pregnancy during which time fetal cells crossed her placenta and caused her to become sensitized to them. The antibodies so produced are transmitted back to the puppies during the first few hours of nursing.

Affected puppies become weak and jaundiced, and pass dark reddish urine containing hemoglobin. Death can occur in twenty-four hours.

Treatment: On suspicion of hemolytic anemia, stop all nursing. Blood transfusions from a compatible donor are required to restore red cells.

Puppies from subsequent litters should not be allowed to receive colostrum from the dam.

The Flat Puppy (Swimmer)

Flat puppies resemble turtles, with their legs sticking out to the sides instead of underneath. Swimmers are flat-chested from lying on their stomachs. The condition is caused by a weakness of the muscles that pull the legs together.

Puppies begin to stand at sixteen days of age and have a steady gait by the time they are three weeks old. If this is not the case, the puppy may be a swimmer. The disorder is more likely to occur in overweight puppies and heavy-boned breeds. It may have a genetic basis. Slippery floors are believed to predispose to the condition. When puppies at first learn to walk, they should be kept on indoor-outdoor carpeting or some other nonslippery surface that provides good traction.

Treatment: Assist a flat puppy several times a day to stand and walk, and encourage the pup to sleep on its side. A hobble made from tape, placed from elbow to elbow, forces a puppy to sleep on its side. It also keeps all legs underneath when the pup attempts to stand.

Some of these puppies make a complete recovery.

Pyloric Stenosis

Congenital pyloric stenosis is caused by a thickening of the ring of muscle at the outlet of the stomach. The cause is unknown. Brachycephalic breeds such as the Boxer and Boston Terrier have a higher incidence.

Puppies with pyloric stenosis usually begin to vomit at or before weaning. They often reingest the vomited meal, only to vomit it again later. The diagnosis is confirmed by a barium swallow X ray. Surgery is necessary to divide the thickened muscle and open the passage.

An acquired form of pyloric stenosis occurs in middle-aged dogs (see DIGESTIVE SYSTEM: *Chronic Gastritis*)

Skin Infection of the Newborn

Scabs, blisters and purulent crusts can develop on the skin of newborn puppies at four to ten days of age. These blisters sometimes contain pus. They are caused by poor sanitation in the whelping box. Usually they appear on the abdomen.

Treatment: Keep the nest clean of food, stools and dried debris. Cleanse scabs with a dilute solution of hydrogen peroxide and wash with a surgical soap. Then apply Panolog ointment.

Conjunctivitis of the Newborn

This condition is caused by a bacterial infection beneath the eyelids. It appears in puppies before the eyes are opened. It is discussed in the chapter EYES.

Hypoglycemia (Low Blood Sugar)

This is a central nervous system disorder caused by a low blood sugar. It occurs mainly in Toy breeds between six and twelve weeks of age. Often it is precipitated by stress.

The first signs are those of listlessness and depression. They are followed by muscular weakness, tremors (especially in the facial muscles) and later convulsions, coma and death. The entire sequence is not always seen. The dog may appear to be depressed or may be weak, wobbly and jerky; or the puppy may be found in a coma.

Hypoglycemia can occur without warning when a puppy is placed in a new home, or while being shipped. It might appear after a puppy misses a meal, chills, becomes exhausted from too much playing or has a digestive upset. These upsets place an added strain on the energy reserves of the liver and bring on symptoms (if the dog is susceptible).

Puppies that are weaned on rice and hamburger are more likely to develop hypoglycemia. Their diet is deficient in certain ingredients needed to sustain the liver.

A similar condition occurs in adult hunting dogs usually when hunting. Care should be taken to feed these dogs before hunting and to increase the protein in their diet.

Treatment: Treatment is directed at restoring blood levels of glucose. Begin at once. Prolonged or repeated attacks can cause permanent damage to the brain. If the puppy is awake, give Karo syrup, honey or sugar in water by mouth. You should begin to see improvement in thirty minutes. When unconscious, a puppy will have to be given a dextrose solution intravenously. It may be necessary to treat for swelling of the brain. A veterinarian should be called at once.

Prevent recurrent attacks by feeding a high-quality kibble diet and add to it sugar, syrup or honey. See that the puppy eats at least every eight hours and receives a daily vitamin.

Breeders should wean puppies on a balanced diet. Food supplements should not exceed 10 percent of the total ration (see *Weaning*). Owners of Toy puppies should not overtire them or allow them to chill.

A condition exists in which hypoglycemia is persistent instead of periodic. It is caused by an enzyme deficiency and is not responsive to treatment.

Hernia

A hernia is a protrusion of an organ, or part of an organ, through an opening in the abdominal wall that would normally close in the course of growth. The two common sites are the groin (inguinal) and around the navel (umbilical). When the bulge can be pushed back into the abdomen, the hernia is *reducible*. When it cannot, the hernia is *incarcerated*. An incarcerated hernia becomes strangulated if the blood supply to the tissues in the sac is pinched off. Accordingly, a painful hard swelling in one of the usual locations could be an incarcerated hernia—which is an emergency. Seek professional help.

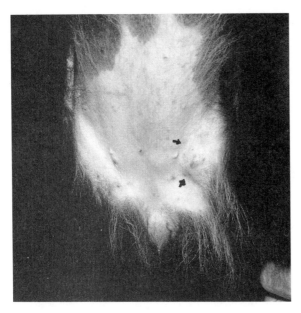

Left *inguinal hernia.* The bulge can be reduced by finger pressure.

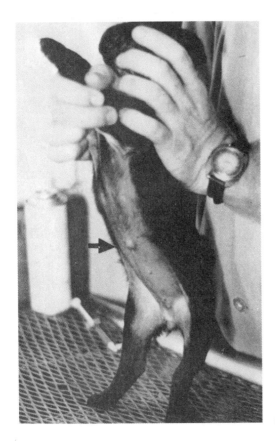

Umbilical hernia in a young puppy.

Hernias have an hereditary basis. There is a genetic predisposition for delayed closure of the abdominal ring in most cases.

With an *inguinal hernia* the bulge appears in the groin (usually in a bitch). It may not be seen until after she is bred or very old, in which case a pregnant or diseased uterus may be incarcerated in the sac. Small inguinal hernias do occur in male puppies. They can be watched closely, as many will close. If not, have them repaired.

Umbilical hernias are seen fairly frequently in puppies at about two weeks of age. An occasional one may be the result of severing the umbilical cord too close to the abdominal wall, but most are caused by a tendency for delayed closure of the umbilical ring.

Binding the abdominal wall with straps does little good. Most get smaller and disappear by themselves by about six months. If you can push a finger through the ring, have it repaired. The operation is not serious; the pup usually goes home the same day. If a female is going to be spayed, repair can be postponed until that time.

WEANING

Weaning time depends upon several factors, which include the size of the litter, the condition of the dam, the availability of mother's milk, and the inclinations of the breeder. Weaning usually can begin at three to six weeks of age and takes about one week to complete.

Begin by offering one or two feedings a day of evaporated milk in equal parts with water; add baby cereal (oatmeal) and one raw egg *yolk* (for iron and protein). This should be made up to a sloppy gruel. Feed it in a low-rimmed metal dish (pie pan). Dip your fingers into the gruel and let the puppies lick it off—or push their noses into it—until they get the message.

To stimulate the appetite, remove the dam an hour or two before feeding. After the meal, let her return to nurse.

Puppies that eat too much gruel are apt to get diarrhea. This is because of a combination of overfeeding and perhaps some degree of intolerance to the milk. Accordingly, at least two feedings a day should still be by nursing.

When the puppies start to eat from a pan, there is less of a demand on the bitch's milk supply. To start the drying-up process, begin to decrease her intake of food. Withhold all food and water the first day; the next day feed one-fourth the normal amount; the third day, one-half, and the fourth day feed three-fourths the normal amount. Restore normal rations the fifth day.

When the puppies are eating the gruel well (eating more than they are spilling), switch to a name-brand puppy kibble mixed with small amounts of hamburger and cottage cheese. These supplements should not exceed 10 percent of the total ration. Although many manufacturers recommend feeding dry or chunky kibble to weaning puppies, experience indicates that small puppies (three to six weeks of age) do not eat chunks. The kibble should be soaked well, or better yet, blended. When the puppy teeth come in at six weeks, puppies will begin to chew dry food.

Weaning now can proceed rapidly. Feed four times a day. Many breeders prefer to alternate kibble feedings with all-milk feedings (powdered or evaporated milk). Keep **water** available all the time. Puppies not getting enough water can come down with a kidney problem that may not appear until later in life.

THE NEW PUPPY

Buying a Healthy Puppy

If you are interested in a pet or family companion, you will want to give some thought as to the type of dog that best suits your needs. A large selection of breed books is available at most public libraries. *The Complete Dog Book* (Howell Book House) is an excellent source and contains useful information on all breeds of dog.

The next thing to consider is whether to buy a male or female. In general, males have a tendency to be more protective, more active and playful and more defensive of their territory. Females in some breeds may be more easily trained, more fastidious, less independent and more attentive to their families. However, any of these traits may or may not be present, depending on the individual puppy.

The best age at which to buy a puppy is when the individual is about eight weeks old. At this age the breeder can usually estimate whether a puppy is going to be a show or breeding prospect. This is also the best age to ship.

Puppies two months old, in particular, are formative. Most new owners prefer to take charge of the care and training of their puppy while still young and impressionable.

The American Kennel Club (51 Madison Avenue, New York, New York 10010) will provide you, upon request, with the name and address of the current secretary of the particular breed club of your choice. Calling or writing to that person will get you a list of breeders. All-breed kennel clubs across the country will also be able to put you in touch with people who can help.

After you locate several breeders who appear to have the kind of puppy you are looking for, write or call each and explain whether you are looking for a family companion and pet, plan to show or breed or have a preference for a male or female pup. A sincere inquiry providing the breeder with some information about the prospective buyer is much more likely to elicit the type of information you are looking for than a hastily scribbled note. Be prepared for the responsible breeder to ask questions about you and your family. The responsible breeder is concerned about the pup's new home.

It is wise to insist on buying the dog pending examination by a veterinarian. Emotional attachments develop rapidly. This can make the return of a puppy to the breeder a difficult task. Conscientious breeders, who are proud of their stock, are willing to stand behind them. They will not object to this request. No breeder should offer you a guarantee that the pup will win in the show ring. Picking a future champion at eight weeks of age is extremely difficult, even for breeders with considerable personal experience. The care, training, feeding, medical care and socialization of the pup after the purchase are every bit as important as the genetic background of the parents.

Many buyers prefer to visit a kennel and make their own selection. There is no need to panic when, on the appointed day, you find yourself standing before a litter of bouncing puppies and find that all appear to be equally lovable. Most puppies appear healthy at first glance but a closer examination may disclose a potential problem that could make the individual undesirable. When choosing an individual for health and soundness, take your time and go over the pup from head to tail.

The Physical Examination

First examine the puppy head-on. The nose should be cool and moist. Squeeze the nostrils together to see if mucus is present. Nasal discharge or frequent sneezing suggest an infection of the respiratory tract. The nostrils should open when the dog inhales. Short-nosed breeds often have collapsed nostrils. They collapse when the dog breathes in. This is especially so in Pugs and Pekingese.

The teeth should meet in a correct bite. The correct bite for most breeds is a *scissors* bite, in which the upper incisors tightly overlap the lowers. If the head of a match can be inserted between the upper and lower incisors, the bite is *overshot* and probably may not correct itself as the dog grows.

In the reverse scissors bite (*undershot* bite), the lower incisors overlap the upper ones. This is acceptable in some short-nosed breeds. If there is doubt, check the Standard for the breed.

The gums should be pink and healthy looking. Pale gums indicate anemia. Inspect the back of the throat. Enlarged tonsils can mean tonsillitis.

Feel on top of the head for a soft spot. If present, the fontanel is open. This is not desirable. In Toy breeds a large dome, sunken eyes and open fontanel suggest hydrocephalus.

The eyes should look straight ahead and not deviate to the side. If tear staining is present on the muzzle, look for eyelids that are rolled in or out, extra eyelashes or conjunctivitis. White spots on the surface of the eye could be scars from prior injuries or infections. The pupils should be dark and have no visible lines or white spots. Cataracts or retained fetal membranes may interfere with vision.

The haw, or third eyelid, may be visible. This should not be taken as a sign of disease unless it is swollen and inflamed.

The ears should stand correctly for the breed. The tips should be healthy and well furred. Crusty tips with bare spots suggest sarcoptic mange.

The ear canal should be clean and sweet smelling. A buildup of wax with a rancid odor may be caused by ear mites. Head shaking and tenderness about the ears indicate an infection of the ear canals.

Feel the chest with the palm of your hand to see if the heart seems especially vibrant. This could be a clue to a heart defect. Puppies should breathe in and out without effort. A flat chest, especially when accompanied by trouble breathing in, indicates an airway obstruction. It is seen most commonly in short-nosed breeds, such as Pugs, Boston Terriers and Pekingese.

Pinch the windpipe gently. This should not elicit a coughing spasm. If it does, the puppy probably suffers from bronchitis.

The skin of the abdomen should be clean and healthy looking. A bulge at the navel probably is caused by an umbilical hernia; while one in the groin, an inguinal hernia.

Male Puppies—Push the foreskin back to confirm that it slides back and forth easily. Adhesions between the prepuce and the head of the penis, as well as strictures of the foreskin, require veterinary attention. Both testicles should be present in the scrotum. A dog with an undescended testicle cannot be shown and should not be used for breeding.

Female puppies—Examine the vulva. Look for pasting of hair or discharge. Juvenile vaginitis is a common problem and requires treatment.

The skin and hair around the anus should be clean and healthy looking. Signs of irritation, such as redness and hair loss, indicate the possibility of worms, chronic diarrhea or a digestive disorder.

The coat should be bright and shiny and carry the correct color and markings for the breed. Excess scale, itching or deposits in the coat suggest mites, fleas and other parasites. Moth-eaten areas of hair loss are typical of mange or ringworm.

Next, examine the puppy for soundness and correct structure. The legs should be straight and well formed. Structural faults include legs that bow in or out, weak pasterns, flat feet with spread toes and that which toe in at the rear. Be sure to ask about and have a vet check for dislocating kneecaps on the rear legs, especially on Toys. The veterinarian will do this by straightening the leg and pushing the kneecap toward the inside. If the patella slips out of its groove easily, and stays out as the knee is rebent, the joint is defective and could cause problems as the dog matures.

The gait of the puppy should be free and smooth. A limp or faltering gait may simply be the result of a sprain or hurt pad, but hip dysplasia and other joint conditions would have to be considered.

At this age puppies should be active, alert, playful and full of vitality. Personalities of puppies vary with breed type, but a sweet disposition is essential to most. An aggressive puppy certainly has no place as a family companion, especially with children. This puppy is unfriendly and may struggle and bite to get loose, or growl when picked up or petted. This dog will require considerable discipline and training.

A puppy that shrinks away when spoken to, or runs away and hides, can be classified as shy and possibly may overcome this later, but taking a chance is not worthwhile. This puppy will not socialize easily.

The ideal puppy for a family pet holds its tail high, follows you about, accepts petting, struggles when picked up but then relaxes and licks your hand.

As good health and good disposition so often go hand in hand, it is perhaps wise, in making the final selection, to pick the individual that appears to be really bursting with vitality and self-confidence.

After you have made your purchase, you will want and should receive future advice and counsel. Any guarantees concerning the puppy should be discussed and agreed upon *before* the check is signed. Before leaving the breeder be sure to ask for and receive the puppy's registration papers, pedigree, health certificate, information on when the puppy's shots were given and a diet sheet.

FEEDING AND NUTRITION

Dog nutrition has received considerable interest during the past few years, and certain large manufacturers of dog foods have conducted extensive research and feeding trials in order to establish nutritious diets that need no supplementation. Federal law requires that all dog food manufacturers provide a listing of ingredients in their rations. However, the required labels do not contain enough information for you to compare one dog food with another. Well-known manufacturers noted for their research generally produce good-quality dog foods you can trust. In general, commercial dry or soft-moist foods are more reliably balanced products than canned rations. Canned meat may be added to the kibble for palatability, but should not exceed 25 percent of the total daily ration.

One of the best ways to gauge the effectiveness of a product is to observe its effect upon a dog's stool. Poor-quality protein passes through a dog's intestinal tract unused, resulting in loose, mushy or diarrheal stools. Very large stools, on the other hand, indicate excessive amounts of fiber and other indigestibles. They can also be caused by overfeeding.

Feeding Older Puppies

Most breeders supply a diet sheet with a new puppy. It should be followed at least for the first few weeks, since an abrupt change in diet can cause digestive upsets. Puppy chows supply the proteins, carbohydrates, fats and minerals required to raise healthy puppies—provided they eat it well. Purchase a name-brand product, one specifically formulated for puppy growth and development. Pups under a year of age require about twice as much protein and about 50 percent more calories per pound than adult dogs. The feeding of young puppies is discussed under *Weaning*.

Puppies six months and older should be fed twice a day, as much as they will eat in twenty minutes. Then pick up the dish. Labels on dog food packages provide recommended daily feeding amounts. They are useful guidelines but not applicable to every puppy. The thing to avoid, which doesn't happen often, is feeding too much. An overweight puppy is in danger of developing structural defects.

Meats, cottage cheese, milk or table scraps may be added for palatability and to supply additional proteins, but should not exceed 25 percent of the total daily ration. This does *not* include pastry, candy, potatoes, greasy foods, splintery bones and other indigestible morsels.

Many breeders of large-boned breeds believe it is advantageous to add vitamin and mineral supplements, including calcium, phosphorus and vitamin D, to a puppy's diet. When feeding a preparation already formulated to meet the needs of a growing puppy, there is danger of inducing a metabolic bone disorder by oversupplementation (see MUSCULOSKELETAL SYSTEM: *Metabolic Bone Disorders*). If your puppy is a poor eater and may need supplements, discuss this with your veterinarian.

Feeding Adults

An older dog will be kept trim by feeding once a day. Caloric requirements differ from dog to dog, are less as the dog grows older and are less in warm weather and during periods of inactivity. Information on the dog food packages can be used as a guide to feeding—but these are only rough estimates and not always applicable to the type of breed or individual dog you own. Nutrition for the elderly dog is discussed in the chapter GERIATRICS.

Examine your dog to see if the body fat is in correct proportion to height and bone. There should be a layer of subcutaneous fat over the ribs, thick enough to provide some padding and insulation, but not too thick. You should be able to feel the ribs as individual structures. Weigh your dog from time to time so as to establish ideal weight and then maintain that level.

Obesity in the adult dog is usually caused by feeding snacks and treats between meals. Most of these are high in sugar and therefore are very palatable. Use table scraps sparingly. Feed them only as a special treat and avoid fatty or spicy foods that can upset your dog's stomach.

TRAINING AND SOCIALIZATION

First establish the proper understanding. Your puppy must be made to realize that you are the teacher and the puppy is pupil.

Although most trainers feel that Obedience training should not begin until a puppy is six months old, the period of puppy socialization, during which a youngster starts to interact in a learning fashion with humans and other dogs, begins at three weeks of age and continues through the first three months of life.

During this important formative period a puppy acquires the social graces and personality traits that make up the adult's character. These traits are largely determined by how you, the owner, react to the pup's emerging behavior. To insure that the lessons you teach have a lasting effect, approach the subject of training and socialization with the following thoughts in mind.

Socialize your puppy to the fullest extent possible. This cannot be postponed. A pup with little or no exposure to people and dogs during the first three months of life adjusts poorly as an adult—despite attempts to compensate for this at a later date.

Take your pup with you in the car and go for walks where you both will see other people. This way your puppy gets used to the noise and distractions of public life and can meet and play with other dogs that are gentle, friendly and well socialized themselves.

When you initiate a training exercise or disciplinary action, be consistent. Insist upon the correct behavior and continue the exercise until the puppy masters the lesson.

Once you start a corrective action, you must see it through to the finish. If you are too compliant, willing to allow the puppy to have its own way, the pup will most certainly interpret your permissiveness as a sign that *you* accept its dominance. This can lead to aggressive problems as the pup grows older.

Reward your puppy with lavish praise and petting for doing well. Dogs instinctively want to please. Approval builds confidence and self-esteem.

Corrective training usually is effective only in those situations in which the pup is caught in the act. A puppy must be able to understand that what you disapprove of is a behavior, not that you dislike your dog. This can be very difficult to establish. You can't explain it to a puppy as you would a child. In many cases punishment, unless a very specific connection can be made, is confusing and has the effect of diminishing a dog's self-esteem. The dog knows it is unworthy but doesn't know why.

The best way to connect with your puppy is by the tone of your voice. Puppies are genetically geared to warning sounds made by their mothers and understand that tonal qualities are warnings to avoid dangerous activity.

Banishment is another safe punishment. It doesn't cower the dog but does impose a separation anxiety that tends to reinforce the social attachment a puppy has for the owner.

A common *mistake* is to show anger. Anger equals loss of control. A puppy senses this loss of control, and an insecure atmosphere is created.

After your reprimand has served its purpose, re-establish a loving relationship with a show of affection. This reassures the puppy that you are still on good terms.

Physical punishment should be avoided in all situations except one: an act of aggression toward any child or adult. In this situation the pup is experimenting with implied or physical force to establish dominance. It cannot be tolerated. It is best understood by giving a similar response. The correct way to administer corporeal punishment is to seize a small dog by the scruff of the neck, lift up and shake soundly. A large dog should wear a collar. Grasp the collar and jerk it forcefully while loudly voicing your displeasure. Put the dog away and leave for two hours. Never strike a puppy with an open hand. This makes a dog shy and distrustful of people.

Do not allow your puppy to play roughly. A puppy that becomes overexcited in play may accidentally nip, scratch or even knock over a small child. Children sometimes tease puppies, in which case it is not the puppy's fault if the children get hurt. But accidents such as these can be avoided if puppies and children are not allowed to roughhouse.

Small bites given in rough play are not acts of aggression and should be dealt with by verbal reprimand. An older pup seems to realize that biting can cause pain and thus develops a soft mouth.

Housebreaking

First be sure that your puppy's stools are soft and well formed. It is difficult to housebreak a puppy that has no control over bowel movements. Loose stools or diarrhea are frequently caused by overfeeding. Reduce the amount of food by 10 percent or more. You should feed only well-balanced commercial dog foods. The basic procedure for toilet training a puppy is similar to potty training a child, except that a puppy will learn more quickly.

Housebreaking can be started as soon as the puppy moves in, but puppies do not begin to exercise some voluntary control over their bladder and bowel functions until they reach five weeks of age. Full bladder control may take somewhat longer. However, they do have a natural instinct to avoid soiling their sleeping quarters. You can use this to advantage.

Confine the puppy to a small area such as a utility room. Pups usually eliminate shortly after eating, when waking from a nap and after playing. Choose these times to take your puppy out of doors, preferably to the same location. When the desired action is accomplished, praise and give a treat. Be sure to take the pup out of doors the last thing at night and the first thing in the morning.

If you can't be at home, you can use newspapers. Confine the pup in a small area and line the floor with newspapers away from the sleeping pad. Use several thicknesses. Remove the soiled papers on top and add new paper to the bottom. The middle layer will retain some odor and remind the pup to use this location. Later, when the dog can exercise more control for longer periods, you can develop a routine for going outdoors. Remove the paper and thoroughly clean the floor.

Rubbing your puppy's nose in mistakes is counterproductive and should not be attempted. Even if caught in the act, a natural reaction is to assume that you object to the pup's going to the bathroom. In fact, you are not objecting to the performance of a natural function, you are objecting to the place the pup chooses. Although this approach may inhibit a dog from going in the house (at least in your presence), it also causes confusion, apprehension and anxiety. It is better to exercise patience or redirect behavior to going outside.

Walking on a Leash

Your puppy should be taught to walk freely on a leash and have good manners, especially if you are planning to show. No judge is amused by a dog that cuts capers in the show ring.

Start first with a soft nylon or leather collar and switch later to a light choke collar. Leave the collar on for short periods only, then attach a leash that can be dragged behind. Next, pick up the leash and begin to lead the puppy with occasional firm tugs, interspersed with a lot of pats and "well dones." Accustom your puppy to walk on the left side, to move out smartly and stay abreast—neither lunging nor lagging. As the exercise progresses, exert a little more force with each tug.

A slip (choke) collar should be removed after an exercise. A dog alone wearing a slip collar is in danger. The dog's foot could get caught between the collar and the neck, or the collar could become snagged in a fence.

Come When Called

Another important exercise is to teach your puppy to come promptly when you call. Basically this is an extension of leash training. Let your puppy out to the end of a long lead. As you call the pup's name, give the rope a quick tug. When your dog moves toward you, shorten the rope. Eventually the dog will have to come to you all the way. Respond to this by giving lavish praise and a choice tidbit. Repeat this exercise over and over, until your puppy is letter-perfect—then remove the lead.

Never call a dog for punishment. If your puppy refuses to obey the command to **come**, show your displeasure by leading the dog to its pen. Your dog must learn that obedience is inevitable. Whenever you give a command, be sure to make it stick!

Chewing

Puppies chew in order to develop strong teeth and jaws. A puppy can be given a rawhide toy to gnaw and should not be allowed to start working on the furniture. If you catch your dog in the act, substitute a toy and make it clear that the toy is for chewing, not the furniture. Various spray-on products leave an unpleasant scent that will effectively discourage chewing. They work well if you take the time to apply them.

Barking

Chronic or neurotic barking is a sign of boredom or lack of attention. Take your puppy for rides in the car or daily trips to the park. Chaining is conducive to barking *and* an open invitation to a bad disposition and poor physical development. Keep your puppy in a fenced yard or a suitable enclosure, giving opportunity for exercise and play. Barking in the house will stop if a dog can't get to a window to see or hear what is going on outside.

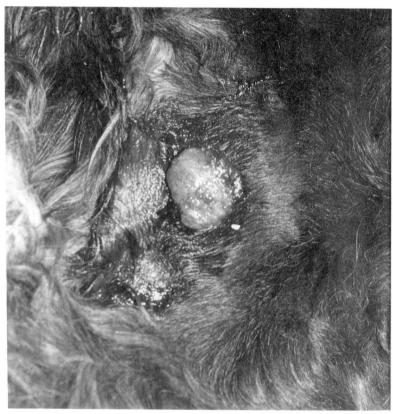

A *sebaceous adenoma*. Only a biopsy can determine whether it is benign or malignant.

18

Tumors and Cancers

MOST PEOPLE associate the word *tumor* with a growth occurring on the skin or somewhere inside the body. However, any sort of lump,
bump, growth or swelling (such as an abscess) is a tumor. Those that are true
growths are called *neoplasms*.

Benign neoplasms are growths that grow slowly, are surrounded by a
capsule, are not invasive, do not destroy and don't spread to other parts. They
are cured by surgical removal, provided that the entire tumor has been removed.

Malignant neoplasms are the same as *cancers* (also called *carcinomas*,
sarcomas or *lymphomas*, depending on the cell type). Cancers usually enlarge
rapidly (a few weeks or month). They are not encapsulated. They appear to
infiltrate (invade) surrounding tissues and may ulcerate and bleed. They tend to
spread via the bloodstream and lymphatic system to remote parts of the body.
This is called *metastasizing*.

Cancer is graded according to its degree of malignancy. Low-grade cancers
continue to grow locally and attain a large size. They metastasize late in the
course of the illness. High-grade cancers metastasize early when the primary
focus is still quite small or barely detectable.

Cancers are approached in the following manner: Suppose a bitch has a
lump in her breast. Since it is solid, it is probably a neoplasm that could be
benign or malignant. The decision is made to *biopsy* the lump. This is a surgical
operation during which the lump, or a part of the lump, is removed and sent to
the pathologist. A pathologist is a medical doctor who has been trained to make
a diagnosis by visual inspection of tissue under a microscope. An experienced
pathologist can tell whether the tumor is a cancer and can often provide additional
information as to the degree of malignancy. This serves the purpose of making

the diagnosis and, in many cases, gives the rationale for the most appropriate treatment.

What Is Cancer?

Although much has been learned, the exact cause of cancer is unknown. All cells in the body die and have to be replaced. This process of reduplication is called *mitosis*. A single cell splits into two cells, each identical to the parent. The process is controlled by genes and chromosomes in the cell. Anything that interferes with mitosis at the genetic level can lead to the production of a mutant cell. Many agents are known to do this, including toxins, chemicals, ionizing rays, viruses and other irritants.

Under appropriate circumstances the mutant cell, which seems to grow much faster than the parent cell, reduplicates itself. This, then, could become a cancer. A cancer acts like a parasite. It depletes the host and replaces normally functioning tissue.

It has been suggested that cancers arise more often than we suspect. The theory is that most of them don't get established because the host's immune system recognizes them as "nonself" and so makes antibodies that destroy them.

Long-standing irritants to tissues are a definite cause of some cancers. The irritant agent appears to speed up tissue repair (and therefore the rate of local mitotic activity), and/or interferes with immune mechanisms that destroy new-born cancer cells.

Examples of agents known to increase the risk of cancer in people are ultraviolet rays (skin cancer); X-rays (thyroid cancer); nuclear radiation (leukemia); chemicals (aniline dyes causing bladder cancer); cigarettes and coal tars (causing lung and skin cancer); viruses (causing experimental cancer in laboratory animals and sarcoma in AIDS victims) and parasites (a cause of bladder cancer). Some cancers have a known familial incidence.

A prior injury or blow is sometimes thought to be the cause of cancer. Trauma can be a cause of certain benign swellings. However, it is seldom, if ever, the cause of a cancer. The injury calls attention to the area and the cancer is discovered incidentally.

Some benign tumors, such as warts and oral papillomas, are clearly caused by a virus infection. Other benign tumors, such as lipomas, adenomas of the breast and other organs, simply just grow there for reasons unknown at the present time.

Treatment of Tumors and Cancers

The effectiveness of any form of treatment often depends upon early recognition by the owner that the dog may have a cancer.

Complete surgical removal of a cancer that has not yet spread is the most satisfactory treatment available. Cancers that have spread to regional lymph nodes still may be cured if the lymph nodes can also be removed. Even when the disease is widespread, local excision of a bleeding or infected cancer can provide relief of pain and improve the quality of life.

Electrocautery and cryosurgery are two techniques by which tumors on the surface of the body can be controlled or cured by burning and freezing. This provides an alternative to surgical removal, but special equipment is required.

Radiation therapy is useful in the management of some surface tumors and in deeply situated tumors where control cannot be achieved by surgery. Cures are possible. Radiotherapy must be carried out in a medical center. It requires expensive equipment and the services of a trained radiotherapist.

Chemotherapy employs anticancer drugs given at regular intervals. These drugs, even when carefully controlled, have major side effects. They are useful in the management of some widely spread cancers. Hormone therapy also has proven successful in the management of some tumors.

Cancer in the Dog

About half the cancers in dogs are visible as growths or sores on the outer surface of the body (on or beneath the skin, in the perianal area, in the mouth and in breast tissue). Signs that a tumor could be a cancer are visible growth, ulceration of the skin with bleeding and a sore that does not heal.

A firm gray (or pink) open sore, especially on the feet and legs, should be regarded with suspicion. The same is true for pigmented lumps or flat moles that start to enlarge and then spread out and begin to bleed (melanoma). A hard mass that appears fixed to bone (or could be a growth of the bone itself) is cause for concern. One other sign is a lump or knot in a place where none should be (the breast). *If you observe any of these signs, be sure to discuss them with your veterinarian.*

Some tumors occur internally where you would be unlikely to detect them until they were quite large. Early detection of these cancers rests upon a suspicion that a symptom caused by some internal disorder could be caused by a cancer. Since two out of every three such cancers develop in the gastrointestinal and reproductive tracts, you should consider the possibility of cancer when your dog has difficulty eating and digesting food, or when there is an unexplained bowel disturbance, such as constipation or the passage of blood. Cancer in the reproductive tract of females causes few signs, but you should look for vaginal discharge and bleeding.

The signs and symptoms of common tumors affecting the internal organs are discussed in the chapters dealing with these organs.

COMMON SURFACE TUMORS

Cysts (Wens, Sebaceous Cysts)

Sebaceous cysts are common in dogs. They occur all over the body. Certain breeds are affected more often than others. They are Kerry Blue Terriers, Schnauzers and spaniels. A sebaceous cyst is made up of a thick capsule that surrounds a lump of cheesy material called sebum. It may grow to an inch. Eventually it is likely to become infected and will have to be drained, unless it

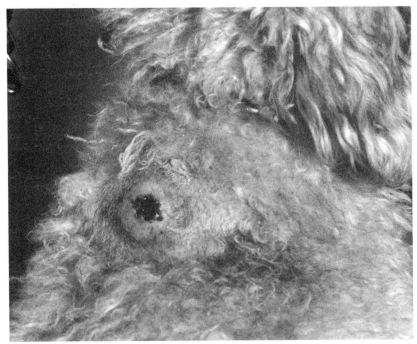

An abscessed *sebaceous cyst.* These are frequently mistaken for tumors.

has already drained spontaneously. This sometimes leads to a cure. Most cysts should be removed.

Cysts Between the Toes (Interdigital Cysts)

Cysts may be found between the toes. They represent inflammatory changes in sweat glands in the feet. They often become infected and require long-term antibiotic treatment.

Warts and Papillomas

Warts are not nearly so common in dogs as they are in people. They are more common on the older dog. For information on warts in the mouth, see ORAL CAVITY: *Warts in the Mouth.*

Papillomas are growths that project out from the skin. Some are on a stalk, but others look very much like a piece of chewing gum stuck to the skin. If they become irritated or start to bleed, they should be removed.

Lipomas

A lipoma is a growth made up of mature fat cells surrounded by a fibrous capsule that sets it apart from the surrounding body fat. It can be recognized by its round, smooth appearance and soft, fatlike consistency. It is not painful. Lipomas grow slowly and may get to be several inches in diameter. Both sexes are affected, but lipomas are more common in overweight dogs, especially females.

Surgical removal is indicated only for cosmetic reasons or to rule out some other tumor, such as a cancer.

Basal Cell Tumor

This is a common benign tumor of the skin. Generally it is found as a solitary ulcerating nodule on the head and neck of dogs over the age of seven years. Surgical removal is curative.

Hematomas

A hematoma is a collection of blood beneath the skin. It is caused by a blow or contusion. Small hematomas may resolve spontaneously. Large ones may need to be opened and drained. Ear flap hematomas require special care (see EARS: *Swollen Ear Flap*).

Calcifying hematomas are hard swellings that resemble bone tumors. They usually occur on the top of the skull of large breed dogs that are prone to strike their heads on the underside of a piece of furniture. As the injury breaks the periosteum over the bone, the hematoma calcifies like a fracture site. Calcifying hematomas are difficult to remove and often recur.

Tender Knot

A small knot may be present at the site of an injection and is often present for a few days in puppies that have been given their vaccinations. It seldom requires treatment. A painful swelling beneath the skin may be an abscess.

Skin Cancer

Several types of skin cancer affect the dog. It is important to distinguish these from benign tumors. This is difficult to do on the basis of appearance alone. Surgical removal of a lump or bump is often required to establish the diagnosis.

The skin tumors are common in the dog, and although not always malignant, all have a malignant potential.

Sebaceous Adenomas are the most common. They arise from oil-producing skin glands. They occur in older individuals. Cocker Spaniels seem to be affected more often than other breeds. They are light-colored, usually less than an inch long, and present a cauliflowerlike appearance. The surface of the skin may be ulcerated. About 25 percent are low-grade cancers. Large adenomas should be removed.

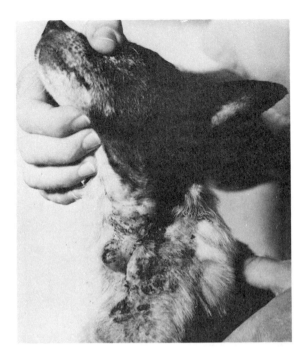

Mast cell tumor on the neck of a terrier.

Mast cell tumors are common in older dogs. They are prevalent in Boxers and Boston Terriers. The average dog with a mast cell tumor is eight years old. Look for these tumors on the hind legs, lower abdomen and foreskin of the penis.

Typically, they are multinodular growths less than an inch in length. About one out of three is malignant. Cancer is more likely when growth is rapid and size is greater than one inch. Malignant mast cell tumors metastasize to distant organs. Cortisone may be given to decrease temporarily the size of mast cell tumors. The treatment of choice is surgical removal.

Squamous cell carcinoma is a cauliflowerlike neoplasm or a hard, flat, grayish-looking ulcer that does not heal. Its size is variable. It occurs on the feet and legs and sometimes elsewhere. Hair may be lost about the tumor because of constant licking. A white hair coat and chronic irritation are predisposing factors. This tumor is locally invasive but seldom spreads. It should be removed.

Melanoma is a malignant neoplasm that takes its name from the brown or black pigment usually associated with it. Often it develops in a pre-existing mole. You should suspect melanoma when a mole starts to enlarge or spread out, becomes elevated above the surface of the skin or starts to bleed. Melanomas are more common in Scottish Terriers, Boston Terriers and Cocker Spaniels. A suspicious mole should be removed. Melanoma spreads widely, often at an early stage.

Histiocytomas are rapidly growing buttonlike tumors that occur in younger dogs. They are most common on the feet, face and ears. In appearance, they

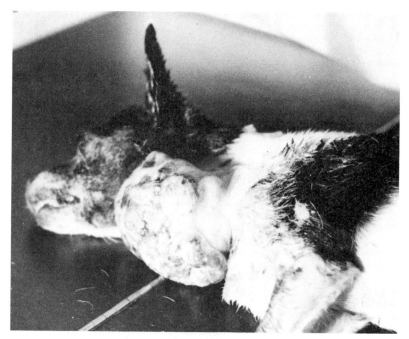

The same growth one month later, showing rapid progression.

are dome-shaped, raised, red, irritated looking and painful to the touch. Some histiocytomas grow smaller and disappear on their own in a few weeks. Others may need to be removed.

REPRODUCTIVE TRACT TUMORS

Tumors of the Testicle

Testicular tumors are relatively common. Signs are those of an enlarging testicle or mass in the scrotum. The vast majority of these tumors occur in *undescended* testicles. In an undescended testicle, swelling will be seen in the inguinal canal. Most testicular tumors do not metastasize.

Leydig cell tumors are small and of little consequence. *Sertoli* cell tumors secrete estrogen and cause feminization of the male with enlargement of the breasts, a pendulous foreskin and a bilateral symmetrical hair loss. High blood estrogen levels can cause bone marrow depression and anemia. *Seminomas* can become quite large. A small number are malignant.

Treatment: Removal of the testicle is curative, except in the unusual case of malignancy. When present, signs of feminization usually disappear two to three months after castration.

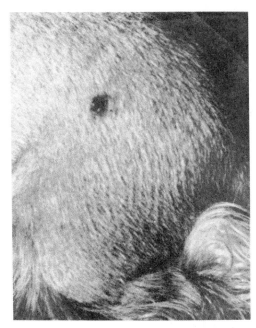

A pigmented skin growth that is suspicious of *melanoma*.

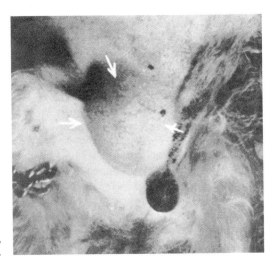

Tumor in an undescended testicle, located in the inguinal region.

Tumors of the Vulva and Vagina

The vaginal and vulvar area is the most common site for tumors in the female genital tract. These tumors tend to occur in the older, sexually intact female. Most of them are benign, but they can become large enough to produce swelling and deformity of the perineum. Vaginal tumors can block the birth canal and cause problems in whelping.

An unusual neoplasm called the *transmissible venereal tumor* (TVT) occurs in both males and females. Visible tumor is present on the vulva, within the vagina, or on the penis of the male within seven days of coitus. These tumors appear as cauliflowerlike neoplasms that grow to an inch in size. About half of them will regress spontaneously in three to six months.

Treatment: Complete removal of vaginal and vulvar tumors usually is curative. A local recurrence can be managed successfully by radiation and/or chemotherapy. TVT is quite responsive to both these modalities.

Tumors of the Ovary

Ovarian tumors are rare. Most are discovered accidentally during a spay. Occasionally one will get large enough to produce a palpable mass or swelling of the abdomen.

Granulosa cell tumors may secrete estrogen, thereby producing signs of hyperestrinism with abnormal heat cycles, enlargement of the vulva and abscess of the uterus.

Adenocarcinoma is a cancer. On average, it occurs in females at eight years of age.

Treatment: Removal of ovarian tumors by hysterectomy will cure benign tumors. The cure rate for malignant tumors is about 50 percent.

Breast Tumors and Swelling

Following heat or false pregnancy, the breasts may remain enlarged or feel lumpy. If you press on the breasts, you may notice that you can express a yellowish, or at times a milky, fluid. This condition is called *mammary hyperplasia*. It is caused by a hormone imbalance. It is seen most often in older females that have never had a litter, and in females that have not been bred for some time. Mammary hyperplasia does not occur in females that have been spayed. Mammary hyperplasia may disappear spontaneously in one to two months. If it persists, a breast tumor or an ovarian problem may be present. Have your bitch checked by a veterinarian.

Breast tumors are clinically the most significant neoplasms encountered in veterinary practice. About half of these will prove to be malignant. The others are benign adenomas. The back breasts are affected most often. The leading sign is a painless enlargement or a knot in the breast. Most females so affected are over six years of age, with an average age of ten. A biopsy is the only way to distinguish between benign and malignant tumors.

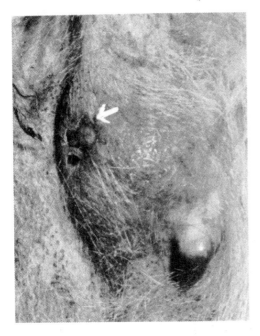

Breast cancer: Note the skin ulceration.

Breast cancers spread widely, with the lungs being the favorite sites for metastases. A chest X-ray is advisable to rule out metastases before embarking on radical surgery.

Surgical removal is the treatment of choice for all breast neoplasms. The success of a cancer operation depends upon the stage of the tumor at the time of the operation. Unfortunately, this cannot always be determined until later. Better chances of cure are associated with early detection and prompt treatment. You should examine your female's breasts at least once a month, especially when she is older. If you detect a suspicious swelling or a solitary lump, ask your veterinarian to examine her. Spaying your dog before her third heat period (at about two and a half years of age) significantly lowers her chances of getting a breast cancer.

BONE TUMORS

Both benign and malignant bone tumors occur in the dog. By far the most likely bone tumor is *osteogenic sarcoma*. While this cancer can strike at any age, usually it is a disease of the middle years. Males are affected more often than females. There is a definite predilection for the large breeds: St. Bernards, Newfoundlands, Great Danes, Great Pyrenees, Irish Setters, Boxers and others. Rarely, if ever, does it occur in the very small breeds.

The long bones of the front and rear legs are the most common locations

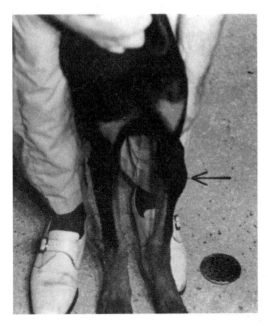

Swelling of the leg caused by *bone tumor.*

for osteogenic sarcoma. The flat bones of the ribs are next. Frequently, the first sign is a limp in a mature male dog having no history of injury. Often this sign receives little attention until swelling of the leg below the tumor is observed. Pressure over the tumor causes varying degrees of pain. X-rays are diagnostic as this form of cancer spreads early and to the lungs. There is no satisfactory cure. Amputation and chemotherapy alleviate pain, but usually do not prolong life.

Chondrosarcoma is the second most common malignant bone tumor in dogs. The average age of onset is six years. It tends to involve the ribs, nasal bones and pelvis. It presents as a large, hard, painless swelling at the junction between bone and cartilage. Complete surgical removal affords relief and may be curative. This tumor also metastasizes to the lungs but is less aggressive than osteogenic sarcoma.

Fibrosarcoma is rare in dogs. It presents as a swelling, usually just above the knee joint. Treatment is like that for chondrosarcoma.

A number of benign bone tumors occur uncommonly. They are osteomas, chondromas and osteochondromas.

Osteomas are protruding tumors composed of dense but otherwise normal bone. They occur about the skull and face.

Chondromas are growths of cartilage. They involve flat bones such as the ribs and pelvis.

Osteochondromas, also called exostoses, are cartilage covered bone tumors that appear on the ribs or vertebrae of young dogs. They can be solitary or multiple. Some of them appear to be inherited.

Surgical removal of benign bone tumors is recommended only when their growth impinges on some other structure, and occasionally for the sake of appearance.

19

Geriatrics

$\mathbf{A}$ PROGRESSIVE and irreversible deterioration of cellular and organ function occurs in the tissues of all animals as time passes. Although its effects are familiar to everyone, the exact mechanism by which organic systems eventually run out of protoplasmic vitality is an unsolved mystery.

It is estimated that about 10 percent of the dog population is over ten years of age. But all dogs do not age at the same rate. A dog's biologic age depends on genetic background, nutritional status, the presence of coexistent diseases and environmental stresses. Of great importance is the care the dog has received throughout life. Well-cared-for pets suffer fewer infirmities as they grow older. But when sickness, illness or injury is neglected, the aging process is accelerated.

Large dogs seem to age more rapidly than smaller ones. St. Bernards, German Shepherds, Great Danes and other large breeds reach old age at ten to twelve years. Toy breeds are old at fourteen to sixteen years.

Although aging is inevitable and irreversible, some of the infirmities attributed to old age may, in fact, be caused by disease—therefore correctable or at least treatable.

The care of the older dog is directed at preventing premature aging, avoiding physical and emotional stress and meeting special nutritional needs. Dogs older than six years of age should have a complete physical examination every six months. Usually it will include a urinalysis, stool exam and complete blood count. At times, liver and kidney function tests, chest X ray and electrocardiogram are indicated. Any disease or abnormal condition that may be present can be dealt with before it leads to a more serious infirmity. Cataracts, strictures, bone deposits and other causes of incipient disability are often amenable to surgical correction or medical management. Heart medications, analgesics, enzymes and hormones can relieve discomfort and improve organ performance.

CARING FOR THE OLDER DOG

Behavioral Changes

Older dogs are more complacent, less energetic, less curious and more restricted in their scope of activity. They are forgetful. They tend to sleep a lot. They become fixed in their habits and are less tolerant of changes in the daily routine. Crankiness and irritability are common. Boarding and hospitalization, in particular, are poorly tolerated. At such times old dogs eat poorly, become overanxious, bark excessively and don't get the rest they need. If possible, it is advisable to care for them at home under the guidance of your veterinarian in order to avoid stress and anxiety. Having a neighbor drop by once or twice a day to care for the dog may be better than boarding.

Physical Changes

With reduced activity and loss of muscular tone, the neck and body of an older dog take on a more bulky appearance and the extremities appear thinner, especially the thighs and upper parts of the front legs. The abdomen may sag, back begin to sway and elbows wing out. There may be muscle tremors at times of physical exertion.

There is nothing more beneficial to an older dog than a regular exercise program. Lack of daily exercise in dogs over eight years of age is a major cause of impaired organ function. Exercise improves muscle tone and strength, keeps the joints supple, helps to prevent weight gain and promotes a youthful attitude. However, an older dog should not be exercised beyond what current physical condition will allow. If a dog is sedentary or out of condition, begin gradually and add more exercise as conditioning improves.

Most older dogs suffer to some degree from osteoarthritis. Stiffness in the joints is made worse by drafts and by sleeping on cold, damp ground or on cement pads. Their beds should be indoors in a warm dry spot. Arthritic dogs, especially large, heavy ones, should be given a padded surface on which to sleep. Toy dogs may need to be covered at night.

Much of the lack of activity in osteoarthritis is caused by muscle soreness. Although there is no way to stop the progress of arthritis, analgesics such as buffered or enteric coated aspirin can relieve the muscle soreness and enable the dog to enjoy a daily exercise program and lead a more active life (see MUSCULOSKELETAL SYSTEM: *Arthritis*). The buffered or enteric coated aspirin should be given with meals to avoid any possible upset stomach. However, buffered or coated aspirin usually does not irritate the stomach.

The coat of an older dog mats easily and the skin becomes dry and scaly because of reduced activity of the oil-producing glands. Small skin tumors are common. Pads of the feet may be thick, overgrown and cracked. Stiff old dogs have trouble keeping their anal and genital areas clean. Frequent grooming and bathing is necessary to keep them clean and free of parasites and skin diseases. The addition of Alpha-Keri bath oil to the final rinse helps to soften the skin and keep it in better condition. Toe nails need to be trimmed more often unless they are worn down by activity. Basic health care is discussed in the chapter SKIN: *Avoiding Coat and Skin Problems.*

Gradual loss of hearing occurs commonly as dogs age. There is no treatment for senile deafness, but there might be a blockage in the ear canal or some other contributing cause that can be improved by treatment. This subject is discussed in the chapter EARS.

Loss of vision is a common problem in aging dogs. *Senile* (old age) cataracts are frequent. Most dogs over eight years of age have some degree of haziness in their lenses. Loss of vision may be caused by retinal disease or another eye disorder.

Surgical removal of cataracts usually is reserved for dogs having difficulty getting around because of loss of sight. Most dogs adjust well to a gradual loss of vision if they retain the ability to hear. Cataracts and other eye disorders leading to loss of sight are taken up in the EYES chapter.

Tooth and gum disease is common in older dogs and interferes with eating. With proper treatment, suffering is relieved, the dog is more comfortable and nutritional status improves. Loose teeth should be removed. If your dog has lost teeth and is unable to chew dry dog food, soak the food for twenty minutes before feeding it, or feed canned food formulated for older dogs.

Dry biscuits help to reduce plaque and calculus. But bones and bone chips should not be given to the older dog. They make the stool hard and can lead to bowel difficulties. Dogs of all ages should be put on a program of good dental hygiene as outlined in the chapter ORAL CAVITY.

Urinary tract difficulties are common in older dogs. Obligatory excretion of increased amounts of urine occurs because the kidneys have lost the power to concentrate the wastes. This is offset by drinking larger amounts of water.

Often the dog with failing kidneys is unable to keep from wetting in the house, especially at night. There should be an opportunity to go outside several times a day, first thing in the morning, last thing in the evening and perhaps during the night.

There is a temptation to reduce water intake. However, water should be made available at all times because without water the dog may go into kidney failure (see URINARY SYSTEM: *Kidney Failure*). Special diets (such as Hills k/d) can be of great help to a dog with impaired kidney function. They reduce the work load on the kidneys and thus the amount of water the dog must drink. However, if your veterinarian determines that your dog's kidney function is normal, you can take away water in the evening. This may help to eliminate the problem of wetting at night. Other causes of an abnormal pattern of voiding (including "bed-wetting") are discussed in the chapter URINARY SYSTEM.

Enlargement of the prostate gland in the male usually does not cause urinary tract symptoms. When enlarged it can narrow the rectal canal, causing constipation or fecal impaction.

Constipation in the older dog often is the result of improper diet aggravated by reduced bowel activity and weakness of the muscles of the abdominal wall. The dog may have to be given a high-residue diet. The subject is discussed in the chapter DIGESTIVE SYSTEM: *Constipation.*

Weakness of the heart muscle is another common condition associated with advancing age. Heart disease can exist for many years before actual signs of failure occur. Early signs of heart failure are loss of pep and condition, lethargy, muscular weakness, shortness of breath and a cough that begins at night or occurs after exercise or excitement. The subject is discussed in the chapter CIRCULATORY SYSTEM: *Heart Failure*.

Being overweight is a serious complicating factor in heart disease. Fat dogs must be made to lose weight. A low-salt diet (such as Hills h/d) may be a real aid in treating dogs with congestive heart failure. Heart medications and diuretics also can be of considerable assistance.

Old dogs adjust poorly to physical and emotional stress. Their hearts, livers, kidneys and metabolism often are not able to meet the increased demands placed upon them. Sudden decompensation can occur. Special care must be taken with the older dog to prevent chilling. When wet, the dog should be toweled dry and kept in a warm room. An older dog also is less tolerant to extremes of heat. Changes in diet or drinking water, too, can cause stress. The older dog's digestive tract and its bacterial flora are geared to the present diet. When changes are necessary, make them slowly. Add small amounts of the new diet while gradually reducing the old. The secret to the care of the old dog is moderation in all things: Make changes by evolution, not revolution.

Nutrition

The single most important dietary consideration in prolonging the life of the older dog is to prevent obesity.

Since an older dog is less active, fewer calories are needed than when the dog was younger. Without a reduction in number of calories, the older dog is likely to gain weight—which puts an additional strain on a limited organ reserve. This contributes to a shortened life span. Feeding "treats" between meals and adding table scraps are two of the main reasons why dogs get too fat.

Caloric requirements for the older dog have to be determined on an individual basis. You must take into consideration *ideal* weight (i.e., neither too fat nor too thin), activity level and the dog's emotional makeup. High-strung dogs require more food than their more sedate counterparts.

In general, an elderly dog of average size needs only about twenty-five to thirty calories per pound body weight per day. Canned dog foods supply about 500 calories in a pound of ration; moist or "chunky" dog food, about 1300 calories; dry kibble, about 1600 calories. Since the older dog must eat *less food*, it is important that this food be of the highest quality to provide an adequate daily supply of nutrients. An ideal diet would supply a somewhat higher concentration of protein than an ordinary adult maintenance diet and a somewhat lower concentration of fat. In this regard it would be qualitatively closer to a ration formulated for the growth of puppies (although proportionately the older dog would eat much less than a growing puppy).

While high-quality protein is important for the older dog, do not feed a diet too rich in meat or one containing protein of poor quality. This creates an increased nitrogen load that must be handled by the liver and kidneys. Dogs with weak kidneys can be thrown into failure by feeding them more protein than they can handle. Energy needs are better met by giving easily digestible carbohydrates—cooked to break down starch granules. High-quality protein suitable for the digestive tract of an older dog can be supplied by adding small amounts of cooked hamburger, boiled egg, cottage cheese or skim milk to a kibble base. If your dog seems to be losing weight or appears to need more calories, try adding small amounts of carbohydrate (cooked cereals, cooked rice or farina).

While fats increase the palatability of food, they are difficult for the older dog to digest and are high in calories. Some fat is required to aid the intestinal absorption of vitamins and to provide for the manufacture of essential fatty acids, but adequate amounts are supplied by commercial dog foods. Fat supplements should not be added to the ration.

Old dogs need *more minerals and vitamins*. B vitamins are lost in the urine of dogs having reduced kidney function; also, absorption of vitamins through the intestinal tract decreases as the individual ages. Calcium and phosphorus in correct balance (1.2 to 1) helps to prevent softening of the bones. Therefore, many old dogs probably need a vitamin/mineral supplement. But it should be *balanced* to meet metabolic needs. Your veterinarian can recommend an appropriate supplement to meet the specific requirements of your dog.

It is desirable when feeding the older dog to divide the daily ration into two equal parts and feed the first half in the morning and the second in the evening.

Dog foods especially formulated for the *maintenance* needs of elderly dogs are available commercially. Gaines Cycle Senior is one example. If you use such a product, you may not need to add vitamins and minerals unless there is a specific medical reason to do so. Feed according to the directions on the package.

The elderly dog that has become obese should be put on a weight loss program. This is best accomplished by increasing daily exercise and decreasing the number of calories in your dog's diet. For a small dog whose ideal weight is judged to be ten pounds, provide twenty-five calories per pound; for a twenty-pound dog, twenty calories per pound; for a fifty-pound dog, seventeen calories per pound; for a seventy-five-pound dog, fifteen calories per pound. Once the ideal weight is attained, feed your dog a maintenance ration.

Weight Loss

1. A *maintenance* diet for the elderly dog: Reduce the daily ration by ¼.

2. ¼ pound cooked lean meat (discard the fat)
   ½ cup cottage cheese
   2 cups cooked carrots
   2 cups cooked green beans
   Vitamin/mineral supplement
   This diet provides 300 calories per pound of food.

Special Diets

Prescription diets such as those from Hills Pet Products may be required for dogs with heart disease, kidney disease, intestinal disease or obesity. They must be prescribed by your veterinarian.

A NEW PUPPY

The addition of a new puppy to the household can be a rejuvenating experience for the elderly dog. When handled properly, most old dogs delight in the companionship, and through renewed interest and added exercise, they seem to recapture their youth. Jealousy is prevented by giving attention to the old dog first. Always affirm your old dog's seniority privileges.

PUTTING YOUR DOG TO SLEEP (EUTHANASIA)

The time may come when you are faced with the prospect of having to put your pet to sleep. This is a difficult decision to make—both for you and for your veterinarian. Many an old and even infirm dog can be made quite comfortable with just a little more thoughtfulness and tender loving care than the average healthy dog needs. Old dogs can still enjoy months or years of happiness in the company of loved ones.

But when life ceases to be a joy and a pleasure, when the dog suffers from a painful and progressive condition for which there is no hope of betterment, then perhaps at this time we owe the dog the final kindness to die easily and painlessly. This is accomplished by an intravenous injection of an anesthetic agent in sufficient amount to cause immediate loss of consciousness and cardiac arrest.

20

Drugs and Medications

ANESTHETICS AND ANESTHESIA

Anesthetics are drugs used to block the sensation of pain. They are divided into two general categories—locals and generals.

Local anesthetics are used for operations on the surface of the body where they are infiltrated locally into the tissue or around a regional nerve. They may be applied topically to mucus membranes. While local anesthetics (such as Xylocaine) have the fewest risks and side effects, they are not suitable for most major operations.

General anesthetics render the dog unconscious. They can be given by injection or inhalation. Light doses sedate or relax the dog and may be suitable for short procedures (such as removing porcupine quills from the mouth). Inhaled gases (such as Halothane) are administered through a tube placed in the trachea.

The dose of an anesthetic is computed by weight of the dog. Certain breeds appear to have a low tolerance for barbiturates and other anesthetics. Whippets, Afghan Hounds, Great Pyrenees and perhaps others may require less anesthetic than other breeds of comparable weight. Discuss this with your veterinarian.

The dosage of any given anesthetic will vary greatly, even among dogs of the same size. Therefore, these drugs must be given only by someone trained to determine the degree of sedation the drugs produce. Combinations of anesthetics often are used to lessen the potential side effects.

The removal of an anesthetic agent is by the lungs, liver or kidney. Impaired function of these organs can cause dose-related problems. If your dog has a history of lung, liver or kidney or heart disease, be sure to discuss it with your veterinarian.

A major risk of general anesthesia is having a dog vomit when going to sleep or waking up. The vomitus refluxes into the windpipe and lungs, producing asphyxiation. This can be avoided by keeping the stomach empty for twelve hours before scheduled surgery. Accordingly, if you know your dog is going to have an operation, *don't give anything to eat or drink* after 6:00 P.M. the night before.

PAIN RELIEVERS

Analgesics are drugs used to relieve pain. While there are many painkillers, buffered or enteric coated aspirin (acetylsalicylic acid) is the safest and best analgesic for home veterinary care in the *dog*, but should *not* be given to *cats*. Its best use, perhaps, is in the arthritic dog, to relieve stiffness and promote joint mobility.

Demerol, morphine, codeine and other *narcotics* are subject to federal regulation and cannot be purchased without a prescription. The effect of these drugs on dogs is highly variable. They should be used under medical supervision.

Tylenol is an analgesic primarily used for its fever-reducing properties. Fever should be treated in dogs only when it is high enough to produce damage by itself.

Butazolidin is used for its anti-inflammatory effects. Your veterinarian may wish to prescribe it in certain disorders of the bones and joints.

Pain-killers are contraindicated in sprains and other acute conditions of muscles, tendons and joints, where relief of pain might permit the use of a leg that should be kept at rest.

While buffered or enteric coated aspirin is the safest analgesic, it is not without complications and can cause gastric upsets. When used for a prolonged period of time, it can cause gastric ulcers and bleeding from the upper gastrointestinal tract.

Nonsteroidal anti-inflammatory drugs such as Ibuprofen (Motrin or Advil) do not appear to be any more effective than buffered or enteric coated aspirin in dogs; and they are more likely to cause gastrointestinal bleeding.

TRANQUILIZERS

Tranquilizers are drugs used to relieve anxiety, treat motion sickness and sedate a dog for ease of handling and treatment. The exact mode of action of tranquilizers is variable. Some act on the brain to modify behavior and increase the threshold for nausea and vomiting. Others achieve their effects primarily through sedation. They are of the antihistamine class and should only be given on the advice of a veterinarian.

Tranquilizers are safe and effective when used as directed and in the right situation. Nevertheless, even in the best of circumstances, untoward results can occur. Tranquilizers used on humans should not be given to dogs without first discussing their use with your veterinarian. Long-term tranquilization is not recommended. Except for motion sickness, thunderstorms and other temporary upsets of this sort, behavior disorders in dogs are best treated by identifying the cause of the problem and taking steps to correct it. Tranquilizers should not be given to acutely injured dogs, as they lower blood pressure.

DRUGS IN PREGNANCY AND LACTATION

Certain antibiotics can affect the growth and development of unborn or newborn puppies. Tetracyclines, kanamycin and griseofulvin are three examples. They should not be used in pregnancy if substitutes are available.

Medicines and drugs given to a nursing mother can be passed on to puppies in the milk. The amount depends upon the blood concentration and whether the drug is soluble in fat. Fat-soluble drugs are stored in the body fat and will be secreted in the milk for prolonged periods. Most of the insecticides fall into this category. Drugs that are not fat-soluble usually do not cause problems.

Keep in mind that because a newborn's liver and kidneys are immature and cannot detoxify and eliminate drugs as readily as those of an adult, a drug given to an adult on a per weight basis might not be safe to give to a very young puppy on a per weight basis.

If your bitch or her puppies are taking drugs or medications, be sure to consult your veterinarian regarding safety and appropriate dosage.

COMMON HOUSEHOLD DRUGS
FOR HOME VETERINARY USE

Dose by Weight of Dog

Buffered or enteric coated aspirin: 1 five-grain tablet per 30 lbs every six hours.
Charcoal: 1 tablespoon in 4 ounces of water per 30 lbs.
Cheracol-D (Cough Syrup): 1 teaspoon per 30 lbs every four hours
Dramamine: 25 to 50 mg one hour *before* traveling.
Glauber's Salt (Sodium Sulfate): 1 teaspoon per 10 lbs.
Hydrogen Peroxide (3%): 2 teaspoons per 30 lbs every ten minutes for three doses, or until the dog vomits.
Kaopectate: 1 teaspoon per 5 lbs every four hours.
Milk of Magnesia: 1 teaspoon per 5 to 10 lbs every six hours.
Mineral Oil: 1 teaspoon per 5 lbs. Add to feed.
Mylanta: 6 to 12 ounces, depending on the size of the dog.
Tylenol: ½ to 1 tablet every six hours.

HOW TO GIVE MEDICATIONS

Pills (Capsules and Tablets)

To give a pill, open your dog's mouth as described in the chapter ORAL CAVITY: *How to Examine the Mouth*. Insert the pill well to the back of the tongue in the *midline*. (If you get the pill to the side of the tongue, dogs will work them

The correct way to give a pill—in the middle and well at the back of the mouth. *(J. Clawson)*

forward and spit them out.) Close the dog's mouth and hold it shut while stroking the throat until the dog swallows. If the dog licks its nose, the pill has probably been swallowed.

Note: If pills are broken up into powders they make an unpleasant taste that is poorly tolerated. Some pills have a protective coating that is important for delayed release in the intestine. Avoid breaking up pills if at all possible.

Liquids

Liquid preparations are administered into a pouch between the molars and the cheek. Bottles, syringes and eyedroppers are suitable for giving liquids. With practice, spoons can be used.

First tilt the chin up at 45 degrees and place the neck of the bottle into the cheek pouch. Seal the lips around it with your fingers and pour in the liquid. Large amounts can be given in this way. Hold the muzzle firmly while the dog swallows.

Injections

If it becomes necessary to give your dog injections, it is highly desirable to have the procedure discussed and demonstrated to you by your veterinarian. One of the dangers of giving a foreign substance by injection is that of producing a sudden allergic or acute *anaphylactic* reaction in which the dog goes into shock

396

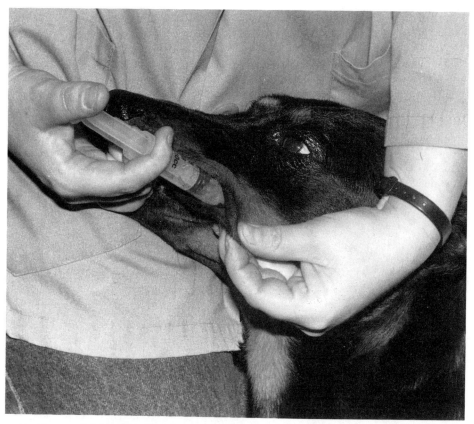

Liquids are administered into a pouch between the molar teeth and the cheek. *(J. Clawson)*

through circulatory collapse. This is a type of hypersensitivity reaction of the immediate type (see SKIN: *Allergies*). The most common agent producing anaphylactic shock is penicillin. Penicillin is used as a preservative in some vaccines. As a precaution, do not administer a drug by injection that has produced any sort of reaction in the past, including hives. Treatment of anaphylactic shock involves intravenous adrenaline and oxygen. This is one reason why it is best to have your veterinarian give injections—as he or she has the drugs on hand to treat such reactions in time.

Some injections are given under the skin (subcutaneous) and others into the muscle (intramuscular). Read the directions on the product to determine the route of administration. Most injections are not painful to the dog, although intramuscular injections may hurt as the medication is injected. A good assistant is a help. If there is any likelihood the dog may bite, use a muzzle. (see EMERGENCIES: *Handling and Restraint of an Injured Dog*).

Draw the medicine up into the syringe and point the needle toward the ceiling while pressing the plunger to expel any air.

The technique for giving an injection is to select a site and swab the skin with a piece of cotton soaked in alcohol. The back of the neck or shoulder is a good place for a *subcutaneous* injection because the skin is loose here and readily

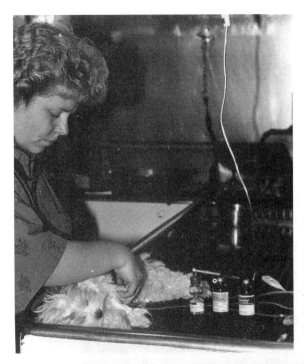

A rare case of *anaphylactic shock*, in this case following a routine vaccination. *(Liisa Carlson)*

Thirty minutes later, the dog has responded to emergency treatment.

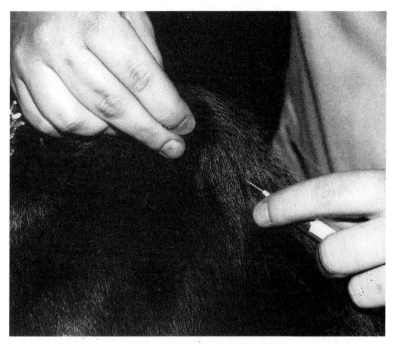

Subcutaneous injections are given beneath the skin over the shoulder.

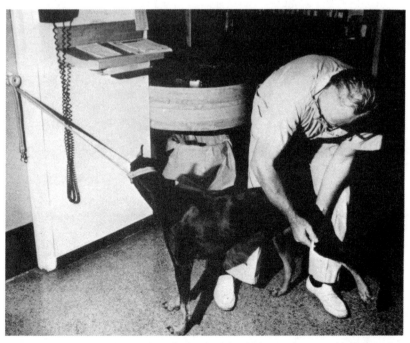

Give intramuscular injections into the back of the thigh muscle. *(J. Clawson)*

399

forms a fold when pinched. Grasp a fold of skin to form a ridge. Firmly push the needle point through the skin into the subcutaneous fat in a course somewhat parallel to the surface of the skin. Before any injection is given, always pull back on the plunger and look for blood. If blood appears, withdraw the syringe and repeat the procedure. Some medicines could cause death if given into a vessel. In the absence of blood, push in the plunger. Withdraw the needle and rub the skin for a few seconds to disperse the medicine.

Intramuscular injections are given in the muscle of the outside of the thigh behind the femur, halfway between the knee joint and the hip. Injections into vessels, nerves and joints can be avoided by giving the shot in the described location, shown in the photograph. Remember to withdraw the plunger and check for blood in the syringe before giving the injection.

Enemas

Enemas are used to treat constipation. The subject is discussed in DIGESTIVE SYSTEM: *Constipation*. Enemas should not be given until a veterinarian has made the diagnosis and prescribed the treatment. Enemas ordinarily are not prescribed on a routine basis. There are better ways to treat chronic constipation.

A soapy enema is made by stirring a piece of soap in water until it turns milky. Enemas also can be made with a half teaspoonful of table salt, or a teaspoonful of baking soda, added to eight ounces of water. The water should be at about body temperature.

The equipment you will need is an enema can or bag and a catheter or a piece of tubing with a nozzle at one end. Lubricate the nozzle and insert it into the anal canal, one to three inches, depending on the size of the dog. Enemas are given at a rate of one ounce of fluid per ten pounds of body weight.

Suppositories

Your veterinarian may prescribe a suppository to treat constipation. Also, medications can be given by suppository when the oral route is not satisfactory (for example, when a dog is vomiting).

A suppository is lubricated with Vaseline and slipped all the way into the rectum, where it dissolves. Suppositories for constipation contain a mild irritant that draws water into the rectum and stimulates a bowel movement. Dulcolax is a good one for this purpose. You can buy it at any drugstore. For small dogs, break the suppository in half. Suppositories should *not* be given to a dog in pain who might have an acute abdomen.

Eye Medication

This is discussed in the chapter Eyes.

Ear Medication

This is discussed in the chapter Ears.

21

Antibiotics and
Infections

ANTIBIOTICS are extracts of basic plants such as molds and fungi. They are capable of destroying some microorganisms that cause disease.

The age of modern antibiotics began with the discovery of penicillin by Sir Alexander Fleming. In 1928, Fleming made a fortuitous and accidental discovery. He observed that a strain of penicillin mold that had fallen on a culture plate could prevent the growth of a colony of bacteria. Although he tried to isolate extracts of the fungus to treat infections, the broths proved too weak.

It remained for a group in Oxford, England, in 1939, under the direction of Sir Howard W. Florey, to isolate potent antibiotic extracts from the mold *penicillium notatum*. The impact of this success on the control of infection sent scientists back to the soil in search of other natural substances having antibiotic activity. This led to the discovery of tetracycline and chloromycetin, as well as many other antibiotics in use today. Taking the basic nucleus of an antibiotic grown in deep broth cultures, researchers added side chains by chemical synthesis. This created a whole new spectrum of synthetic drugs.

Antibiotics fall into two general categories. Those that are *bacteriostatic*, or *fungistatic*, inhibit the growth of microorganisms but don't kill them outright. *Bacteriocidal* and *fungicidal* drugs destroy the microorganisms.

Bacteria also are classified according to their ability to cause disease. *Pathogenic* bacteria are capable of producing a particular illness or infection. *Nonpathogenic* bacteria live on (or within) the host but don't cause illness under normal circumstances. They are referred to as *normal flora*. Some of them produce substances necessary to the well-being of the host. For example, bacteria in the bowel synthesize vitamin K, which is absorbed into the animal's blood-stream and is necessary for normal blood clotting.

Antibiotics are specific for certain pathogenic bacteria. The number now available brings with it new possibilities for animal sensitivity and allergy, and multiplies the potential hazards of mismanagement.

WHY ANTIBIOTICS MAY NOT BE EFFECTIVE

Misdiagnosis of Infection

At times, signs of inflammation (such as heat, redness and swelling) can exist without infection. Sunburn is one example. Infection can be *presumed* to exist when one sees inflammation *and* purulent discharge (pus). Usually there will be an offensive odor. Other signs are fever and elevated white cell count. Specific infections are discussed in other chapters.

Inappropriate Selection

An antibiotic must be effective against the specific microorganism. Some-times a choice can be made on the basis of the character of the illness. The best way to determine susceptibility is to recover the organism, culture it and identify it by colony appearance and microscopic characteristics. Antibiotic discs are applied to the culture plate to see if the growth of colonies is inhibited. Antibiotics are graded according to whether the microorganism is *sensitive*, *indifferent* or *insensitive*. Unfortunately, laboratory findings do not always coincide with results in the host. Nevertheless, antibiotic culture and sensitivity testing is the surest way of selecting the best agent.

Inadequate Wound Care

Antibiotics enter the bloodstream and are carried to the source of the infection. Abscesses, wounds containing devitalized tissue and wounds with foreign bodies (dirt, splinters) are resistant areas. Under such circumstances, antibiotics can't get into the wound. Accordingly, it is important to drain ab-scesses, debride or clean dirty wounds and remove foreign bodies.

Route of Administration

An important medical decision rests in selecting the best route for adminis-tration. Some antibiotics have to be given on an empty stomach or again with a meal. Insufficient absorption from the gastrointestinal tract is one cause of inade-quate blood levels. Some antibiotics are not absorbed when taken with antacids or milk. In severe infections, antibiotics are given intravenously, or by intramus-cular injection to circumvent the problem.

In the treatment of urinary tract infections, other substances may have to be given by mouth to change the pH of the urine and assure that the antibiotics won't precipitate.

402

Dose and Frequency of Administration

The total daily dose is computed by weighing the dog, then dividing the dose into equal parts and giving each one at spaced-out intervals. When the total dose is too low, or not given often enough, the result is less than favorable.

Other factors that have to be taken into account when computing the daily dose are the severity of the infection, the dog's age, overall health and stamina and whether the dog is taking another antibiotic or drug that could depress the ability to fight infection (such as cortisone).

COMPLICATIONS OF ANTIBIOTICS

All drugs should be viewed as poisons, and therefore should always be discussed with your veterinarian. Even buffered aspirin can kill if a dog takes enough of it. The side effects of drugs may be more dangerous than the disease.

Antibiotics should never be given without justifiable indications. Common complications of antibiotics are discussed below and listed in the table *Antibiotics Your Veterinarian May Prescribe*. (This list is by no means complete.)

Allergy

Antibiotics, more than any other class of drugs, can cause allergic reactions. Allergies are discussed in the SKIN chapter. Signs of allergy are hives, rash, itching and scratching and watering of the eyes. Wheezing, collapse and death can occur.

Toxicity

There is a certain margin of safety between a therapeutic dose and a toxic dose. Toxicity is caused by overdose or impaired elimination. With advanced liver and kidney disease, these organs fail to break down and excrete the antibiotic. Young pups require a lower dose by weight than adult dogs because their kidneys are immature.

One cause of overdosage is giving an antibiotic for too long a time.

Toxicity can affect one or more systems:

Ears—Damage to the otic nerves leads to ringing in the ears, hearing loss and deafness. Loss can be permanent.

Liver—Toxicity can lead to jaundice and liver failure.

Kidneys—Toxicity causes nitrogen retention, uremia and kidney failure.

Bone marrow—Toxicity depresses the formation of red cells, white cells and platelets. Fatalities do occur.

Signs of toxicity are difficult to recognize in the dog. They can be far advanced before they come to the owner's attention.

Secondary Infections

Antibiotics alter a normal flora, which serves as a protection against pathogens. Harmful bacteria multiply and cause disease.

Enterocolitis (severe diarrhea) follows the use of certain antibiotics that change the normal flora of the bowel.

Emergence of Resistant Strains

Strains of bacteria that exhibit resistance to antibiotics evolve when antibiotics are used: (a) for a long time, (b) in too low a dose and (c) when the antibiotic is bacteriostatic. Microorganisms resistant to one antibiotic often are resistant to others of the same class.

ANTIBIOTICS AND CORTISONE

Cortisone and other steroids have an anti-inflammatory effect—that is, they reduce *signs* of infection (swelling, redness and tenderness) but do not treat the *infection*. They help to relieve the pain and irritation associated with an inflammation. (For example, to relieve the itching of allergy and some skin diseases.) Steroids often are combined with antibiotics, particularly in topical preparations for use in the eye or ear and on the skin.

Because they have anti-inflammatory properties, steroids mask the signs of infection while giving the impression the dog is getting better. At times this can lead to continuation of tissue damage. Preparations containing steroids should not be used in the eye except under medical supervision.

Steroids have another side effect that is particularly undesirable. *They depress the normal host immune response. This allows infection to go unchecked.*

Other untoward effects of steroids are discussed in SKIN: *Cortisone Excess.*

Antibiotics Your Veterinarian May Prescribe

Antibiotic	Dose (By Weight of Dog)	Used in Infections of:	Adverse Reactions
Penicillins	10,000 u/lb q 12 or 24 hr, IM	Skin, Mouth, Tonsils, Uterus, Wounds	Allergy
Ampicillin	5–10 mg/lb q 6 hr, orally	Same as penicillin Genitourinary tract Respiratory tract	Allergy
Cephalosporins	Depends on the drug	Urinary tract Respiratory tract	Kidney damage (Expensive for owner)
Amiglycosides Neomycin	10 mg/lb q 6 hr, orally Topically 3 to 4 times daily	Diarrhea (orally) Eye*, Ear, Skin (topically)	Kidney damage Allergy

Kanamycin	3 mg/lb q 6 hr, IM or SC	Puppy septicemia	Kidney damage Deafness Brain injury in newborns
Streptomycin	5 mg/lb q 8 hr, IM	Navel infection Leptospirosis	Deafness
Gentamicin	1 mg/lb q 8 hr, IM or SC	Skin, Respiratory tract Urinary tract Eye*, Ear	Kidney damage Deafness
Tetracyclines	10 mg/lb q 8 hr, orally 3½ mg/lb q 12 hr, IM	Leptospirosis Brucellosis Respiratory tract Kennel cough Skin	Stained teeth (unborn puppies) Retarded bone growth (puppies)
Chloromycetin	10 mg/lbs q 8 hr, orally Eye preparations: 3 times daily	Skin, Mouth Respiratory tract Eye* (topically)	Bone marrow depression Urinary tract
Panolog	Topically 2 or 3 times daily. Drops and cream.	Ear Skin	
Erythromycin	5 mg/lb q 8 hr, orally	Penicillin substitute when dog is allergic to penicillin	Rare
Lincomycin	7 mg/lb q 8 hr, orally 5 mg/lb q 12 hr, IM	Skin, Wounds Penicillin substitute	Diarrhea
Tylosin	5 mg/lb q 8 hr, orally 2½ mg/lb 12 hr, IM	Same as Erythromycin	Same as for Erythromycin
Sulfa Drugs	Depends on the drug	Urinary tract Gastrointestinal tract Eye*	Forms crystals in urine. Anemia, Allergy
Furacin	Apply 2 or 3 times daily (topically)	Burns Puppy vaginitis	
Griseofulvin	25 mg/lb daily with fat for 4 to 6 weeks	Ringworm	Don't use in pregnancy
Nystatin	100,000 u/lb q 6 hr, orally	Thrush	

NOTE: Unless otherwise stated, antibiotics should be continued **48 hours** after the dog becomes free of signs and symptoms. If the condition does not improve in 48 hours, check with your veterinarian before continuing the antibiotic.

SC means subcutaneous. **IM** means intramuscularly.

*Preparations used in the eye must be labeled specifically for *ophthalmological use*.

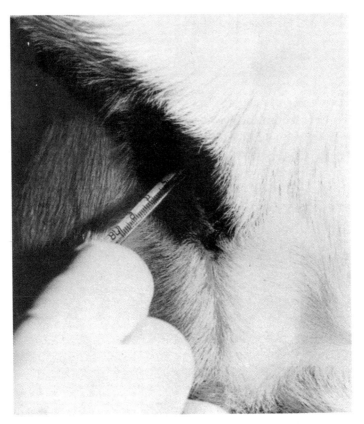

Taking the rectal temperature. *(J. Clawson)*

Appendix

NORMAL PHYSIOLOGIC DATA

Normal Temperature

Adult Dog: 100 to 102.5 degrees F (rectal). (Average: 101.3 degrees F.) Newborn Puppies: see PEDIATRICS: *Physiology*.

How to Take Your Dog's Temperature

The only effective way to take your dog's temperature is by rectal thermometer. Shake down the thermometer until the bulb registers 96 degrees F. Lubricate the bulb with Vaseline. Raise your dog's tail and hold it firmly to keep your dog from sitting down; then gently insert the bulb into the anal canal with a twisting motion. Insert the thermometer one to three inches, depending upon the size of the dog.

Hold the thermometer in place for three minutes. Then remove it, wipe clean and read the temperature by the height of the silver column of mercury on the thermometer scale.

Clean the thermometer with alcohol before using it again. This prevents the transfer of diseases.

(**Note:** Should the thermometer break off, usually because the dog sits down, do not attempt to find and extract the broken end. Give one to two teaspoonsful of mineral oil by mouth to facilitate passage and notify your veterinarian.)

Pulse

Normal: 60 to 160 beats per minute for adult dogs; up to 180 beats per minute in toy breeds; and 220 beats per minute for puppies.

(Note: To learn how to take your dog's pulse, see CIRCULATORY SYSTEM: *Pulse*.)

Respiration

Normal: 10 to 30 breaths per minute at rest.

Gestation

59 to 66 days (average 63 days).

Comparative Age of Dogs to Humans
(Average of All Breeds)

Age of Dog in Years	Age of Human in Years
1	15
2	24
3	28
4	32
5	36
6	40
7	44
8	48
9	52
10	56
11	60
12	64
13	68
14	72
15	76
16	80

Table of
STANDARDS FOR TAIL DOCKING
Compiled by M. JOSEPHINE DEUBLER, V.M.D., Ph.D.
School of Veterinary Medicine, University of Pennsylvania

IMPORTANT NOTE: This table gives *approximate* guides for docking *when done before the puppy is one week old*. It has been compiled from information in the official breed standards, or—where information is not given in the standards—from opinions of judges, veterinarians, breeders and professional handlers. Because of the ambiguous descriptions used in many standards, and because breed fashions change, veterinarians are cautioned to *use these figures as sugges-*

tions only. Always obtain specific instructions from the owner as to length of dock.

An improperly docked tail may ruin a puppy for show purposes. If one is in doubt, consultation with an established breeder is suggested. There may be variations among puppies, and a knowledge of breed characteristics is important in determining the correct length to dock.

Reprinted from KIRK'S CURRENT VETERINARY THERAPY, *Volume VI, with special permission of the publisher, W. B. Saunders Company.*

Tail Docking Lengths

Breed	Length at less than 1 week of age
Sporting Breeds	
Brittany	Leave 1 inch
Clumber Spaniel	Leave ¼–⅓
Cocker Spaniel	Leave ⅓ (about ¾ inch)
English Cocker Spaniel	Leave ⅓
English Springer Spaniel	Leave ⅓
Field Spaniel	Leave ⅓
German Shorthaired Pointer	Leave ⅖*
German Wirehaired Pointer	Leave ⅖*
Sussex Spaniel	Leave ⅓
Vizsla	Leave ⅔*
Weimaraner	Leave ⅗ (about 1½ inches)
Welsh Springer Spaniel	Leave ⅓–½
Wirehaired Pointing Griffon	Leave ⅓*
Working Breeds	
Bouvier de Flandres	Leave ½–¾ inch
Boxer	Leave ½–¾
Doberman Pinscher	Leave ¾ inch (two vertebrae)
Giant Schnauzer	Leave 1¼ inches (three vertebrae)
Old English Sheepdog	If necessary—close to body (leave one vertebra)
Rottweiler	If necessary—close to body (leave one vertebra)
Standard Schnauzer	Leave 1 inch (two vertebrae)
Pembroke Welsh Corgi	Close to body (leave one vertebra)
Terrier Breeds	
Airedale Terrier	Leave ⅔–¾* **
Australian Terrier	Leave ⅖*
Fox Terrier (Smooth and Wirehaired)	Leave ⅔–¾* **
Irish Terrier	Leave ¾*
Kerry Blue Terrier	Leave ½–⅔
Lakeland Terrier	Leave ⅔**
Norwich Terrier	Leave ¼–⅓
Miniature Schnauzer	Leave about ¾ inch—not more than 1 inch
Sealyham Terrier	Leave ⅓–½
Soft-Coated Wheaten Terrier	Leave ½–¾
Welsh Terrier	Leave ⅔**

Toy Breeds

Affenpinscher	Close to body (leave ⅓ inch)
Brussels Griffon	Leave ¼–⅓
English Toy Spaniel (both varieties)	Leave ⅓
Miniature Pinscher	Leave ½ inch (two vertebrae)
Toy Poodle	Leave ½–⅔ (about 1 inch)
Silky Terrier	Leave about ⅓ (about ½ inch)
Yorkshire Terrier	Leave about ⅓ (about ½ inch)

Non-Sporting Breeds

Miniature Poodle	Leave ½–⅔ (about 1⅛ inches)
Standard Poodle	Leave ½–⅔ (about 1½ inches)
Schipperke	Close to body (if present)

Miscellaneous Breeds (not registered by AKC)

Cavalier King Charles Spaniel	Optional. Leave at least ⅔. Always leave white tip in broken-colored dogs.
Spinoni Italiani	Leave ⅗

*Taken from official breed Standard.

**The tip of the docked tail should be approximately level with the top of the skull with the puppy in show position.

TRIBUTE TO A DOG

The one absolutely unselfish friend that man can have in this selfish world, the one that never deserts him, the one that never proves ungrateful or treacherous, is his dog. A man's dog stands by him in prosperity and in poverty, in health and in sickness. He will sleep on the cold ground, where the wintry winds blow and the snow drives fiercely, if only he may be near his master's side. He will kiss the hand that has no food to offer; he will lick the wounds and sores that come in encounter with the roughness of the world. He guards the sleep of his pauper master as if he were a prince. When all other friends desert, he remains. When riches take wings and reputation falls to pieces, he is as constant in his love as the sun in its journey through the heavens.''

Senator George Vest, 1870

Index of Tables and Charts

General Index

418

Stool(s)
    appearance of, 203–4
    average number, 207
    blood-streaked, 209, **210**, 377. *See also*
        Diarrhea, bloody
    eating (coprophagia), 210
    straining at, **207–8**, 210, 295
Stud dog, 301–3
Stys, 120
Suffocation, 7–8
Sunburn, 5, **160–61**
    prevention, 108, 110
Suppository, how to give, 400
Sweat glands, 67, 157
Swimmer (flat puppy), 362
Swollen head, 189

Tail docking, 408–10
Tapeworms, 37–39
Tar in hair, 72
Tartar (dental calculus), 182
Tearing mechanism, 128–31
Tear stains, 130
    See also Eye discharge
Teeth, 177–87
    decay of, 159, 175–76, **182–84**, 389
Teething in puppies, **177**
Temperature
    drop before whelping, 331
    how to take, 407
    normal, 407
    puppy, 347–48, **351**
    subnormal, 6, 24
    See also Fever
Tendon injuries, 271
Testicles, 310, **315–16**
    tumors of, 382
Testosterone (male hormone), 216, 305,
    311, 321
Tetanus (lockjaw), 47
Threadworms, 39
Throat, 187–89
Thrush, 171
Thyroid gland, 91
Tick paralysis, 261
Ticks, 50, 63, 64, 65, **82–83**, 261
    in ear, 149
Tie, 306–7
    prolonged, 308
Toad poisoning, 20
Tongue, 174
    string around, 175
Tonsillitis, 187–88
Tourniquet, **26**
Toxic Epidermal Necrolysis, 110
Toxic milk, 360
Toxoplasmosis, 61–62
Training a puppy, 370–73
Tranquilizers, 197–98, 309, 345, **394**

Transporting an injured dog, 8–11, 252,
    260, 263
Tremor of white dogs, 256
Trench mouth, 171
Trichinosis, 40
Trichomoniasis, 62
Trypanosomiasis, 63
Tubal ligation, 323
Tube feeding, 357–58
Tuberculosis, 48
Tularemia, 50
Tumors (growths) and Cancers, **375–86**
    Anus and Rectum, 215–16
    Bone, 271, **384–86**
    Brain, 254
    Breast, 383–84
    Esophagus, 195
    Eye, 124
    Intestine, 209
    Lung, 222, 230
    Mouth, 173–74
    Nasal cavity, 164
    Ovary, 93, **383**
    Skin, 379–80
    Stomach, 197
    Testicle, 382

Ulcer, stomach, 199
Umbilical cord, 332, 360
Undescended testicles, **315–16**, 382
Uremic poisoning. *See* Kidney failure
Urethra, 287, 288, **292–96**
Urinary incontinence, causes of, **294–95**
    See also **Index of Signs and Symptoms**
Urinary System, **289–95**
Urinating, with pain or difficulty. *See* **Index
    of Signs and Symptoms**
Urine, 287
    blood in, 18, 288, 292
Uterine infection, 318, 324, 341
Uterus, during labor, 335–36
Uveitis (soft eye), 138

Vaccinations, **42–45**, 47, 379
    when to give, 45
Vaccines, **42–45**, 329, 353
Vaginal cytology (to predict ovulation),
    304, **306**, 309
Vaginal discharge. *See* **Index of Signs and
    Symptoms**
    during heat, **303–6**
Vaginal infection, **316**, 361
    See also Bladder and Uterine Infection
Vaginal prolapse, 317
Valvular heart disease, 236–37
Vasectomy, 324
Vena cava syndrome, 240
Venereal diseases. *See* Sexually Transmitted
    Diseases